CASE CLOSED

VOLUME 50

Gosho Aoyama

Case Briefing:

Subject: **Jimmy Kudo, a.k.a. Conan Edogawa**
Occupation: **High School Student/Detective**
Special Skills: **Analytical thinking and deductive reasoning, Soccer**
Equipment: **Bow Tie Voice Transmitter, Super Sneakers, Homing Glasses, Stretchy Suspenders**

The subject is hot on the trail of a pair of suspicious men in black when he is attacked from behind and administered a strange substance which physically transforms him into a first grader. When the subject confides in the eccentric inventor Dr. Agasa, they decide to keep the subject's true identity a secret for the safety of everyone around him. Assuming the new identity of first-grader Conan Edogawa, the subject continues to assist the police force on their most baffling cases. The only problem is that most crime-solving professionals won't take a little kid's advice!

Table of Contents

CASE CLOSED

CONFIDEN

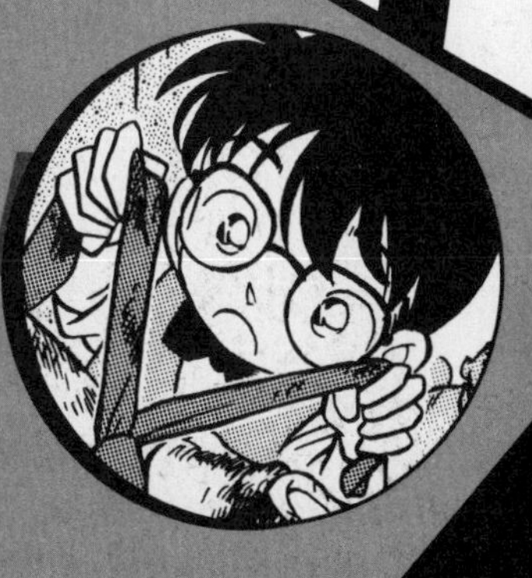

CASE CLOSED

Volume 50
Shonen Sunday Edition

Story and Art by GOSHO AOYAMA

MEITANTEI CONAN Vol. 50
by Gosho AOYAMA
© 1994 Gosho AOYAMA
All rights reserved.
Original Japanese edition published by SHOGAKUKAN.
English translation rights in the United States of America, Canada,
the United Kingdom and Ireland arranged with SHOGAKUKAN.

Translation
Tetsuichiro Miyaki

Touch-up & Lettering
Freeman Wong

Cover & Graphic Design
Andrea Rice

Editor
Shaenon K. Garrity

Printed in Canada

Published by VIZ Media, LLC
P.O. Box 77010
San Francisco, CA 94107

10 9 8 7 6 5 4 3 2 1
First printing, April 2014

www.viz.com

FILE 1: THE MENACING MIXER

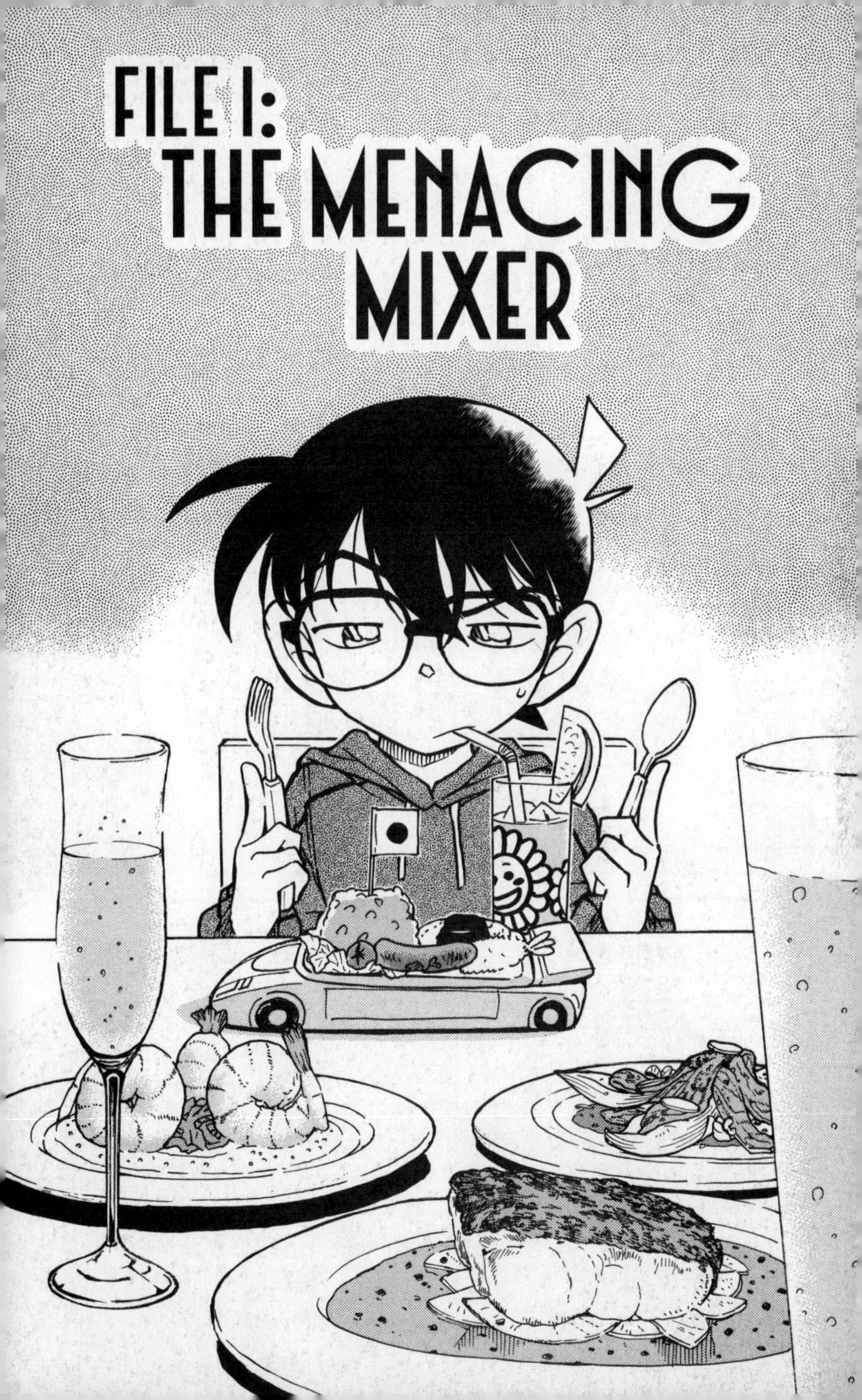

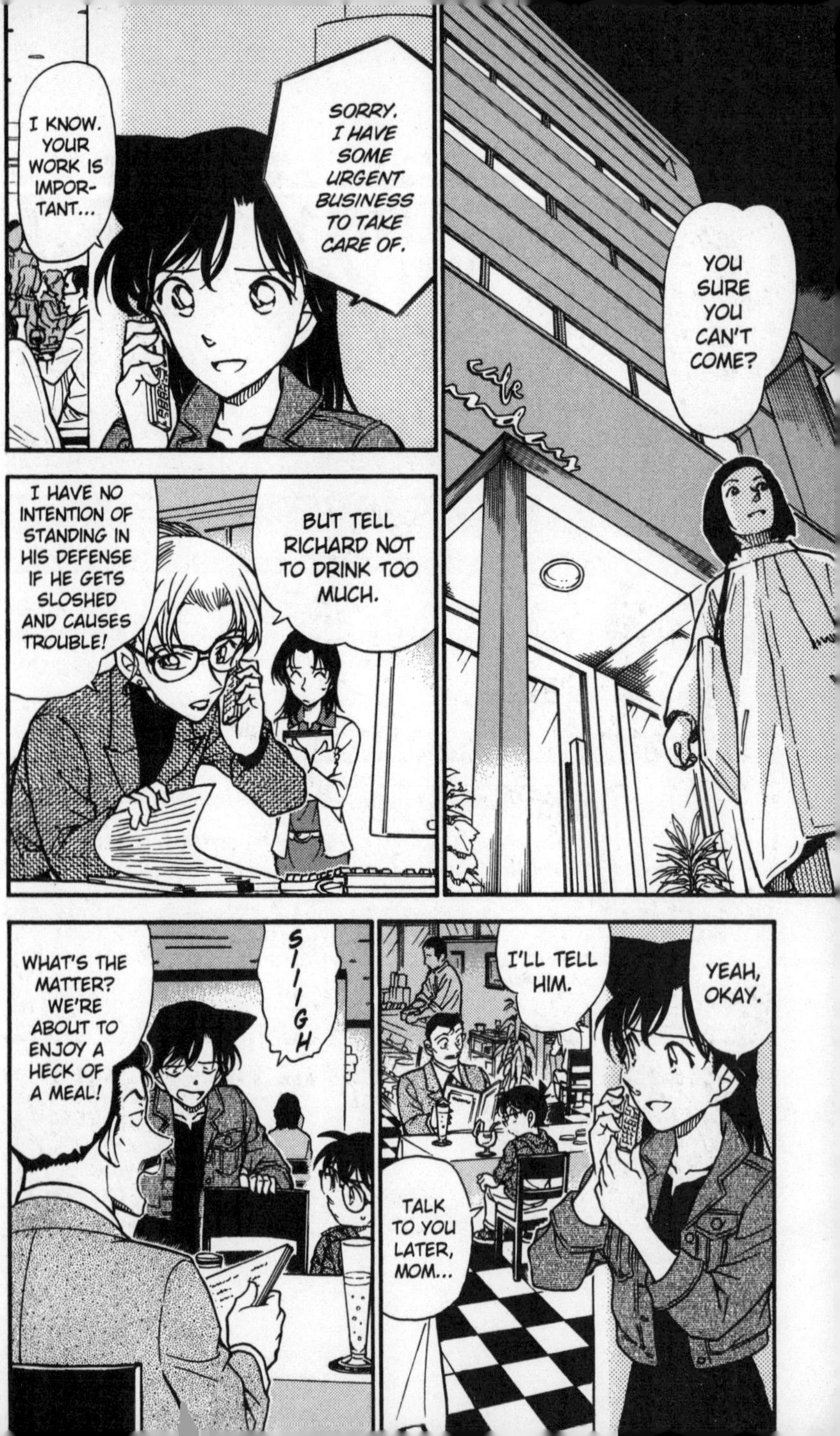

YOU SURE YOU CAN'T COME?
SORRY. I HAVE SOME URGENT BUSINESS TO TAKE CARE OF.
I KNOW. YOUR WORK IS IMPORTANT...
BUT TELL RICHARD NOT TO DRINK TOO MUCH.
I HAVE NO INTENTION OF STANDING IN HIS DEFENSE IF HE GETS SLOSHED AND CAUSES TROUBLE!
YEAH, OKAY.
I'LL TELL HIM.
TALK TO YOU LATER, MOM...
SIIIGH
WHAT'S THE MATTER? WE'RE ABOUT TO ENJOY A HECK OF A MEAL!

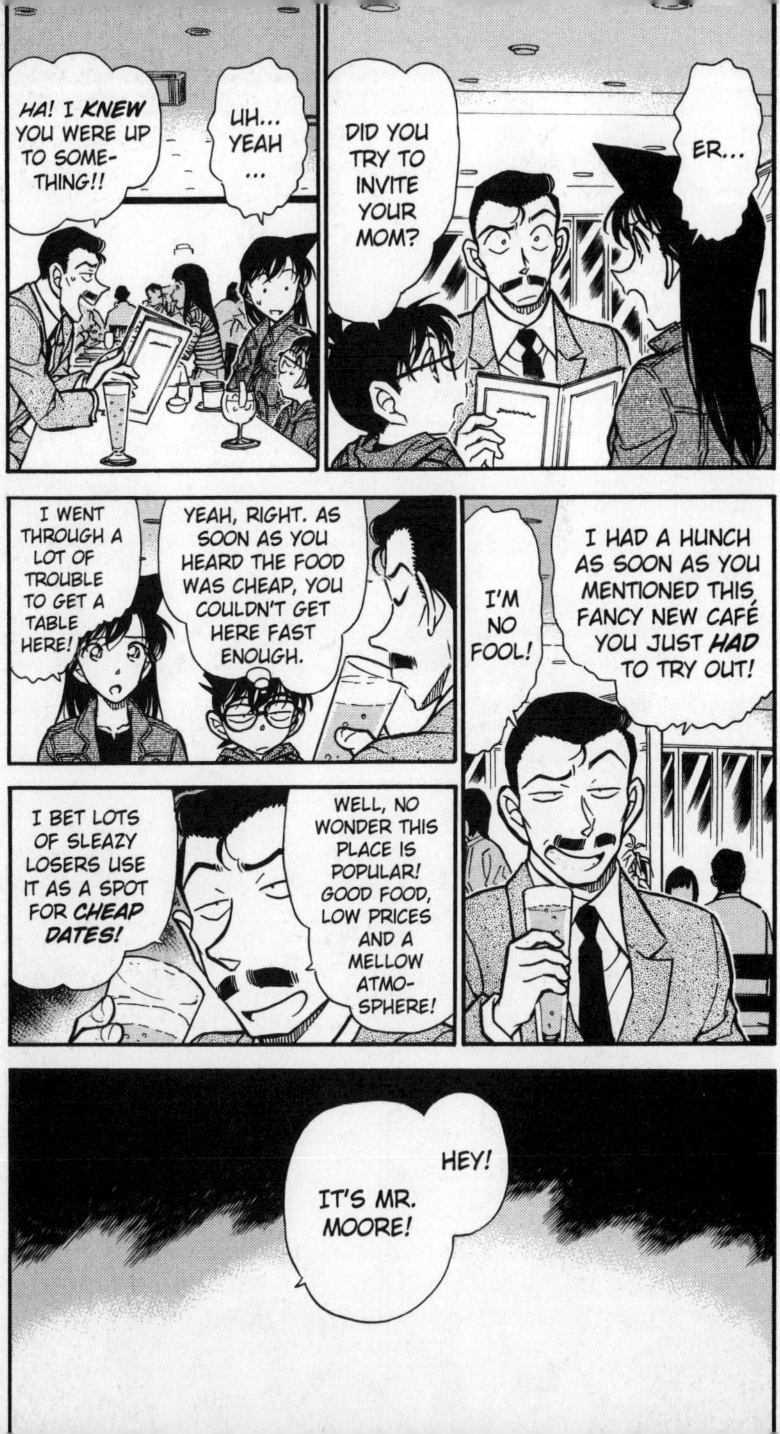

ER...
DID YOU TRY TO INVITE YOUR MOM?
UH... YEAH...
HA! I KNEW YOU WERE UP TO SOME-THING!!
I HAD A HUNCH AS SOON AS YOU MENTIONED THIS FANCY NEW CAFÉ YOU JUST HAD TO TRY OUT!
I'M NO FOOL!
YEAH, RIGHT. AS SOON AS YOU HEARD THE FOOD WAS CHEAP, YOU COULDN'T GET HERE FAST ENOUGH.
I WENT THROUGH A LOT OF TROUBLE TO GET A TABLE HERE!
WELL, NO WONDER THIS PLACE IS POPULAR! GOOD FOOD, LOW PRICES AND A MELLOW ATMO-SPHERE!
I BET LOTS OF SLEAZY LOSERS USE IT AS A SPOT FOR CHEAP DATES!
HEY!
IT'S MR. MOORE!

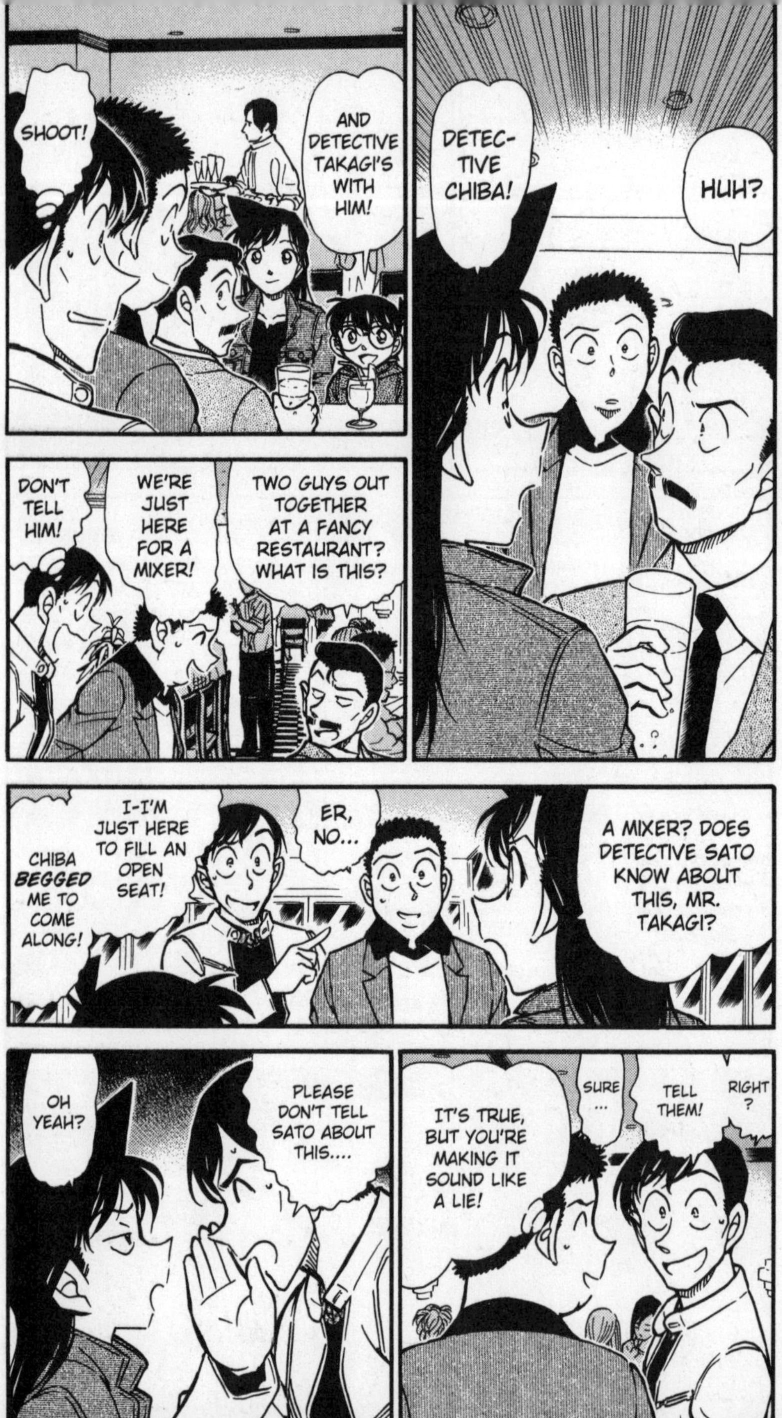
DETECTIVE CHIBA!
HUH?
AND DETECTIVE TAKAGI'S WITH HIM!
SHOOT!
TWO GUYS OUT TOGETHER AT A FANCY RESTAURANT? WHAT IS THIS?
WE'RE JUST HERE FOR A MIXER!
DON'T TELL HIM!
A MIXER? DOES DETECTIVE SATO KNOW ABOUT THIS, MR. TAKAGI?
ER, NO...
I-I'M JUST HERE TO FILL AN OPEN SEAT!
CHIBA **BEGGED** ME TO COME ALONG!
RIGHT?
TELL THEM!
SURE...
IT'S TRUE, BUT YOU'RE MAKING IT SOUND LIKE A LIE!
PLEASE DON'T TELL SATO ABOUT THIS....
OH YEAH?

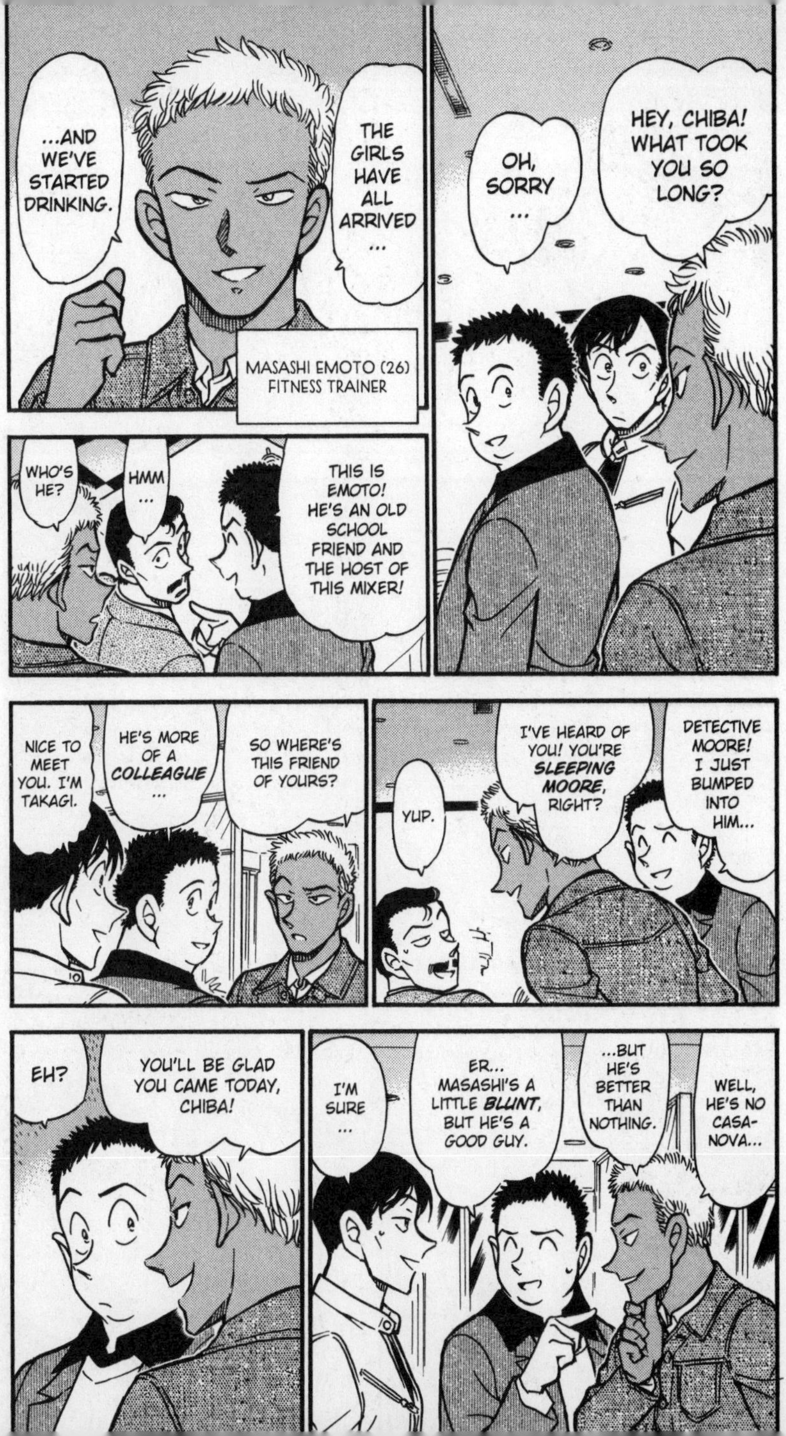
HEY, CHIBA! WHAT TOOK YOU SO LONG?
OH, SORRY...
THE GIRLS HAVE ALL ARRIVED...
...AND WE'VE STARTED DRINKING.
MASASHI EMOTO (26) FITNESS TRAINER
THIS IS EMOTO! HE'S AN OLD SCHOOL FRIEND AND THE HOST OF THIS MIXER!
HMM...
WHO'S HE?
DETECTIVE MOORE! I JUST BUMPED INTO HIM...
I'VE HEARD OF YOU! YOU'RE SLEEPING MOORE, RIGHT?
YUP.
SO WHERE'S THIS FRIEND OF YOURS?
HE'S MORE OF A COLLEAGUE...
NICE TO MEET YOU. I'M TAKAGI.
WELL, HE'S NO CASANOVA...
...BUT HE'S BETTER THAN NOTHING.
ER... MASASHI'S A LITTLE BLUNT, BUT HE'S A GOOD GUY.
I'M SURE...
YOU'LL BE GLAD YOU CAME TODAY, CHIBA!
EH?

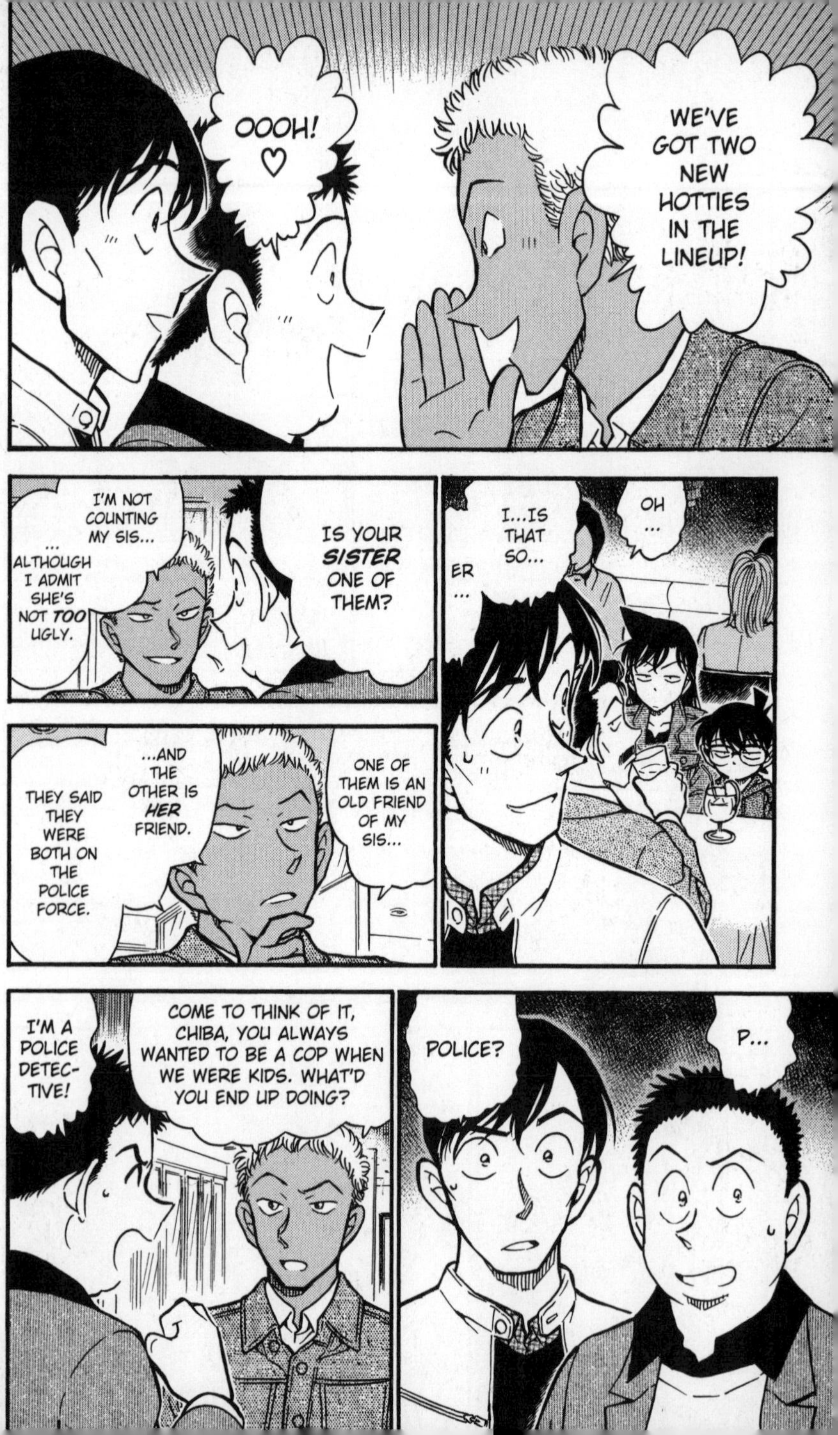
WE'VE GOT TWO NEW HOTTIES IN THE LINEUP!
OOOH! ♥
OH ...
ER ...
I...IS THAT SO...
IS YOUR *SISTER* ONE OF THEM?
I'M NOT COUNTING MY SIS...
... ALTHOUGH I ADMIT SHE'S NOT *TOO* UGLY.
ONE OF THEM IS AN OLD FRIEND OF MY SIS...
...AND THE OTHER IS *HER* FRIEND.
THEY SAID THEY WERE BOTH ON THE POLICE FORCE.
P...
POLICE?
COME TO THINK OF IT, CHIBA, YOU ALWAYS WANTED TO BE A COP WHEN WE WERE KIDS. WHAT'D YOU END UP DOING?
I'M A POLICE DETECTIVE!

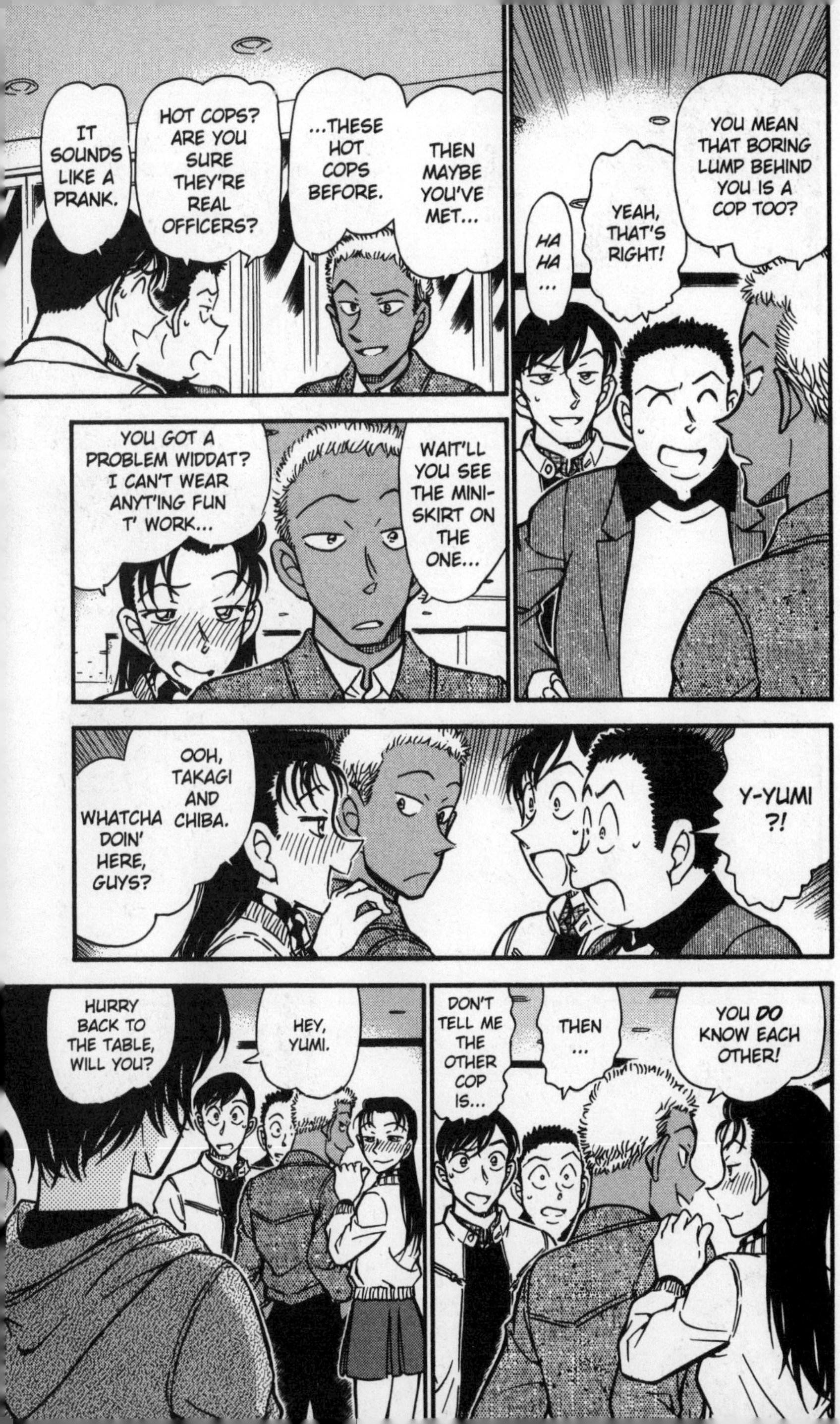
YOU MEAN THAT BORING LUMP BEHIND YOU IS A COP TOO?
YEAH, THAT'S RIGHT!
HA HA ...
THEN MAYBE YOU'VE MET...
...THESE HOT COPS BEFORE.
HOT COPS? ARE YOU SURE THEY'RE REAL OFFICERS?
IT SOUNDS LIKE A PRANK.
WAIT'LL YOU SEE THE MINI-SKIRT ON THE ONE...
YOU GOT A PROBLEM WIDDAT? I CAN'T WEAR ANYT'ING FUN T' WORK...
Y-YUMI ?!
OOH, TAKAGI AND CHIBA.
WHATCHA DOIN' HERE, GUYS?
YOU DO KNOW EACH OTHER!
THEN ...
DON'T TELL ME THE OTHER COP IS...
HEY, YUMI.
HURRY BACK TO THE TABLE, WILL YOU?

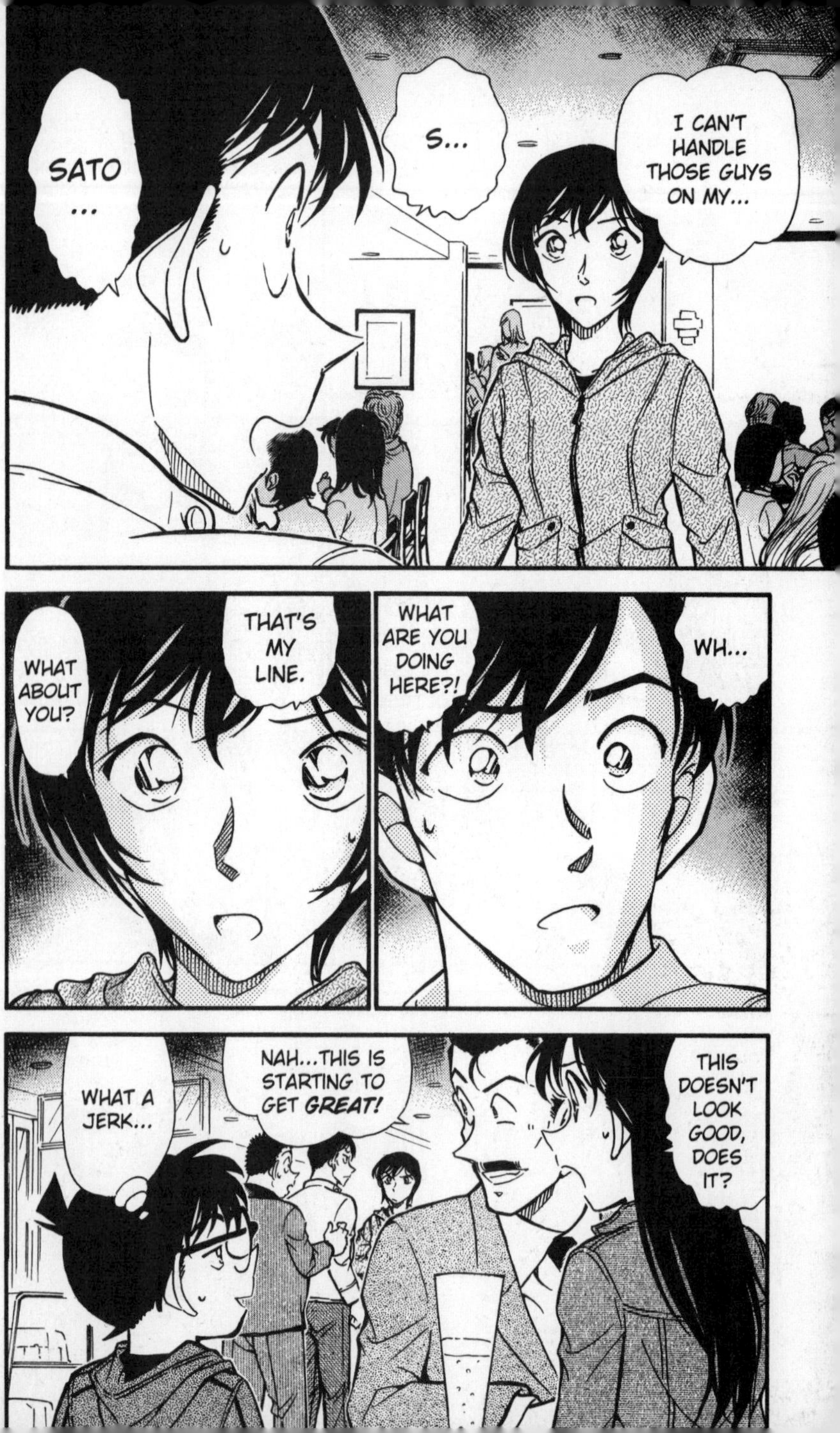
I CAN'T HANDLE THOSE GUYS ON MY...
S...
SATO ...
WH...
WHAT ARE YOU DOING HERE?!
THAT'S MY LINE.
WHAT ABOUT YOU?
THIS DOESN'T LOOK GOOD, DOES IT?
NAH...THIS IS STARTING TO GET **GREAT!**
WHAT A JERK...

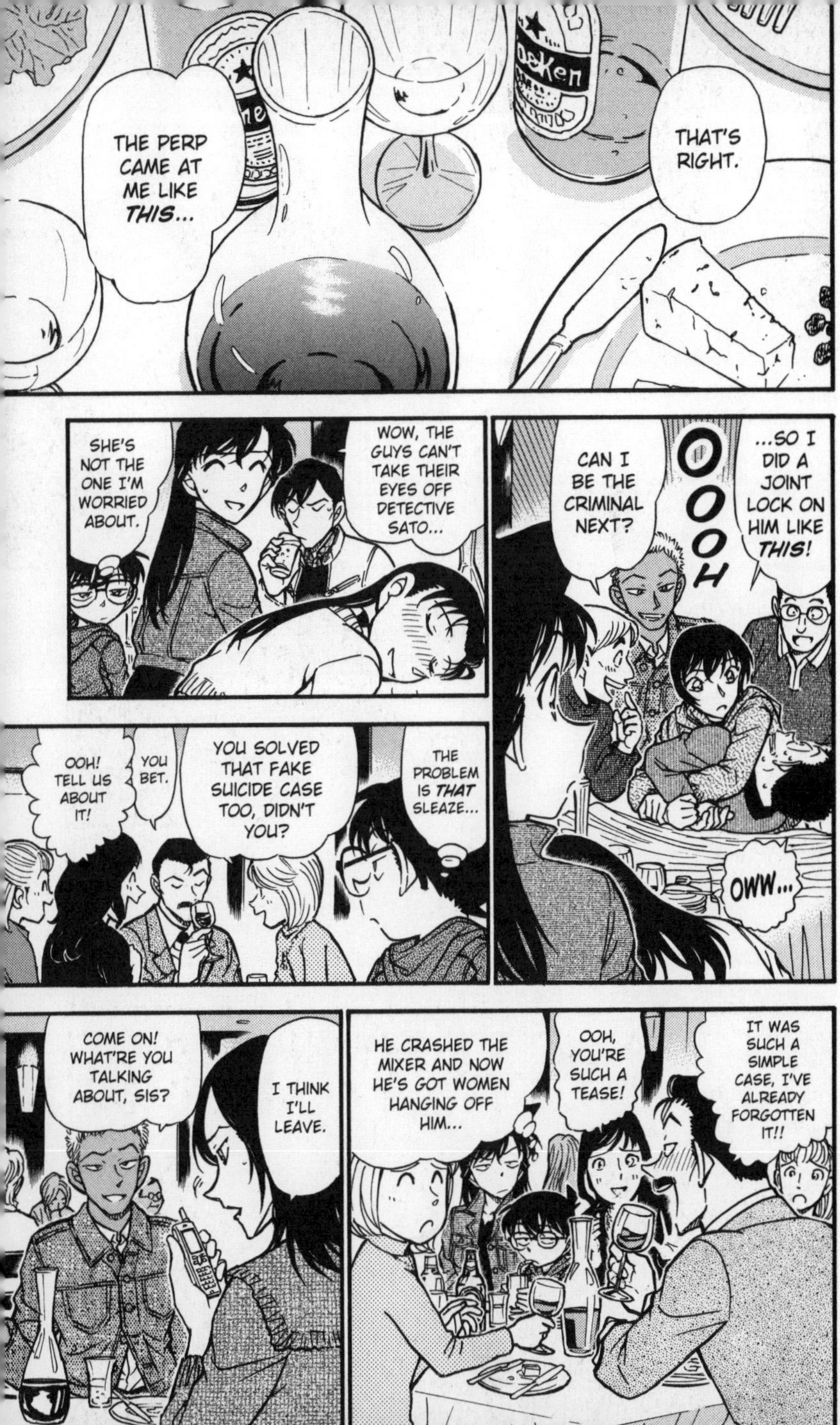
THAT'S RIGHT.
THE PERP CAME AT ME LIKE *THIS*...
...SO I DID A JOINT LOCK ON HIM LIKE *THIS*!
OOOOH
CAN I BE THE CRIMINAL NEXT?
OWW...
WOW, THE GUYS CAN'T TAKE THEIR EYES OFF DETECTIVE SATO...
SHE'S NOT THE ONE I'M WORRIED ABOUT.
THE PROBLEM IS *THAT* SLEAZE...
YOU SOLVED THAT FAKE SUICIDE CASE TOO, DIDN'T YOU?
YOU BET.
OOH! TELL US ABOUT IT!
IT WAS SUCH A SIMPLE CASE, I'VE ALREADY FORGOTTEN IT!!
OOH, YOU'RE SUCH A TEASE!
HE CRASHED THE MIXER AND NOW HE'S GOT WOMEN HANGING OFF HIM...
I THINK I'LL LEAVE.
COME ON! WHAT'RE YOU TALKING ABOUT, SIS?

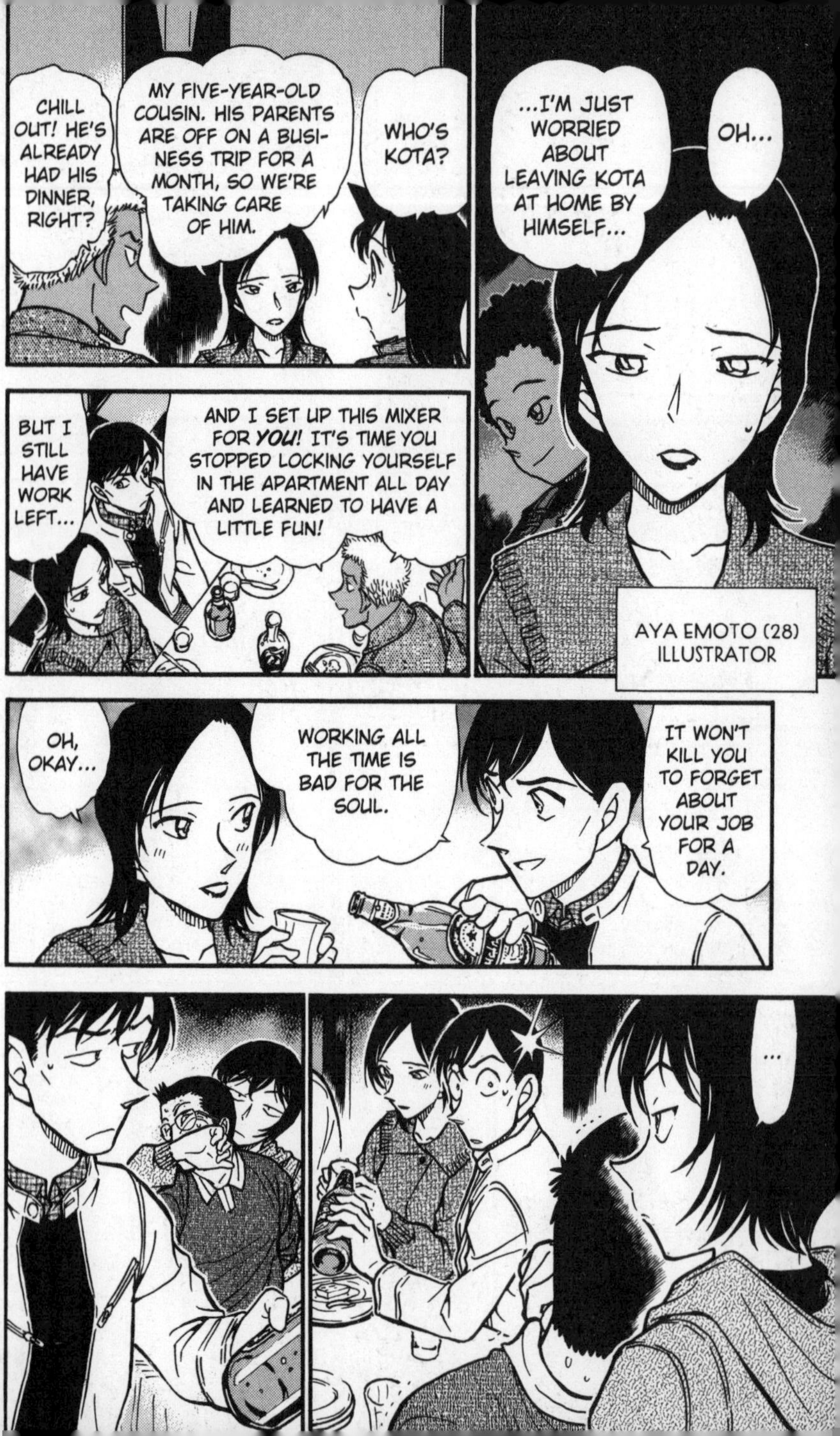
OH...
...I'M JUST WORRIED ABOUT LEAVING KOTA AT HOME BY HIMSELF...
AYA EMOTO (28) ILLUSTRATOR
WHO'S KOTA?
MY FIVE-YEAR-OLD COUSIN. HIS PARENTS ARE OFF ON A BUSI-NESS TRIP FOR A MONTH, SO WE'RE TAKING CARE OF HIM.
CHILL OUT! HE'S ALREADY HAD HIS DINNER, RIGHT?
AND I SET UP THIS MIXER FOR *YOU!* IT'S TIME YOU STOPPED LOCKING YOURSELF IN THE APARTMENT ALL DAY AND LEARNED TO HAVE A LITTLE FUN!
BUT I STILL HAVE WORK LEFT...
IT WON'T KILL YOU TO FORGET ABOUT YOUR JOB FOR A DAY.
WORKING ALL THE TIME IS BAD FOR THE SOUL.
OH, OKAY...
...

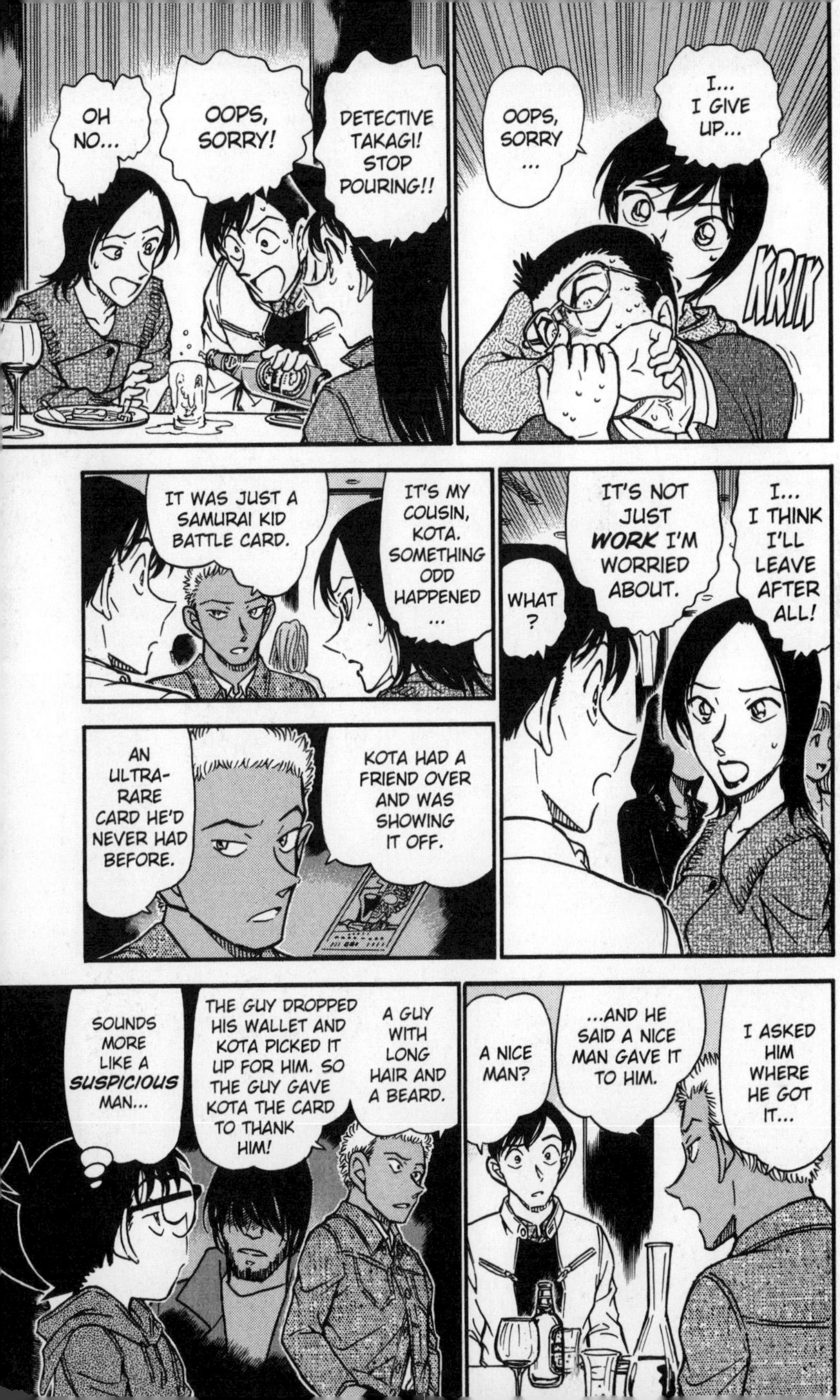
I... I GIVE UP...
OOPS, SORRY ...
KRIK
DETECTIVE TAKAGI! STOP POURING!!
OOPS, SORRY!
OH NO...
I... I THINK I'LL LEAVE AFTER ALL!
IT'S NOT JUST **WORK** I'M WORRIED ABOUT.
WHAT ?
IT'S MY COUSIN, KOTA. SOMETHING ODD HAPPENED ...
IT WAS JUST A SAMURAI KID BATTLE CARD.
KOTA HAD A FRIEND OVER AND WAS SHOWING IT OFF.
AN ULTRA-RARE CARD HE'D NEVER HAD BEFORE.
I ASKED HIM WHERE HE GOT IT...
...AND HE SAID A NICE MAN GAVE IT TO HIM.
A NICE MAN?
A GUY WITH LONG HAIR AND A BEARD.
THE GUY DROPPED HIS WALLET AND KOTA PICKED IT UP FOR HIM. SO THE GUY GAVE KOTA THE CARD TO THANK HIM!
SOUNDS MORE LIKE A ***SUSPICIOUS*** MAN...

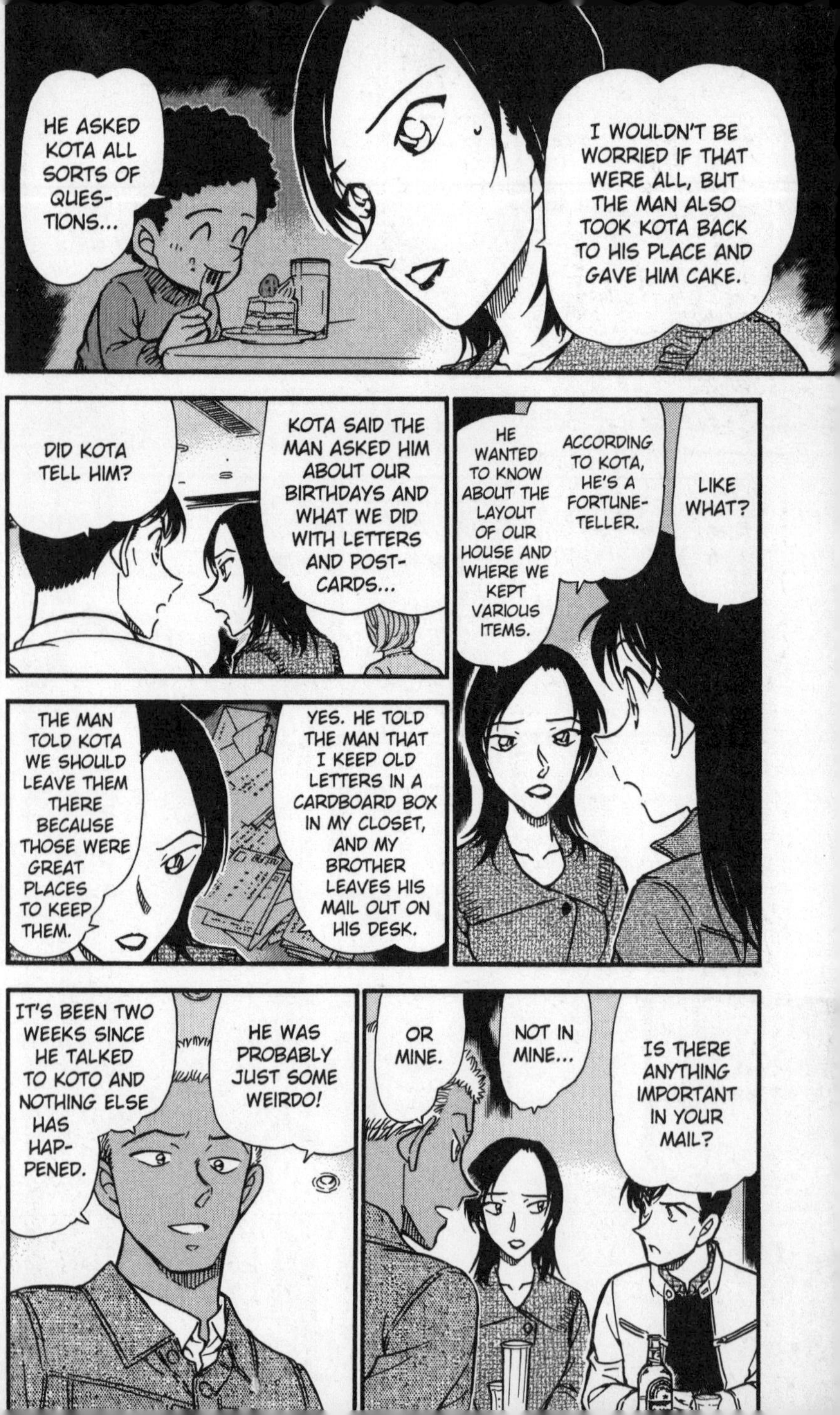
I WOULDN'T BE WORRIED IF THAT WERE ALL, BUT THE MAN ALSO TOOK KOTA BACK TO HIS PLACE AND GAVE HIM CAKE.
HE ASKED KOTA ALL SORTS OF QUES- TIONS...
LIKE WHAT?
ACCORDING TO KOTA, HE'S A FORTUNE- TELLER.
HE WANTED TO KNOW ABOUT THE LAYOUT OF OUR HOUSE AND WHERE WE KEPT VARIOUS ITEMS.
KOTA SAID THE MAN ASKED HIM ABOUT OUR BIRTHDAYS AND WHAT WE DID WITH LETTERS AND POST- CARDS...
DID KOTA TELL HIM?
YES. HE TOLD THE MAN THAT I KEEP OLD LETTERS IN A CARDBOARD BOX IN MY CLOSET, AND MY BROTHER LEAVES HIS MAIL OUT ON HIS DESK.
THE MAN TOLD KOTA WE SHOULD LEAVE THEM THERE BECAUSE THOSE WERE GREAT PLACES TO KEEP THEM.
IS THERE ANYTHING IMPORTANT IN YOUR MAIL?
NOT IN MINE...
OR MINE.
HE WAS PROBABLY JUST SOME WEIRDO!
IT'S BEEN TWO WEEKS SINCE HE TALKED TO KOTO AND NOTHING ELSE HAS HAP- PENED.

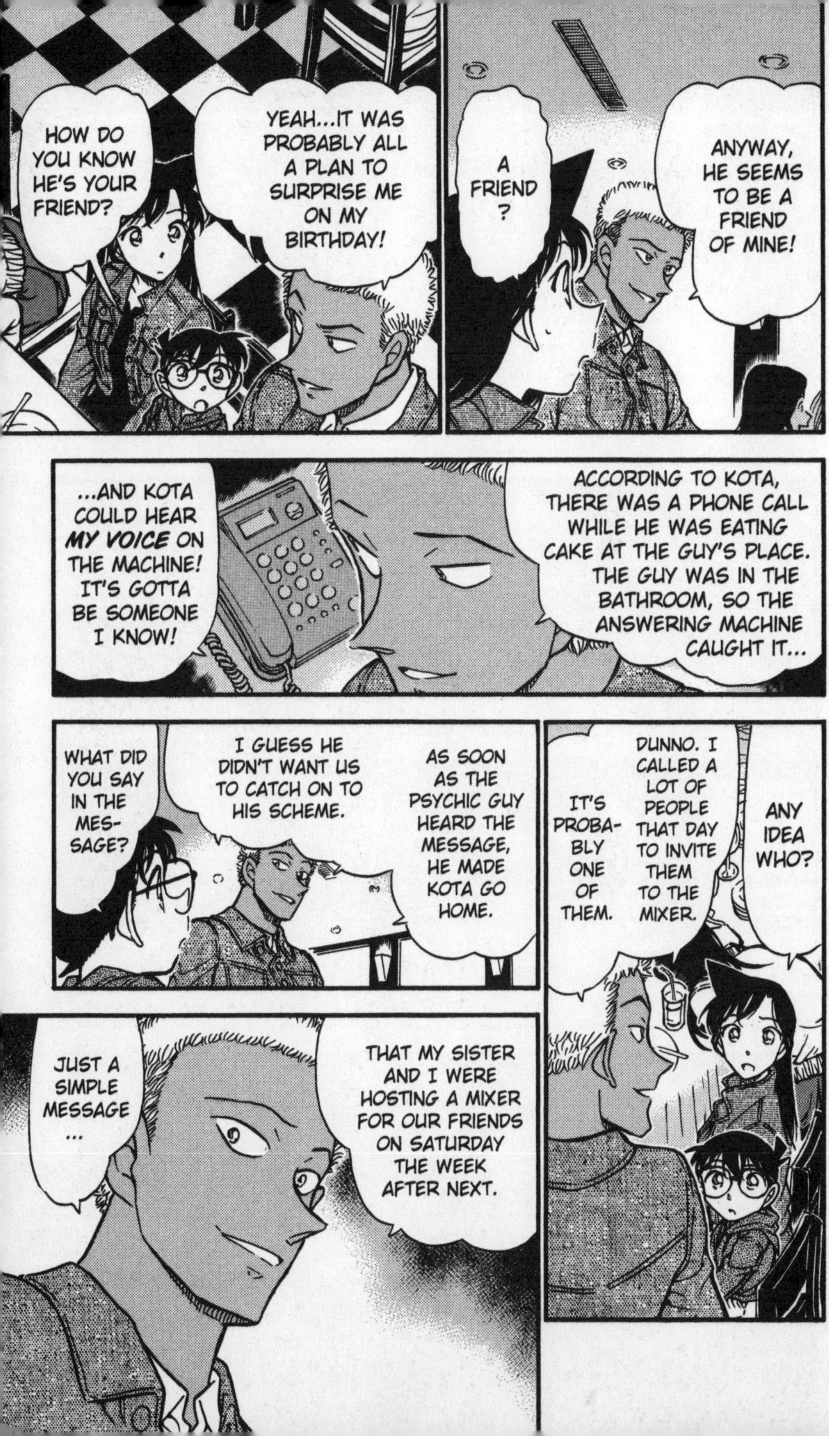
ANYWAY, HE SEEMS TO BE A FRIEND OF MINE!
A FRIEND ?
YEAH...IT WAS PROBABLY ALL A PLAN TO SURPRISE ME ON MY BIRTHDAY!
HOW DO YOU KNOW HE'S YOUR FRIEND?
ACCORDING TO KOTA, THERE WAS A PHONE CALL WHILE HE WAS EATING CAKE AT THE GUY'S PLACE. THE GUY WAS IN THE BATHROOM, SO THE ANSWERING MACHINE CAUGHT IT...
...AND KOTA COULD HEAR *MY VOICE* ON THE MACHINE! IT'S GOTTA BE SOMEONE I KNOW!
ANY IDEA WHO?
DUNNO. I CALLED A LOT OF PEOPLE THAT DAY TO INVITE THEM TO THE MIXER.
IT'S PROBA-BLY ONE OF THEM.
AS SOON AS THE PSYCHIC GUY HEARD THE MESSAGE, HE MADE KOTA GO HOME.
I GUESS HE DIDN'T WANT US TO CATCH ON TO HIS SCHEME.
WHAT DID YOU SAY IN THE MES-SAGE?
THAT MY SISTER AND I WERE HOSTING A MIXER FOR OUR FRIENDS ON SATURDAY THE WEEK AFTER NEXT.
JUST A SIMPLE MESSAGE ...

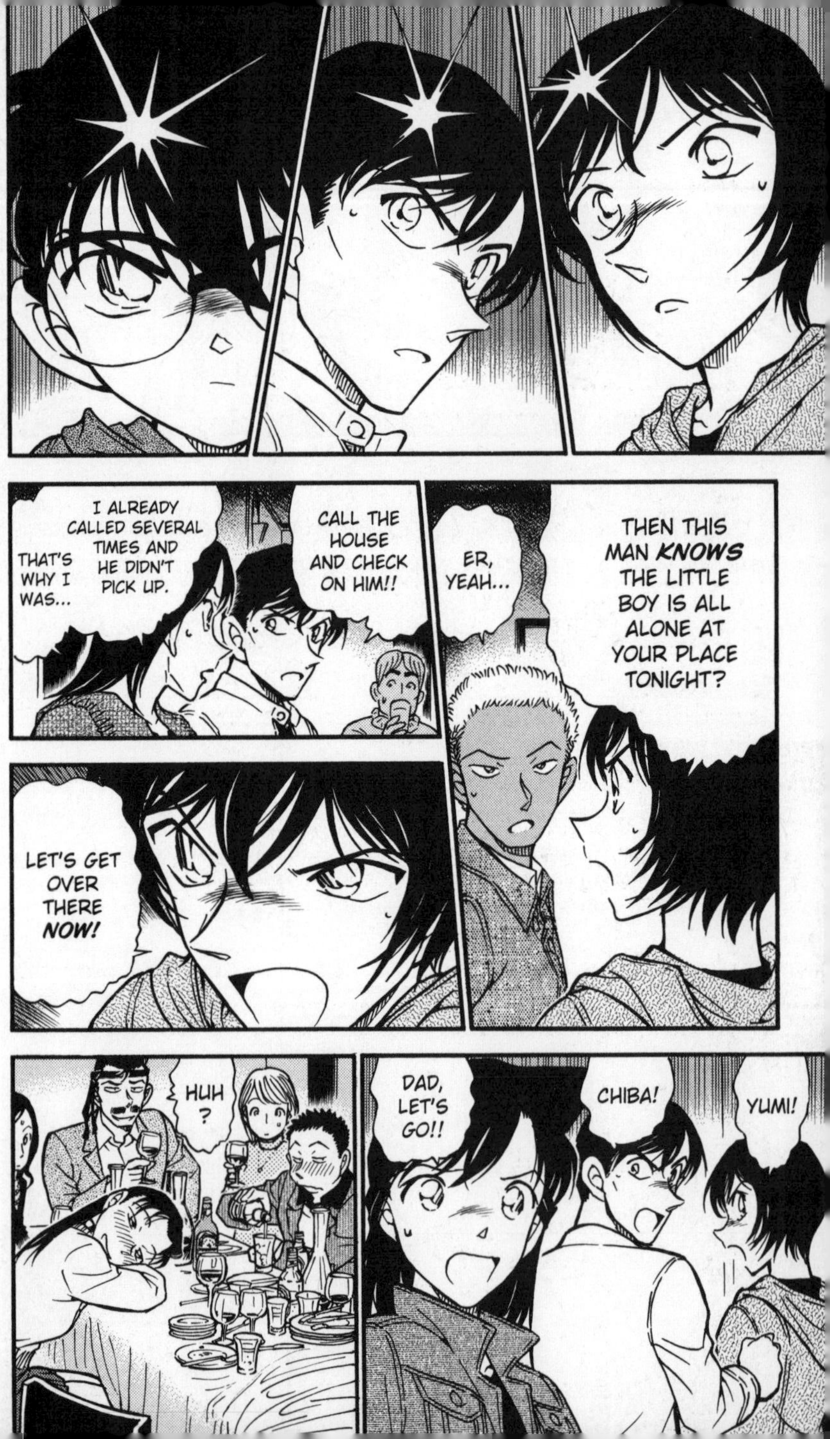
THEN THIS MAN **KNOWS** THE LITTLE BOY IS ALL ALONE AT YOUR PLACE TONIGHT?
ER, YEAH...
CALL THE HOUSE AND CHECK ON HIM!!
I ALREADY CALLED SEVERAL TIMES AND HE DIDN'T PICK UP.
THAT'S WHY I WAS...
LET'S GET OVER THERE **NOW!**
YUMI!
CHIBA!
DAD, LET'S GO!!
HUH?

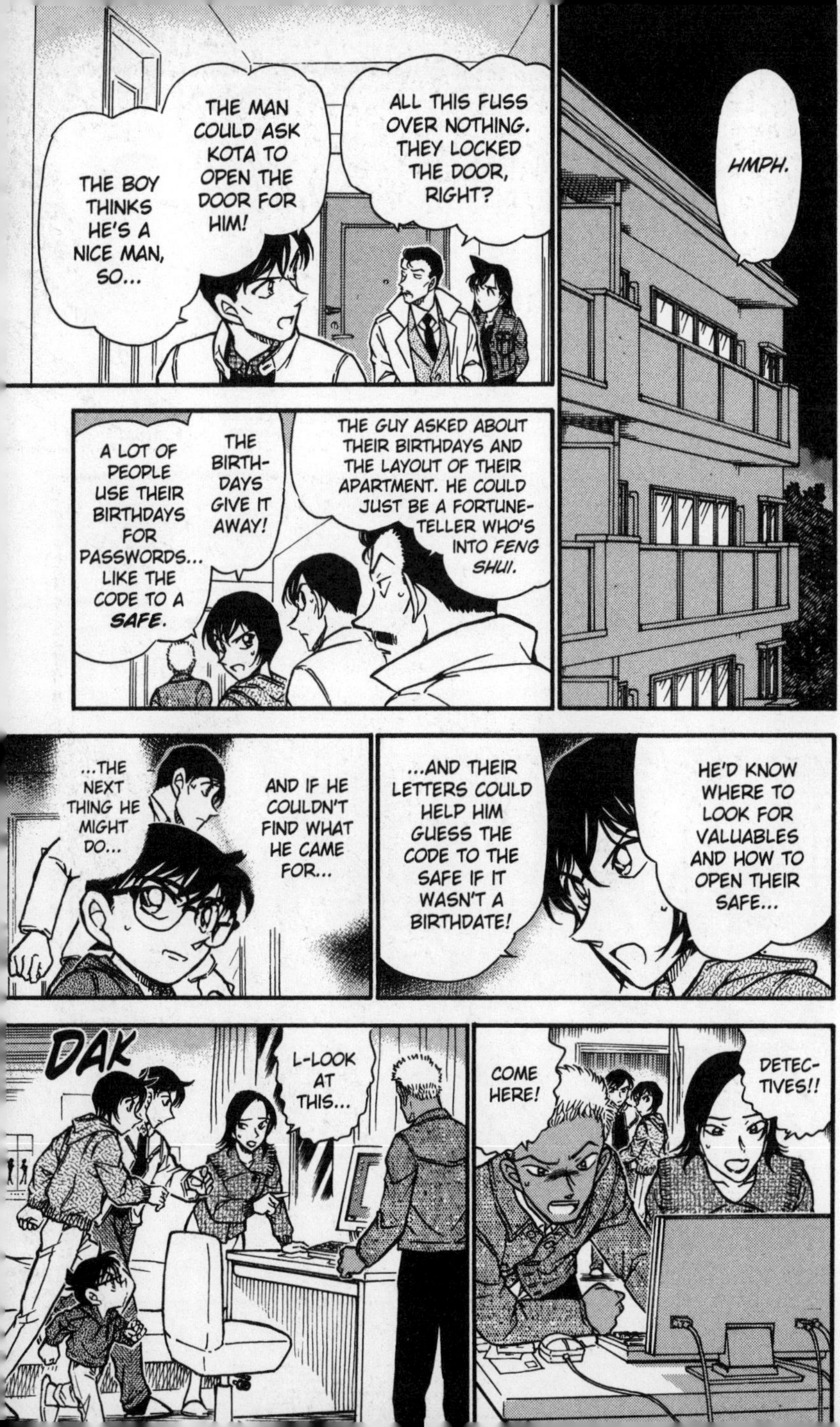
HMPH.
ALL THIS FUSS OVER NOTHING. THEY LOCKED THE DOOR, RIGHT?
THE MAN COULD ASK KOTA TO OPEN THE DOOR FOR HIM!
THE BOY THINKS HE'S A NICE MAN, SO...
THE GUY ASKED ABOUT THEIR BIRTHDAYS AND THE LAYOUT OF THEIR APARTMENT. HE COULD JUST BE A FORTUNE-TELLER WHO'S INTO *FENG SHUI*.
THE BIRTHDAYS GIVE IT AWAY!
A LOT OF PEOPLE USE THEIR BIRTHDAYS FOR PASSWORDS... LIKE THE CODE TO A **SAFE**.
HE'D KNOW WHERE TO LOOK FOR VALUABLES AND HOW TO OPEN THEIR SAFE...
...AND THEIR LETTERS COULD HELP HIM GUESS THE CODE TO THE SAFE IF IT WASN'T A BIRTHDATE!
AND IF HE COULDN'T FIND WHAT HE CAME FOR...
...THE NEXT THING HE MIGHT DO...
DETEC-TIVES!!
COME HERE!
L-LOOK AT THIS...
DAK

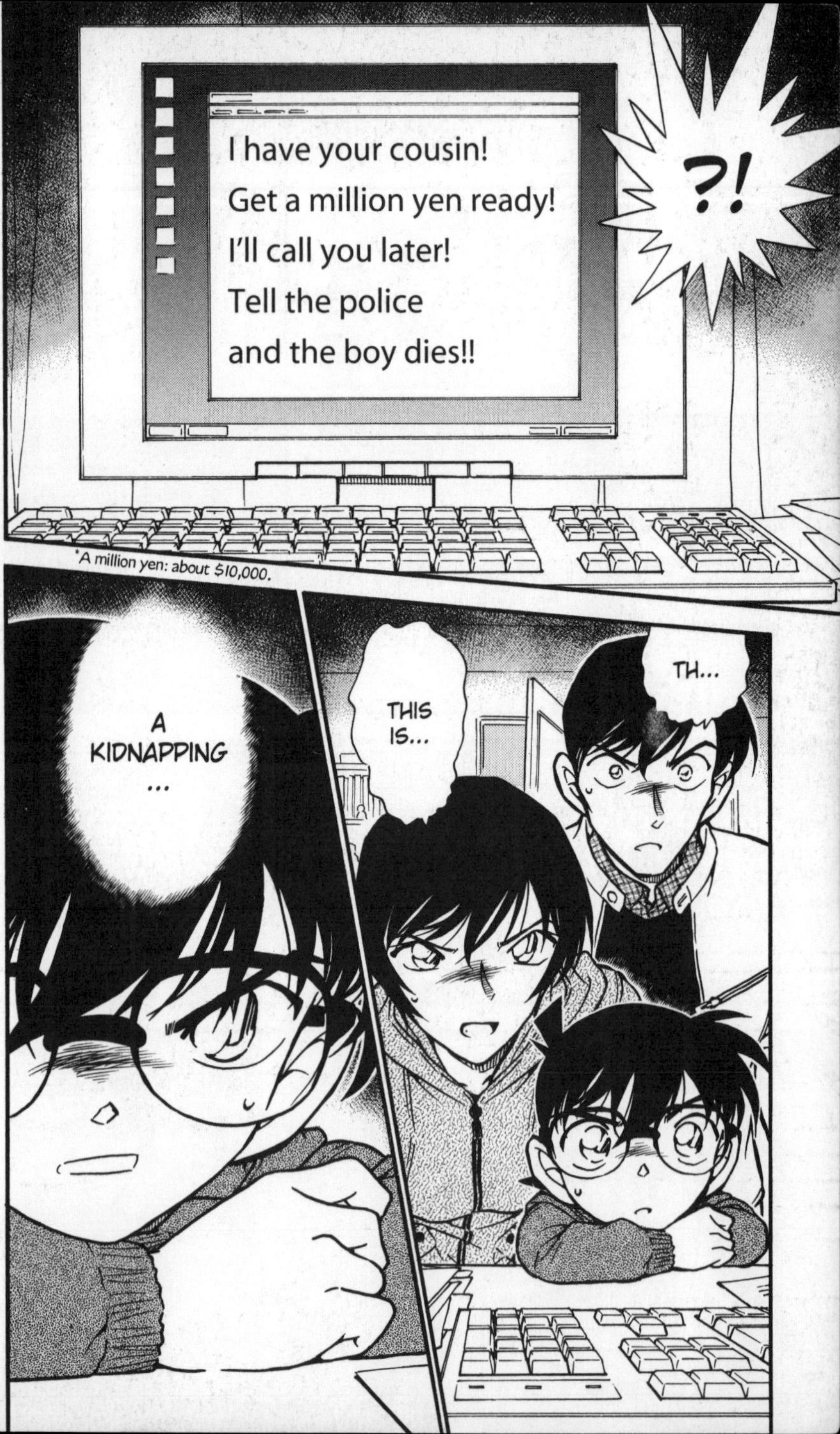
I have your cousin!
Get a million yen ready!
I'll call you later!
Tell the police
and the boy dies!!
?!
TH...
THIS IS...
A KIDNAPPING...
*A million yen: about $10,000.

FILE 2: THE SECRET VISIT

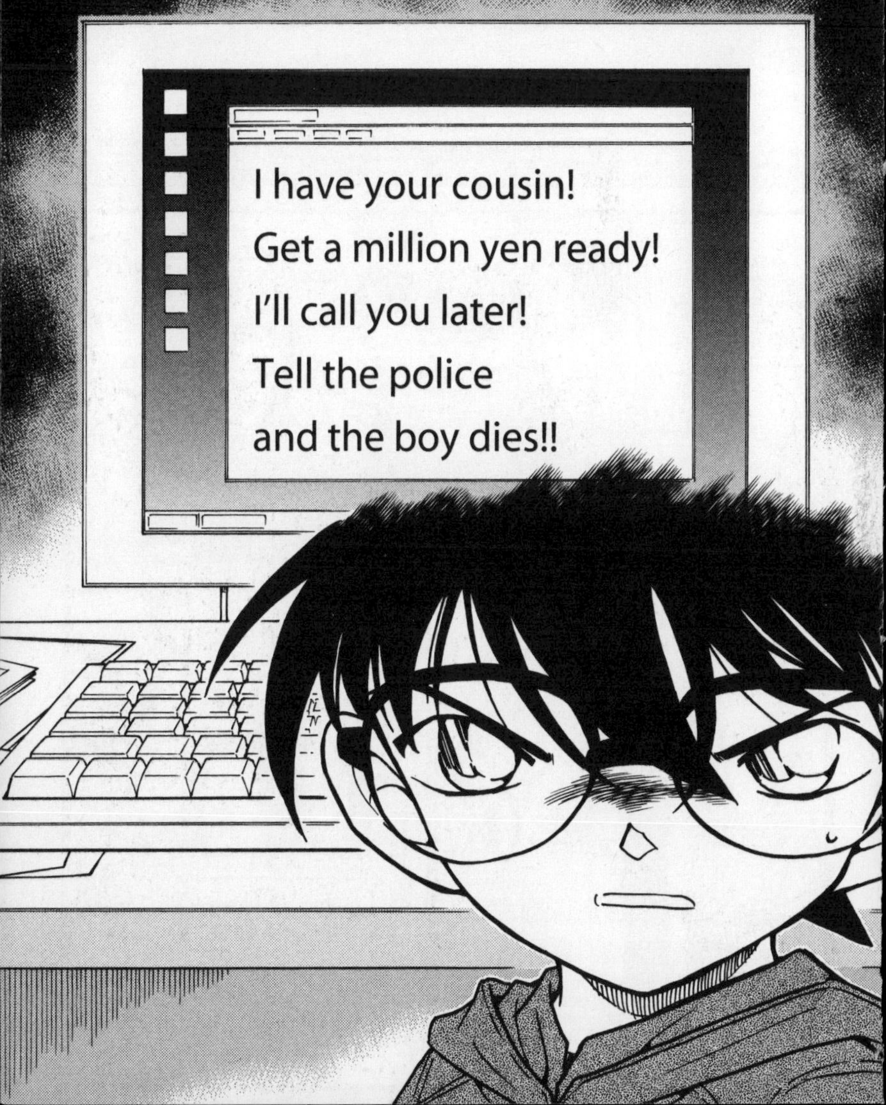

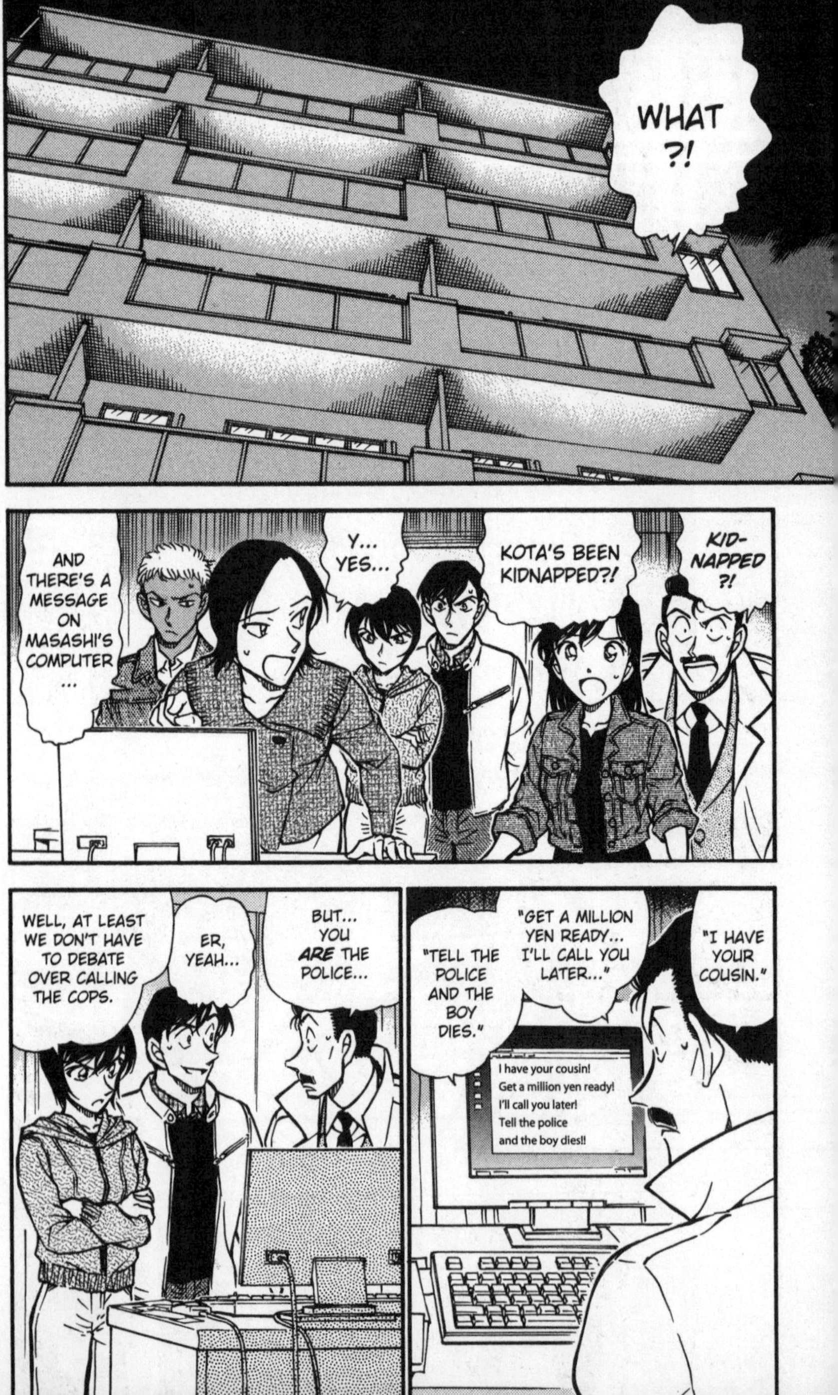
WHAT ?!
KID-NAPPED ?!
KOTA'S BEEN KIDNAPPED?!
Y... YES...
AND THERE'S A MESSAGE ON MASASHI'S COMPUTER ...
"I HAVE YOUR COUSIN."
"GET A MILLION YEN READY... I'LL CALL YOU LATER..."
"TELL THE POLICE AND THE BOY DIES."
I have your cousin!
Get a million yen ready!
I'll call you later!
Tell the police
and the boy dies!!
BUT... YOU ARE THE POLICE...
ER, YEAH...
WELL, AT LEAST WE DON'T HAVE TO DEBATE OVER CALLING THE COPS.

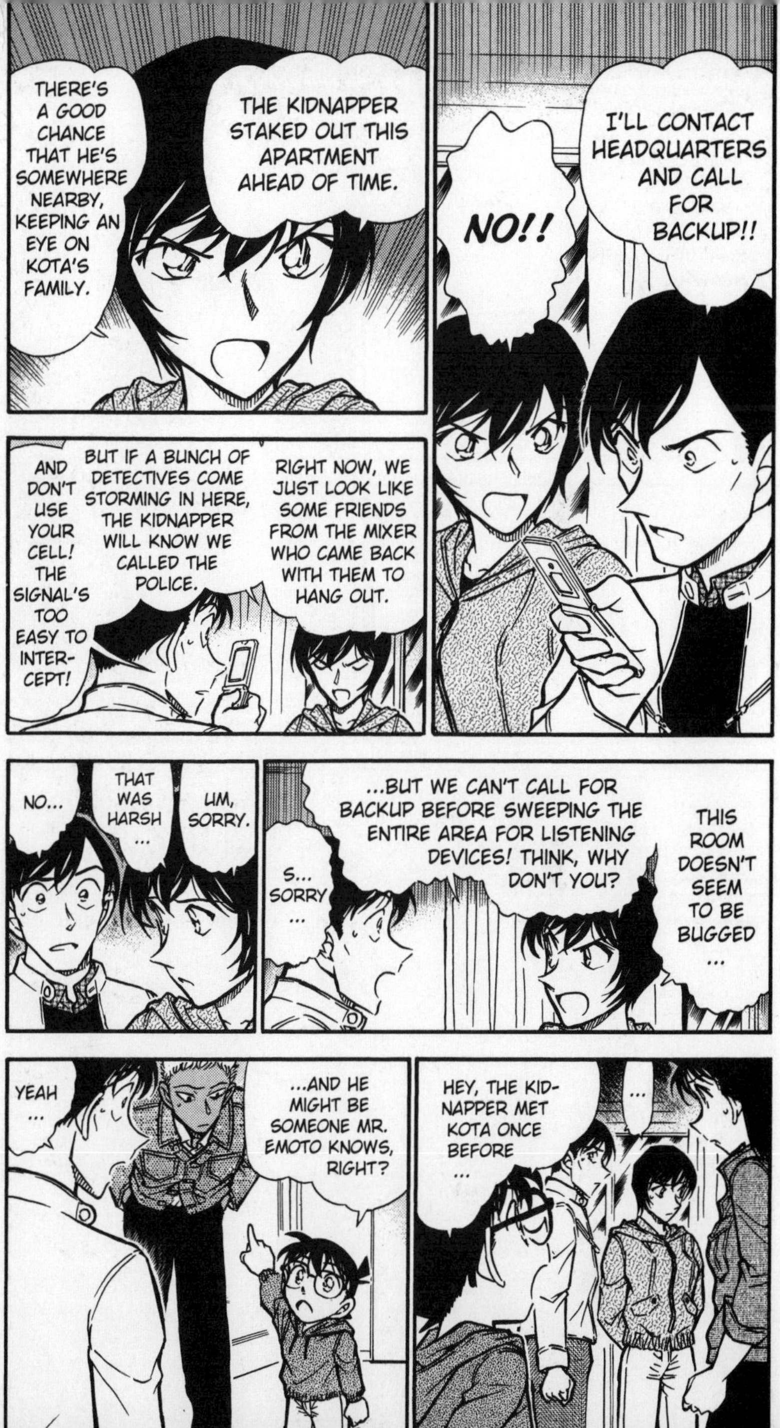
I'LL CONTACT HEADQUARTERS AND CALL FOR BACKUP!!
NO!!
THE KIDNAPPER STAKED OUT THIS APARTMENT AHEAD OF TIME.
THERE'S A GOOD CHANCE THAT HE'S SOMEWHERE NEARBY, KEEPING AN EYE ON KOTA'S FAMILY.
RIGHT NOW, WE JUST LOOK LIKE SOME FRIENDS FROM THE MIXER WHO CAME BACK WITH THEM TO HANG OUT.
BUT IF A BUNCH OF DETECTIVES COME STORMING IN HERE, THE KIDNAPPER WILL KNOW WE CALLED THE POLICE.
AND DON'T USE YOUR CELL! THE SIGNAL'S TOO EASY TO INTER-CEPT!
THIS ROOM DOESN'T SEEM TO BE BUGGED...
...BUT WE CAN'T CALL FOR BACKUP BEFORE SWEEPING THE ENTIRE AREA FOR LISTENING DEVICES! THINK, WHY DON'T YOU?
S... SORRY...
UM, SORRY.
THAT WAS HARSH...
NO...
...
HEY, THE KID-NAPPER MET KOTA ONCE BEFORE...
...AND HE MIGHT BE SOMEONE MR. EMOTO KNOWS, RIGHT?
YEAH...

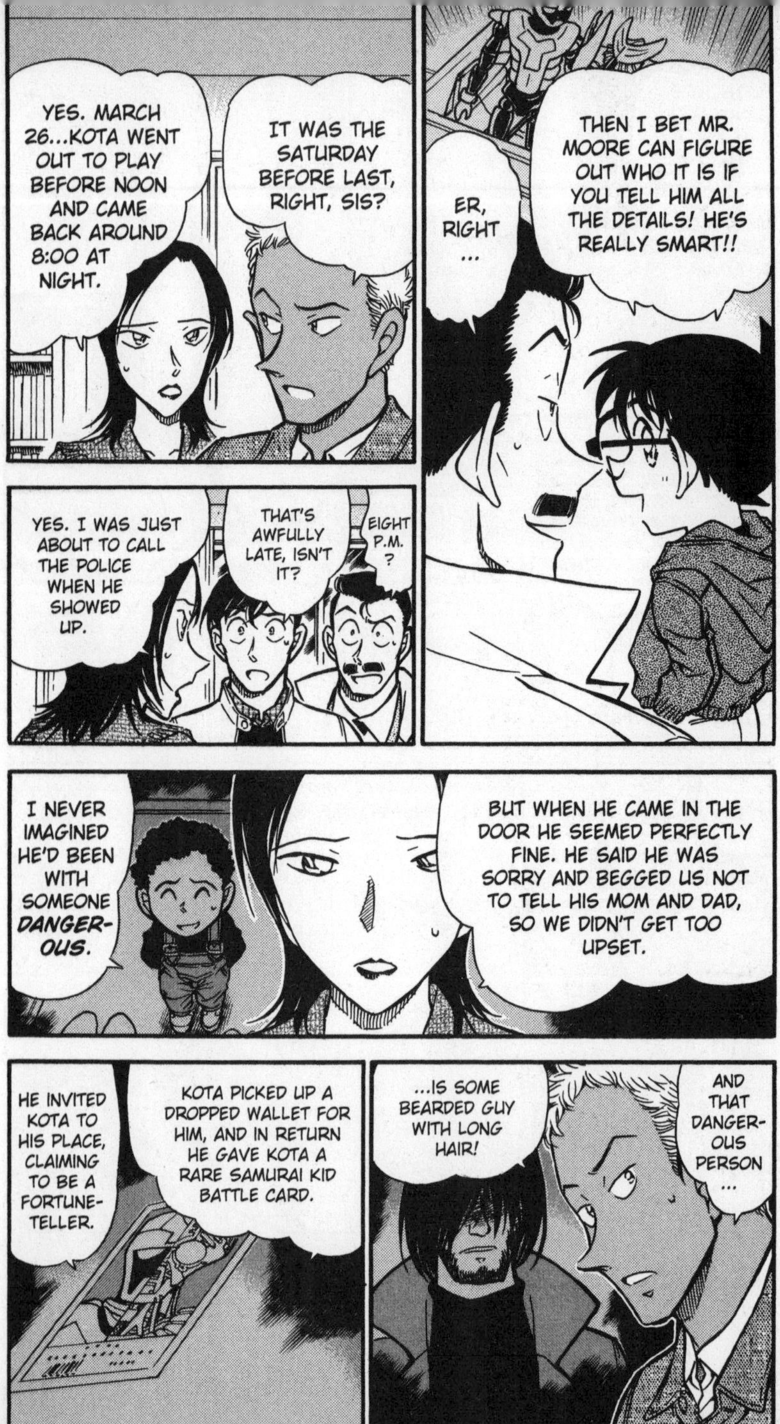
THEN I BET MR. MOORE CAN FIGURE OUT WHO IT IS IF YOU TELL HIM ALL THE DETAILS! HE'S REALLY SMART!!
ER, RIGHT ...
IT WAS THE SATURDAY BEFORE LAST, RIGHT, SIS?
YES. MARCH 26...KOTA WENT OUT TO PLAY BEFORE NOON AND CAME BACK AROUND 8:00 AT NIGHT.
EIGHT P.M. ?
THAT'S AWFULLY LATE, ISN'T IT?
YES. I WAS JUST ABOUT TO CALL THE POLICE WHEN HE SHOWED UP.
BUT WHEN HE CAME IN THE DOOR HE SEEMED PERFECTLY FINE. HE SAID HE WAS SORRY AND BEGGED US NOT TO TELL HIS MOM AND DAD, SO WE DIDN'T GET TOO UPSET.
I NEVER IMAGINED HE'D BEEN WITH SOMEONE ***DANGEROUS***.
AND THAT DANGEROUS PERSON ...
...IS SOME BEARDED GUY WITH LONG HAIR!
KOTA PICKED UP A DROPPED WALLET FOR HIM, AND IN RETURN HE GAVE KOTA A RARE SAMURAI KID BATTLE CARD.
HE INVITED KOTA TO HIS PLACE, CLAIMING TO BE A FORTUNE-TELLER.

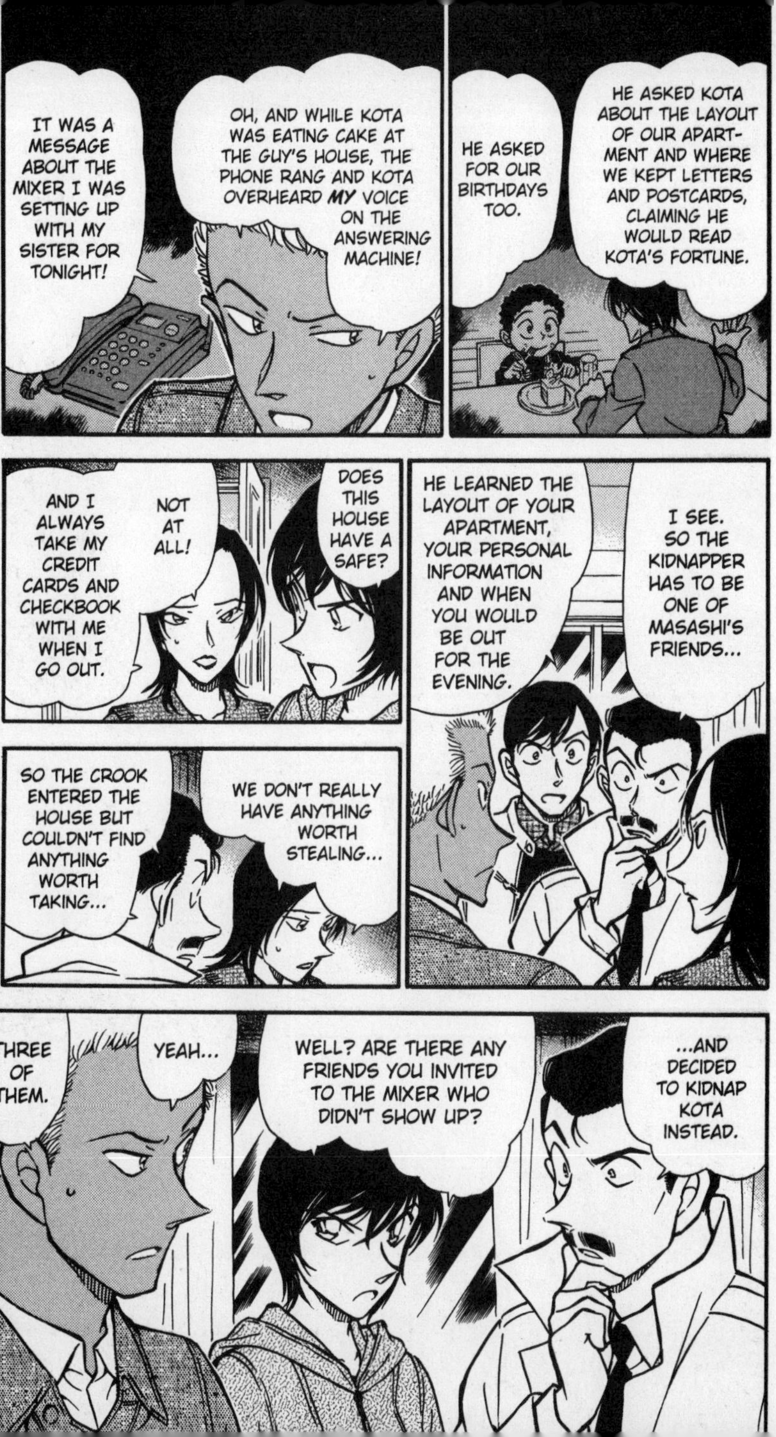
HE ASKED KOTA ABOUT THE LAYOUT OF OUR APARTMENT AND WHERE WE KEPT LETTERS AND POSTCARDS, CLAIMING HE WOULD READ KOTA'S FORTUNE.
HE ASKED FOR OUR BIRTHDAYS TOO.
OH, AND WHILE KOTA WAS EATING CAKE AT THE GUY'S HOUSE, THE PHONE RANG AND KOTA OVERHEARD *MY* VOICE ON THE ANSWERING MACHINE!
IT WAS A MESSAGE ABOUT THE MIXER I WAS SETTING UP WITH MY SISTER FOR TONIGHT!
I SEE. SO THE KIDNAPPER HAS TO BE ONE OF MASASHI'S FRIENDS...
HE LEARNED THE LAYOUT OF YOUR APARTMENT, YOUR PERSONAL INFORMATION AND WHEN YOU WOULD BE OUT FOR THE EVENING.
DOES THIS HOUSE HAVE A SAFE?
NOT AT ALL!
AND I ALWAYS TAKE MY CREDIT CARDS AND CHECKBOOK WITH ME WHEN I GO OUT.
WE DON'T REALLY HAVE ANYTHING WORTH STEALING...
SO THE CROOK ENTERED THE HOUSE BUT COULDN'T FIND ANYTHING WORTH TAKING...
...AND DECIDED TO KIDNAP KOTA INSTEAD.
WELL? ARE THERE ANY FRIENDS YOU INVITED TO THE MIXER WHO DIDN'T SHOW UP?
YEAH...
THREE OF THEM.

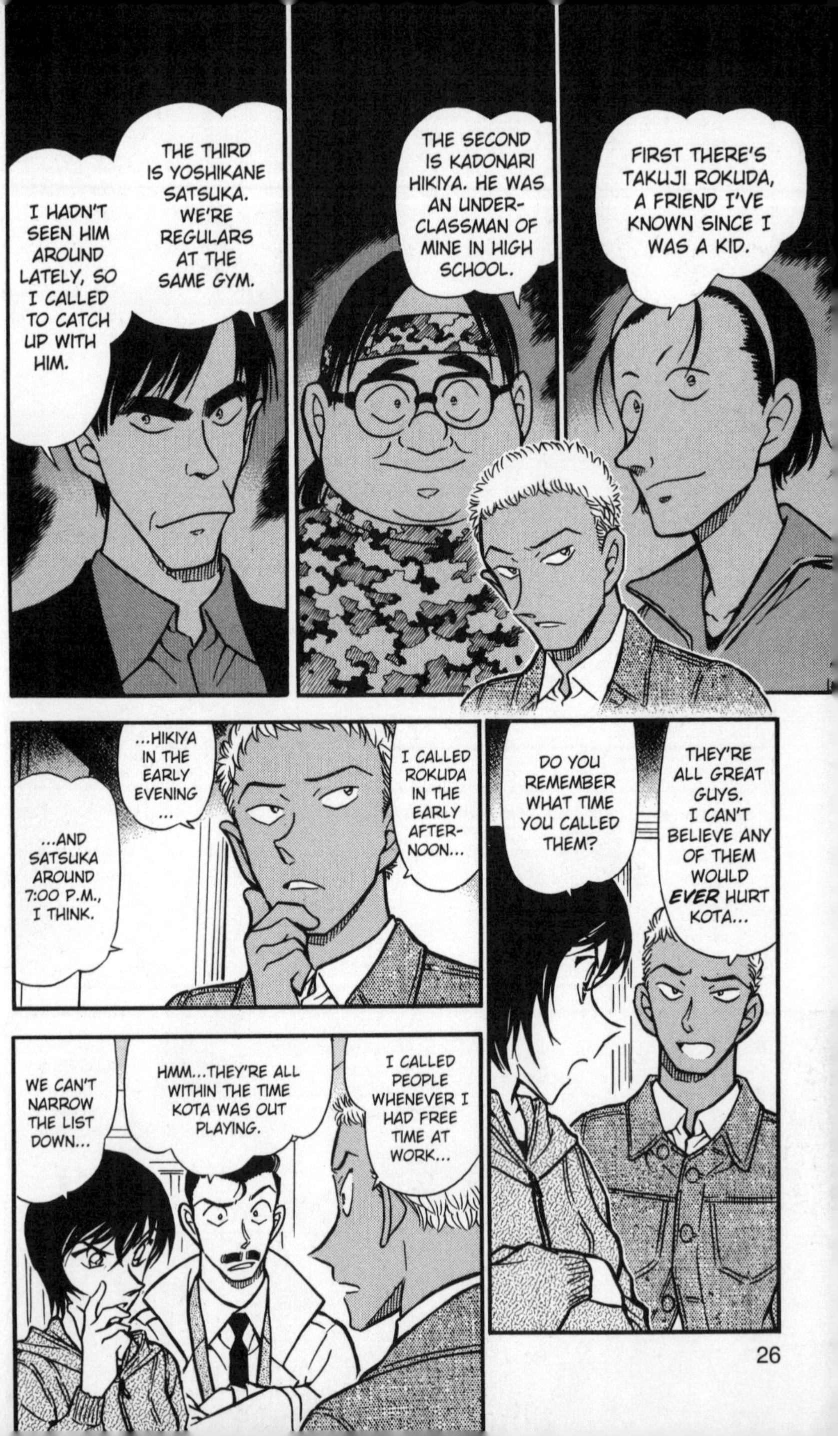
FIRST THERE'S TAKUJI ROKUDA, A FRIEND I'VE KNOWN SINCE I WAS A KID.
THE SECOND IS KADONARI HIKIYA. HE WAS AN UNDER-CLASSMAN OF MINE IN HIGH SCHOOL.
THE THIRD IS YOSHIKANE SATSUKA. WE'RE REGULARS AT THE SAME GYM.
I HADN'T SEEN HIM AROUND LATELY, SO I CALLED TO CATCH UP WITH HIM.
THEY'RE ALL GREAT GUYS. I CAN'T BELIEVE ANY OF THEM WOULD *EVER* HURT KOTA...
DO YOU REMEMBER WHAT TIME YOU CALLED THEM?
I CALLED ROKUDA IN THE EARLY AFTER-NOON...
...HIKIYA IN THE EARLY EVENING...
...AND SATSUKA AROUND 7:00 P.M., I THINK.
I CALLED PEOPLE WHENEVER I HAD FREE TIME AT WORK...
HMM...THEY'RE ALL WITHIN THE TIME KOTA WAS OUT PLAYING.
WE CAN'T NARROW THE LIST DOWN...

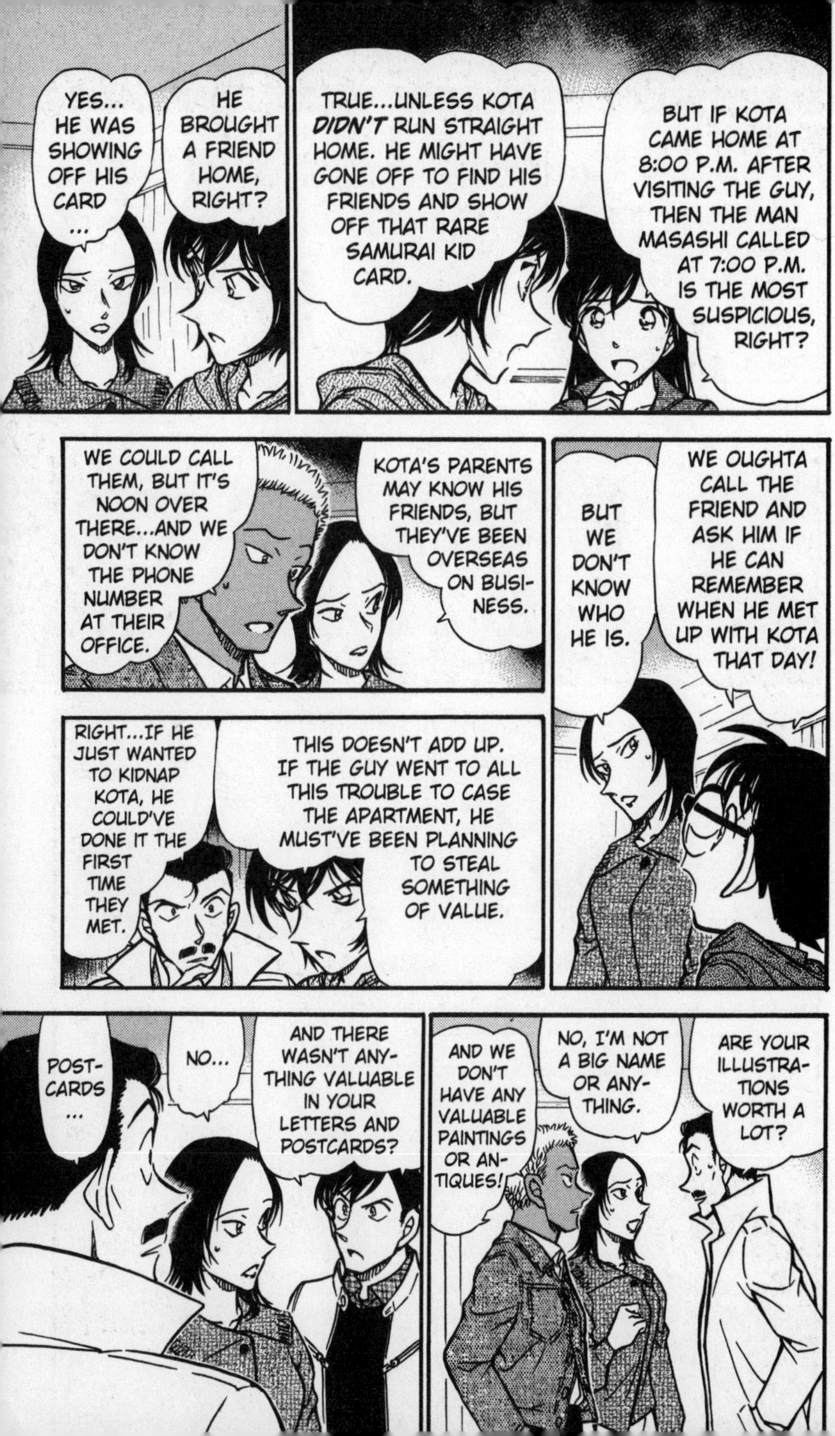
BUT IF KOTA CAME HOME AT 8:00 P.M. AFTER VISITING THE GUY, THEN THE MAN MASASHI CALLED AT 7:00 P.M. IS THE MOST SUSPICIOUS, RIGHT?
TRUE...UNLESS KOTA *DIDN'T* RUN STRAIGHT HOME. HE MIGHT HAVE GONE OFF TO FIND HIS FRIENDS AND SHOW OFF THAT RARE SAMURAI KID CARD.
HE BROUGHT A FRIEND HOME, RIGHT?
YES... HE WAS SHOWING OFF HIS CARD ...
WE OUGHTA CALL THE FRIEND AND ASK HIM IF HE CAN REMEMBER WHEN HE MET UP WITH KOTA THAT DAY!
BUT WE DON'T KNOW WHO HE IS.
KOTA'S PARENTS MAY KNOW HIS FRIENDS, BUT THEY'VE BEEN OVERSEAS ON BUSI-NESS.
WE COULD CALL THEM, BUT IT'S NOON OVER THERE...AND WE DON'T KNOW THE PHONE NUMBER AT THEIR OFFICE.
THIS DOESN'T ADD UP. IF THE GUY WENT TO ALL THIS TROUBLE TO CASE THE APARTMENT, HE MUST'VE BEEN PLANNING TO STEAL SOMETHING OF VALUE.
RIGHT...IF HE JUST WANTED TO KIDNAP KOTA, HE COULD'VE DONE IT THE FIRST TIME THEY MET.
ARE YOUR ILLUSTRA-TIONS WORTH A LOT?
NO, I'M NOT A BIG NAME OR ANY-THING.
AND WE DON'T HAVE ANY VALUABLE PAINTINGS OR AN-TIQUES!
AND THERE WASN'T ANY-THING VALUABLE IN YOUR LETTERS AND POSTCARDS?
NO...
POST-CARDS ...

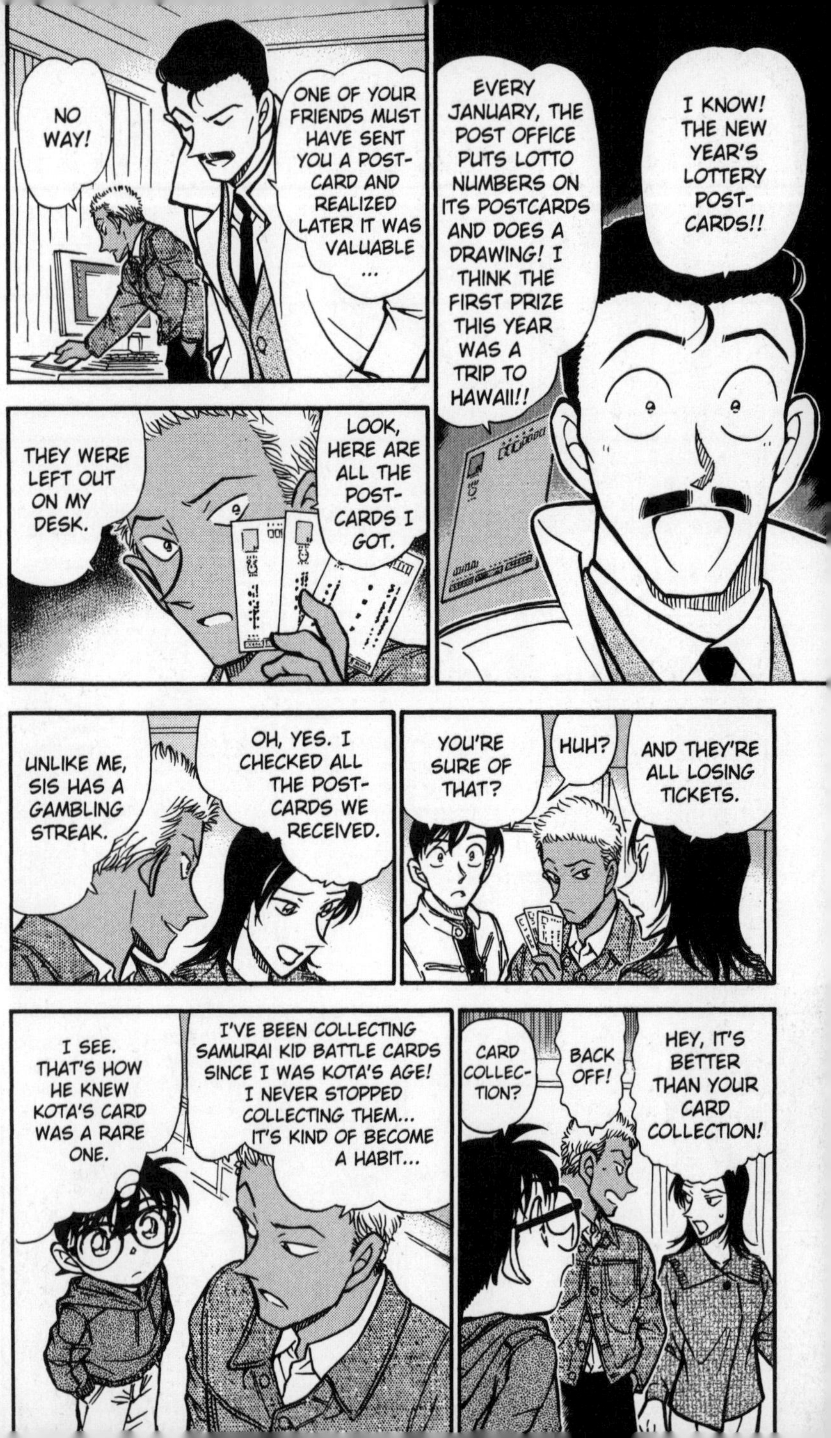
I KNOW! THE NEW YEAR'S LOTTERY POST-CARDS!!
EVERY JANUARY, THE POST OFFICE PUTS LOTTO NUMBERS ON ITS POSTCARDS AND DOES A DRAWING! I THINK THE FIRST PRIZE THIS YEAR WAS A TRIP TO HAWAII!!
ONE OF YOUR FRIENDS MUST HAVE SENT YOU A POST-CARD AND REALIZED LATER IT WAS VALUABLE ...
NO WAY!
LOOK, HERE ARE ALL THE POST-CARDS I GOT.
THEY WERE LEFT OUT ON MY DESK.
AND THEY'RE ALL LOSING TICKETS.
HUH?
YOU'RE SURE OF THAT?
OH, YES. I CHECKED ALL THE POST-CARDS WE RECEIVED.
UNLIKE ME, SIS HAS A GAMBLING STREAK.
HEY, IT'S BETTER THAN YOUR CARD COLLECTION!
BACK OFF!
CARD COLLEC-TION?
I'VE BEEN COLLECTING SAMURAI KID BATTLE CARDS SINCE I WAS KOTA'S AGE! I NEVER STOPPED COLLECTING THEM... IT'S KIND OF BECOME A HABIT...
I SEE. THAT'S HOW HE KNEW KOTA'S CARD WAS A RARE ONE.

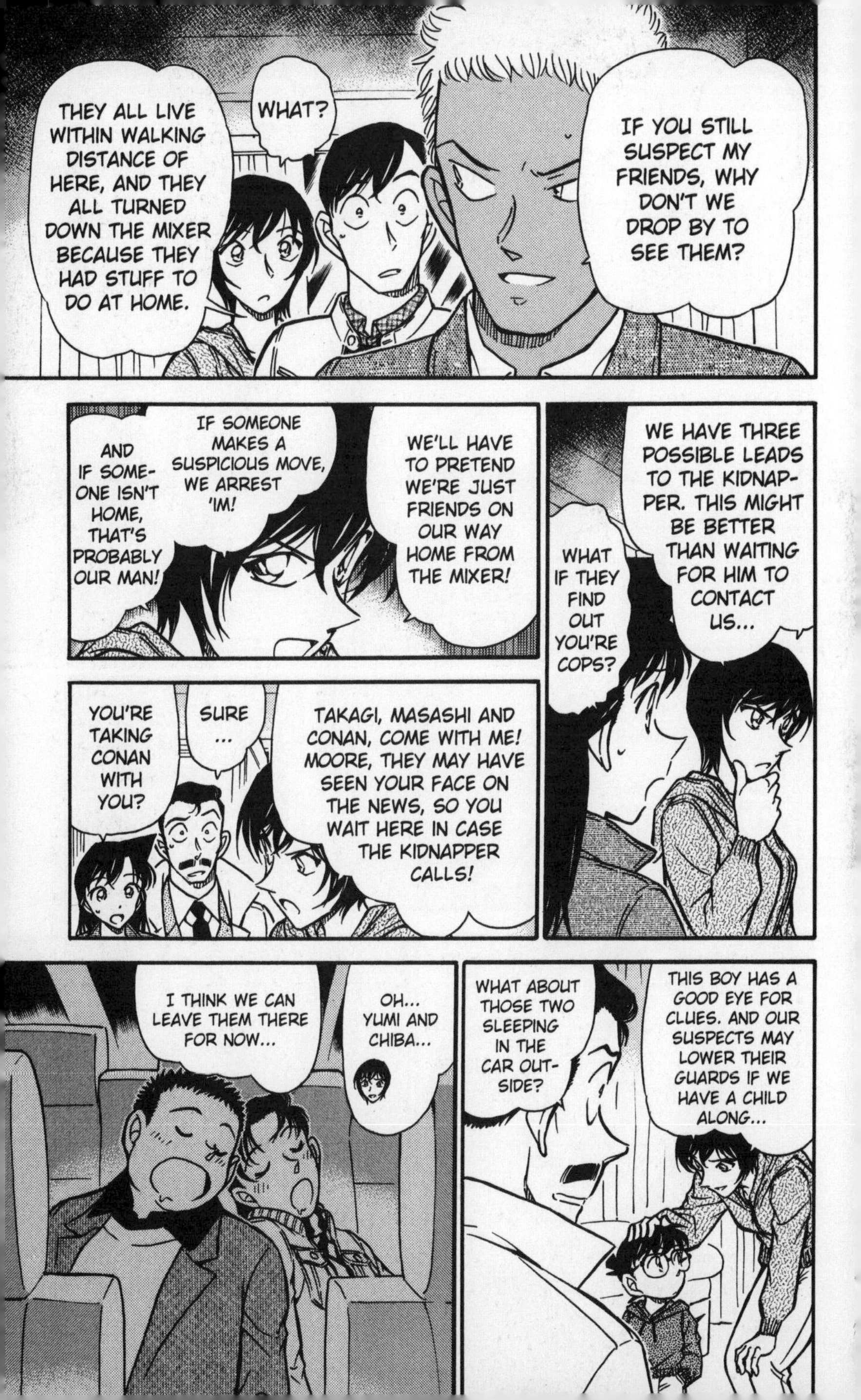
IF YOU STILL SUSPECT MY FRIENDS, WHY DON'T WE DROP BY TO SEE THEM?
WHAT?
THEY ALL LIVE WITHIN WALKING DISTANCE OF HERE, AND THEY ALL TURNED DOWN THE MIXER BECAUSE THEY HAD STUFF TO DO AT HOME.
WE HAVE THREE POSSIBLE LEADS TO THE KIDNAP-PER. THIS MIGHT BE BETTER THAN WAITING FOR HIM TO CONTACT US...
WHAT IF THEY FIND OUT YOU'RE COPS?
WE'LL HAVE TO PRETEND WE'RE JUST FRIENDS ON OUR WAY HOME FROM THE MIXER!
IF SOMEONE MAKES A SUSPICIOUS MOVE, WE ARREST 'IM!
AND IF SOME-ONE ISN'T HOME, THAT'S PROBABLY OUR MAN!
TAKAGI, MASASHI AND CONAN, COME WITH ME! MOORE, THEY MAY HAVE SEEN YOUR FACE ON THE NEWS, SO YOU WAIT HERE IN CASE THE KIDNAPPER CALLS!
SURE ...
YOU'RE TAKING CONAN WITH YOU?
THIS BOY HAS A GOOD EYE FOR CLUES. AND OUR SUSPECTS MAY LOWER THEIR GUARDS IF WE HAVE A CHILD ALONG...
WHAT ABOUT THOSE TWO SLEEPING IN THE CAR OUT-SIDE?
OH... YUMI AND CHIBA...
I THINK WE CAN LEAVE THEM THERE FOR NOW...

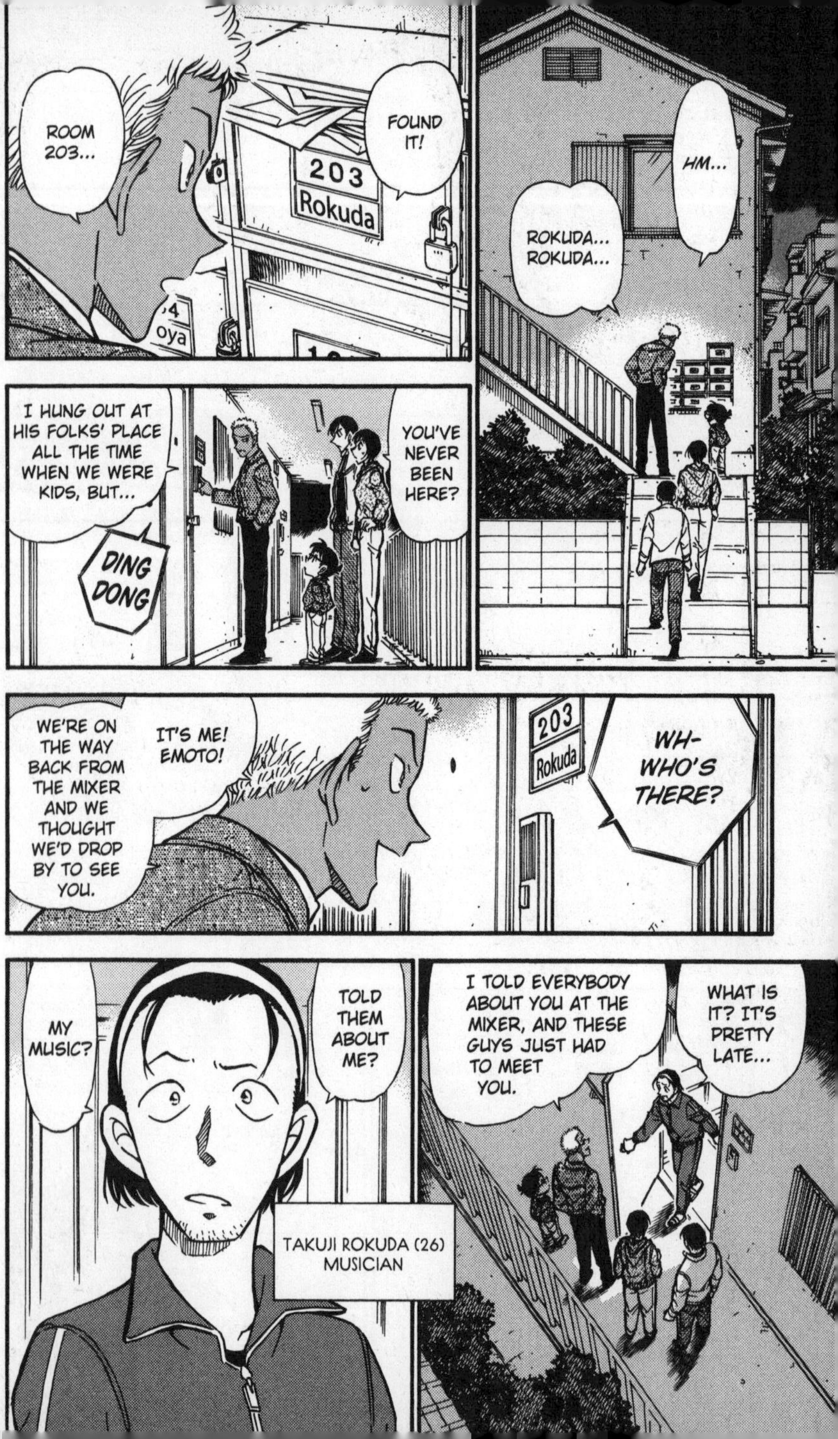
HM...
ROKUDA... ROKUDA...
FOUND IT!
203
Rokuda
ROOM 203...
YOU'VE NEVER BEEN HERE?
I HUNG OUT AT HIS FOLKS' PLACE ALL THE TIME WHEN WE WERE KIDS, BUT...
DING DONG
203
Rokuda
WH-WHO'S THERE?
IT'S ME! EMOTO!
WE'RE ON THE WAY BACK FROM THE MIXER AND WE THOUGHT WE'D DROP BY TO SEE YOU.
WHAT IS IT? IT'S PRETTY LATE...
I TOLD EVERYBODY ABOUT YOU AT THE MIXER, AND THESE GUYS JUST HAD TO MEET YOU.
TOLD THEM ABOUT ME?
MY MUSIC?
TAKUJI ROKUDA (26)
MUSICIAN

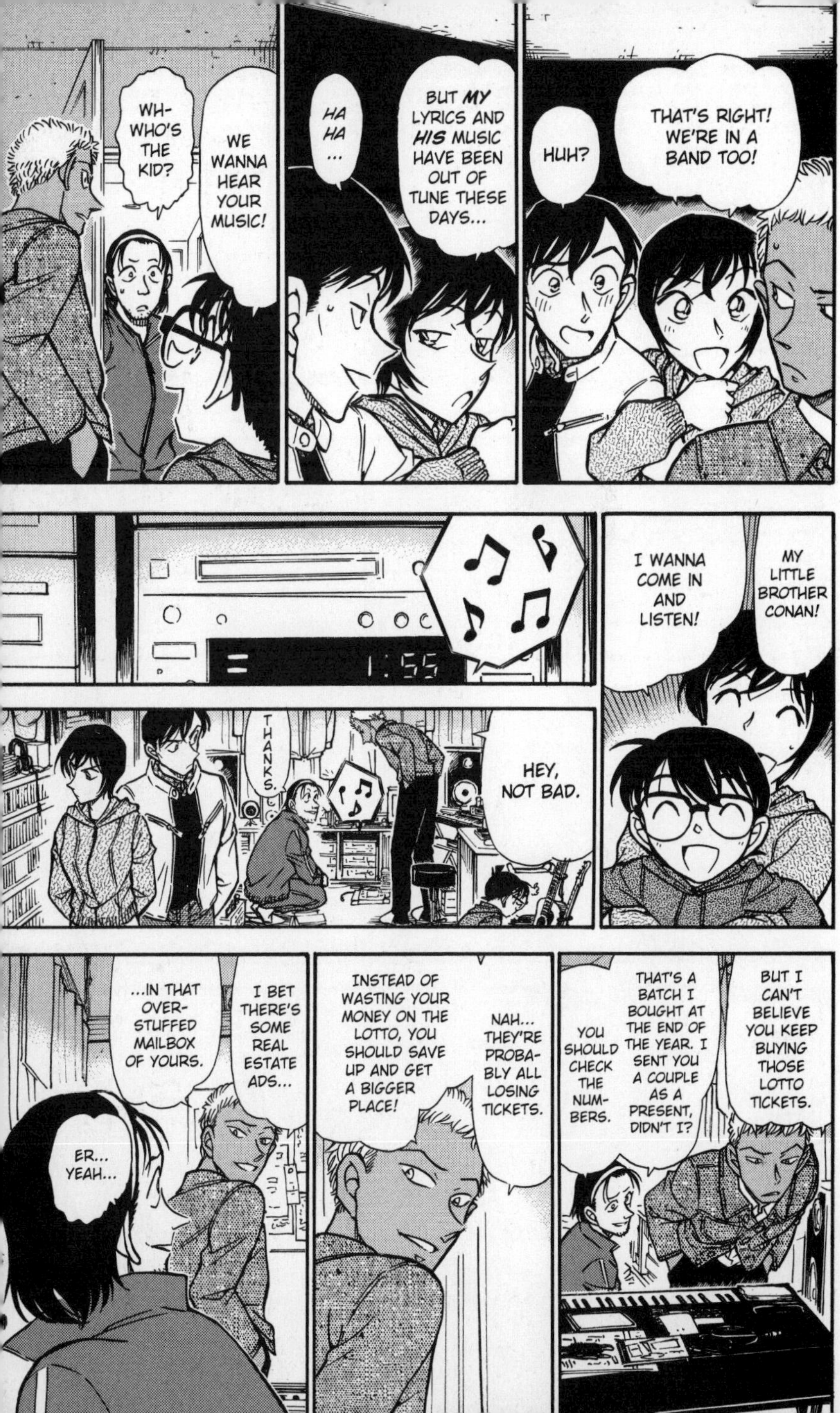
THAT'S RIGHT! WE'RE IN A BAND TOO!
HUH?
BUT MY LYRICS AND HIS MUSIC HAVE BEEN OUT OF TUNE THESE DAYS...
HA HA ...
WE WANNA HEAR YOUR MUSIC!
WH-WHO'S THE KID?
MY LITTLE BROTHER CONAN!
I WANNA COME IN AND LISTEN!
1:55
HEY, NOT BAD.
THANKS.
BUT I CAN'T BELIEVE YOU KEEP BUYING THOSE LOTTO TICKETS.
THAT'S A BATCH I BOUGHT AT THE END OF THE YEAR. I SENT YOU A COUPLE AS A PRESENT, DIDN'T I?
YOU SHOULD CHECK THE NUMBERS.
NAH... THEY'RE PROBABLY ALL LOSING TICKETS.
INSTEAD OF WASTING YOUR MONEY ON THE LOTTO, YOU SHOULD SAVE UP AND GET A BIGGER PLACE!
I BET THERE'S SOME REAL ESTATE ADS...
...IN THAT OVERSTUFFED MAILBOX OF YOURS.
ER... YEAH...

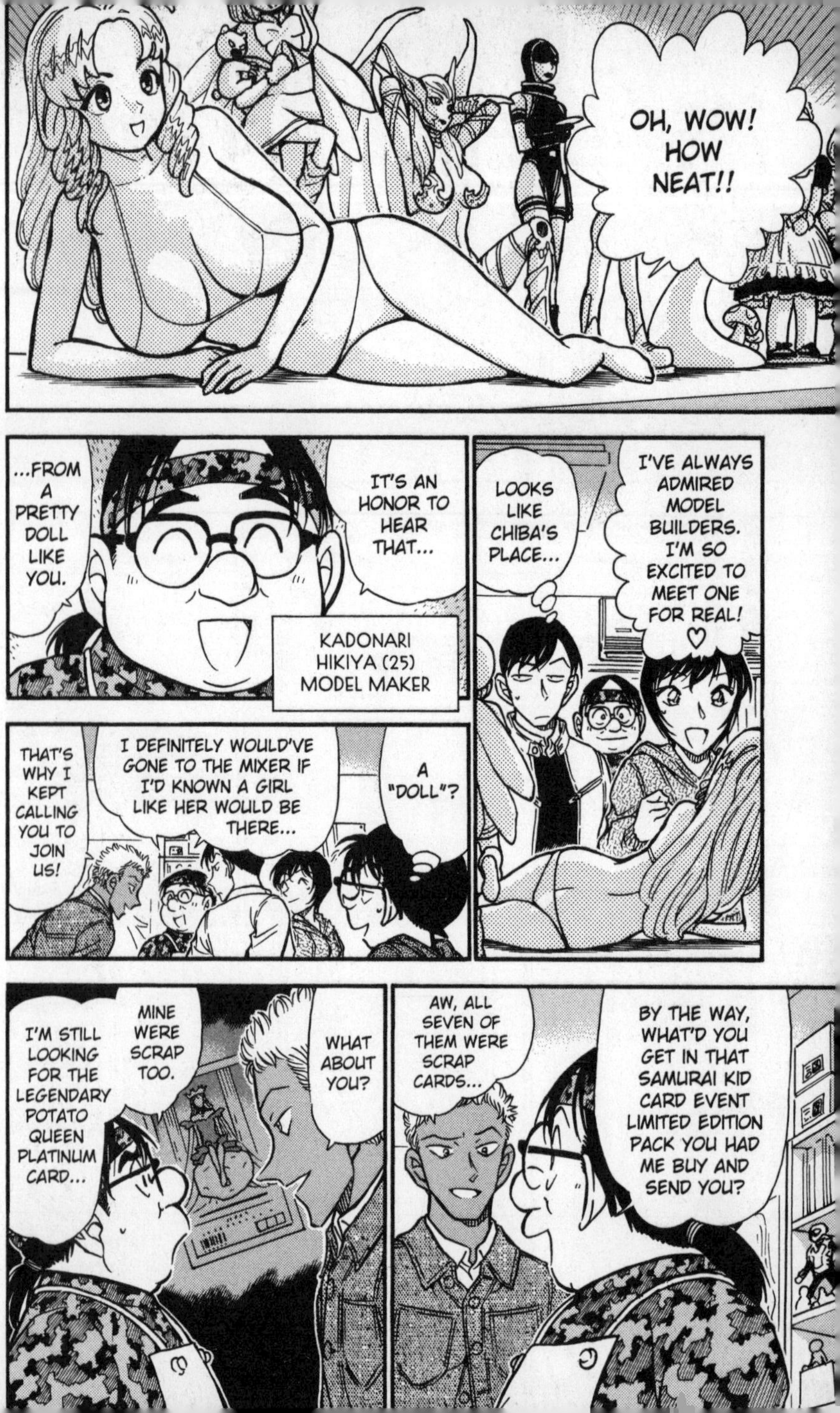
OH, WOW! HOW NEAT!!
I'VE ALWAYS ADMIRED MODEL BUILDERS. I'M SO EXCITED TO MEET ONE FOR REAL! ♥
LOOKS LIKE CHIBA'S PLACE...
IT'S AN HONOR TO HEAR THAT...
...FROM A PRETTY DOLL LIKE YOU.
KADONARI HIKIYA (25) MODEL MAKER
A "DOLL"?
I DEFINITELY WOULD'VE GONE TO THE MIXER IF I'D KNOWN A GIRL LIKE HER WOULD BE THERE...
THAT'S WHY I KEPT CALLING YOU TO JOIN US!
BY THE WAY, WHAT'D YOU GET IN THAT SAMURAI KID CARD EVENT LIMITED EDITION PACK YOU HAD ME BUY AND SEND YOU?
AW, ALL SEVEN OF THEM WERE SCRAP CARDS...
WHAT ABOUT YOU?
MINE WERE SCRAP TOO.
I'M STILL LOOKING FOR THE LEGENDARY POTATO QUEEN PLATINUM CARD...

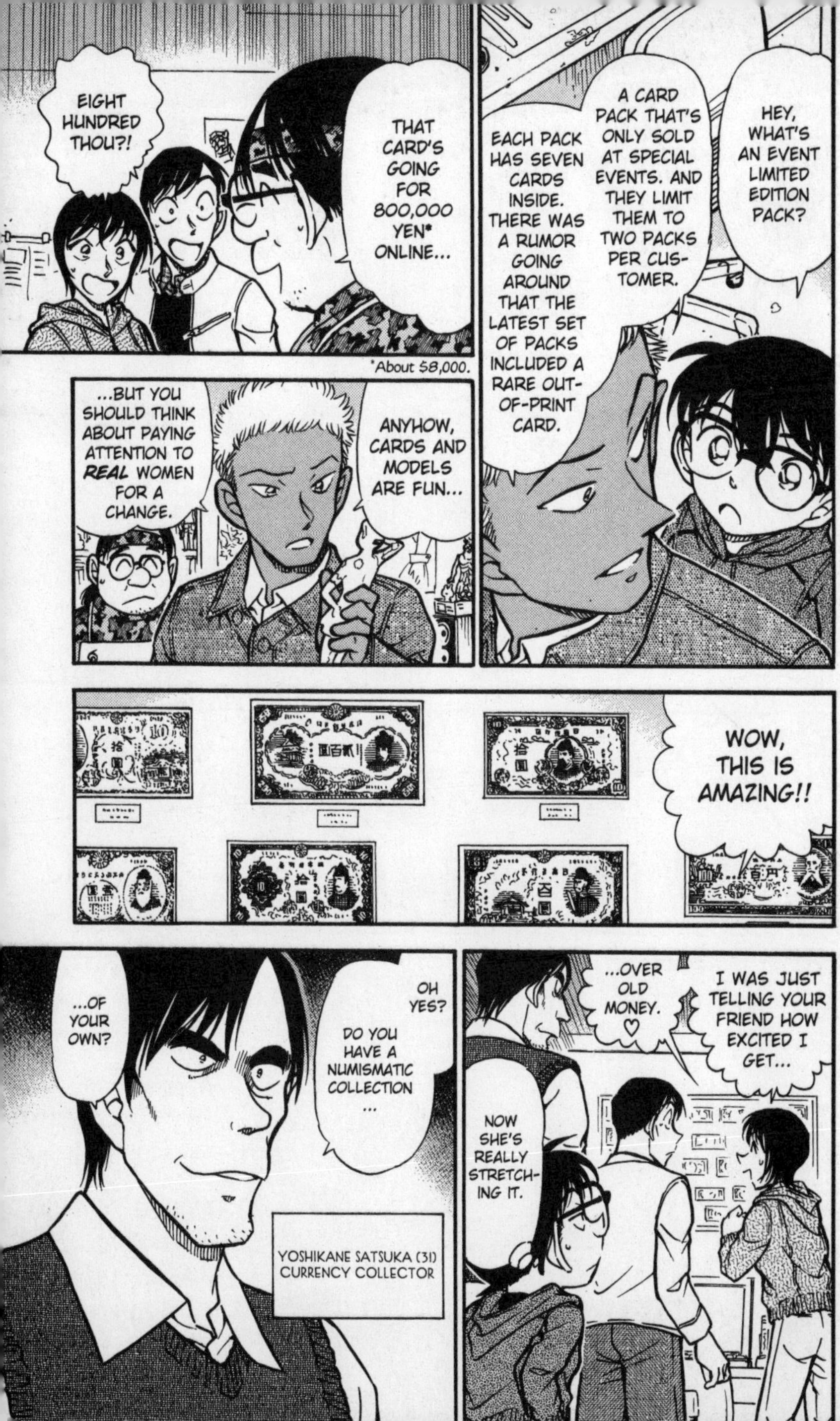
HEY, WHAT'S AN EVENT LIMITED EDITION PACK?
A CARD PACK THAT'S ONLY SOLD AT SPECIAL EVENTS. AND THEY LIMIT THEM TO TWO PACKS PER CUSTOMER.
EACH PACK HAS SEVEN CARDS INSIDE. THERE WAS A RUMOR GOING AROUND THAT THE LATEST SET OF PACKS INCLUDED A RARE OUT-OF-PRINT CARD.
THAT CARD'S GOING FOR 800,000 YEN* ONLINE...
EIGHT HUNDRED THOU?!
ANYHOW, CARDS AND MODELS ARE FUN...
...BUT YOU SHOULD THINK ABOUT PAYING ATTENTION TO *REAL* WOMEN FOR A CHANGE.
WOW, THIS IS AMAZING!!
I WAS JUST TELLING YOUR FRIEND HOW EXCITED I GET...
...OVER OLD MONEY. ♡
NOW SHE'S REALLY STRETCHING IT.
OH YES?
DO YOU HAVE A NUMISMATIC COLLECTION...
...OF YOUR OWN?
YOSHIKANE SATSUKA (31) CURRENCY COLLECTOR

*About $8,000.

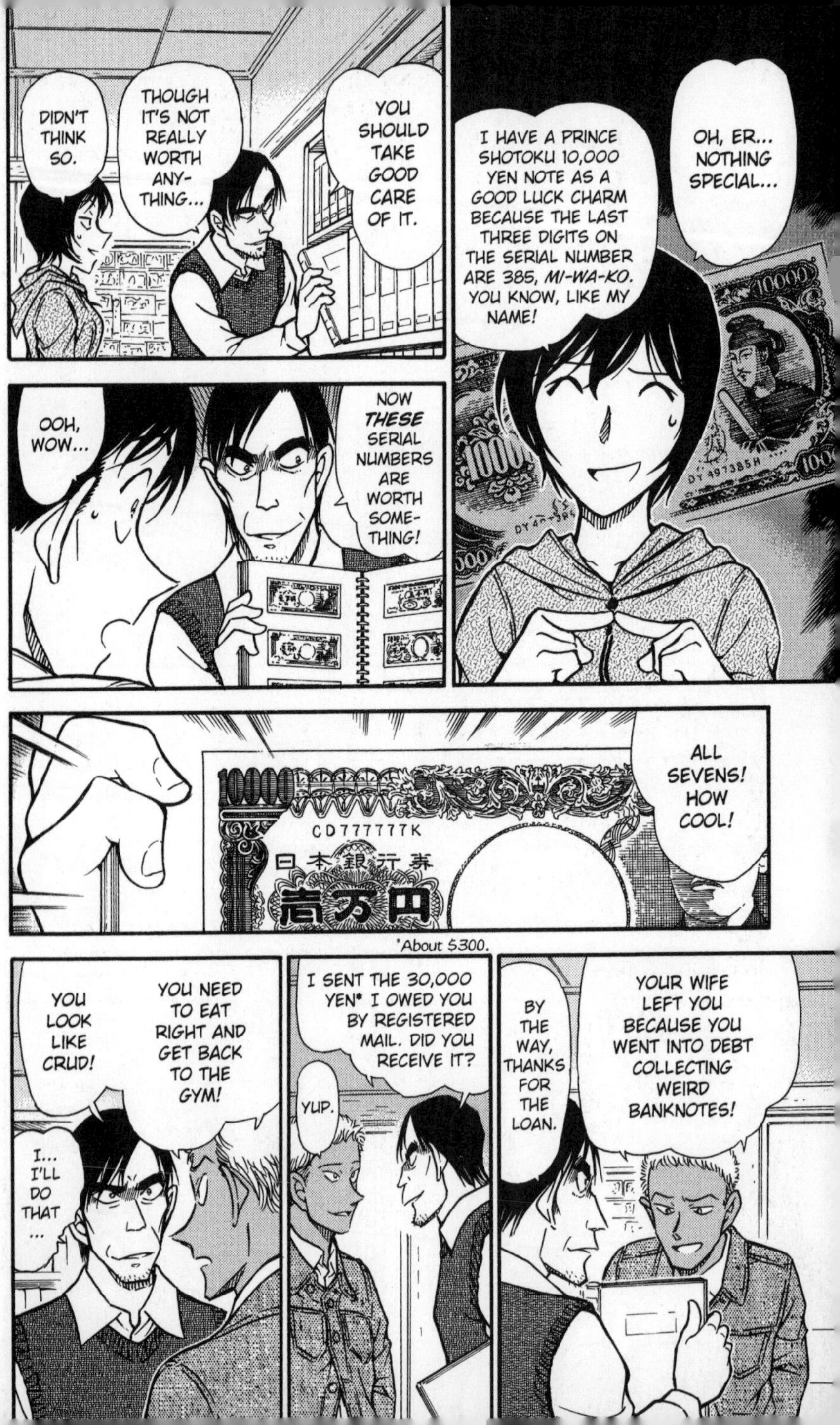
OH, ER... NOTHING SPECIAL...
I HAVE A PRINCE SHOTOKU 10,000 YEN NOTE AS A GOOD LUCK CHARM BECAUSE THE LAST THREE DIGITS ON THE SERIAL NUMBER ARE 385, *MI-WA-KO*. YOU KNOW, LIKE MY NAME!
YOU SHOULD TAKE GOOD CARE OF IT.
THOUGH IT'S NOT REALLY WORTH ANY-THING...
DIDN'T THINK SO.
NOW ***THESE*** SERIAL NUMBERS ARE WORTH SOME-THING!
OOH, WOW...
ALL SEVENS! HOW COOL!
CD777777K
日本銀行券
壱万円
YOUR WIFE LEFT YOU BECAUSE YOU WENT INTO DEBT COLLECTING WEIRD BANKNOTES!
BY THE WAY, THANKS FOR THE LOAN.
I SENT THE 30,000 YEN* I OWED YOU BY REGISTERED MAIL. DID YOU RECEIVE IT?
YUP.
YOU NEED TO EAT RIGHT AND GET BACK TO THE GYM!
YOU LOOK LIKE CRUD!
I... I'LL DO THAT ...

*About $300.

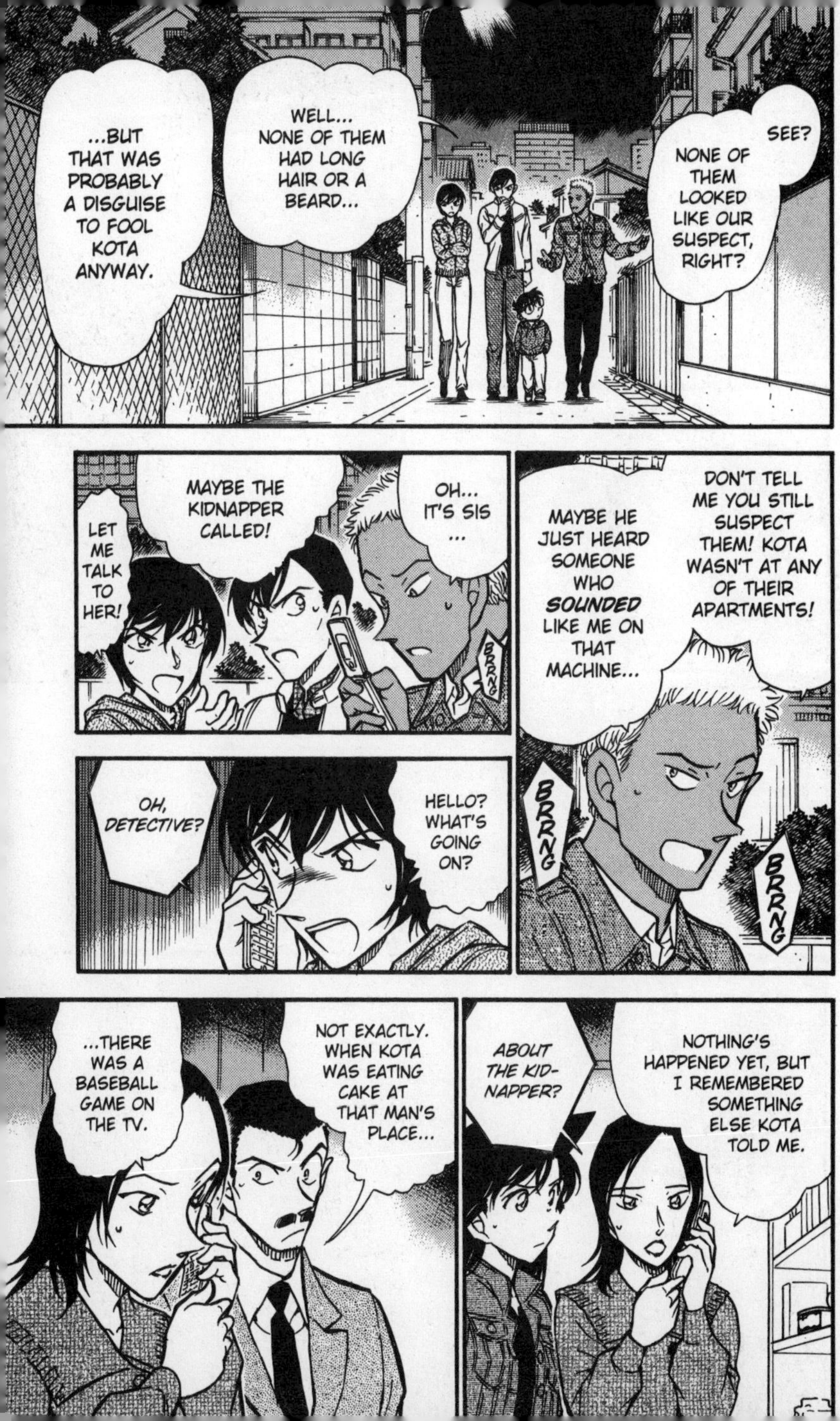
SEE? NONE OF THEM LOOKED LIKE OUR SUSPECT, RIGHT?
WELL... NONE OF THEM HAD LONG HAIR OR A BEARD...
...BUT THAT WAS PROBABLY A DISGUISE TO FOOL KOTA ANYWAY.
DON'T TELL ME YOU STILL SUSPECT THEM! KOTA WASN'T AT ANY OF THEIR APARTMENTS!
MAYBE HE JUST HEARD SOMEONE WHO *SOUNDED* LIKE ME ON THAT MACHINE...
BRRNG
BRRNG
OH... IT'S SIS ...
BRRNG
MAYBE THE KIDNAPPER CALLED!
LET ME TALK TO HER!
HELLO? WHAT'S GOING ON?
OH, DETECTIVE?
NOTHING'S HAPPENED YET, BUT I REMEMBERED SOMETHING ELSE KOTA TOLD ME.
ABOUT THE KID-NAPPER?
NOT EXACTLY. WHEN KOTA WAS EATING CAKE AT THAT MAN'S PLACE...
...THERE WAS A BASEBALL GAME ON THE TV.

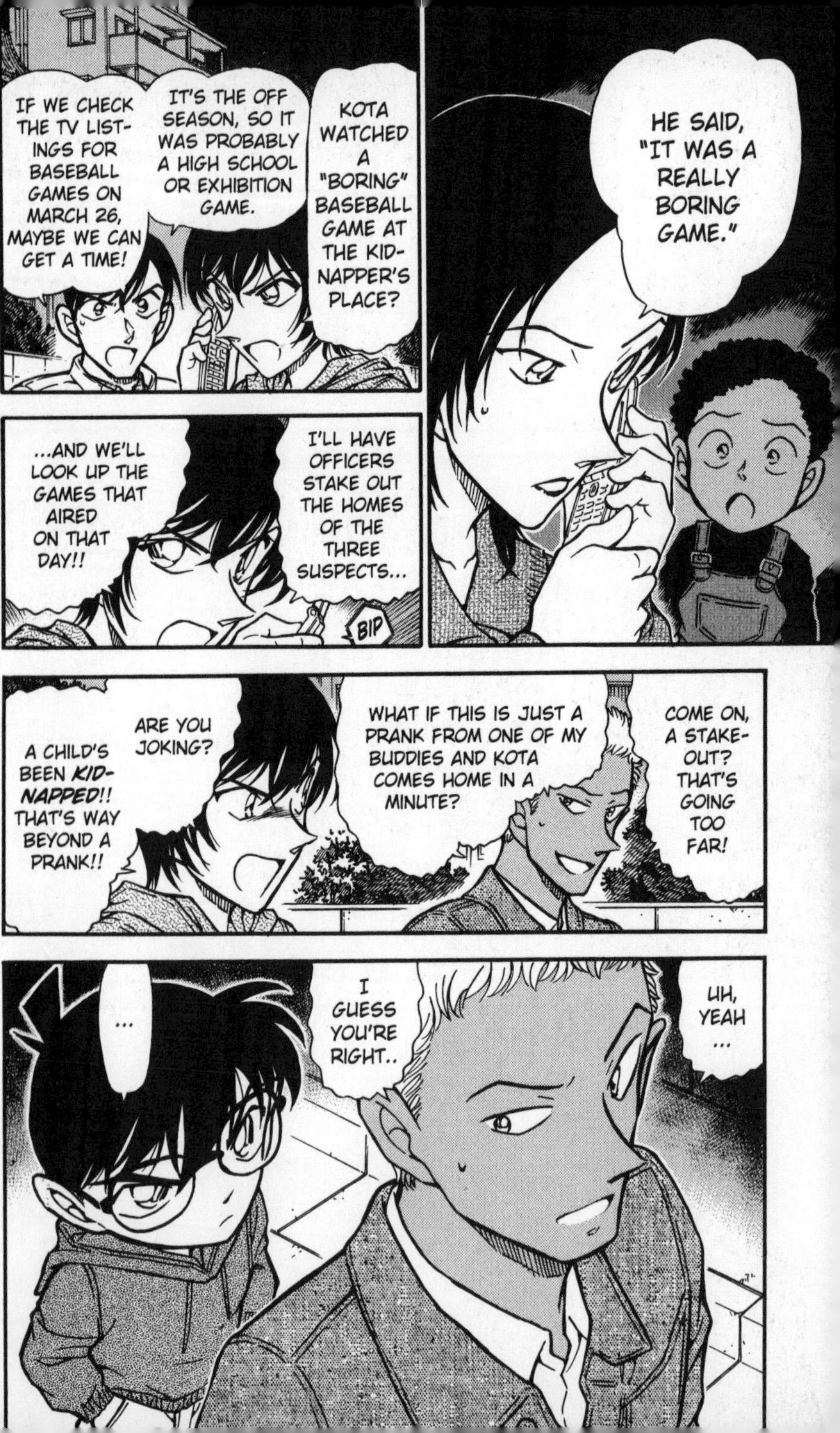
HE SAID, "IT WAS A REALLY BORING GAME."
KOTA WATCHED A "BORING" BASEBALL GAME AT THE KID-NAPPER'S PLACE?
IT'S THE OFF SEASON, SO IT WAS PROBABLY A HIGH SCHOOL OR EXHIBITION GAME.
IF WE CHECK THE TV LIST-INGS FOR BASEBALL GAMES ON MARCH 26, MAYBE WE CAN GET A TIME!
I'LL HAVE OFFICERS STAKE OUT THE HOMES OF THE THREE SUSPECTS...
BIP
...AND WE'LL LOOK UP THE GAMES THAT AIRED ON THAT DAY!!
COME ON, A STAKE-OUT? THAT'S GOING TOO FAR!
WHAT IF THIS IS JUST A PRANK FROM ONE OF MY BUDDIES AND KOTA COMES HOME IN A MINUTE?
ARE YOU JOKING?
A CHILD'S BEEN *KID-NAPPED*!! THAT'S WAY BEYOND A PRANK!!
UH, YEAH ...
I GUESS YOU'RE RIGHT..
...

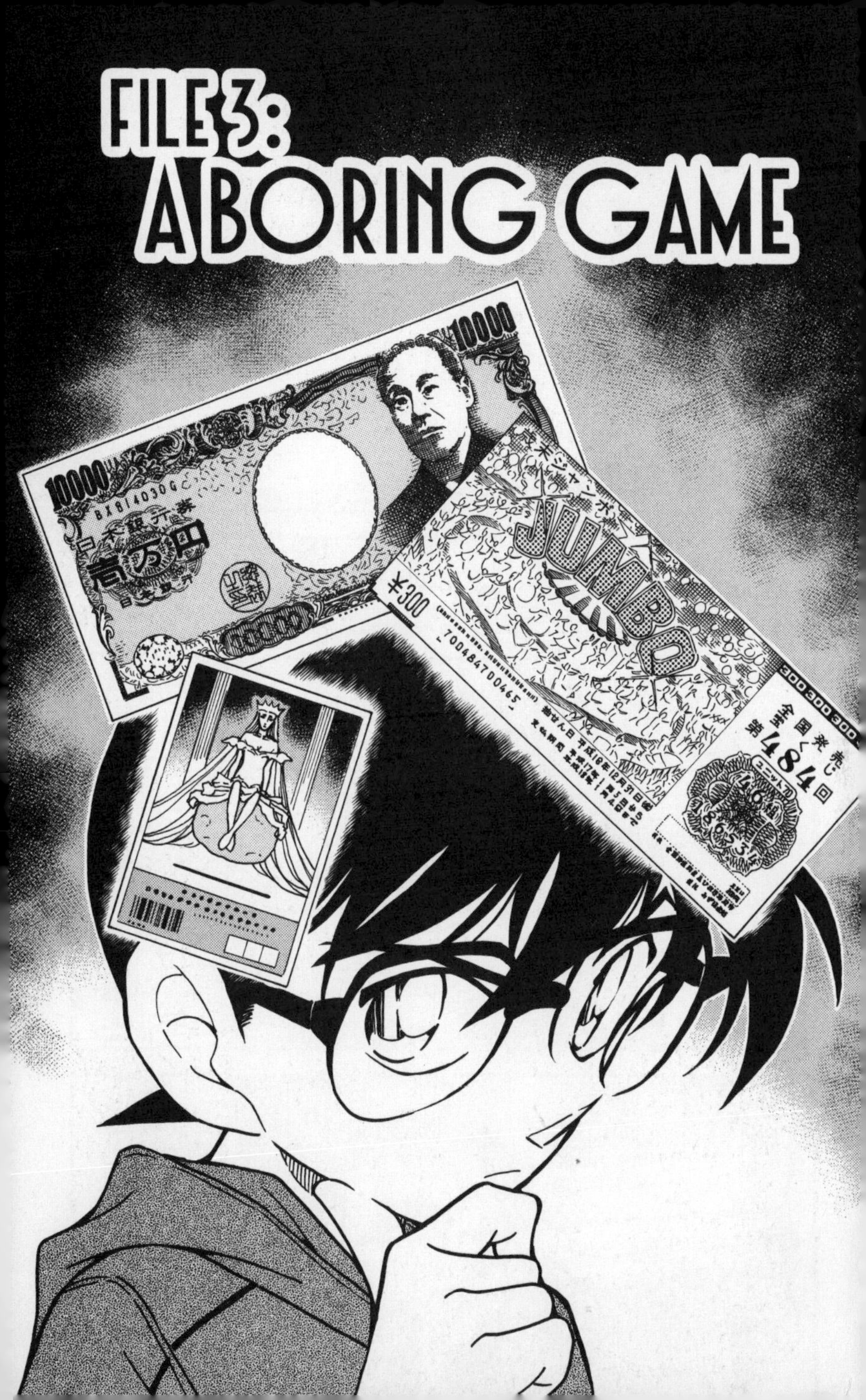
FILE 3:
A BORING GAME
10000
JUMBO
¥300

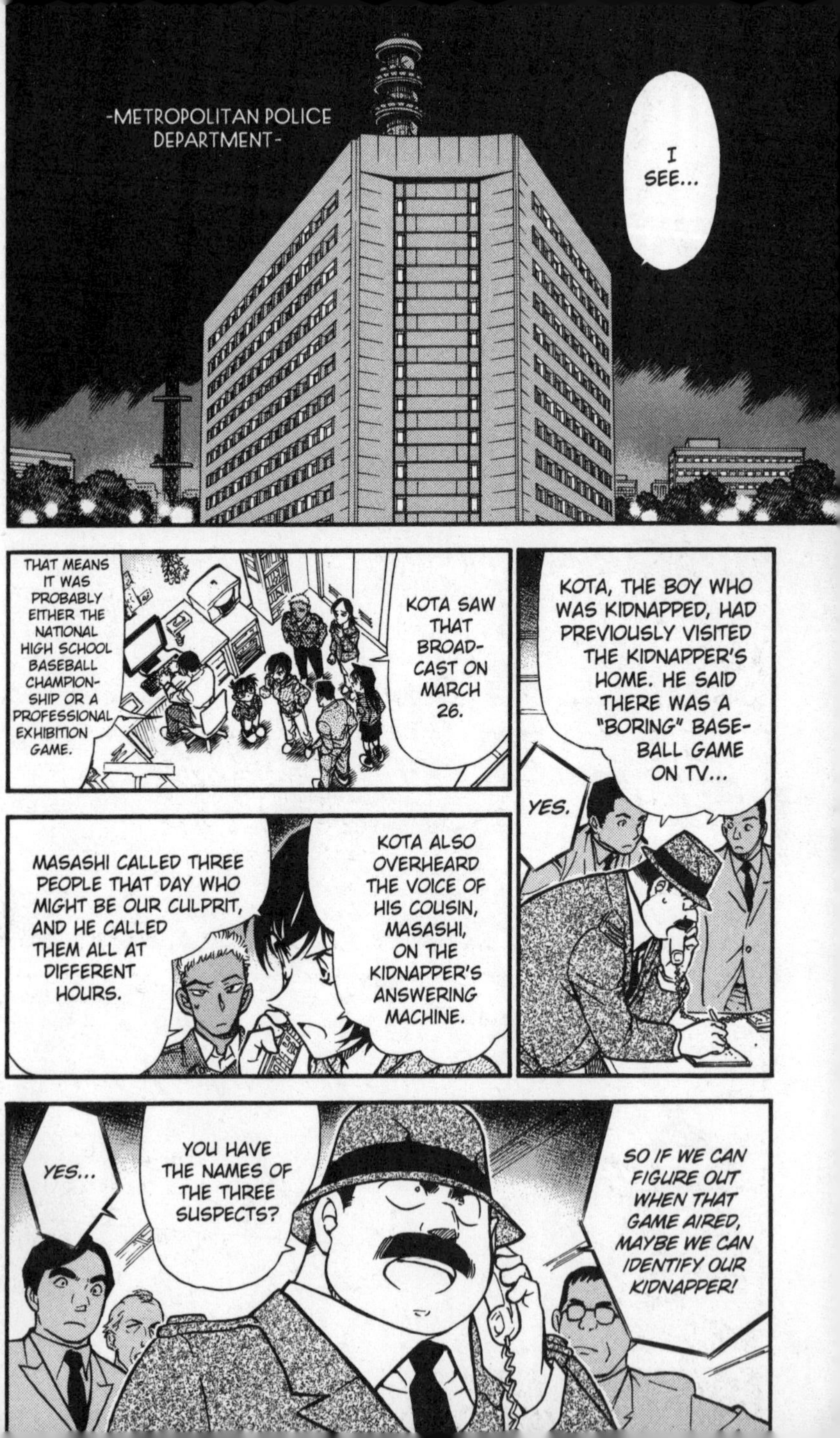
I SEE...
-METROPOLITAN POLICE DEPARTMENT-
KOTA, THE BOY WHO WAS KIDNAPPED, HAD PREVIOUSLY VISITED THE KIDNAPPER'S HOME. HE SAID THERE WAS A "BORING" BASEBALL GAME ON TV...
YES.
KOTA SAW THAT BROADCAST ON MARCH 26.
THAT MEANS IT WAS PROBABLY EITHER THE NATIONAL HIGH SCHOOL BASEBALL CHAMPIONSHIP OR A PROFESSIONAL EXHIBITION GAME.
KOTA ALSO OVERHEARD THE VOICE OF HIS COUSIN, MASASHI, ON THE KIDNAPPER'S ANSWERING MACHINE.
MASASHI CALLED THREE PEOPLE THAT DAY WHO MIGHT BE OUR CULPRIT, AND HE CALLED THEM ALL AT DIFFERENT HOURS.
SO IF WE CAN FIGURE OUT WHEN THAT GAME AIRED, MAYBE WE CAN IDENTIFY OUR KIDNAPPER!
YOU HAVE THE NAMES OF THE THREE SUSPECTS?
YES...

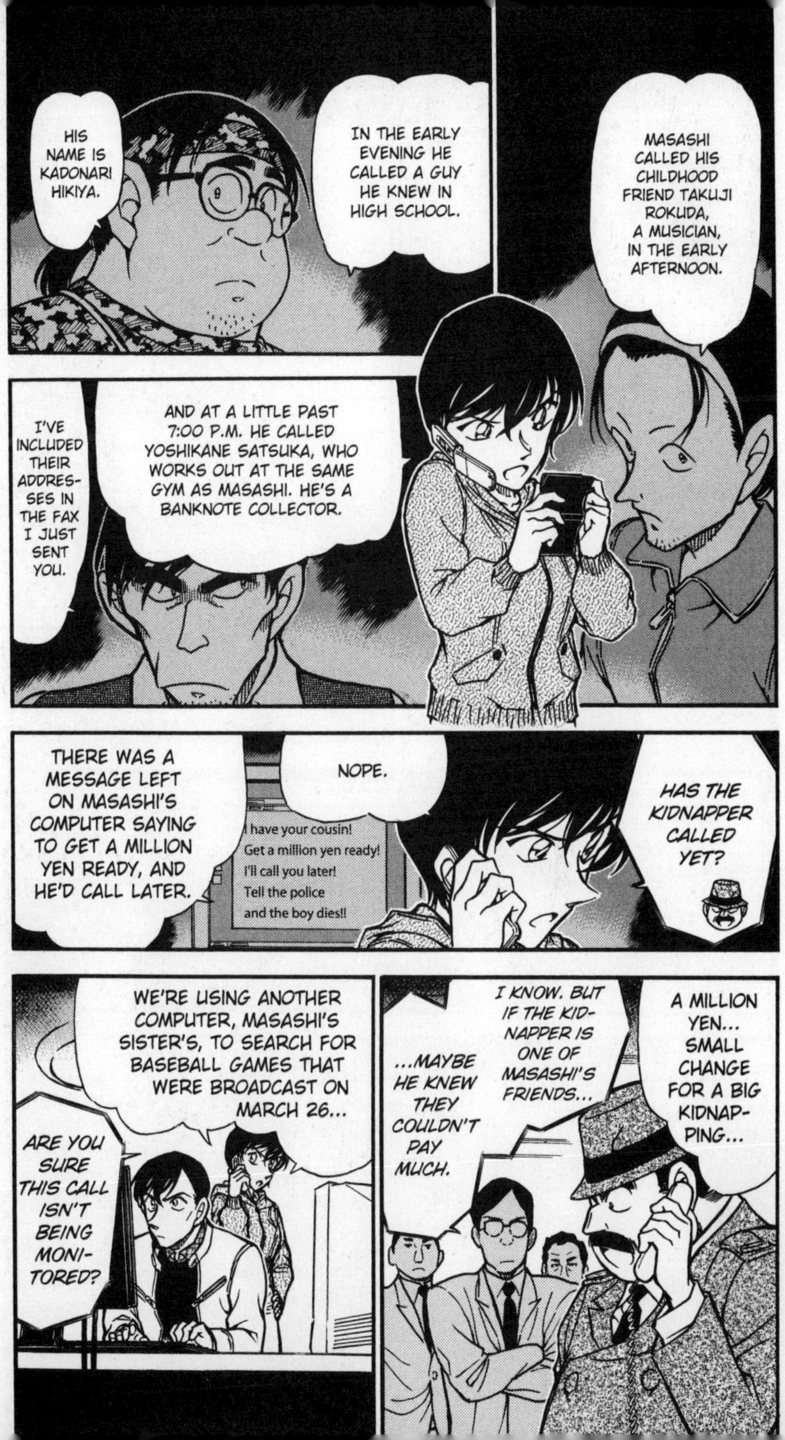
MASASHI CALLED HIS CHILDHOOD FRIEND TAKUJI ROKUDA, A MUSICIAN, IN THE EARLY AFTERNOON.
IN THE EARLY EVENING HE CALLED A GUY HE KNEW IN HIGH SCHOOL.
HIS NAME IS KADONARI HIKIYA.
AND AT A LITTLE PAST 7:00 P.M. HE CALLED YOSHIKANE SATSUKA, WHO WORKS OUT AT THE SAME GYM AS MASASHI. HE'S A BANKNOTE COLLECTOR.
I'VE INCLUDED THEIR ADDRESSES IN THE FAX I JUST SENT YOU.
HAS THE KIDNAPPER CALLED YET?
NOPE.
THERE WAS A MESSAGE LEFT ON MASASHI'S COMPUTER SAYING TO GET A MILLION YEN READY, AND HE'D CALL LATER.
I have your cousin! Get a million yen ready! I'll call you later! Tell the police and the boy dies!!
A MILLION YEN... SMALL CHANGE FOR A BIG KIDNAPPING...
I KNOW. BUT IF THE KIDNAPPER IS ONE OF MASASHI'S FRIENDS...
...MAYBE HE KNEW THEY COULDN'T PAY MUCH.
WE'RE USING ANOTHER COMPUTER, MASASHI'S SISTER'S, TO SEARCH FOR BASEBALL GAMES THAT WERE BROADCAST ON MARCH 26...
ARE YOU SURE THIS CALL ISN'T BEING MONITORED?

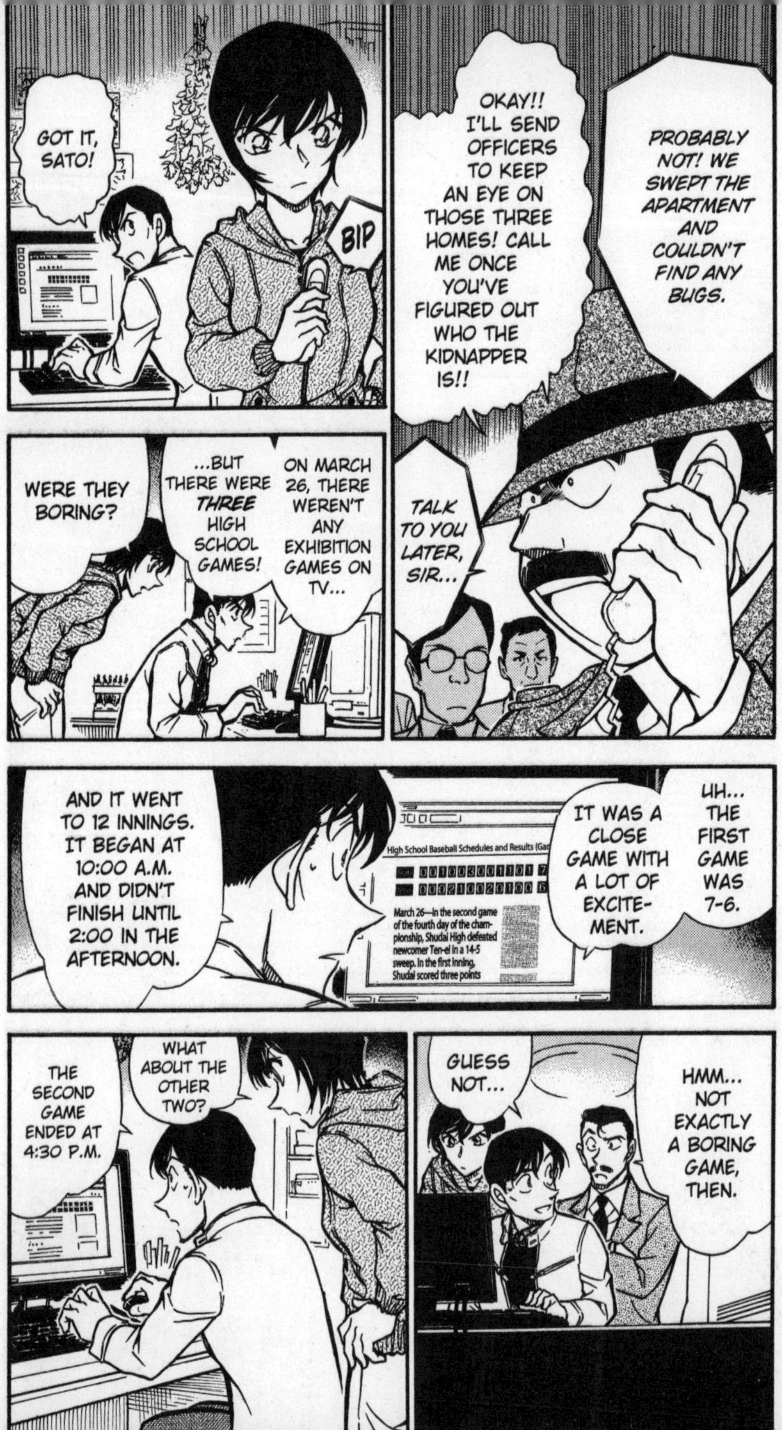
PROBABLY NOT! WE SWEPT THE APARTMENT AND COULDN'T FIND ANY BUGS.
OKAY!! I'LL SEND OFFICERS TO KEEP AN EYE ON THOSE THREE HOMES! CALL ME ONCE YOU'VE FIGURED OUT WHO THE KIDNAPPER IS!!
TALK TO YOU LATER, SIR...
BIP
GOT IT, SATO!
ON MARCH 26, THERE WEREN'T ANY EXHIBITION GAMES ON TV...
...BUT THERE WERE THREE HIGH SCHOOL GAMES!
WERE THEY BORING?
UH... THE FIRST GAME WAS 7-6.
IT WAS A CLOSE GAME WITH A LOT OF EXCITE-MENT.
High School Baseball Schedules and Results (Ga
March 26—In the second game of the fourth day of the championship, Shudai High defeated newcomer Ten-ei in a 14-5 sweep. In the first inning, Shudai scored three points
AND IT WENT TO 12 INNINGS. IT BEGAN AT 10:00 A.M. AND DIDN'T FINISH UNTIL 2:00 IN THE AFTERNOON.
HMM... NOT EXACTLY A BORING GAME, THEN.
GUESS NOT...
WHAT ABOUT THE OTHER TWO?
THE SECOND GAME ENDED AT 4:30 P.M.

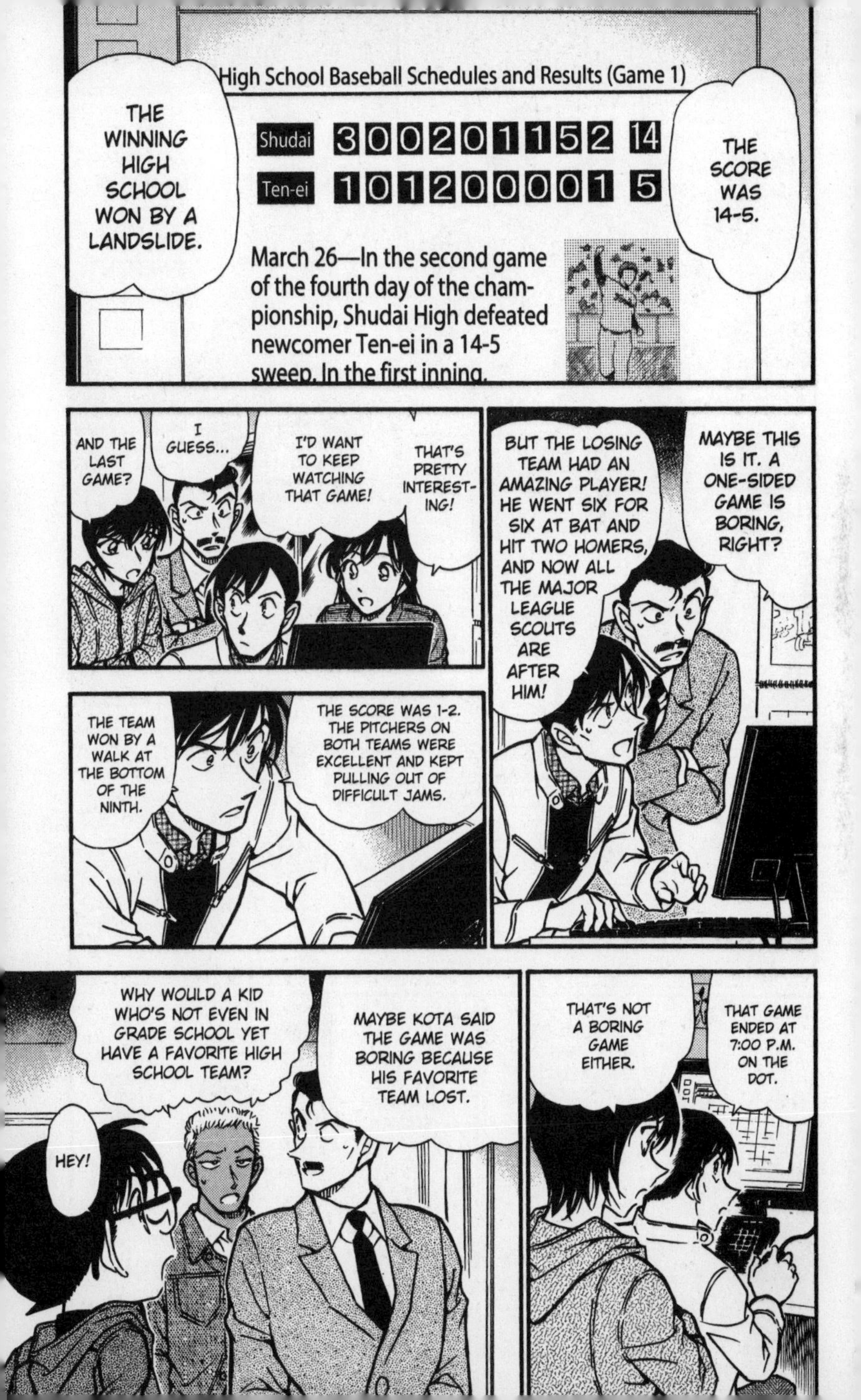
High School Baseball Schedules and Results (Game 1)
Shudai 3 0 0 2 0 1 1 5 2 14
Ten-ei 1 0 1 2 0 0 0 0 1 5
March 26—In the second game of the fourth day of the championship, Shudai High defeated newcomer Ten-ei in a 14-5 sweep. In the first inning,
THE SCORE WAS 14-5.
THE WINNING HIGH SCHOOL WON BY A LANDSLIDE.
MAYBE THIS IS IT. A ONE-SIDED GAME IS BORING, RIGHT?
BUT THE LOSING TEAM HAD AN AMAZING PLAYER! HE WENT SIX FOR SIX AT BAT AND HIT TWO HOMERS, AND NOW ALL THE MAJOR LEAGUE SCOUTS ARE AFTER HIM!
THAT'S PRETTY INTERESTING!
I'D WANT TO KEEP WATCHING THAT GAME!
I GUESS...
AND THE LAST GAME?
THE SCORE WAS 1-2. THE PITCHERS ON BOTH TEAMS WERE EXCELLENT AND KEPT PULLING OUT OF DIFFICULT JAMS.
THE TEAM WON BY A WALK AT THE BOTTOM OF THE NINTH.
THAT GAME ENDED AT 7:00 P.M. ON THE DOT.
THAT'S NOT A BORING GAME EITHER.
MAYBE KOTA SAID THE GAME WAS BORING BECAUSE HIS FAVORITE TEAM LOST.
WHY WOULD A KID WHO'S NOT EVEN IN GRADE SCHOOL YET HAVE A FAVORITE HIGH SCHOOL TEAM?
HEY!

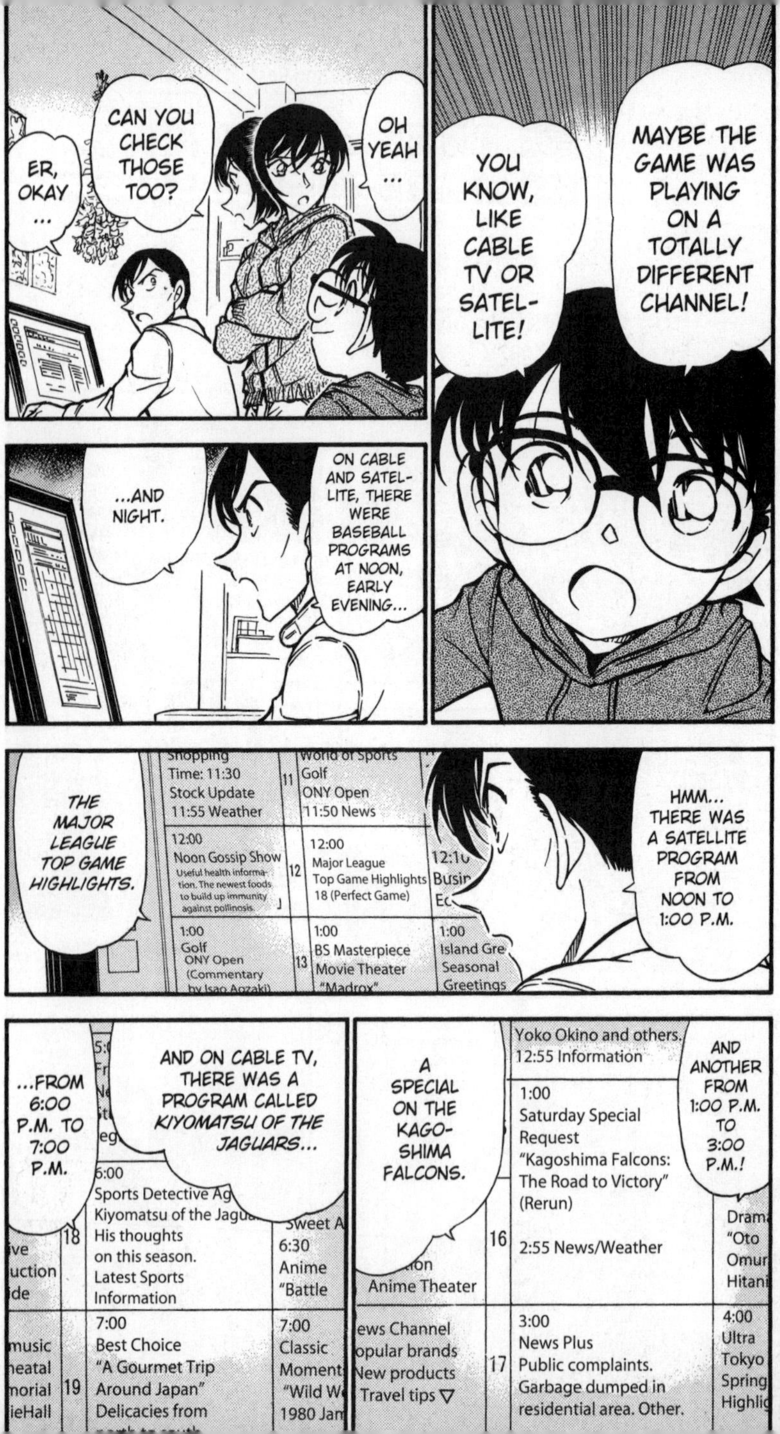

MAYBE THE GAME WAS PLAYING ON A TOTALLY DIFFERENT CHANNEL!
YOU KNOW, LIKE CABLE TV OR SATEL-LITE!
OH YEAH ...
CAN YOU CHECK THOSE TOO?
ER, OKAY ...
ON CABLE AND SATEL-LITE, THERE WERE BASEBALL PROGRAMS AT NOON, EARLY EVENING...
...AND NIGHT.
HMM... THERE WAS A SATELLITE PROGRAM FROM NOON TO 1:00 P.M.
THE MAJOR LEAGUE TOP GAME HIGHLIGHTS.
Time: 11:30
Stock Update
11:55 Weather
Golf
ONY Open
11:50 News
12:00
Noon Gossip Show
Useful health information. The newest foods to build up immunity against pollinosis.
12
12:00
Major League
Top Game Highlights
18 (Perfect Game)
1:00
Golf
ONY Open
(Commentary
1:00
BS Masterpiece
Movie Theater
13
1:00
Seasonal
AND ANOTHER FROM 1:00 P.M. TO 3:00 P.M.!
A SPECIAL ON THE KAGO-SHIMA FALCONS.
Yoko Okino and others.
12:55 Information
1:00
Saturday Special
Request
"Kagoshima Falcons: The Road to Victory"
(Rerun)
16
2:55 News/Weather
Anime Theater
3:00
News Plus
17
Public complaints.
Garbage dumped in residential area. Other.
4:00
Travel tips
AND ON CABLE TV, THERE WAS A PROGRAM CALLED KIYOMATSU OF THE JAGUARS...
...FROM 6:00 P.M. TO 7:00 P.M.
6:00
18
His thoughts
on this season.
Latest Sports
Information
6:30
Anime
7:00
Best Choice
"A Gourmet Trip
19
Around Japan"
Delicacies from
7:00
Classic

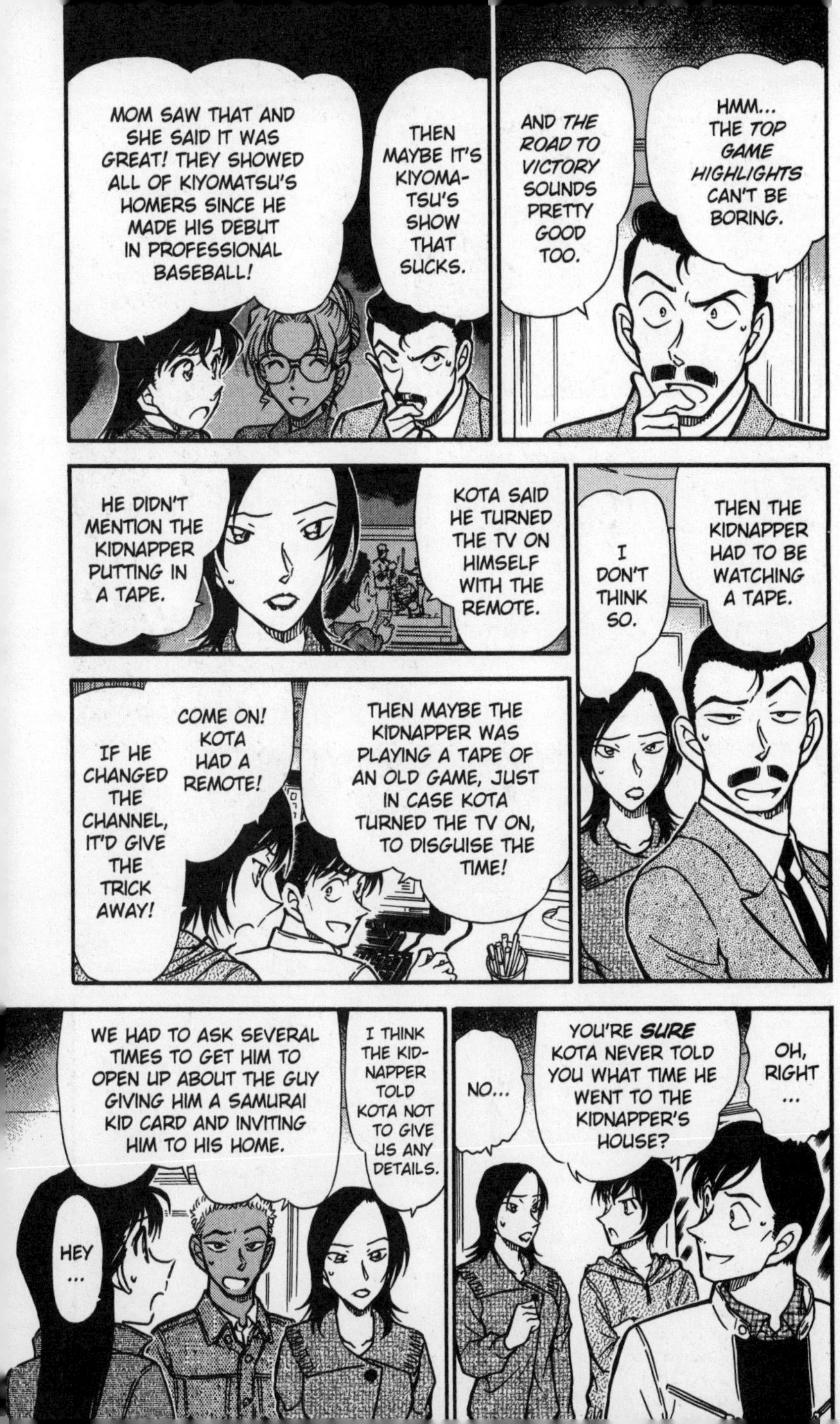
HMM... THE *TOP GAME HIGHLIGHTS* CAN'T BE BORING.
AND *THE ROAD TO VICTORY* SOUNDS PRETTY GOOD TOO.
THEN MAYBE IT'S KIYOMATSU'S SHOW THAT SUCKS.
MOM SAW THAT AND SHE SAID IT WAS GREAT! THEY SHOWED ALL OF KIYOMATSU'S HOMERS SINCE HE MADE HIS DEBUT IN PROFESSIONAL BASEBALL!
THEN THE KIDNAPPER HAD TO BE WATCHING A TAPE.
I DON'T THINK SO.
KOTA SAID HE TURNED THE TV ON HIMSELF WITH THE REMOTE.
HE DIDN'T MENTION THE KIDNAPPER PUTTING IN A TAPE.
THEN MAYBE THE KIDNAPPER WAS PLAYING A TAPE OF AN OLD GAME, JUST IN CASE KOTA TURNED THE TV ON, TO DISGUISE THE TIME!
COME ON! KOTA HAD A REMOTE!
IF HE CHANGED THE CHANNEL, IT'D GIVE THE TRICK AWAY!
OH, RIGHT ...
YOU'RE **SURE** KOTA NEVER TOLD YOU WHAT TIME HE WENT TO THE KIDNAPPER'S HOUSE?
NO...
I THINK THE KID-NAPPER TOLD KOTA NOT TO GIVE US ANY DETAILS.
WE HAD TO ASK SEVERAL TIMES TO GET HIM TO OPEN UP ABOUT THE GUY GIVING HIM A SAMURAI KID CARD AND INVITING HIM TO HIS HOME.
HEY ...

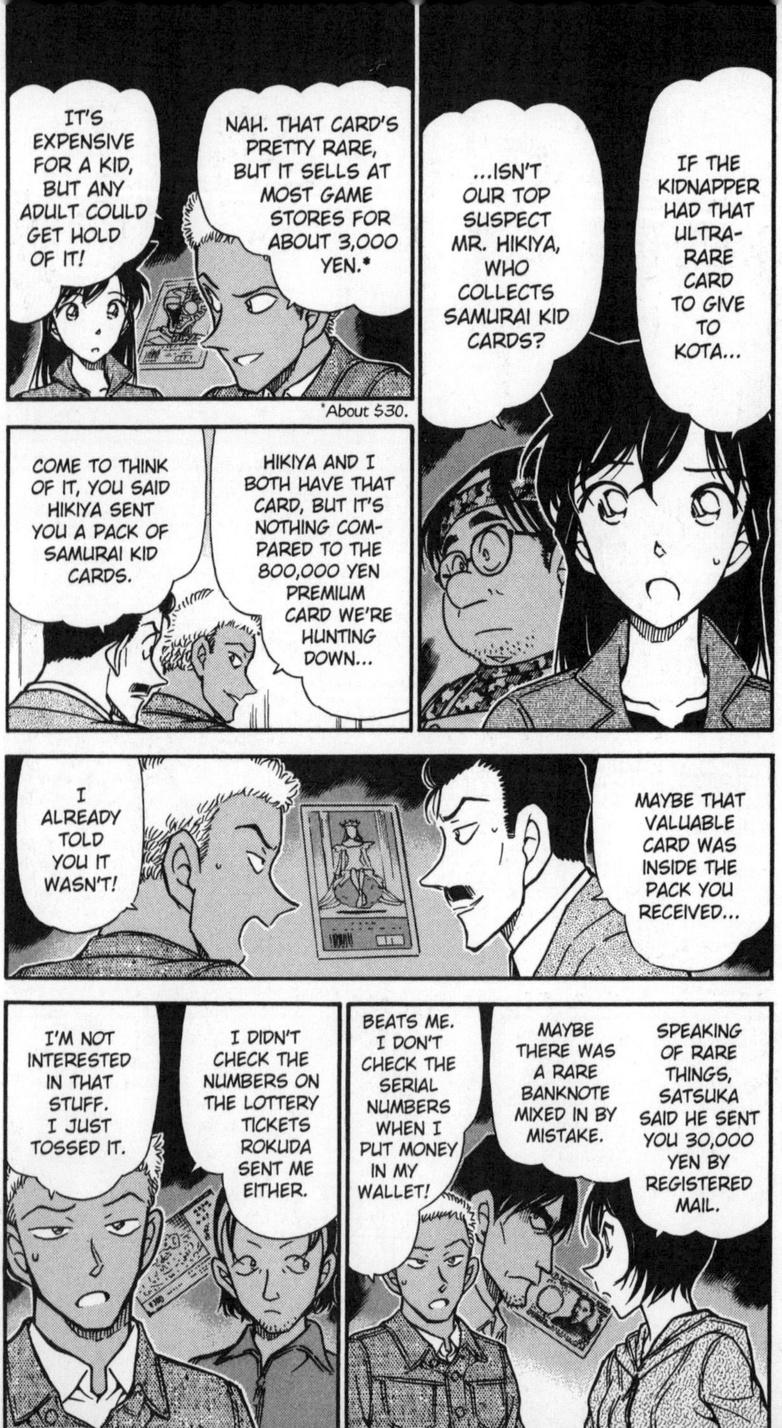
IF THE KIDNAPPER HAD THAT ULTRA-RARE CARD TO GIVE TO KOTA...
...ISN'T OUR TOP SUSPECT MR. HIKIYA, WHO COLLECTS SAMURAI KID CARDS?
NAH. THAT CARD'S PRETTY RARE, BUT IT SELLS AT MOST GAME STORES FOR ABOUT 3,000 YEN.*
IT'S EXPENSIVE FOR A KID, BUT ANY ADULT COULD GET HOLD OF IT!
HIKIYA AND I BOTH HAVE THAT CARD, BUT IT'S NOTHING COMPARED TO THE 800,000 YEN PREMIUM CARD WE'RE HUNTING DOWN...
COME TO THINK OF IT, YOU SAID HIKIYA SENT YOU A PACK OF SAMURAI KID CARDS.
MAYBE THAT VALUABLE CARD WAS INSIDE THE PACK YOU RECEIVED...
I ALREADY TOLD YOU IT WASN'T!
SPEAKING OF RARE THINGS, SATSUKA SAID HE SENT YOU 30,000 YEN BY REGISTERED MAIL.
MAYBE THERE WAS A RARE BANKNOTE MIXED IN BY MISTAKE.
BEATS ME. I DON'T CHECK THE SERIAL NUMBERS WHEN I PUT MONEY IN MY WALLET!
I DIDN'T CHECK THE NUMBERS ON THE LOTTERY TICKETS ROKUDA SENT ME EITHER.
I'M NOT INTERESTED IN THAT STUFF. I JUST TOSSED IT.
*About $30.

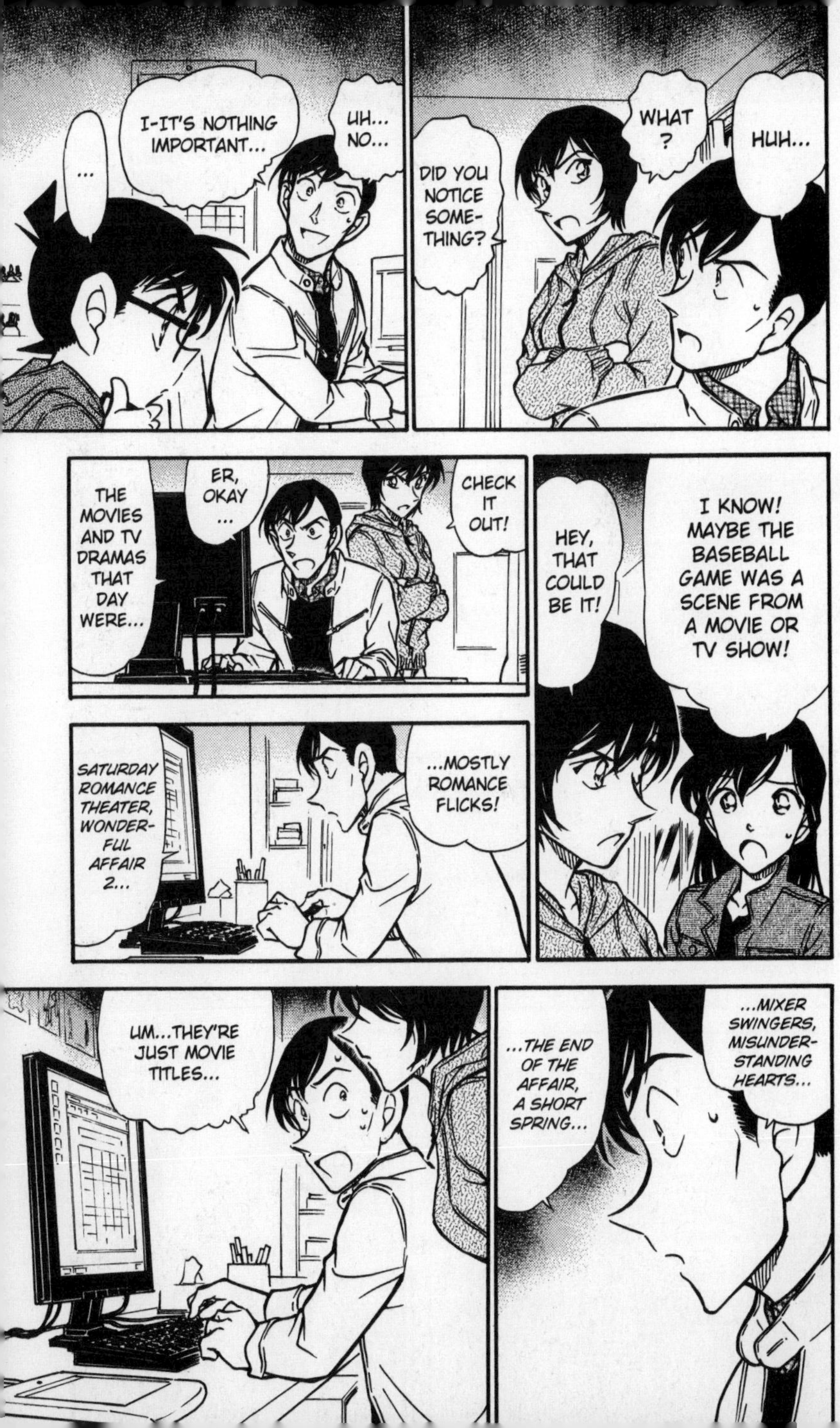
HUH...
WHAT?
DID YOU NOTICE SOMETHING?
UH... NO...
I-IT'S NOTHING IMPORTANT...
...
I KNOW! MAYBE THE BASEBALL GAME WAS A SCENE FROM A MOVIE OR TV SHOW!
HEY, THAT COULD BE IT!
CHECK IT OUT!
ER, OKAY...
THE MOVIES AND TV DRAMAS THAT DAY WERE...
...MOSTLY ROMANCE FLICKS!
SATURDAY ROMANCE THEATER, WONDERFUL AFFAIR 2...
...MIXER SWINGERS, MISUNDERSTANDING HEARTS...
...THE END OF THE AFFAIR, A SHORT SPRING...
UM...THEY'RE JUST MOVIE TITLES...

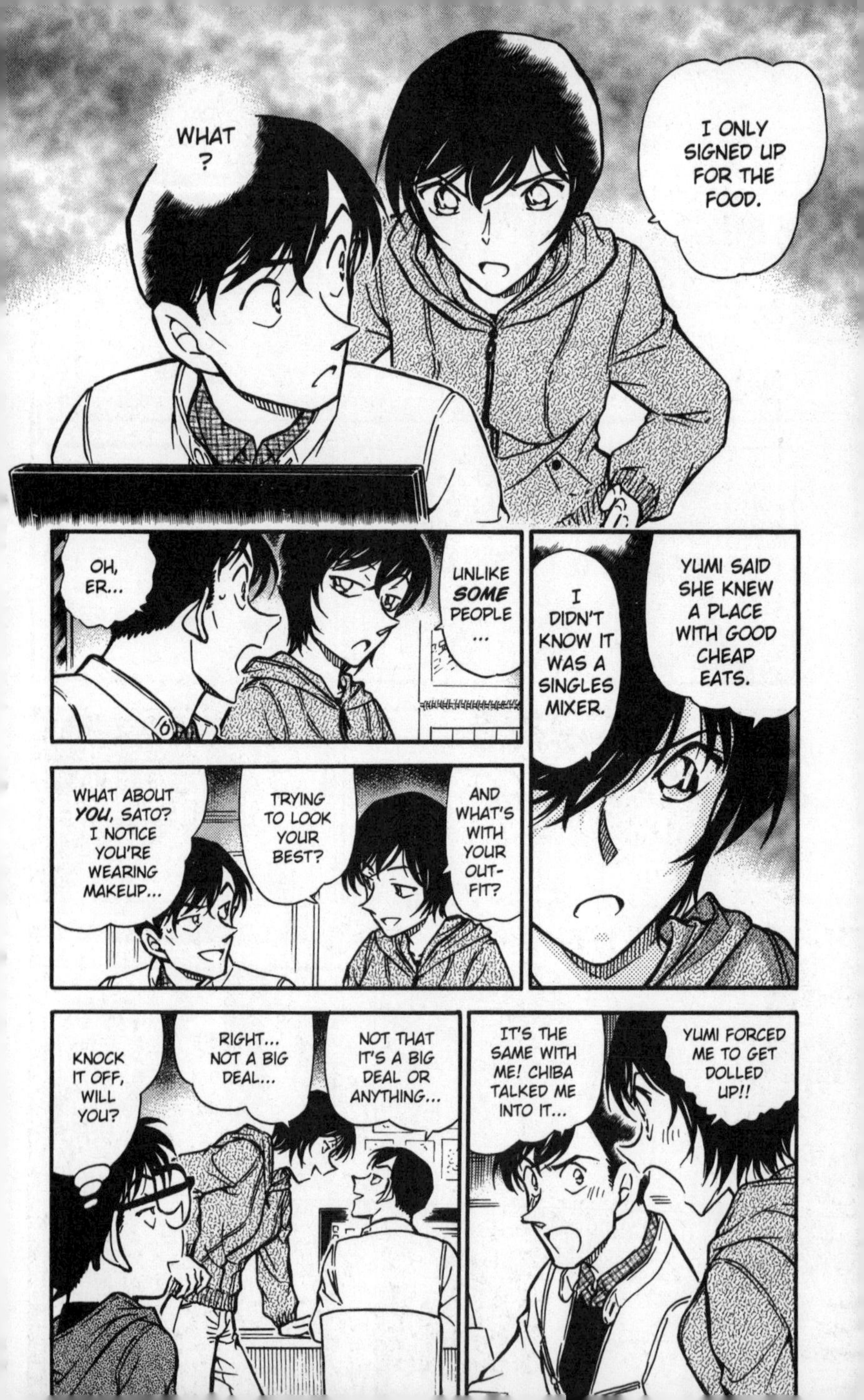
I ONLY SIGNED UP FOR THE FOOD.
WHAT ?
YUMI SAID SHE KNEW A PLACE WITH GOOD CHEAP EATS.
I DIDN'T KNOW IT WAS A SINGLES MIXER.
UNLIKE *SOME* PEOPLE ...
OH, ER...
AND WHAT'S WITH YOUR OUT-FIT?
TRYING TO LOOK YOUR BEST?
WHAT ABOUT *YOU*, SATO? I NOTICE YOU'RE WEARING MAKEUP...
YUMI FORCED ME TO GET DOLLED UP!!
IT'S THE SAME WITH ME! CHIBA TALKED ME INTO IT...
NOT THAT IT'S A BIG DEAL OR ANYTHING...
RIGHT... NOT A BIG DEAL...
KNOCK IT OFF, WILL YOU?

BRRNG
BRRNG
BRRNG
SATO HERE!
IT'S MEGUIRE!! HAVE YOU FIGURED OUT WHICH OF YOUR SUSPECTS IS THE KIDNAPPER?
WELL... ALL THE BASEBALL GAMES THAT DAY TURNED OUT TO BE INTERESTING...
HURRY UP! I'VE GOT OFFICERS WAITING TO MAKE A BUST!!
THAT LITTLE BOY'S LIFE COULD BE IN—
I'M HOME!
WHAT?
IT'S...
C-COULD IT BE...

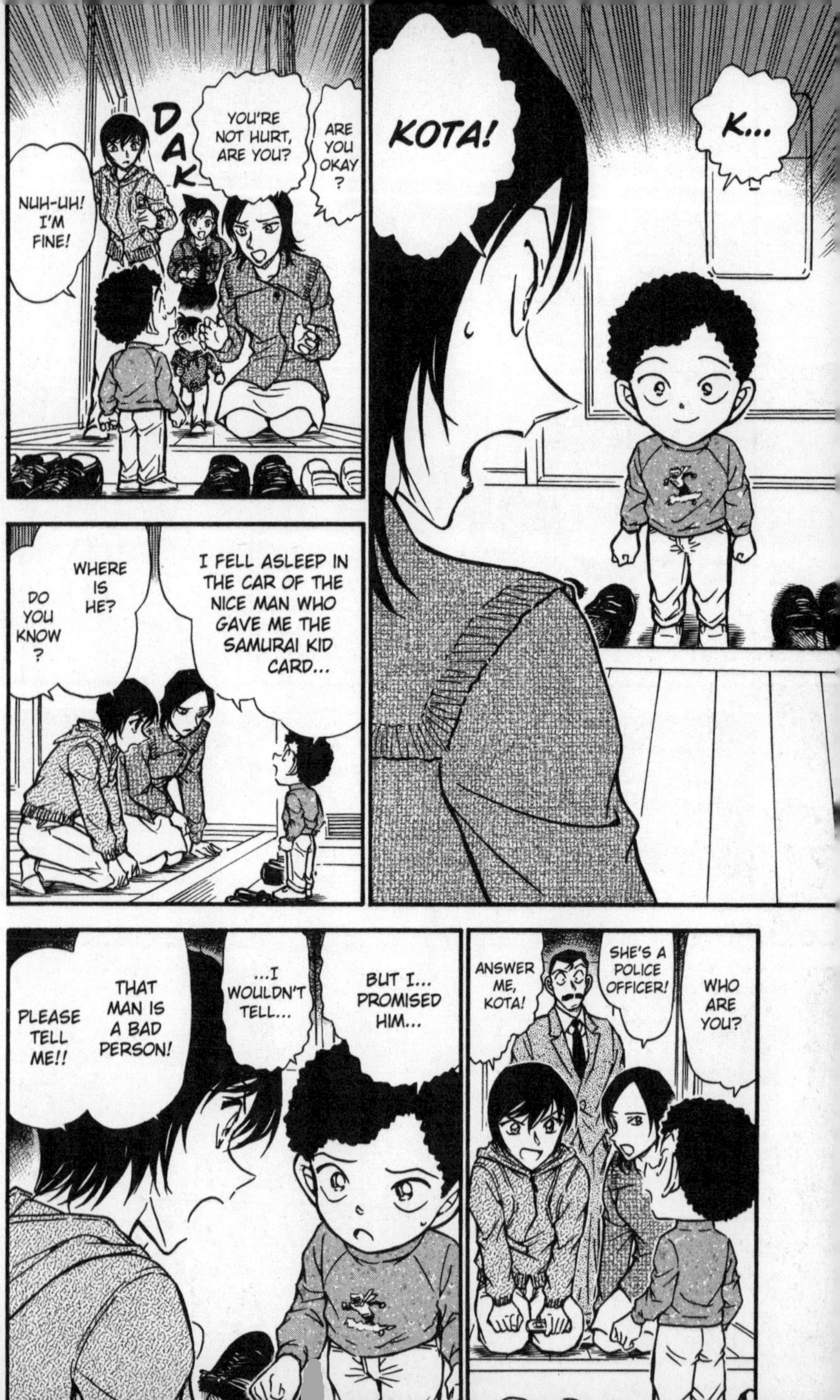
K...
KOTA!
ARE YOU OKAY?
YOU'RE NOT HURT, ARE YOU?
DAK
NUH-UH! I'M FINE!
I FELL ASLEEP IN THE CAR OF THE NICE MAN WHO GAVE ME THE SAMURAI KID CARD...
WHERE IS HE?
DO YOU KNOW?
WHO ARE YOU?
SHE'S A POLICE OFFICER!
ANSWER ME, KOTA!
BUT I... PROMISED HIM...
...I WOULDN'T TELL...
THAT MAN IS A BAD PERSON!
PLEASE TELL ME!!

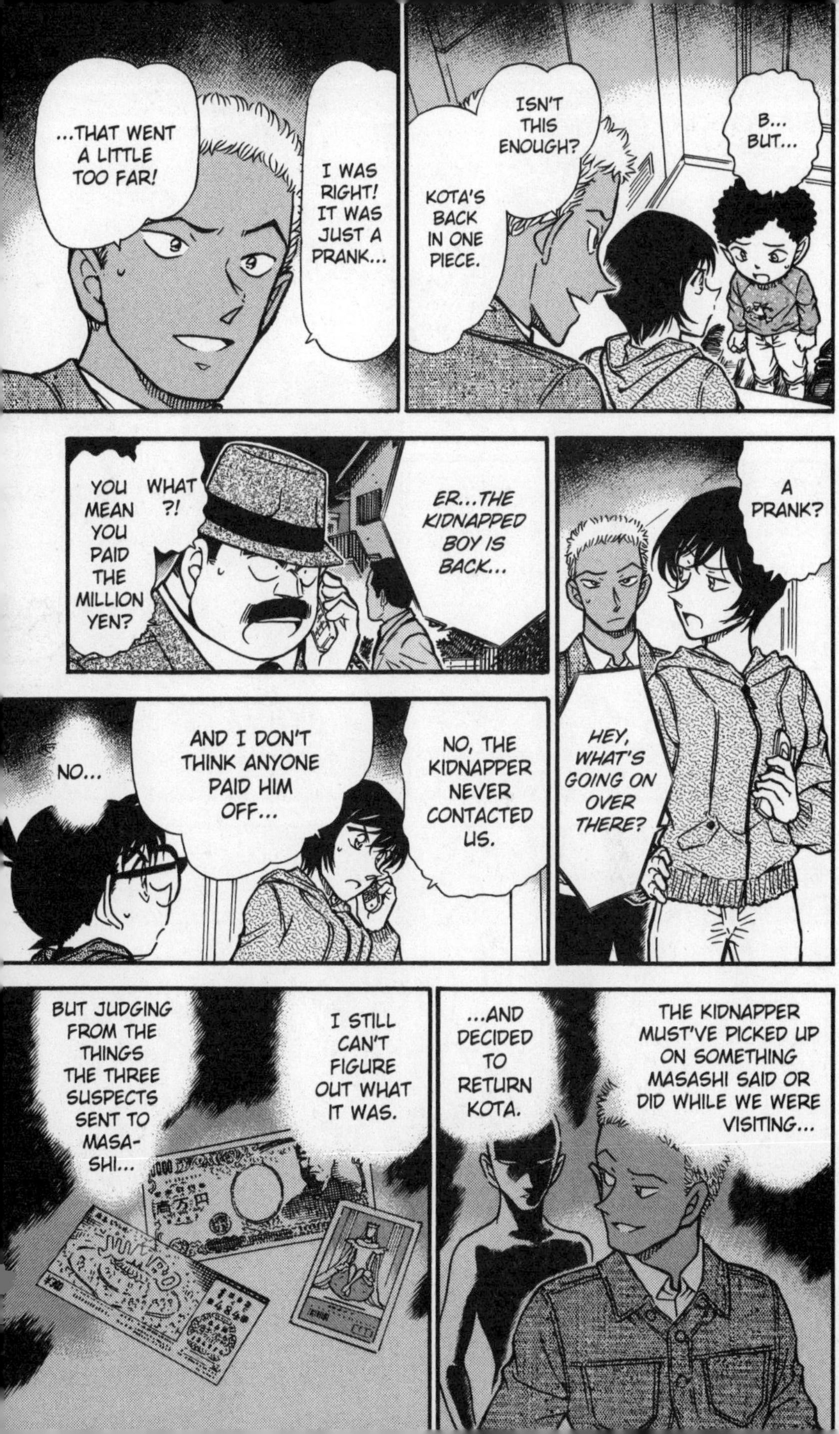
B... BUT...
ISN'T THIS ENOUGH?
KOTA'S BACK IN ONE PIECE.
I WAS RIGHT! IT WAS JUST A PRANK...
...THAT WENT A LITTLE TOO FAR!
A PRANK?
HEY, WHAT'S GOING ON OVER THERE?
ER...THE KIDNAPPED BOY IS BACK...
WHAT?!
YOU MEAN YOU PAID THE MILLION YEN?
NO, THE KIDNAPPER NEVER CONTACTED US.
AND I DON'T THINK ANYONE PAID HIM OFF...
NO...
THE KIDNAPPER MUST'VE PICKED UP ON SOMETHING MASASHI SAID OR DID WHILE WE WERE VISITING...
...AND DECIDED TO RETURN KOTA.
I STILL CAN'T FIGURE OUT WHAT IT WAS.
BUT JUDGING FROM THE THINGS THE THREE SUSPECTS SENT TO MASA-SHI...

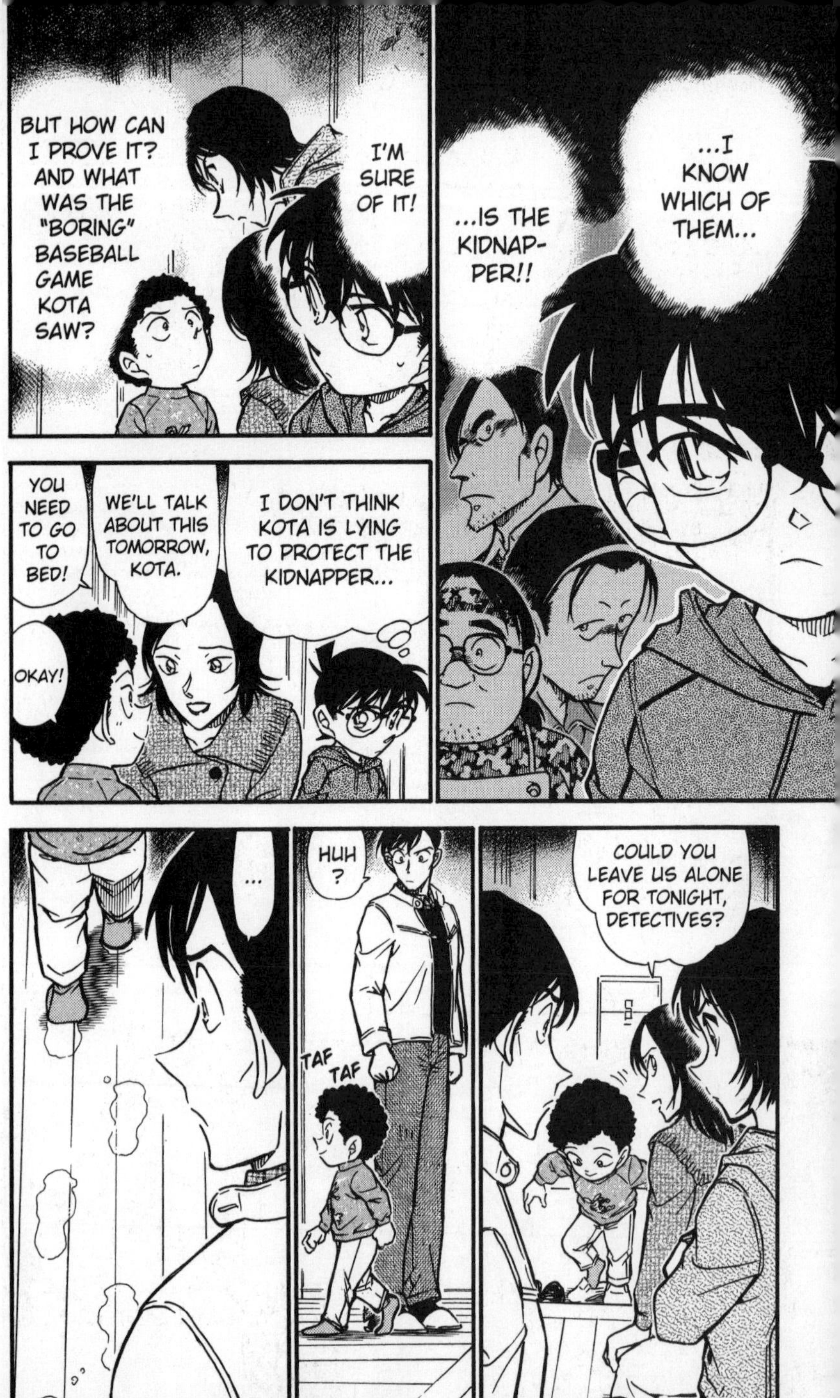
...I KNOW WHICH OF THEM...
...IS THE KIDNAPPER!!
I'M SURE OF IT!
BUT HOW CAN I PROVE IT? AND WHAT WAS THE "BORING" BASEBALL GAME KOTA SAW?
I DON'T THINK KOTA IS LYING TO PROTECT THE KIDNAPPER...
WE'LL TALK ABOUT THIS TOMORROW, KOTA.
YOU NEED TO GO TO BED!
OKAY!
COULD YOU LEAVE US ALONE FOR TONIGHT, DETECTIVES?
HUH?
TAF TAF
...

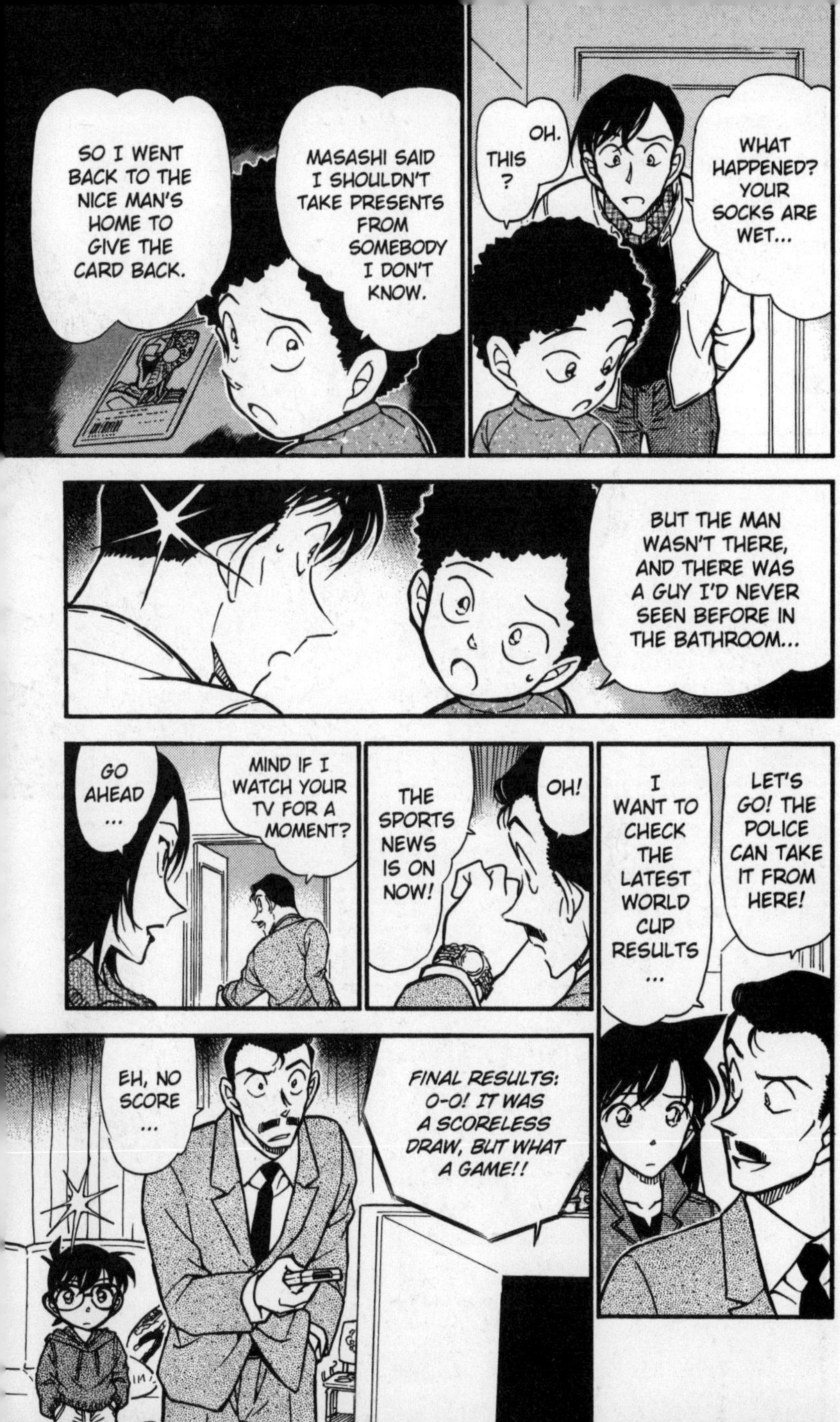
WHAT HAPPENED? YOUR SOCKS ARE WET...
OH. THIS?
MASASHI SAID I SHOULDN'T TAKE PRESENTS FROM SOMEBODY I DON'T KNOW.
SO I WENT BACK TO THE NICE MAN'S HOME TO GIVE THE CARD BACK.
BUT THE MAN WASN'T THERE, AND THERE WAS A GUY I'D NEVER SEEN BEFORE IN THE BATHROOM...
LET'S GO! THE POLICE CAN TAKE IT FROM HERE!
I WANT TO CHECK THE LATEST WORLD CUP RESULTS...
OH!
THE SPORTS NEWS IS ON NOW!
MIND IF I WATCH YOUR TV FOR A MOMENT?
GO AHEAD...
FINAL RESULTS: 0-0! IT WAS A SCORELESS DRAW, BUT WHAT A GAME!!
EH, NO SCORE...

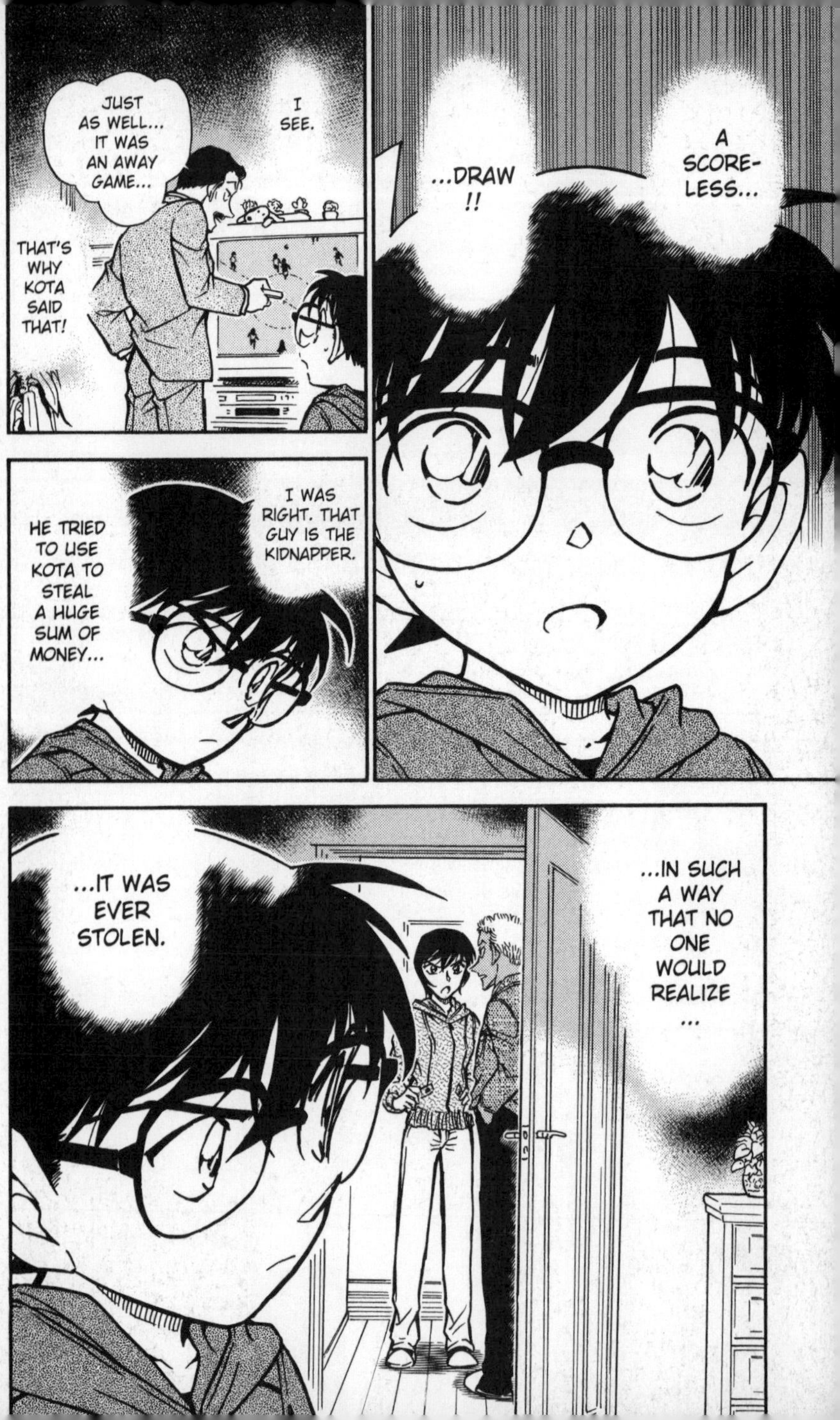
A SCORE-LESS...
...DRAW!!
I SEE.
JUST AS WELL... IT WAS AN AWAY GAME...
THAT'S WHY KOTA SAID THAT!
I WAS RIGHT. THAT GUY IS THE KIDNAPPER.
HE TRIED TO USE KOTA TO STEAL A HUGE SUM OF MONEY...
...IN SUCH A WAY THAT NO ONE WOULD REALIZE...
...IT WAS EVER STOLEN.

FILE 4: JACKPOT!

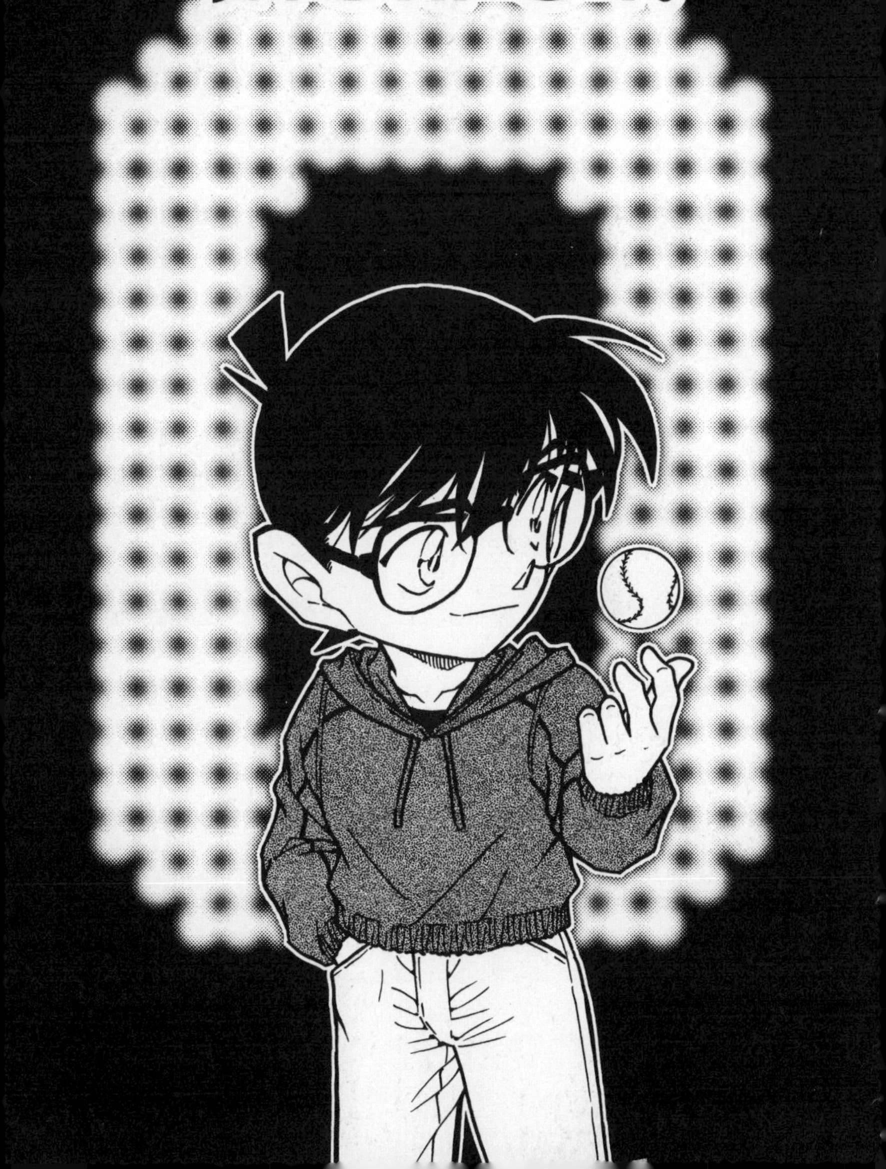

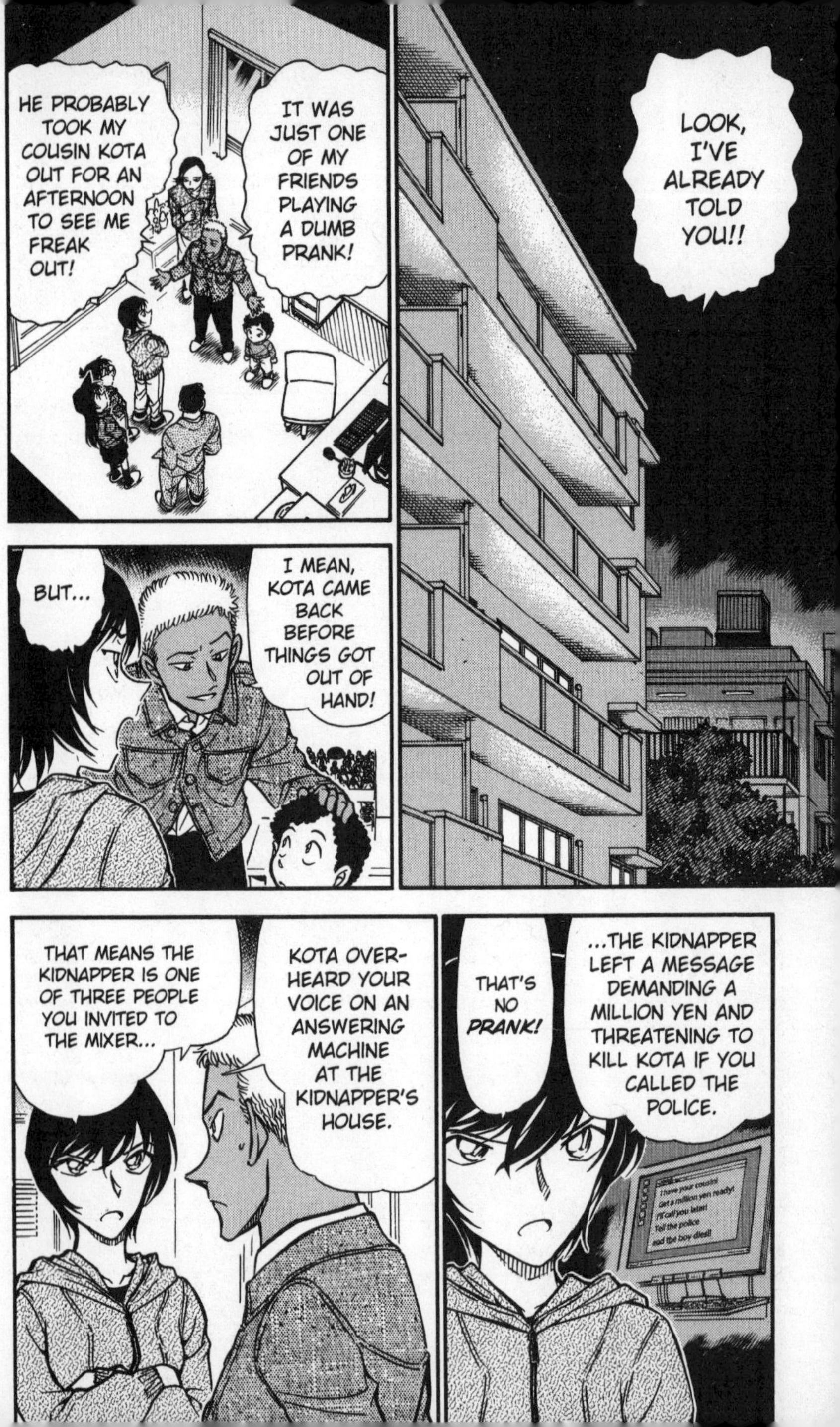
LOOK, I'VE ALREADY TOLD YOU!!
IT WAS JUST ONE OF MY FRIENDS PLAYING A DUMB PRANK!
HE PROBABLY TOOK MY COUSIN KOTA OUT FOR AN AFTERNOON TO SEE ME FREAK OUT!
I MEAN, KOTA CAME BACK BEFORE THINGS GOT OUT OF HAND!
BUT...
...THE KIDNAPPER LEFT A MESSAGE DEMANDING A MILLION YEN AND THREATENING TO KILL KOTA IF YOU CALLED THE POLICE.
THAT'S NO *PRANK!*
I have your cousin!
Get a million yen ready!
I'll call you later!
Tell the police
and the boy dies!
KOTA OVER-HEARD YOUR VOICE ON AN ANSWERING MACHINE AT THE KIDNAPPER'S HOUSE.
THAT MEANS THE KIDNAPPER IS ONE OF THREE PEOPLE YOU INVITED TO THE MIXER...

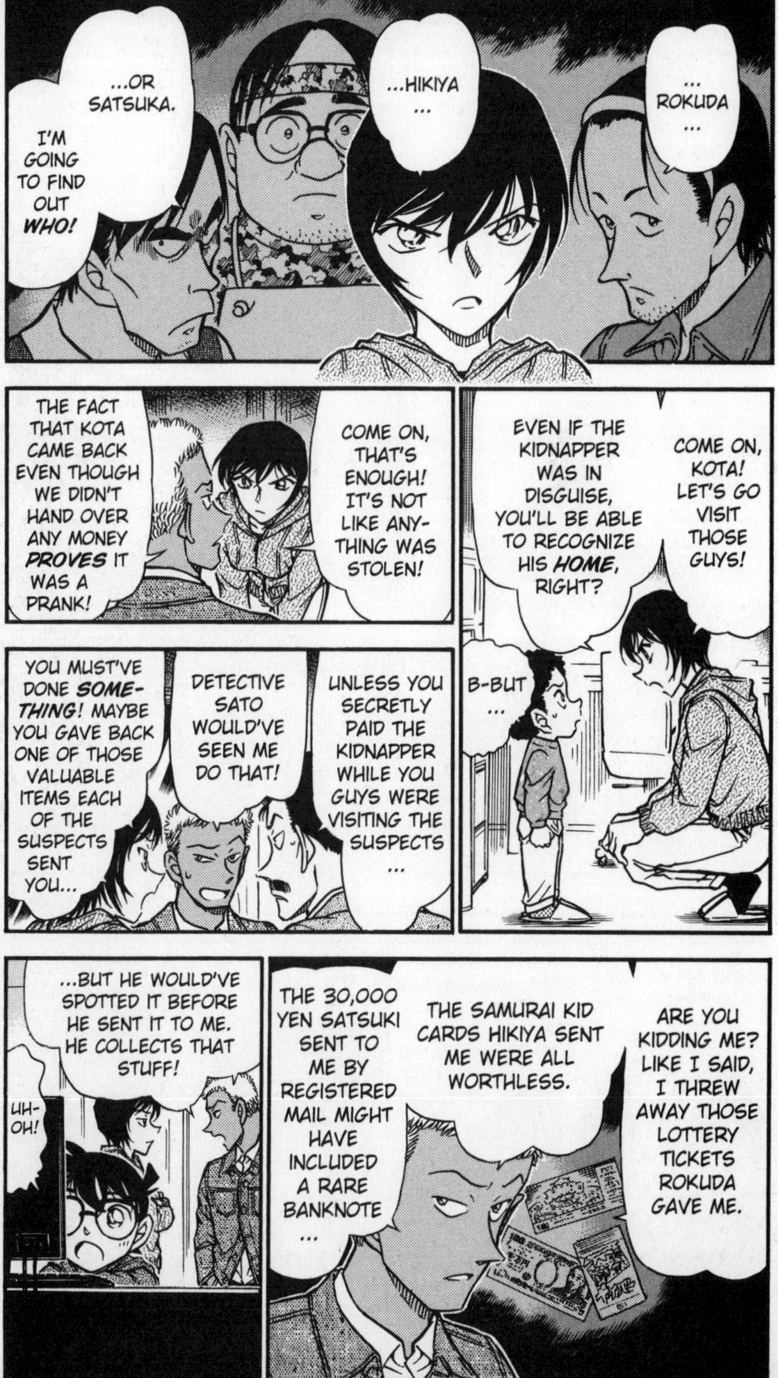
... ROKUDA ...
...HIKIYA ...
...OR SATSUKA.
I'M GOING TO FIND OUT WHO!
COME ON, KOTA! LET'S GO VISIT THOSE GUYS!
EVEN IF THE KIDNAPPER WAS IN DISGUISE, YOU'LL BE ABLE TO RECOGNIZE HIS HOME, RIGHT?
B-BUT ...
COME ON, THAT'S ENOUGH! IT'S NOT LIKE ANYTHING WAS STOLEN!
THE FACT THAT KOTA CAME BACK EVEN THOUGH WE DIDN'T HAND OVER ANY MONEY PROVES IT WAS A PRANK!
UNLESS YOU SECRETLY PAID THE KIDNAPPER WHILE YOU GUYS WERE VISITING THE SUSPECTS ...
DETECTIVE SATO WOULD'VE SEEN ME DO THAT!
YOU MUST'VE DONE SOMETHING! MAYBE YOU GAVE BACK ONE OF THOSE VALUABLE ITEMS EACH OF THE SUSPECTS SENT YOU...
ARE YOU KIDDING ME? LIKE I SAID, I THREW AWAY THOSE LOTTERY TICKETS ROKUDA GAVE ME.
THE SAMURAI KID CARDS HIKIYA SENT ME WERE ALL WORTHLESS.
THE 30,000 YEN SATSUKI SENT TO ME BY REGISTERED MAIL MIGHT HAVE INCLUDED A RARE BANKNOTE ...
...BUT HE WOULD'VE SPOTTED IT BEFORE HE SENT IT TO ME. HE COLLECTS THAT STUFF!
UH-OH!

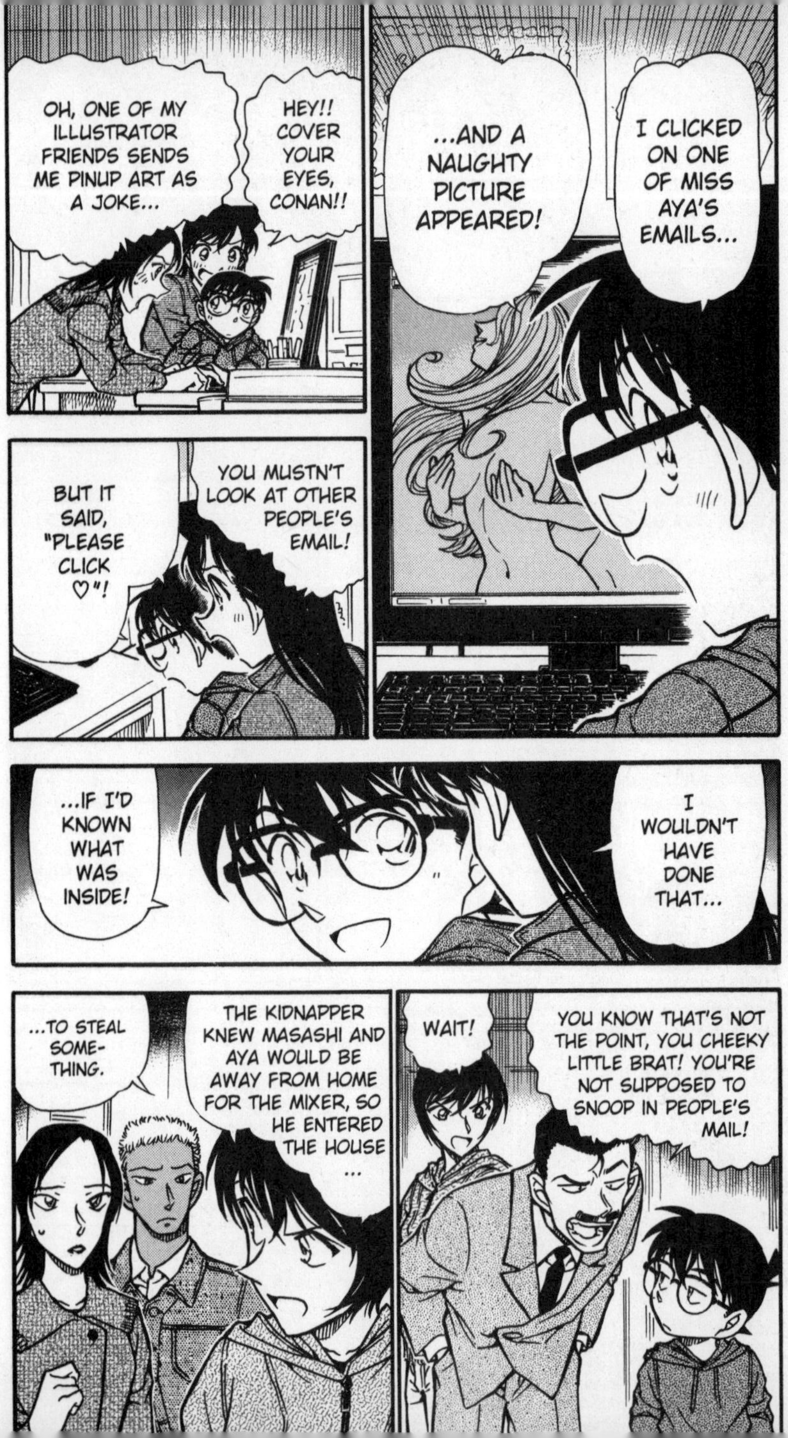
I CLICKED ON ONE OF MISS AYA'S EMAILS...
...AND A NAUGHTY PICTURE APPEARED!
HEY!! COVER YOUR EYES, CONAN!!
OH, ONE OF MY ILLUSTRATOR FRIENDS SENDS ME PINUP ART AS A JOKE...
YOU MUSTN'T LOOK AT OTHER PEOPLE'S EMAIL!
BUT IT SAID, "PLEASE CLICK ♡"!
I WOULDN'T HAVE DONE THAT...
...IF I'D KNOWN WHAT WAS INSIDE!
YOU KNOW THAT'S NOT THE POINT, YOU CHEEKY LITTLE BRAT! YOU'RE NOT SUPPOSED TO SNOOP IN PEOPLE'S MAIL!
WAIT!
THE KIDNAPPER KNEW MASASHI AND AYA WOULD BE AWAY FROM HOME FOR THE MIXER, SO HE ENTERED THE HOUSE ...
...TO STEAL SOME-THING.

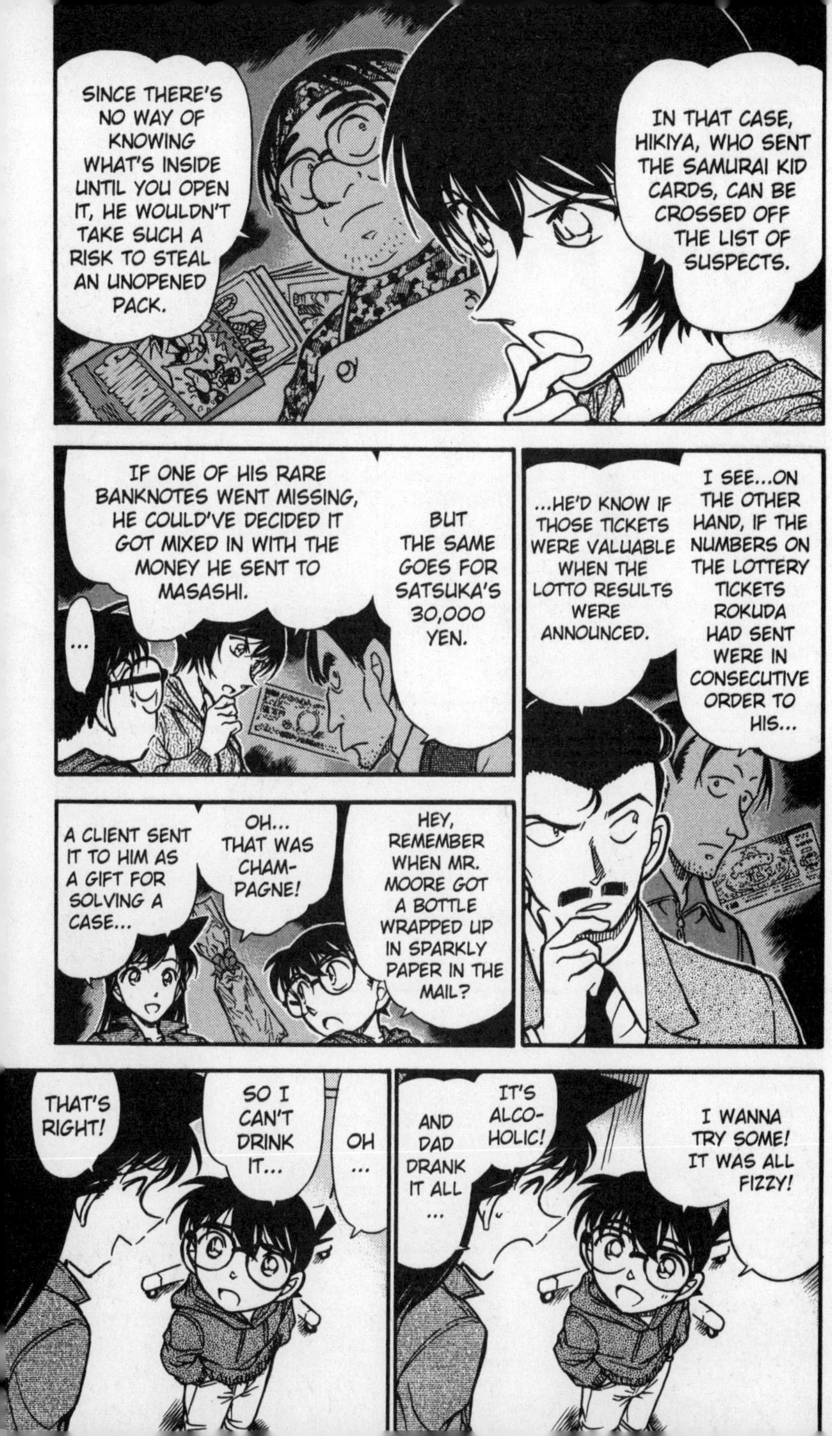
IN THAT CASE, HIKIYA, WHO SENT THE SAMURAI KID CARDS, CAN BE CROSSED OFF THE LIST OF SUSPECTS.
SINCE THERE'S NO WAY OF KNOWING WHAT'S INSIDE UNTIL YOU OPEN IT, HE WOULDN'T TAKE SUCH A RISK TO STEAL AN UNOPENED PACK.
I SEE...ON THE OTHER HAND, IF THE NUMBERS ON THE LOTTERY TICKETS ROKUDA HAD SENT WERE IN CONSECUTIVE ORDER TO HIS...
...HE'D KNOW IF THOSE TICKETS WERE VALUABLE WHEN THE LOTTO RESULTS WERE ANNOUNCED.
BUT THE SAME GOES FOR SATSUKA'S 30,000 YEN.
IF ONE OF HIS RARE BANKNOTES WENT MISSING, HE COULD'VE DECIDED IT GOT MIXED IN WITH THE MONEY HE SENT TO MASASHI.
...
HEY, REMEMBER WHEN MR. MOORE GOT A BOTTLE WRAPPED UP IN SPARKLY PAPER IN THE MAIL?
OH... THAT WAS CHAMPAGNE!
A CLIENT SENT IT TO HIM AS A GIFT FOR SOLVING A CASE...
I WANNA TRY SOME! IT WAS ALL FIZZY!
IT'S ALCOHOLIC!
AND DAD DRANK IT ALL...
OH...
SO I CAN'T DRINK IT...
THAT'S RIGHT!

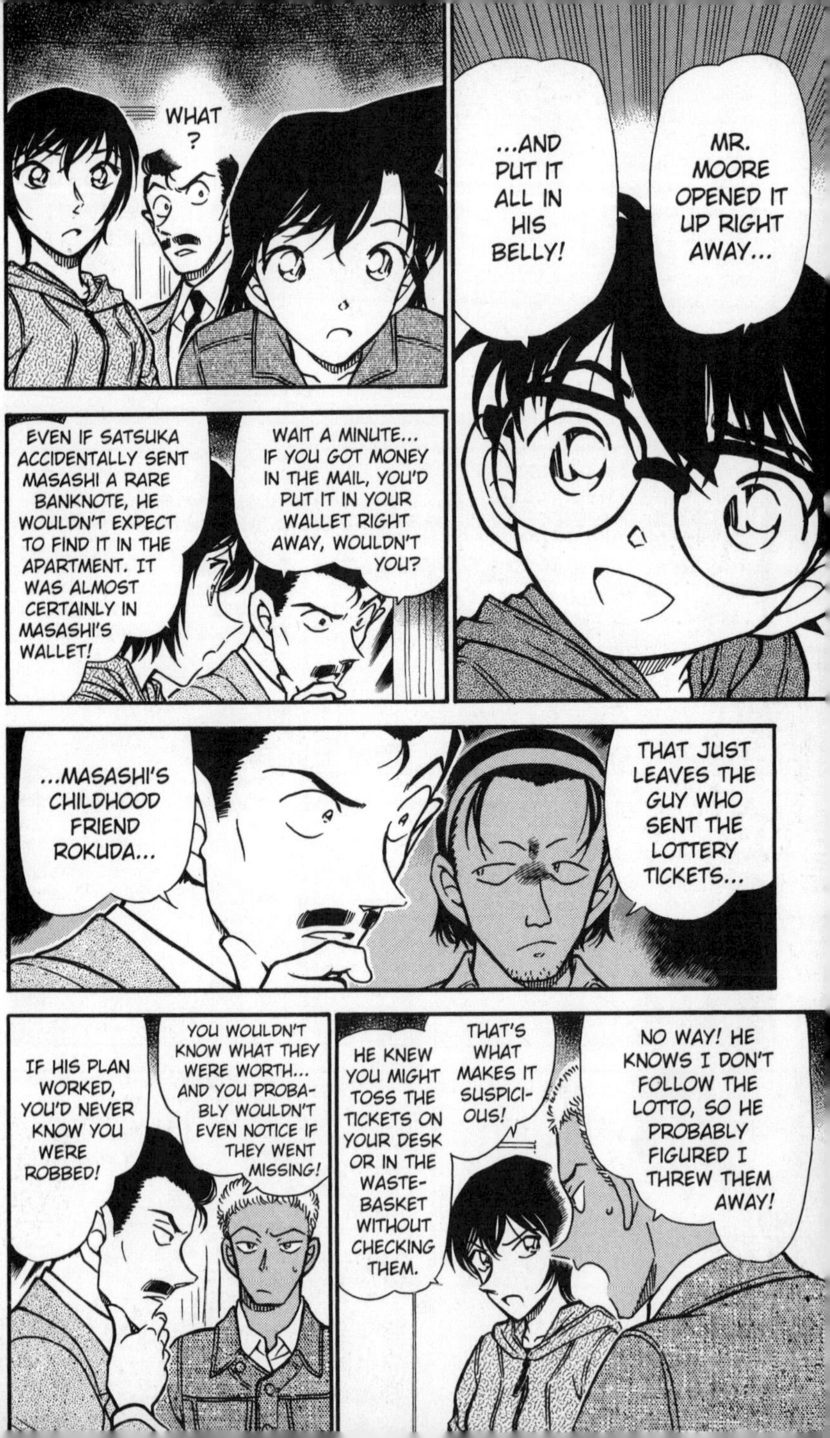
MR. MOORE OPENED IT UP RIGHT AWAY...
...AND PUT IT ALL IN HIS BELLY!
WHAT ?
WAIT A MINUTE... IF YOU GOT MONEY IN THE MAIL, YOU'D PUT IT IN YOUR WALLET RIGHT AWAY, WOULDN'T YOU?
EVEN IF SATSUKA ACCIDENTALLY SENT MASASHI A RARE BANKNOTE, HE WOULDN'T EXPECT TO FIND IT IN THE APARTMENT. IT WAS ALMOST CERTAINLY IN MASASHI'S WALLET!
THAT JUST LEAVES THE GUY WHO SENT THE LOTTERY TICKETS...
...MASASHI'S CHILDHOOD FRIEND ROKUDA...
NO WAY! HE KNOWS I DON'T FOLLOW THE LOTTO, SO HE PROBABLY FIGURED I THREW THEM AWAY!
THAT'S WHAT MAKES IT SUSPICIOUS!
HE KNEW YOU MIGHT TOSS THE TICKETS ON YOUR DESK OR IN THE WASTE-BASKET WITHOUT CHECKING THEM.
YOU WOULDN'T KNOW WHAT THEY WERE WORTH... AND YOU PROBA-BLY WOULDN'T EVEN NOTICE IF THEY WENT MISSING!
IF HIS PLAN WORKED, YOU'D NEVER KNOW YOU WERE ROBBED!

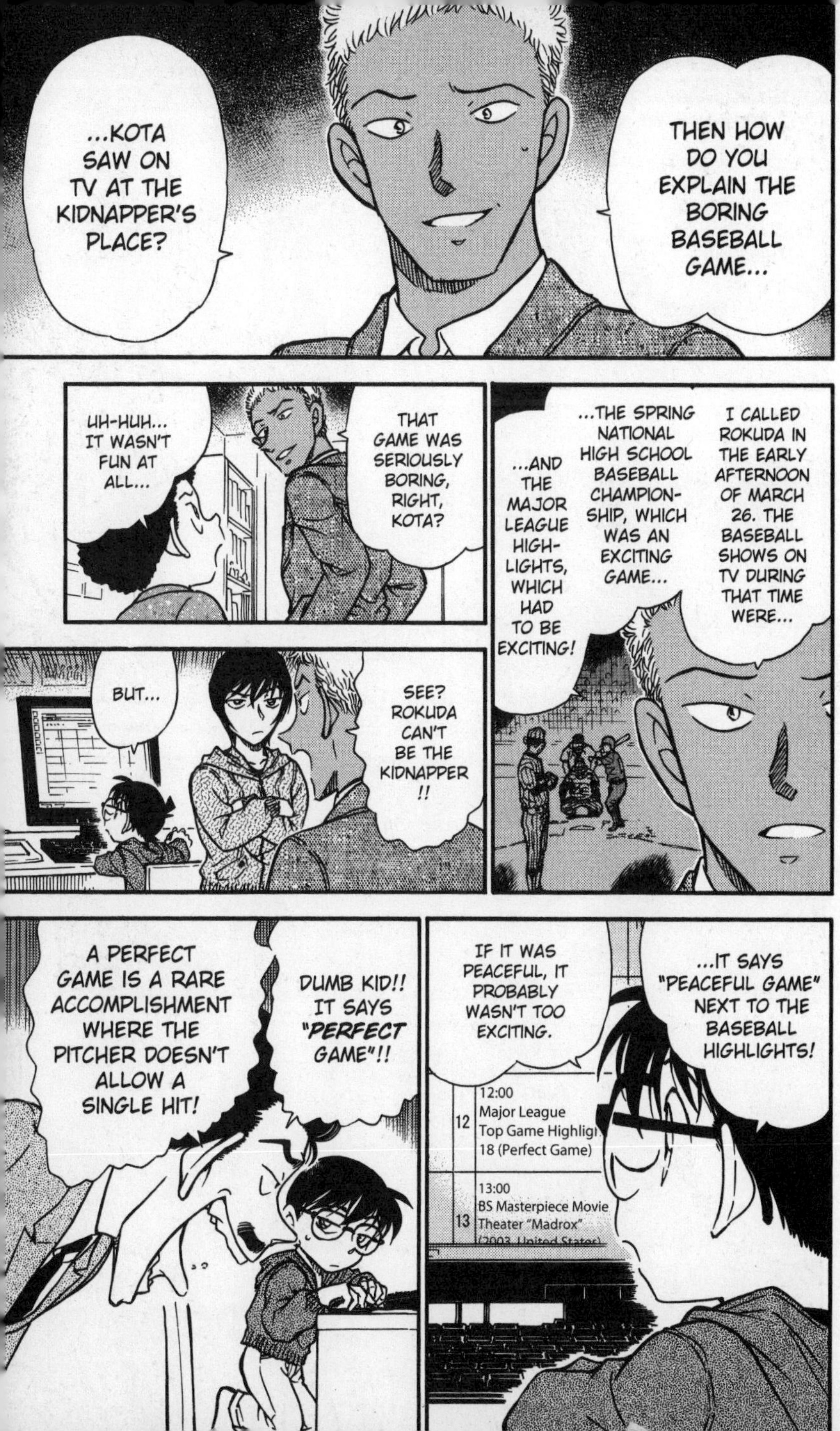
THEN HOW DO YOU EXPLAIN THE BORING BASEBALL GAME...
...KOTA SAW ON TV AT THE KIDNAPPER'S PLACE?
I CALLED ROKUDA IN THE EARLY AFTERNOON OF MARCH 26. THE BASEBALL SHOWS ON TV DURING THAT TIME WERE...
...THE SPRING NATIONAL HIGH SCHOOL BASEBALL CHAMPIONSHIP, WHICH WAS AN EXCITING GAME...
...AND THE MAJOR LEAGUE HIGHLIGHTS, WHICH HAD TO BE EXCITING!
THAT GAME WAS SERIOUSLY BORING, RIGHT, KOTA?
UH-HUH... IT WASN'T FUN AT ALL...
SEE? ROKUDA CAN'T BE THE KIDNAPPER!!
BUT...
...IT SAYS "PEACEFUL GAME" NEXT TO THE BASEBALL HIGHLIGHTS!
IF IT WAS PEACEFUL, IT PROBABLY WASN'T TOO EXCITING.
12
12:00
Major League
Top Game Highligi
18 (Perfect Game)
13
13:00
BS Masterpiece Movie
Theater "Madrox"
DUMB KID!! IT SAYS "*PERFECT* GAME"!!
A PERFECT GAME IS A RARE ACCOMPLISHMENT WHERE THE PITCHER DOESN'T ALLOW A SINGLE HIT!

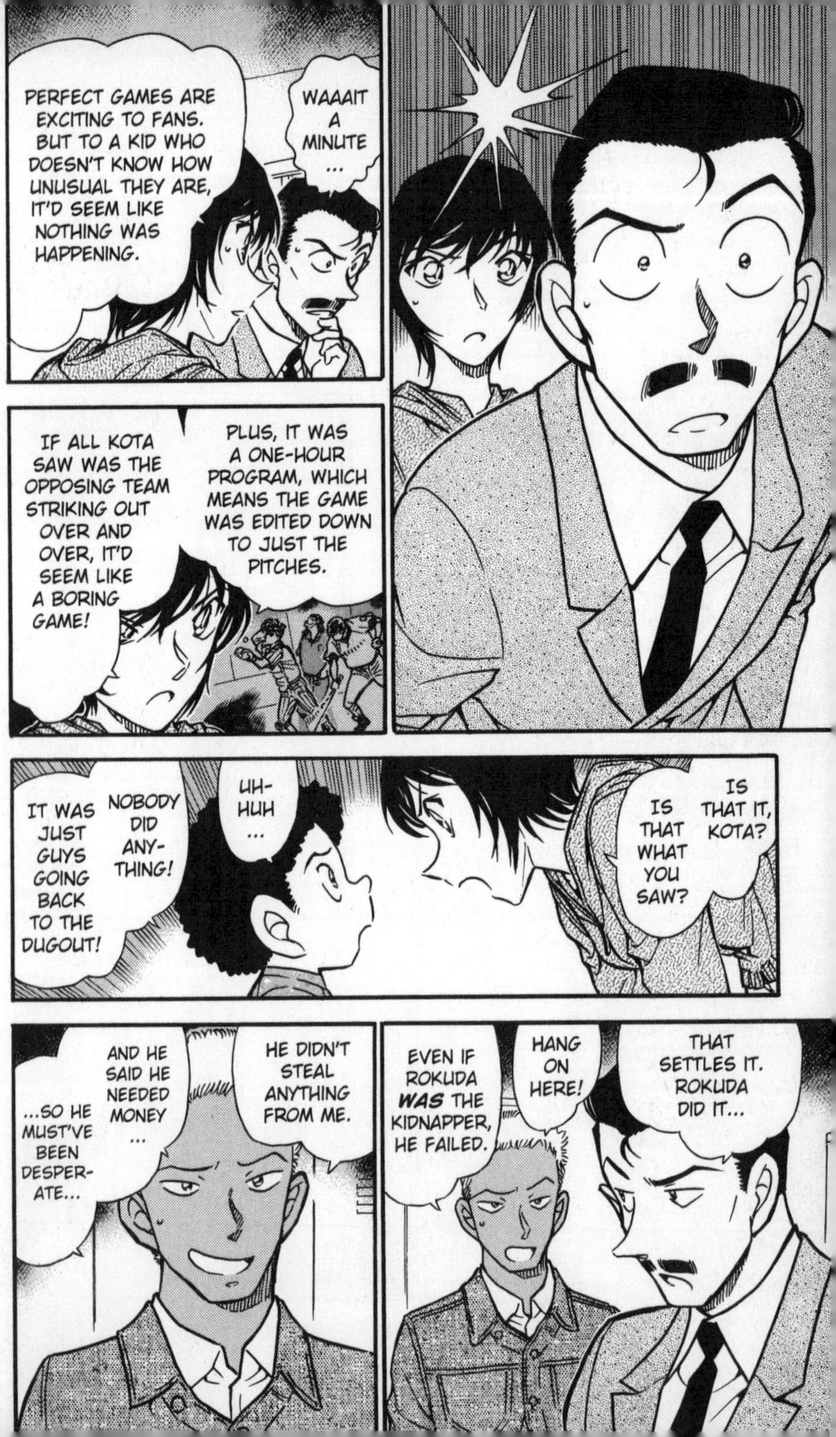
WAAAIT A MINUTE ...
PERFECT GAMES ARE EXCITING TO FANS. BUT TO A KID WHO DOESN'T KNOW HOW UNUSUAL THEY ARE, IT'D SEEM LIKE NOTHING WAS HAPPENING.
PLUS, IT WAS A ONE-HOUR PROGRAM, WHICH MEANS THE GAME WAS EDITED DOWN TO JUST THE PITCHES.
IF ALL KOTA SAW WAS THE OPPOSING TEAM STRIKING OUT OVER AND OVER, IT'D SEEM LIKE A BORING GAME!
IS THAT IT, KOTA?
IS THAT WHAT YOU SAW?
UH-HUH ...
NOBODY DID ANY-THING!
IT WAS JUST GUYS GOING BACK TO THE DUGOUT!
THAT SETTLES IT. ROKUDA DID IT...
HANG ON HERE!
EVEN IF ROKUDA ***WAS*** THE KIDNAPPER, HE FAILED.
HE DIDN'T STEAL ANYTHING FROM ME.
AND HE SAID HE NEEDED MONEY ...
...SO HE MUST'VE BEEN DESPERATE...

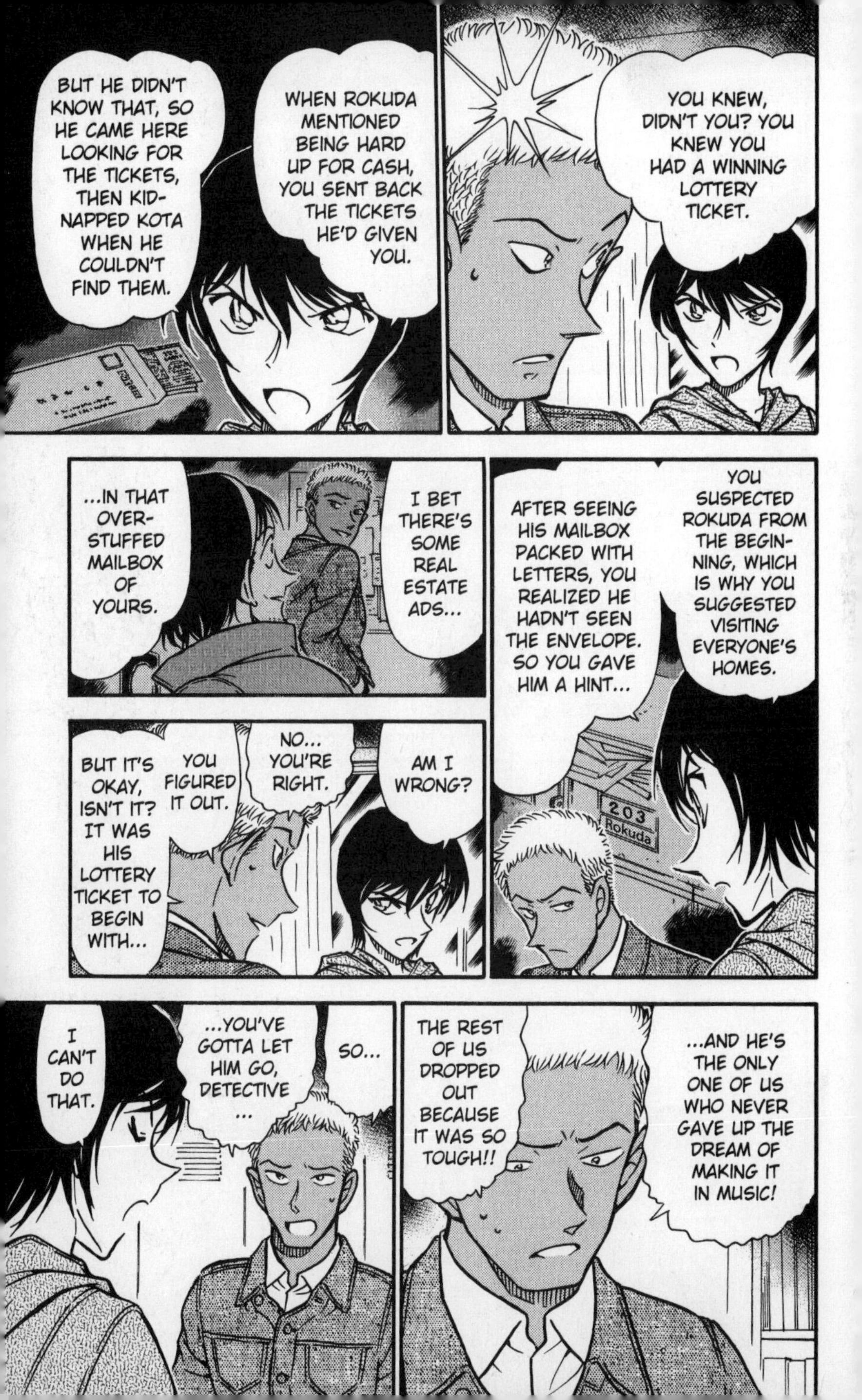
YOU KNEW, DIDN'T YOU? YOU KNEW YOU HAD A WINNING LOTTERY TICKET.
WHEN ROKUDA MENTIONED BEING HARD UP FOR CASH, YOU SENT BACK THE TICKETS HE'D GIVEN YOU.
BUT HE DIDN'T KNOW THAT, SO HE CAME HERE LOOKING FOR THE TICKETS, THEN KID-NAPPED KOTA WHEN HE COULDN'T FIND THEM.
YOU SUSPECTED ROKUDA FROM THE BEGIN-NING, WHICH IS WHY YOU SUGGESTED VISITING EVERYONE'S HOMES.
AFTER SEEING HIS MAILBOX PACKED WITH LETTERS, YOU REALIZED HE HADN'T SEEN THE ENVELOPE. SO YOU GAVE HIM A HINT...
203 Rokuda
I BET THERE'S SOME REAL ESTATE ADS...
...IN THAT OVER-STUFFED MAILBOX OF YOURS.
AM I WRONG?
NO... YOU'RE RIGHT.
YOU FIGURED IT OUT.
BUT IT'S OKAY, ISN'T IT? IT WAS HIS LOTTERY TICKET TO BEGIN WITH...
...AND HE'S THE ONLY ONE OF US WHO NEVER GAVE UP THE DREAM OF MAKING IT IN MUSIC!
THE REST OF US DROPPED OUT BECAUSE IT WAS SO TOUGH!!
SO...
...YOU'VE GOTTA LET HIM GO, DETECTIVE...
I CAN'T DO THAT.

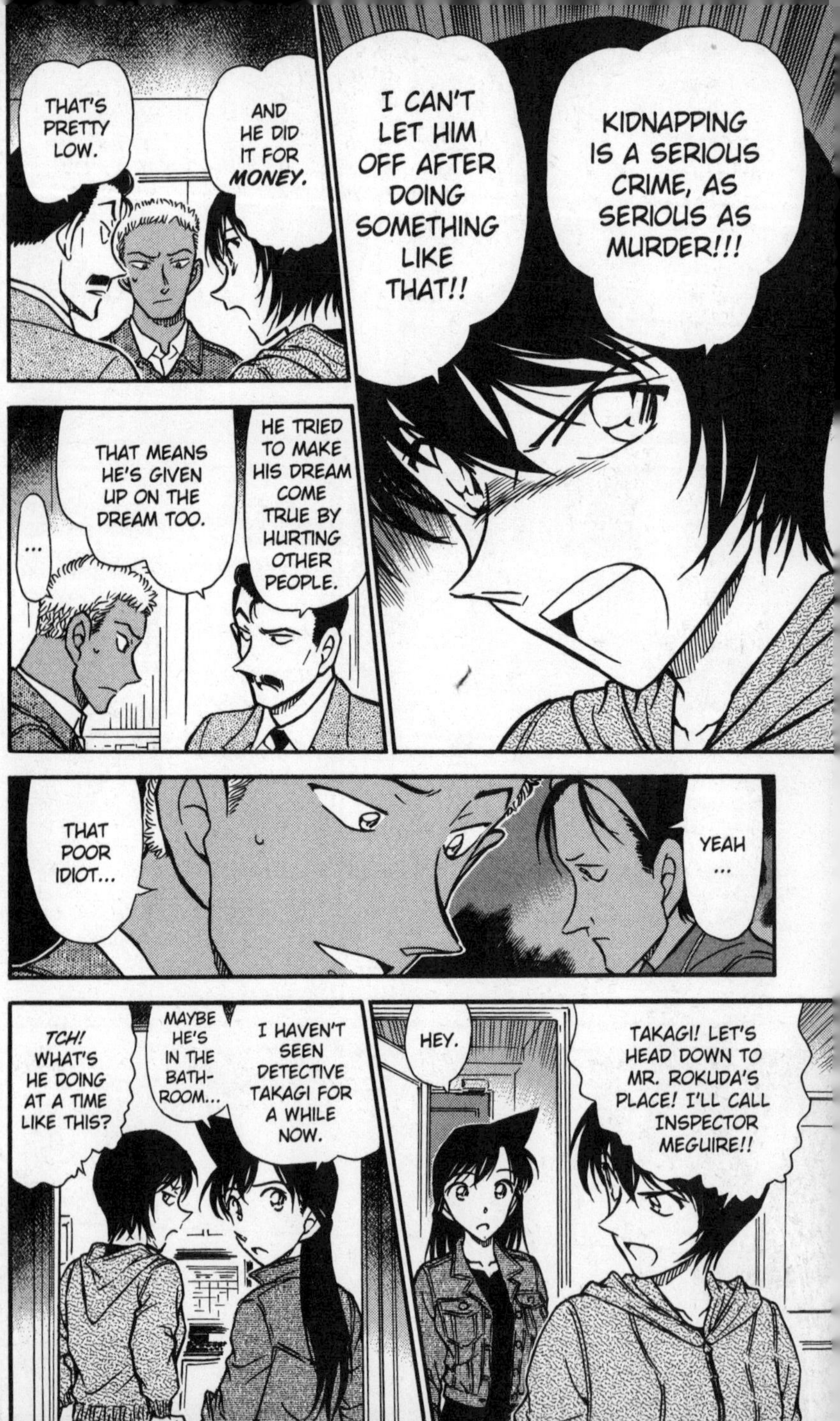
KIDNAPPING IS A SERIOUS CRIME, AS SERIOUS AS MURDER!!!
I CAN'T LET HIM OFF AFTER DOING SOMETHING LIKE THAT!!
AND HE DID IT FOR *MONEY.*
THAT'S PRETTY LOW.
HE TRIED TO MAKE HIS DREAM COME TRUE BY HURTING OTHER PEOPLE.
THAT MEANS HE'S GIVEN UP ON THE DREAM TOO.
...
YEAH ...
THAT POOR IDIOT...
TAKAGI! LET'S HEAD DOWN TO MR. ROKUDA'S PLACE! I'LL CALL INSPECTOR MEGUIRE!!
HEY.
I HAVEN'T SEEN DETECTIVE TAKAGI FOR A WHILE NOW.
MAYBE HE'S IN THE BATH-ROOM...
TCH! WHAT'S HE DOING AT A TIME LIKE THIS?

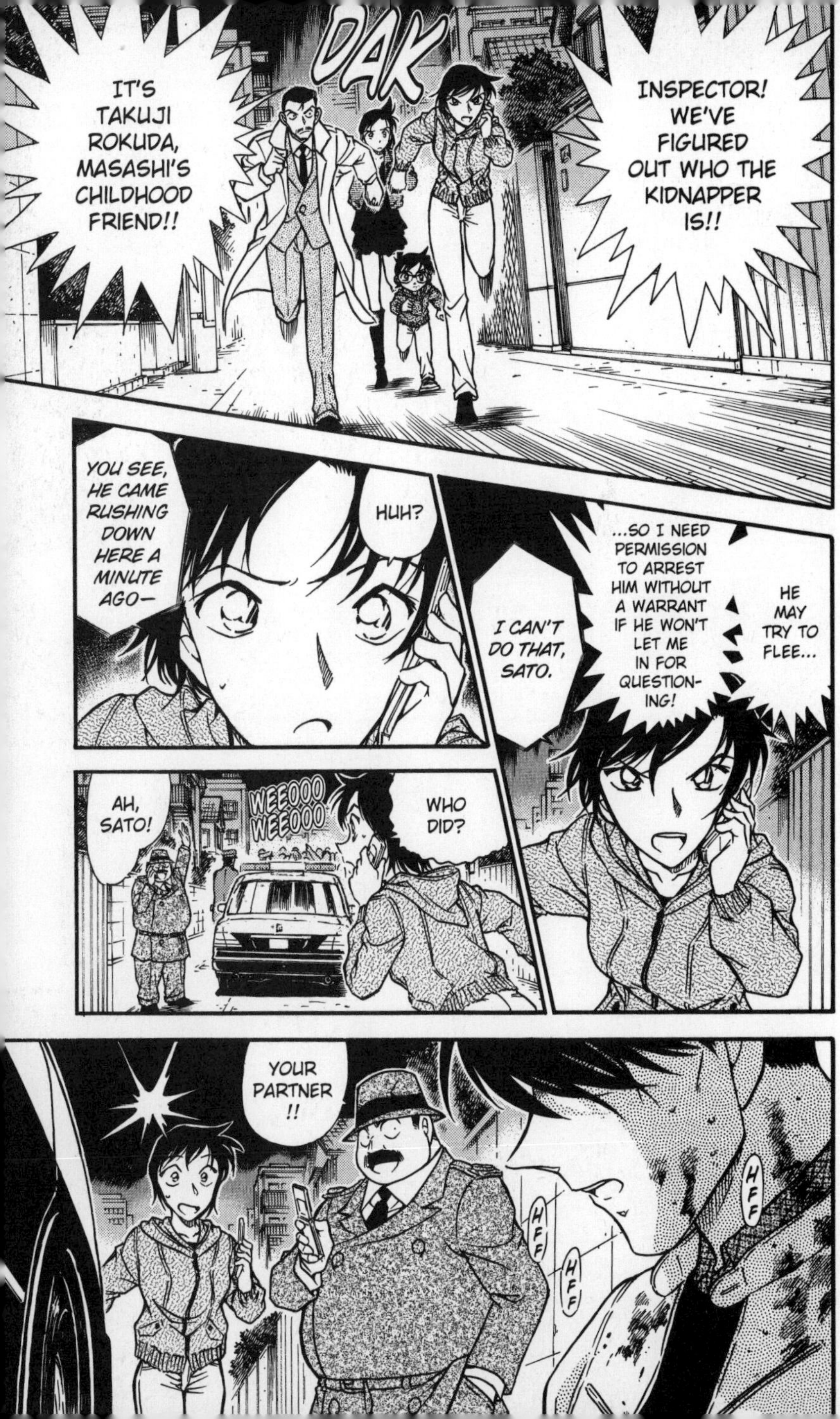
INSPECTOR! WE'VE FIGURED OUT WHO THE KIDNAPPER IS!!
DAK
IT'S TAKUJI ROKUDA, MASASHI'S CHILDHOOD FRIEND!!
HE MAY TRY TO FLEE...
...SO I NEED PERMISSION TO ARREST HIM WITHOUT A WARRANT IF HE WON'T LET ME IN FOR QUESTIONING!
I CAN'T DO THAT, SATO.
HUH?
YOU SEE, HE CAME RUSHING DOWN HERE A MINUTE AGO—
WHO DID?
WEEOOO WEEOOO
AH, SATO!
YOUR PARTNER!!
HFF
HFF
HFF
HFF

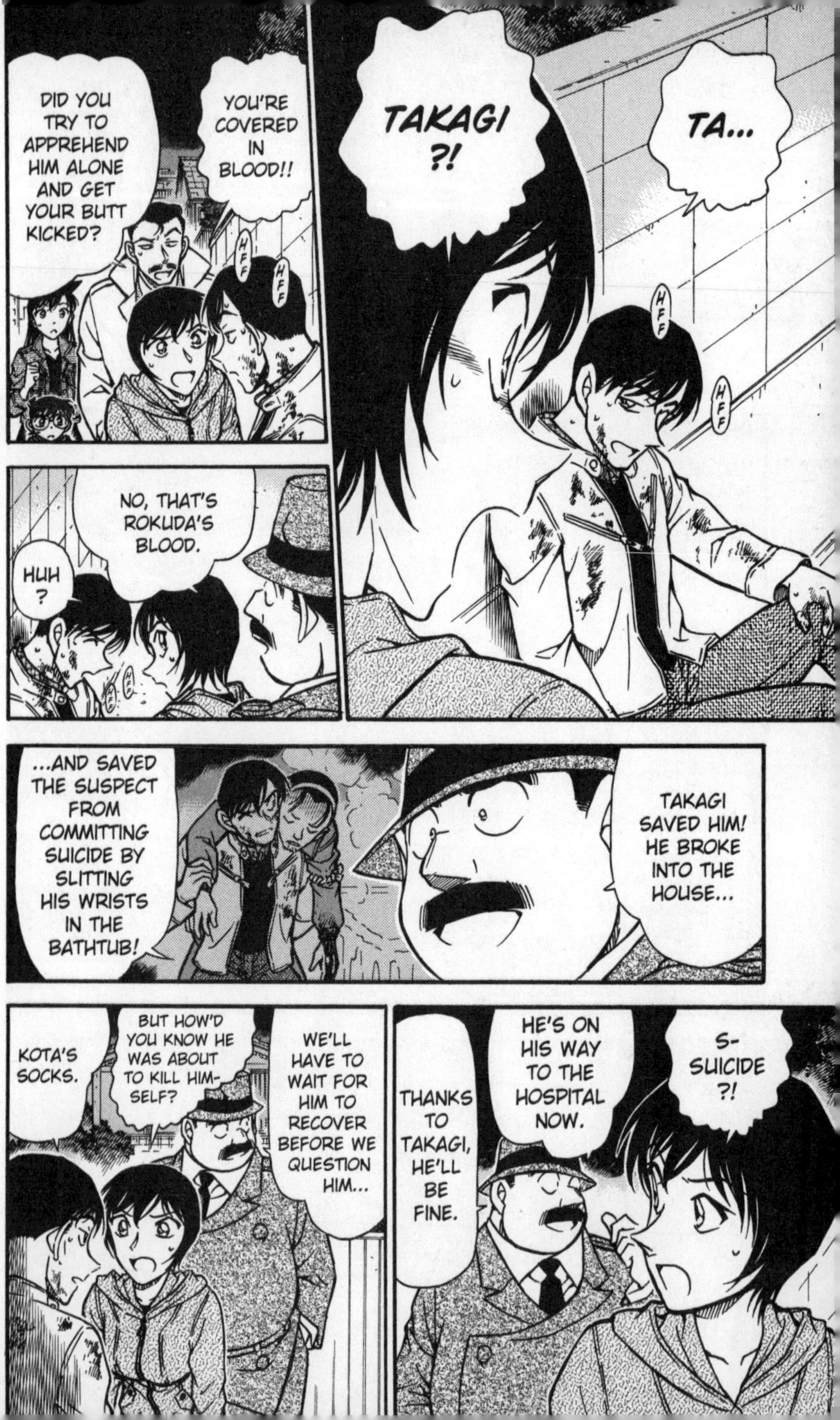
TA...
TAKAGI ?!
HFF
HFF
YOU'RE COVERED IN BLOOD!!
DID YOU TRY TO APPREHEND HIM ALONE AND GET YOUR BUTT KICKED?
HFF
HFF
NO, THAT'S ROKUDA'S BLOOD.
HUH ?
HFF
HFF
TAKAGI SAVED HIM! HE BROKE INTO THE HOUSE...
...AND SAVED THE SUSPECT FROM COMMITTING SUICIDE BY SLITTING HIS WRISTS IN THE BATHTUB!
S- SUICIDE ?!
HE'S ON HIS WAY TO THE HOSPITAL NOW.
THANKS TO TAKAGI, HE'LL BE FINE.
WE'LL HAVE TO WAIT FOR HIM TO RECOVER BEFORE WE QUESTION HIM...
BUT HOW'D YOU KNOW HE WAS ABOUT TO KILL HIM-SELF?
KOTA'S SOCKS.

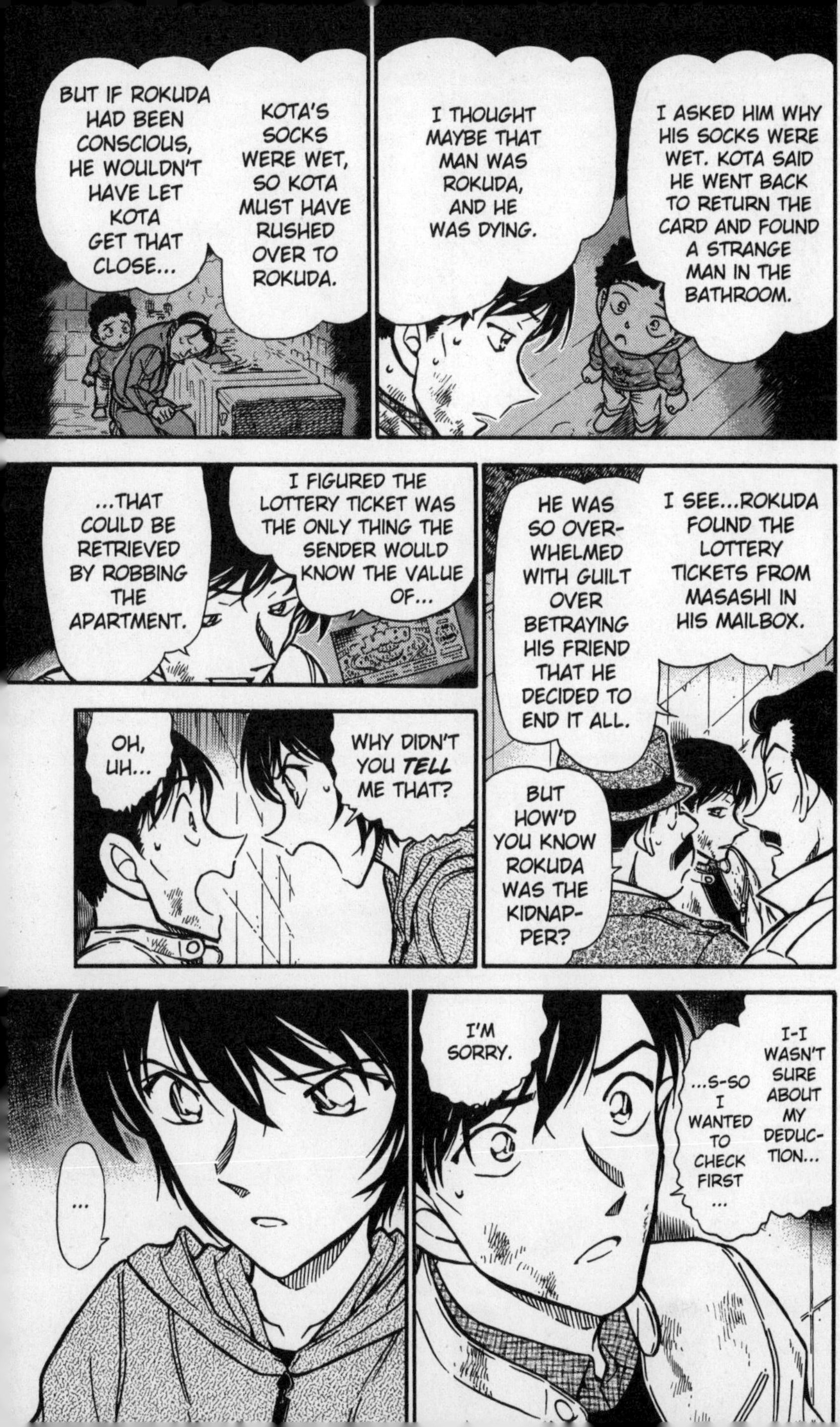
I ASKED HIM WHY HIS SOCKS WERE WET. KOTA SAID HE WENT BACK TO RETURN THE CARD AND FOUND A STRANGE MAN IN THE BATHROOM.
I THOUGHT MAYBE THAT MAN WAS ROKUDA, AND HE WAS DYING.
KOTA'S SOCKS WERE WET, SO KOTA MUST HAVE RUSHED OVER TO ROKUDA.
BUT IF ROKUDA HAD BEEN CONSCIOUS, HE WOULDN'T HAVE LET KOTA GET THAT CLOSE...
I SEE...ROKUDA FOUND THE LOTTERY TICKETS FROM MASASHI IN HIS MAILBOX.
HE WAS SO OVER-WHELMED WITH GUILT OVER BETRAYING HIS FRIEND THAT HE DECIDED TO END IT ALL.
BUT HOW'D YOU KNOW ROKUDA WAS THE KIDNAP-PER?
I FIGURED THE LOTTERY TICKET WAS THE ONLY THING THE SENDER WOULD KNOW THE VALUE OF...
...THAT COULD BE RETRIEVED BY ROBBING THE APARTMENT.
WHY DIDN'T YOU ***TELL*** ME THAT?
OH, UH...
I-I WASN'T SURE ABOUT MY DEDUC-TION...
...S-SO I WANTED TO CHECK FIRST...
I'M SORRY.
...

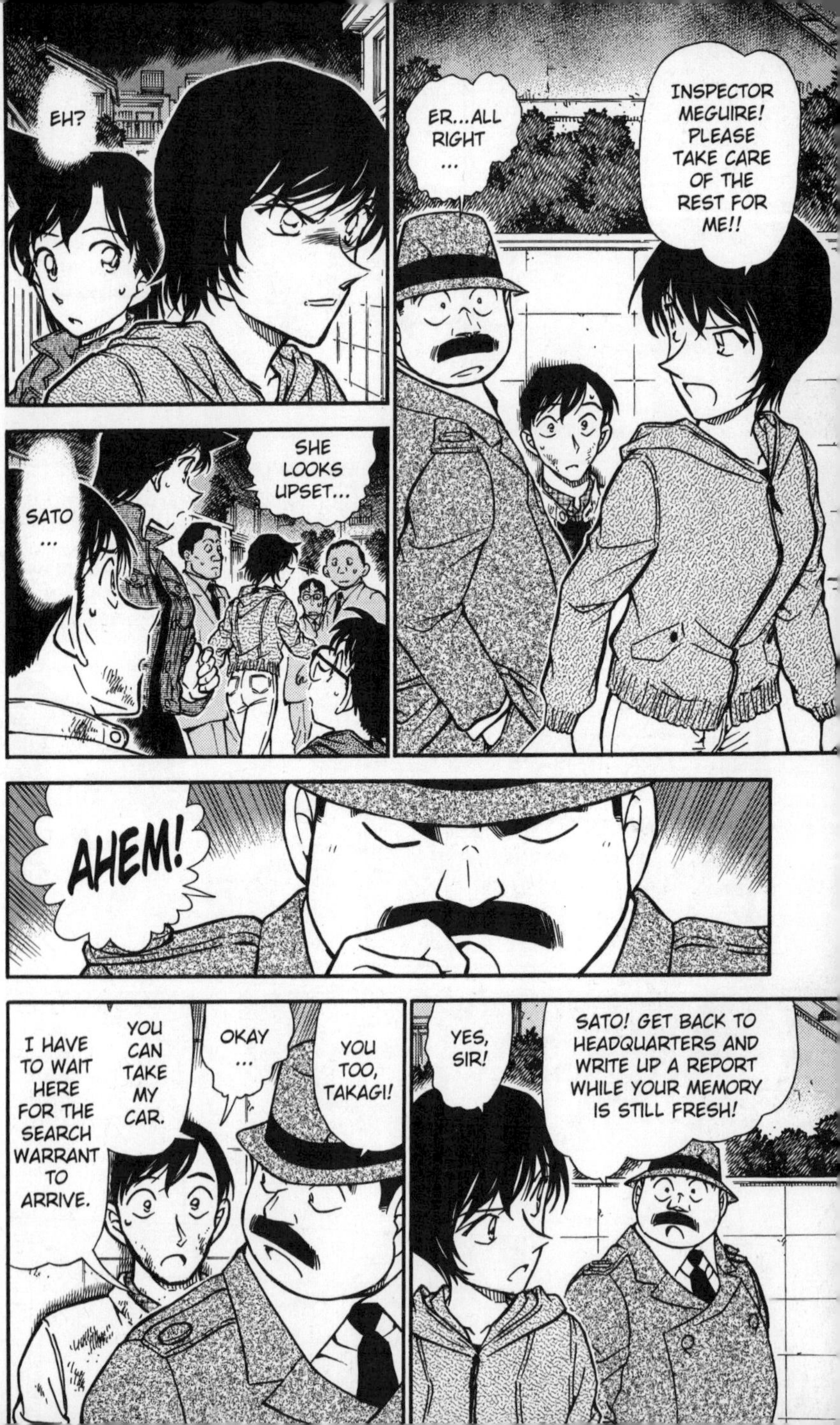
INSPECTOR MEGUIRE! PLEASE TAKE CARE OF THE REST FOR ME!!
ER...ALL RIGHT...
EH?
SHE LOOKS UPSET...
SATO...
AHEM!
SATO! GET BACK TO HEADQUARTERS AND WRITE UP A REPORT WHILE YOUR MEMORY IS STILL FRESH!
YES, SIR!
YOU TOO, TAKAGI!
OKAY...
YOU CAN TAKE MY CAR.
I HAVE TO WAIT HERE FOR THE SEARCH WARRANT TO ARRIVE.

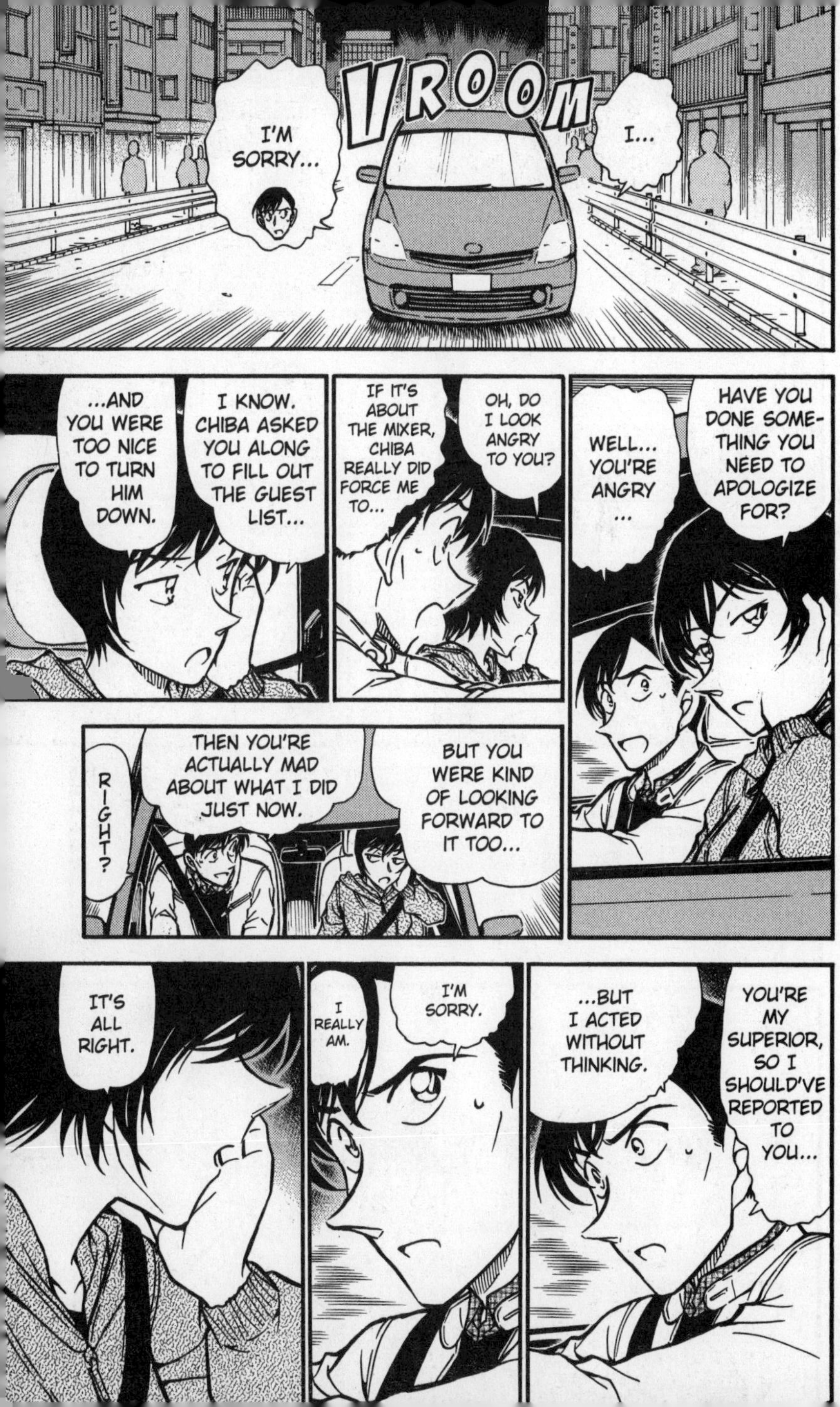
VROOM
I...
I'M SORRY...
HAVE YOU DONE SOME-THING YOU NEED TO APOLOGIZE FOR?
WELL... YOU'RE ANGRY ...
OH, DO I LOOK ANGRY TO YOU?
IF IT'S ABOUT THE MIXER, CHIBA REALLY DID FORCE ME TO...
I KNOW. CHIBA ASKED YOU ALONG TO FILL OUT THE GUEST LIST...
...AND YOU WERE TOO NICE TO TURN HIM DOWN.
BUT YOU WERE KIND OF LOOKING FORWARD TO IT TOO...
THEN YOU'RE ACTUALLY MAD ABOUT WHAT I DID JUST NOW.
RIGHT?
YOU'RE MY SUPERIOR, SO I SHOULD'VE REPORTED TO YOU...
...BUT I ACTED WITHOUT THINKING.
I'M SORRY.
I REALLY AM.
IT'S ALL RIGHT.

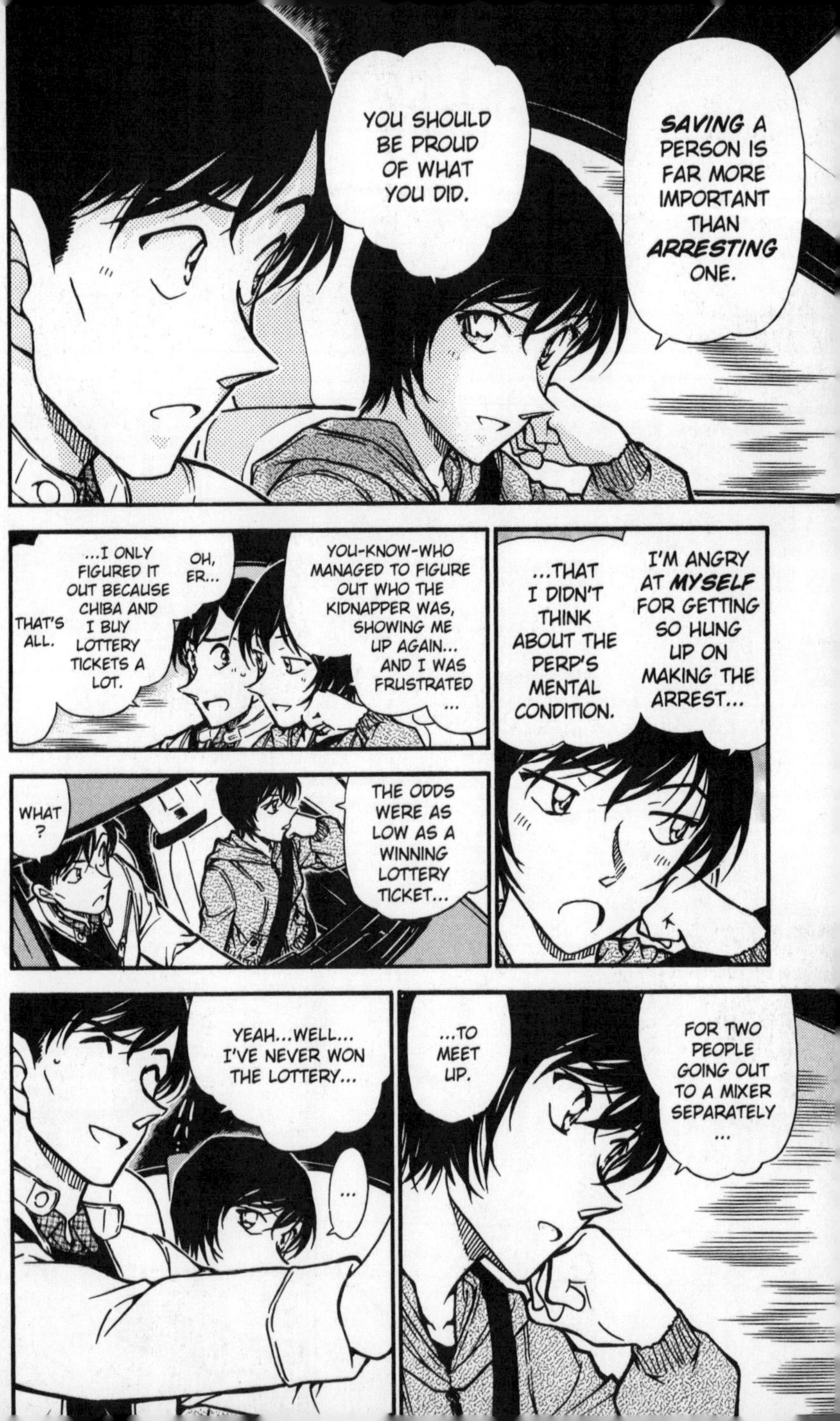
SAVING A PERSON IS FAR MORE IMPORTANT THAN *ARRESTING* ONE.
YOU SHOULD BE PROUD OF WHAT YOU DID.
I'M ANGRY AT *MYSELF* FOR GETTING SO HUNG UP ON MAKING THE ARREST...
...THAT I DIDN'T THINK ABOUT THE PERP'S MENTAL CONDITION.
YOU-KNOW-WHO MANAGED TO FIGURE OUT WHO THE KIDNAPPER WAS, SHOWING ME UP AGAIN... AND I WAS FRUSTRATED ...
OH, ER...
...I ONLY FIGURED IT OUT BECAUSE CHIBA AND I BUY LOTTERY TICKETS A LOT.
THAT'S ALL.
THE ODDS WERE AS LOW AS A WINNING LOTTERY TICKET...
WHAT?
FOR TWO PEOPLE GOING OUT TO A MIXER SEPARATELY ...
...TO MEET UP.
YEAH...WELL... I'VE NEVER WON THE LOTTERY...
...

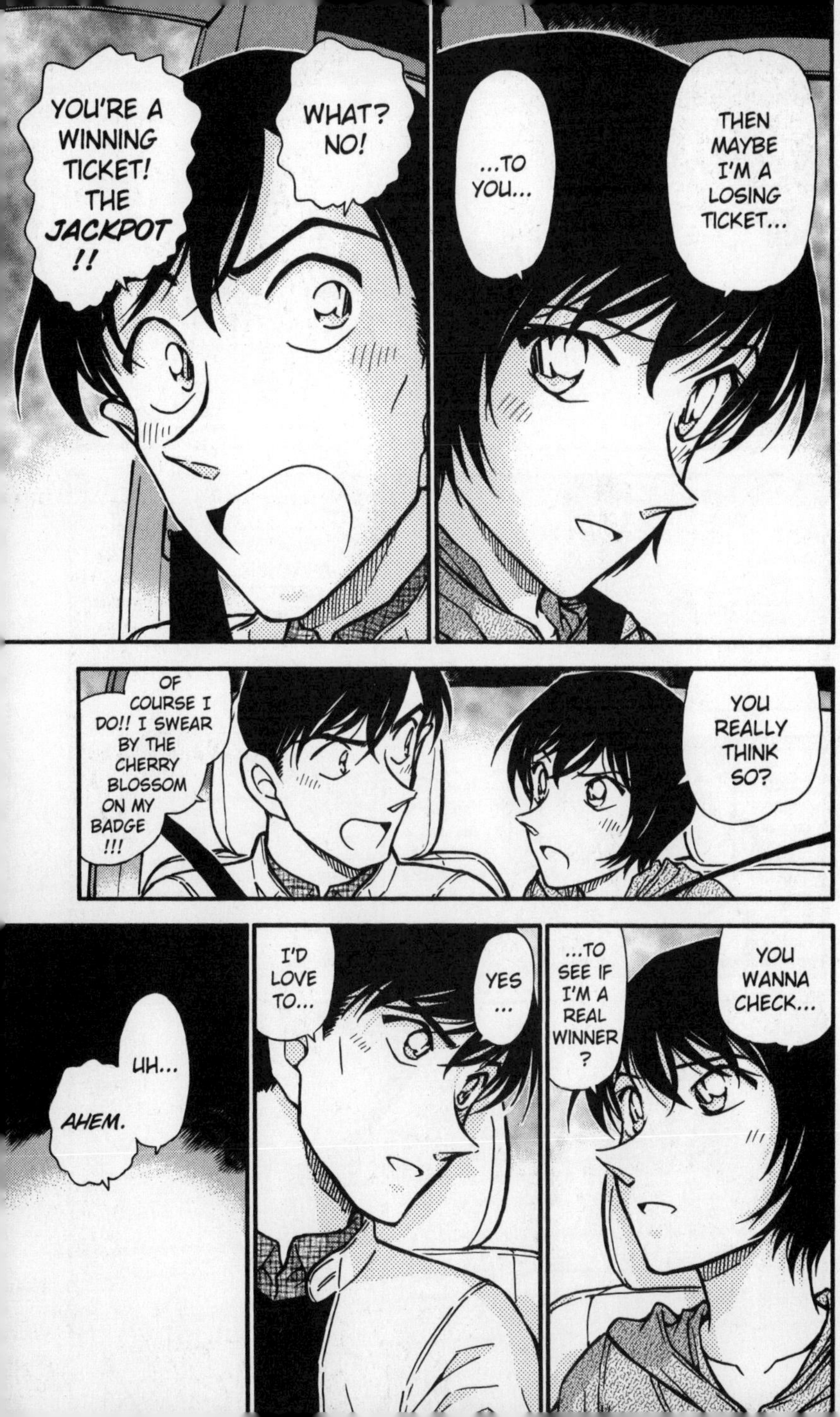
THEN MAYBE I'M A LOSING TICKET...
...TO YOU...
WHAT? NO!
YOU'RE A WINNING TICKET! THE JACKPOT!!
YOU REALLY THINK SO?
OF COURSE I DO!! I SWEAR BY THE CHERRY BLOSSOM ON MY BADGE!!!
YOU WANNA CHECK...
...TO SEE IF I'M A REAL WINNER?
YES...
I'D LOVE TO...
UH...
AHEM.

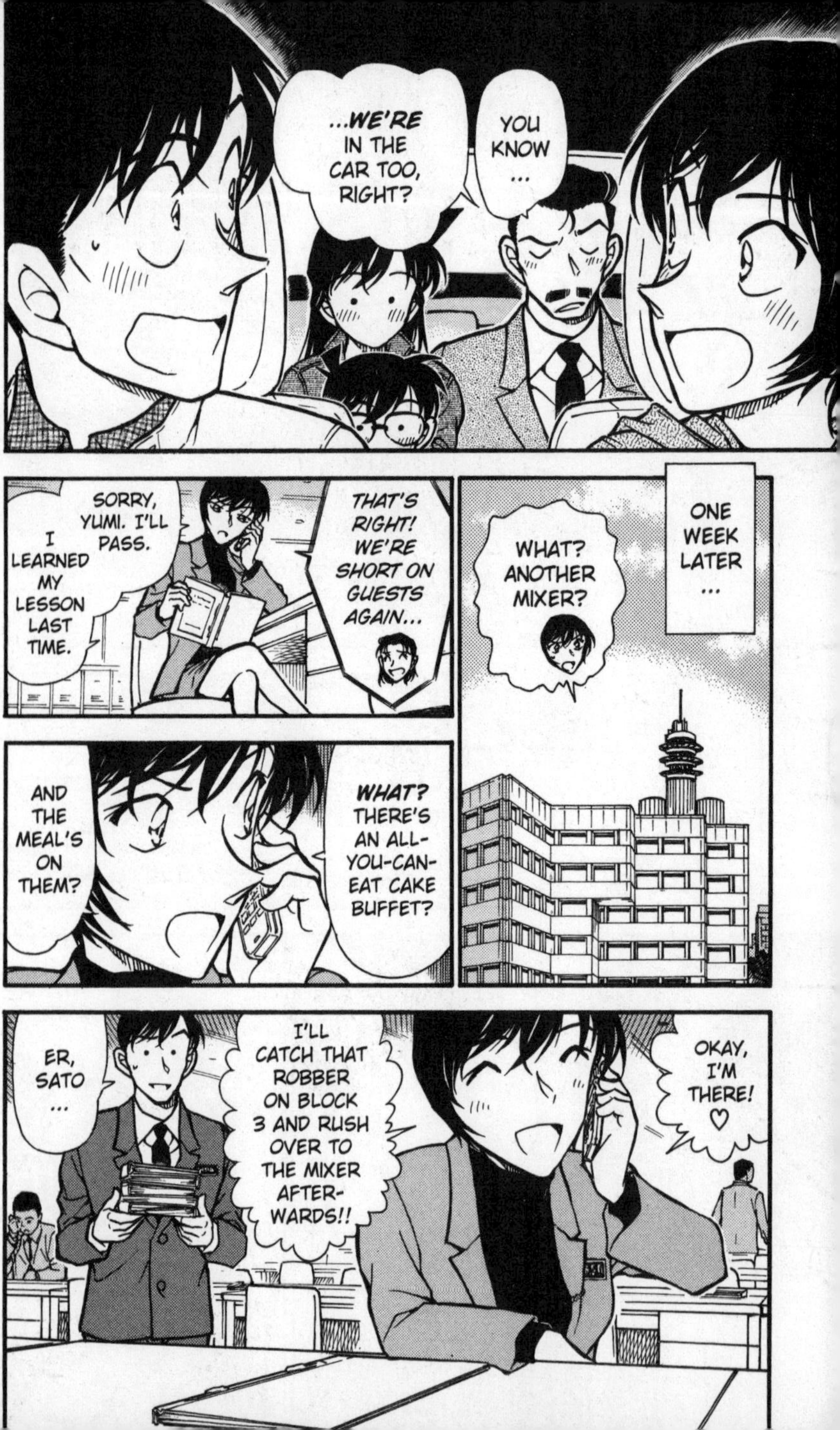
YOU KNOW ...
...WE'RE IN THE CAR TOO, RIGHT?
ONE WEEK LATER ...
WHAT? ANOTHER MIXER?
THAT'S RIGHT! WE'RE SHORT ON GUESTS AGAIN...
SORRY, YUMI. I'LL PASS.
I LEARNED MY LESSON LAST TIME.
WHAT? THERE'S AN ALL-YOU-CAN-EAT CAKE BUFFET?
AND THE MEAL'S ON THEM?
OKAY, I'M THERE! ♡
I'LL CATCH THAT ROBBER ON BLOCK 3 AND RUSH OVER TO THE MIXER AFTER-WARDS!!
ER, SATO ...

FILE 5: A THRILLING INTERVIEW

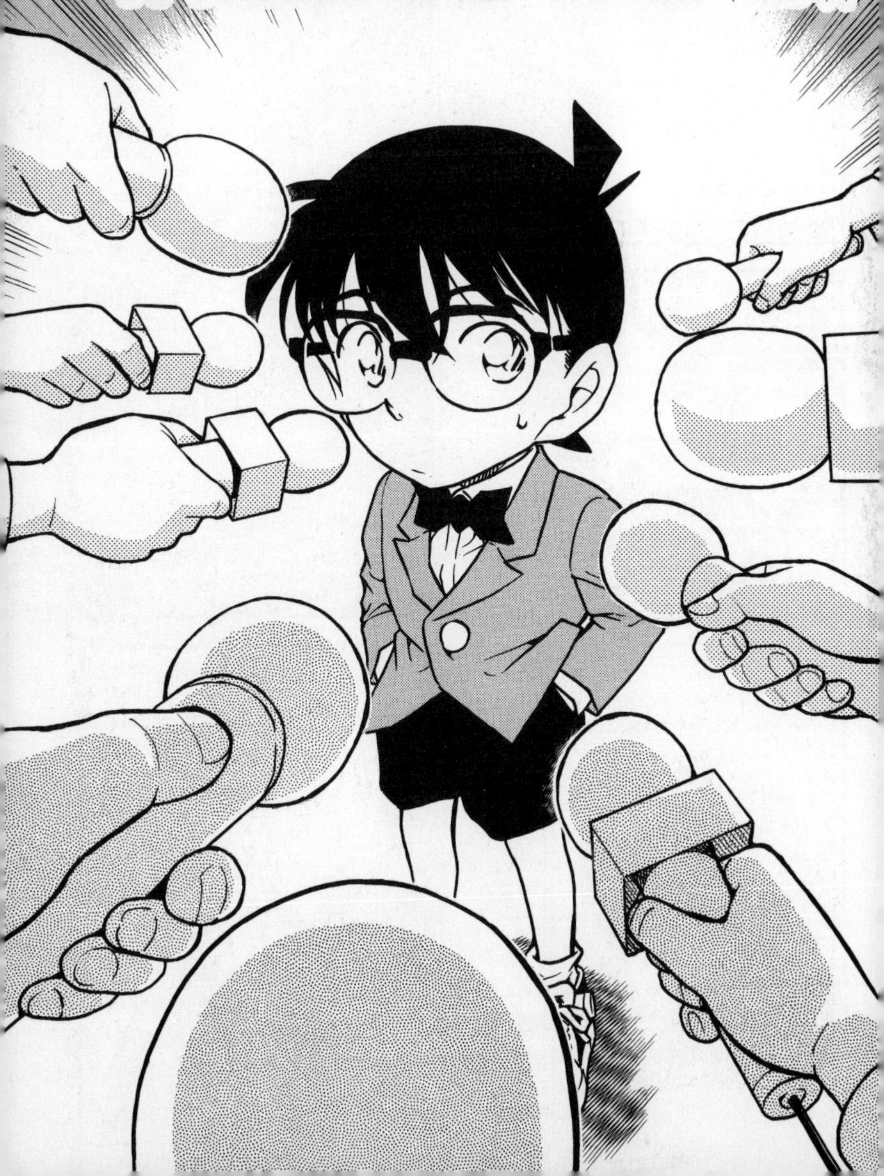

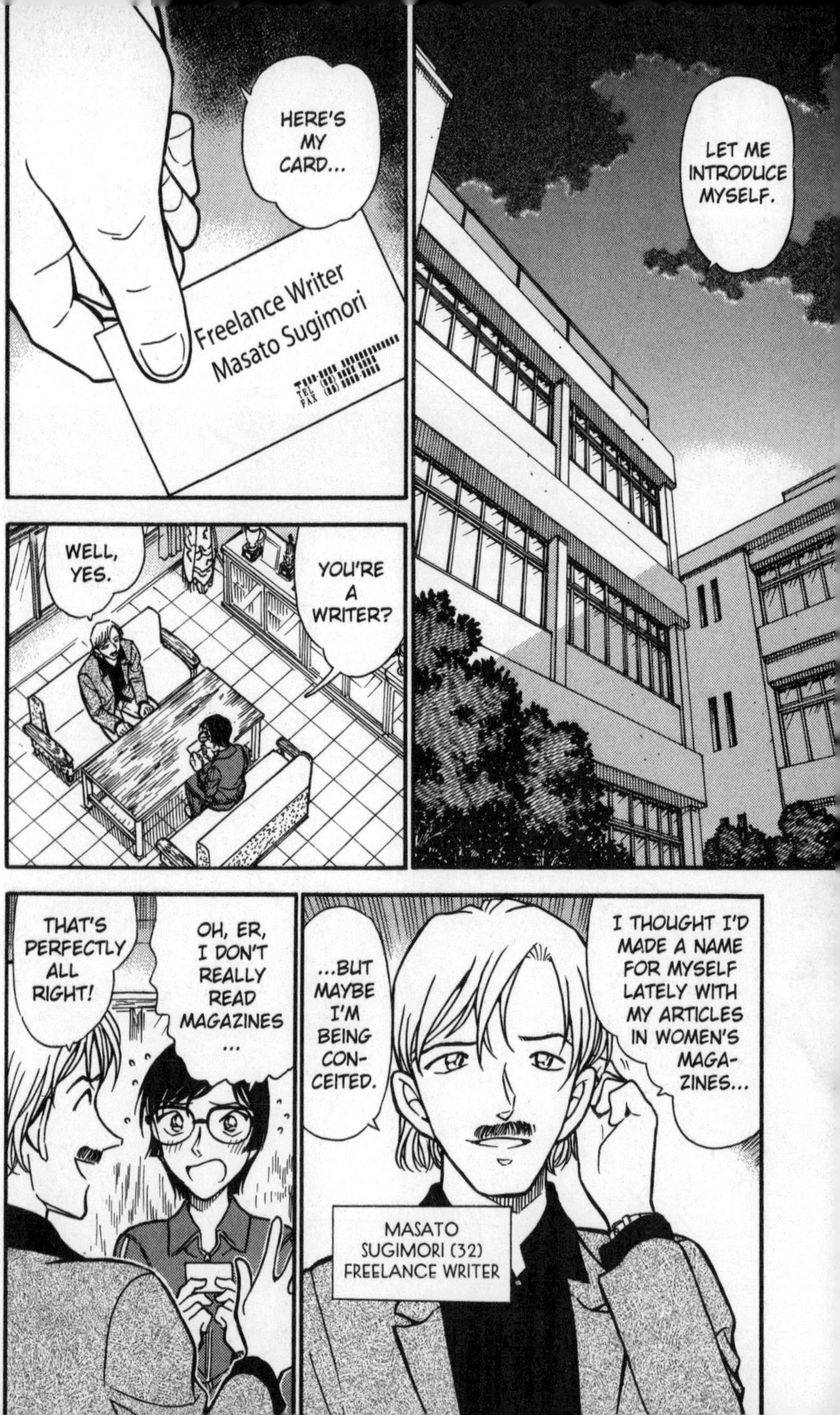
LET ME INTRODUCE MYSELF.
HERE'S MY CARD...
Freelance Writer
Masato Sugimori
YOU'RE A WRITER?
WELL, YES.
I THOUGHT I'D MADE A NAME FOR MYSELF LATELY WITH MY ARTICLES IN WOMEN'S MAGA-ZINES...
...BUT MAYBE I'M BEING CON-CEITED.
MASATO SUGIMORI (32) FREELANCE WRITER
OH, ER, I DON'T REALLY READ MAGAZINES...
THAT'S PERFECTLY ALL RIGHT!

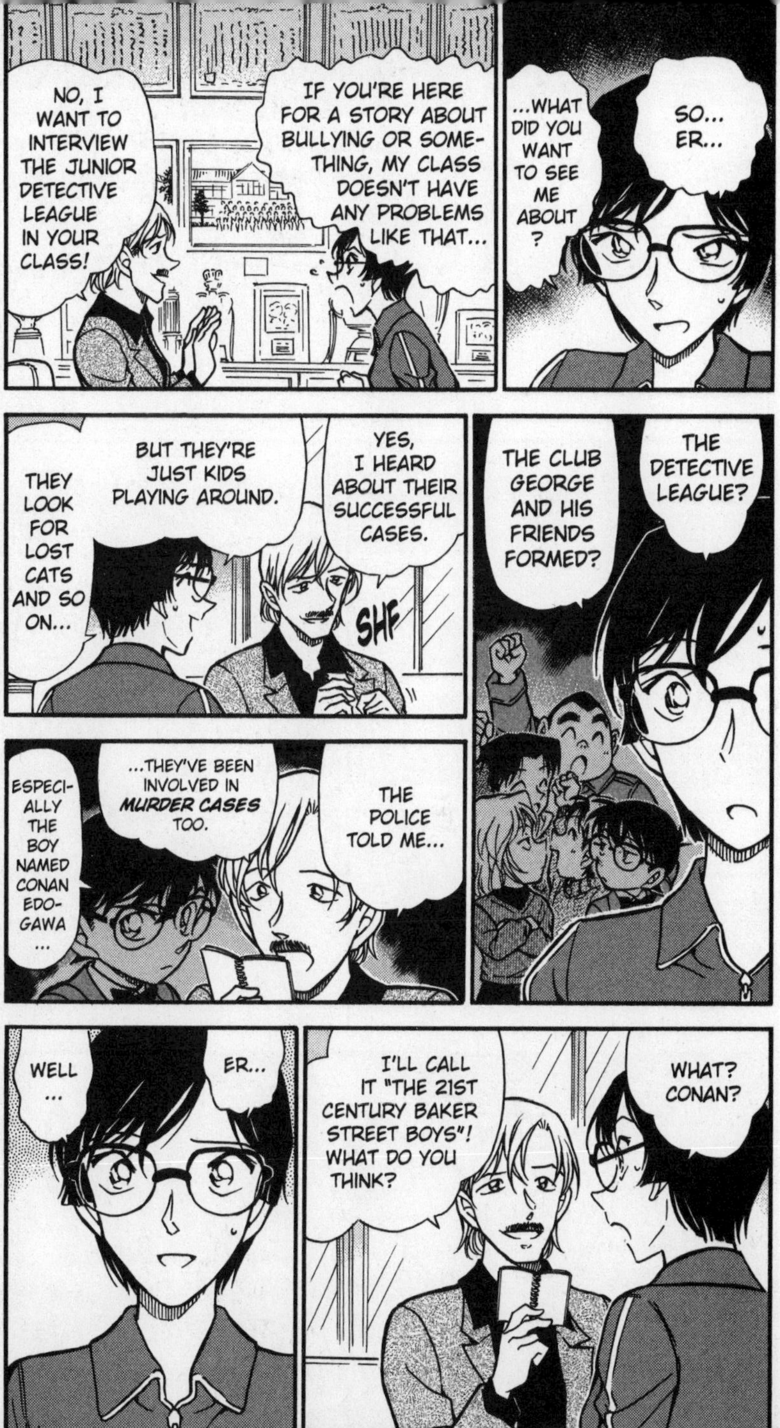
SO... ER...
...WHAT DID YOU WANT TO SEE ME ABOUT?
IF YOU'RE HERE FOR A STORY ABOUT BULLYING OR SOME-THING, MY CLASS DOESN'T HAVE ANY PROBLEMS LIKE THAT...
NO, I WANT TO INTERVIEW THE JUNIOR DETECTIVE LEAGUE IN YOUR CLASS!
THE DETECTIVE LEAGUE?
THE CLUB GEORGE AND HIS FRIENDS FORMED?
YES, I HEARD ABOUT THEIR SUCCESSFUL CASES.
SHF
BUT THEY'RE JUST KIDS PLAYING AROUND.
THEY LOOK FOR LOST CATS AND SO ON...
THE POLICE TOLD ME...
...THEY'VE BEEN INVOLVED IN *MURDER CASES* TOO.
ESPECI-ALLY THE BOY NAMED CONAN EDO-GAWA...
WHAT? CONAN?
I'LL CALL IT "THE 21ST CENTURY BAKER STREET BOYS"! WHAT DO YOU THINK?
ER...
WELL...

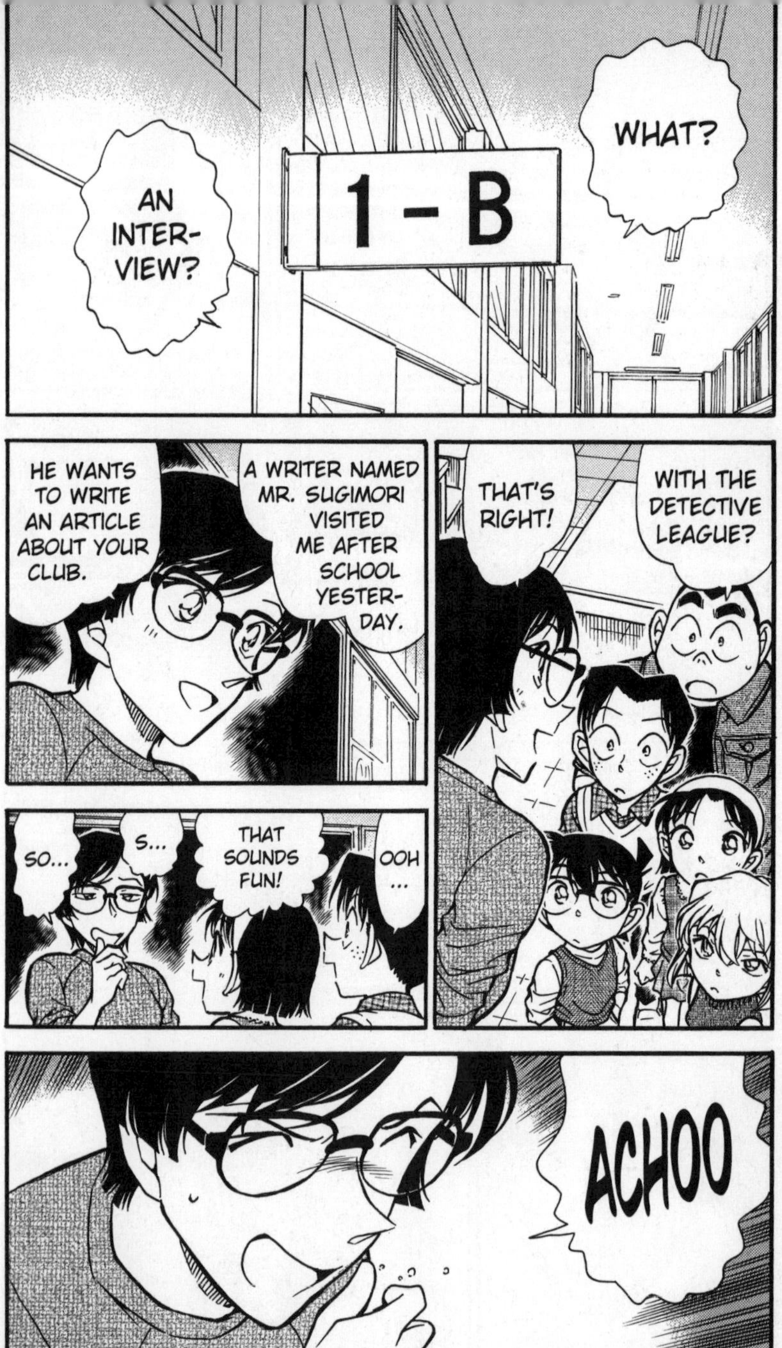
WHAT?
1 - B
AN INTERVIEW?
WITH THE DETECTIVE LEAGUE?
THAT'S RIGHT!
A WRITER NAMED MR. SUGIMORI VISITED ME AFTER SCHOOL YESTERDAY.
HE WANTS TO WRITE AN ARTICLE ABOUT YOUR CLUB.
OOH ...
THAT SOUNDS FUN!
S...
SO...
ACHOO

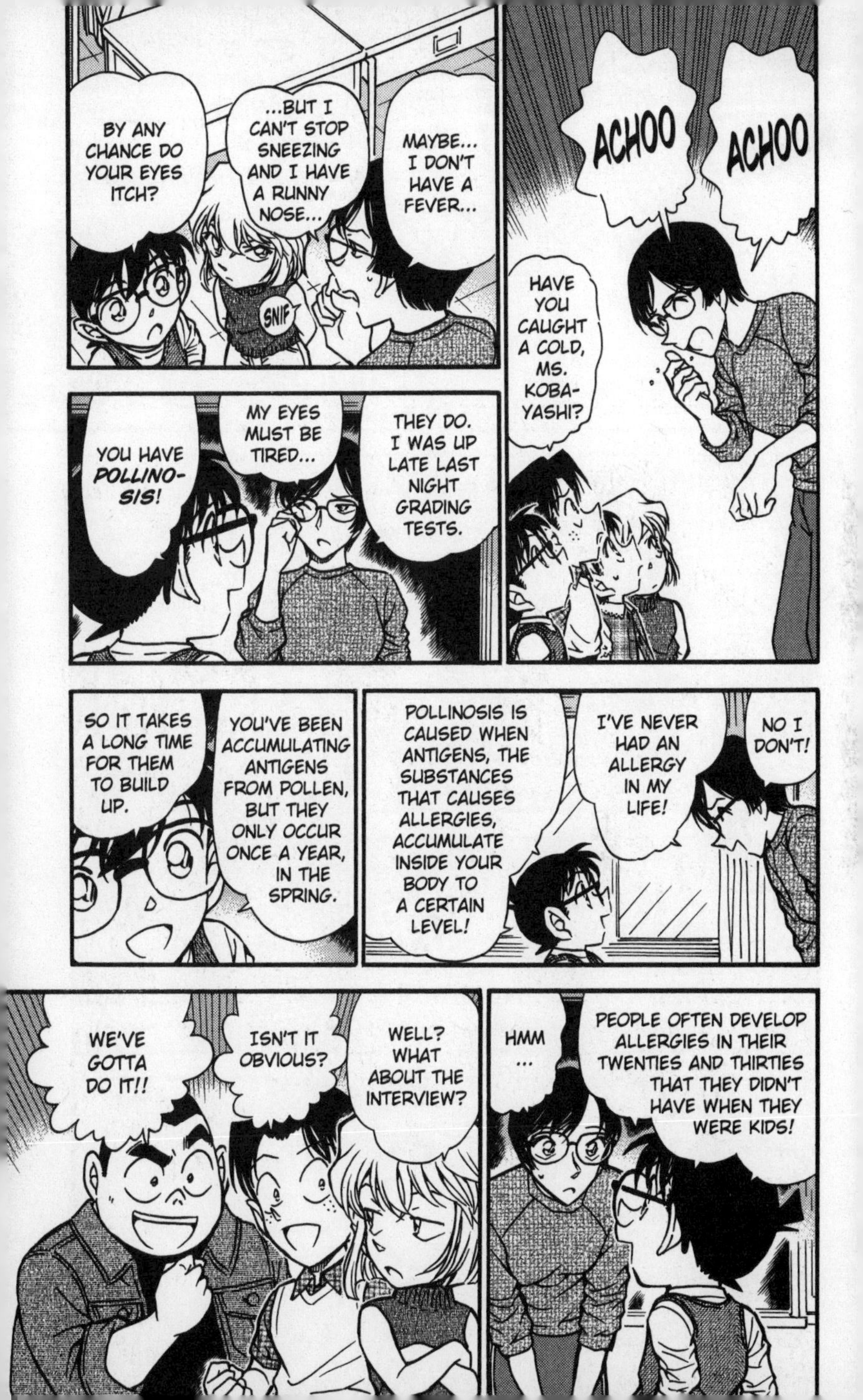
ACHOO
ACHOO
HAVE YOU CAUGHT A COLD, MS. KOBAYASHI?
MAYBE... I DON'T HAVE A FEVER...
...BUT I CAN'T STOP SNEEZING AND I HAVE A RUNNY NOSE...
SNIF
BY ANY CHANCE DO YOUR EYES ITCH?
THEY DO. I WAS UP LATE LAST NIGHT GRADING TESTS.
MY EYES MUST BE TIRED...
YOU HAVE *POLLINOSIS*!
NO I DON'T!
I'VE NEVER HAD AN ALLERGY IN MY LIFE!
POLLINOSIS IS CAUSED WHEN ANTIGENS, THE SUBSTANCES THAT CAUSES ALLERGIES, ACCUMULATE INSIDE YOUR BODY TO A CERTAIN LEVEL!
YOU'VE BEEN ACCUMULATING ANTIGENS FROM POLLEN, BUT THEY ONLY OCCUR ONCE A YEAR, IN THE SPRING.
SO IT TAKES A LONG TIME FOR THEM TO BUILD UP.
PEOPLE OFTEN DEVELOP ALLERGIES IN THEIR TWENTIES AND THIRTIES THAT THEY DIDN'T HAVE WHEN THEY WERE KIDS!
HMM ...
WELL? WHAT ABOUT THE INTERVIEW?
ISN'T IT OBVIOUS?
WE'VE GOTTA DO IT!!

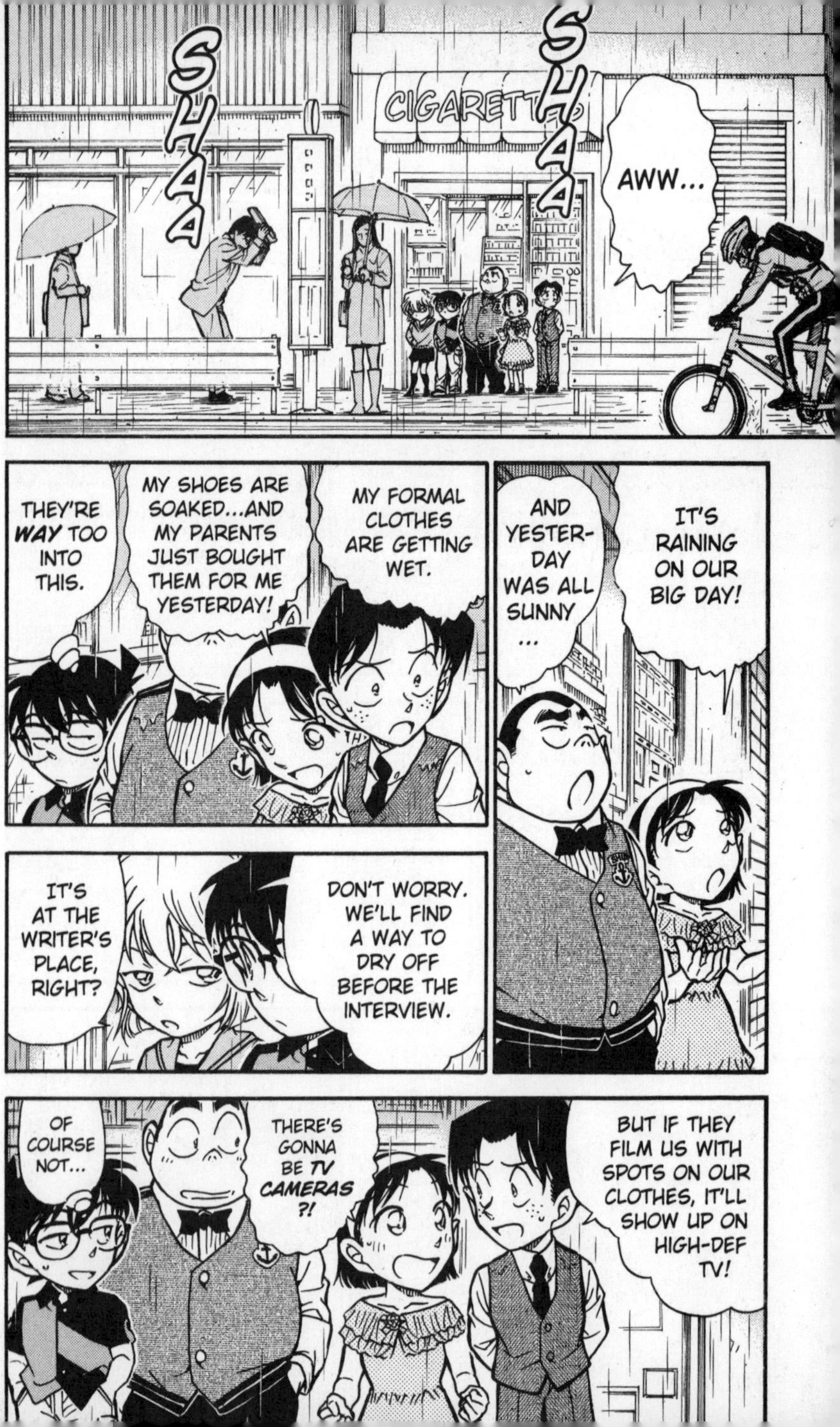
SHAA
AWW...
CIGARETT
SHAA
IT'S RAINING ON OUR BIG DAY!
AND YESTERDAY WAS ALL SUNNY...
MY FORMAL CLOTHES ARE GETTING WET.
MY SHOES ARE SOAKED...AND MY PARENTS JUST BOUGHT THEM FOR ME YESTERDAY!
THEY'RE WAY TOO INTO THIS.
DON'T WORRY. WE'LL FIND A WAY TO DRY OFF BEFORE THE INTERVIEW.
IT'S AT THE WRITER'S PLACE, RIGHT?
BUT IF THEY FILM US WITH SPOTS ON OUR CLOTHES, IT'LL SHOW UP ON HIGH-DEF TV!
THERE'S GONNA BE TV CAMERAS?!
OF COURSE NOT...

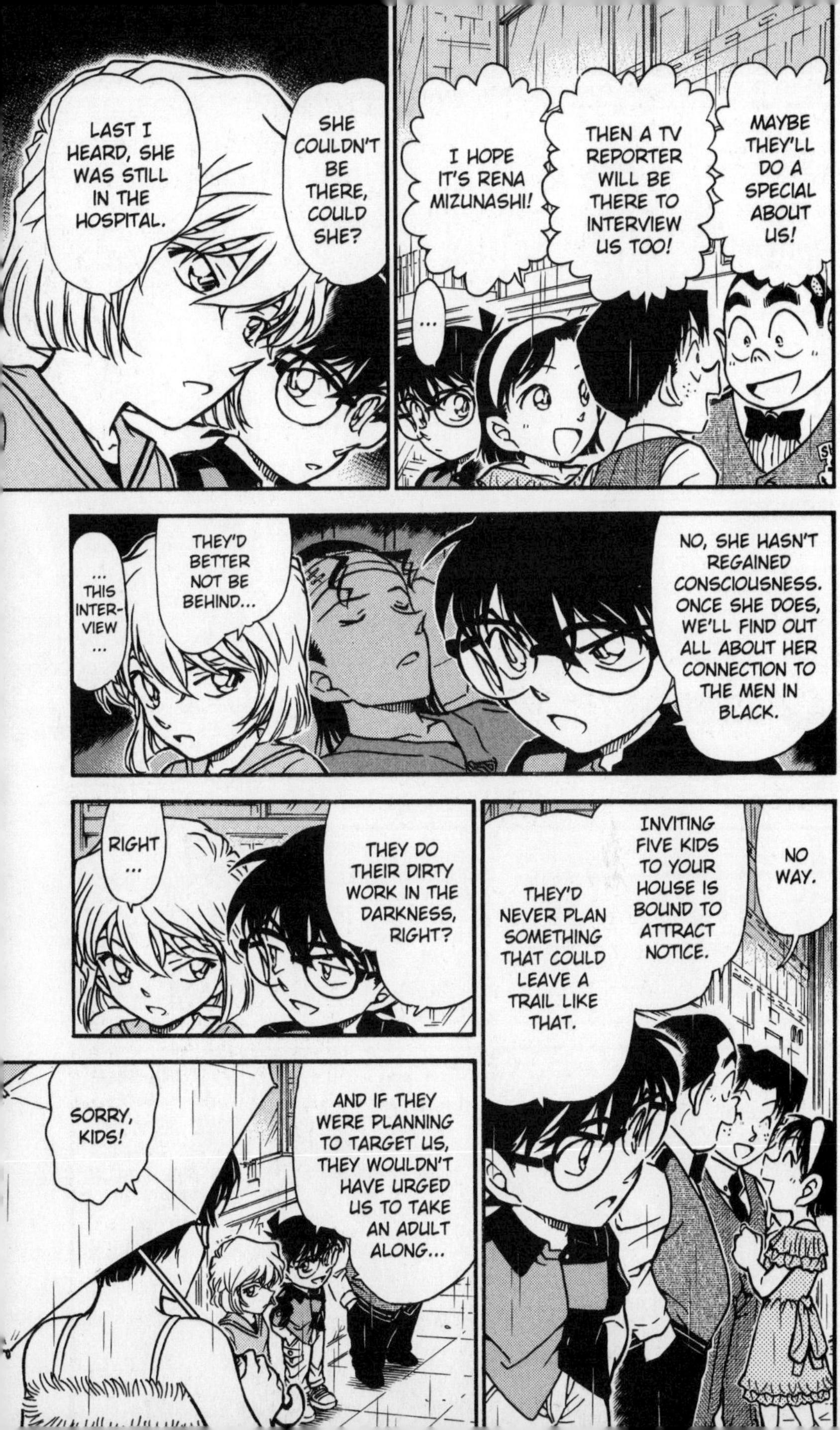
MAYBE THEY'LL DO A SPECIAL ABOUT US!
THEN A TV REPORTER WILL BE THERE TO INTERVIEW US TOO!
I HOPE IT'S RENA MIZUNASHI!
...
SHE COULDN'T BE THERE, COULD SHE?
LAST I HEARD, SHE WAS STILL IN THE HOSPITAL.
NO, SHE HASN'T REGAINED CONSCIOUSNESS. ONCE SHE DOES, WE'LL FIND OUT ALL ABOUT HER CONNECTION TO THE MEN IN BLACK.
THEY'D BETTER NOT BE BEHIND...
... THIS INTER-VIEW ...
NO WAY.
INVITING FIVE KIDS TO YOUR HOUSE IS BOUND TO ATTRACT NOTICE.
THEY'D NEVER PLAN SOMETHING THAT COULD LEAVE A TRAIL LIKE THAT.
THEY DO THEIR DIRTY WORK IN THE DARKNESS, RIGHT?
RIGHT ...
AND IF THEY WERE PLANNING TO TARGET US, THEY WOULDN'T HAVE URGED US TO TAKE AN ADULT ALONG...
SORRY, KIDS!

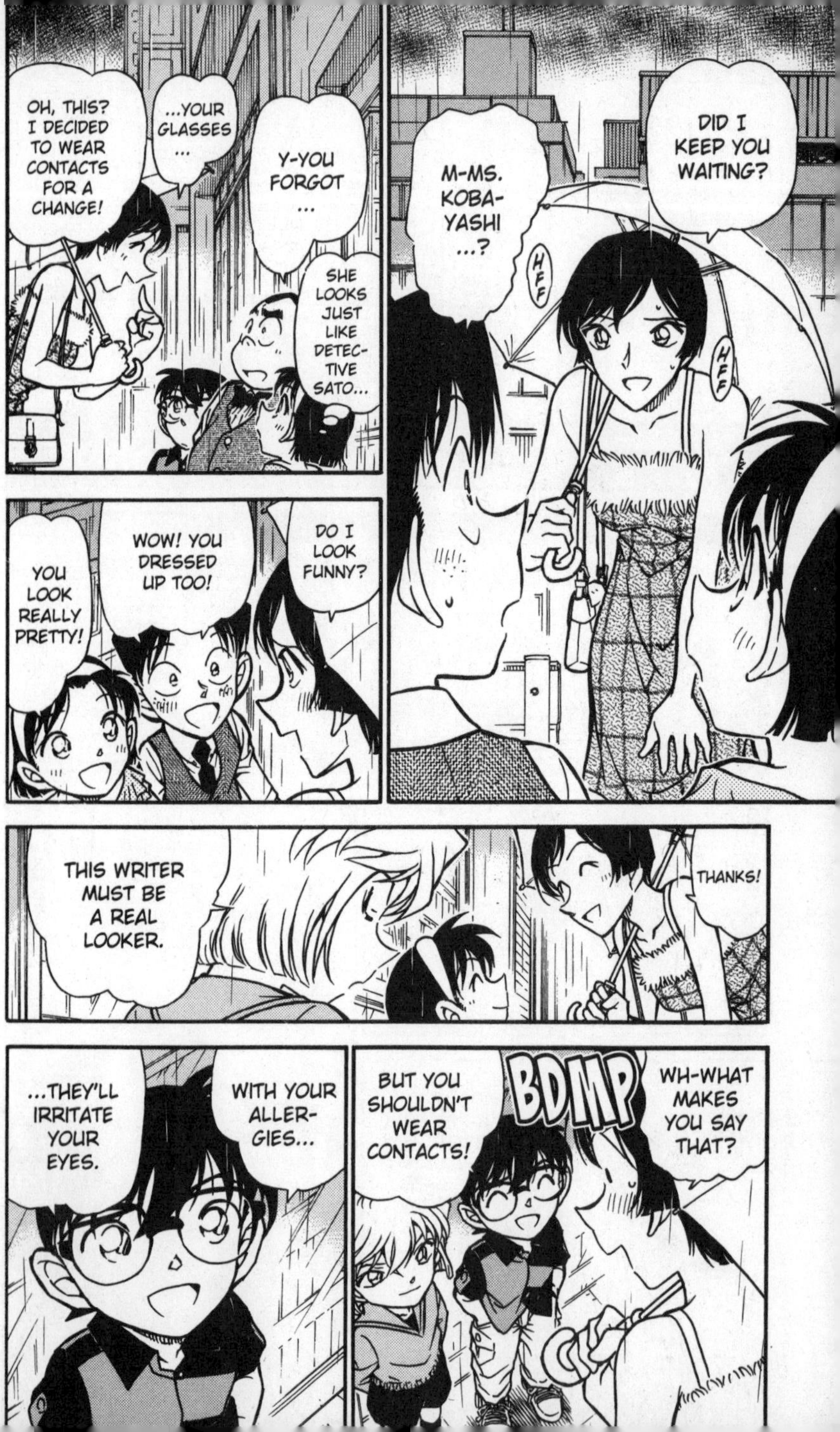
DID I KEEP YOU WAITING?
M-MS. KOBA-YASHI ...?
HFF
HFF
Y-YOU FORGOT ...
...YOUR GLASSES ...
OH, THIS? I DECIDED TO WEAR CONTACTS FOR A CHANGE!
SHE LOOKS JUST LIKE DETEC-TIVE SATO...
DO I LOOK FUNNY?
WOW! YOU DRESSED UP TOO!
YOU LOOK REALLY PRETTY!
THANKS!
THIS WRITER MUST BE A REAL LOOKER.
BUT YOU SHOULDN'T WEAR CONTACTS!
BDMP
WH-WHAT MAKES YOU SAY THAT?
WITH YOUR ALLER-GIES...
...THEY'LL IRRITATE YOUR EYES.

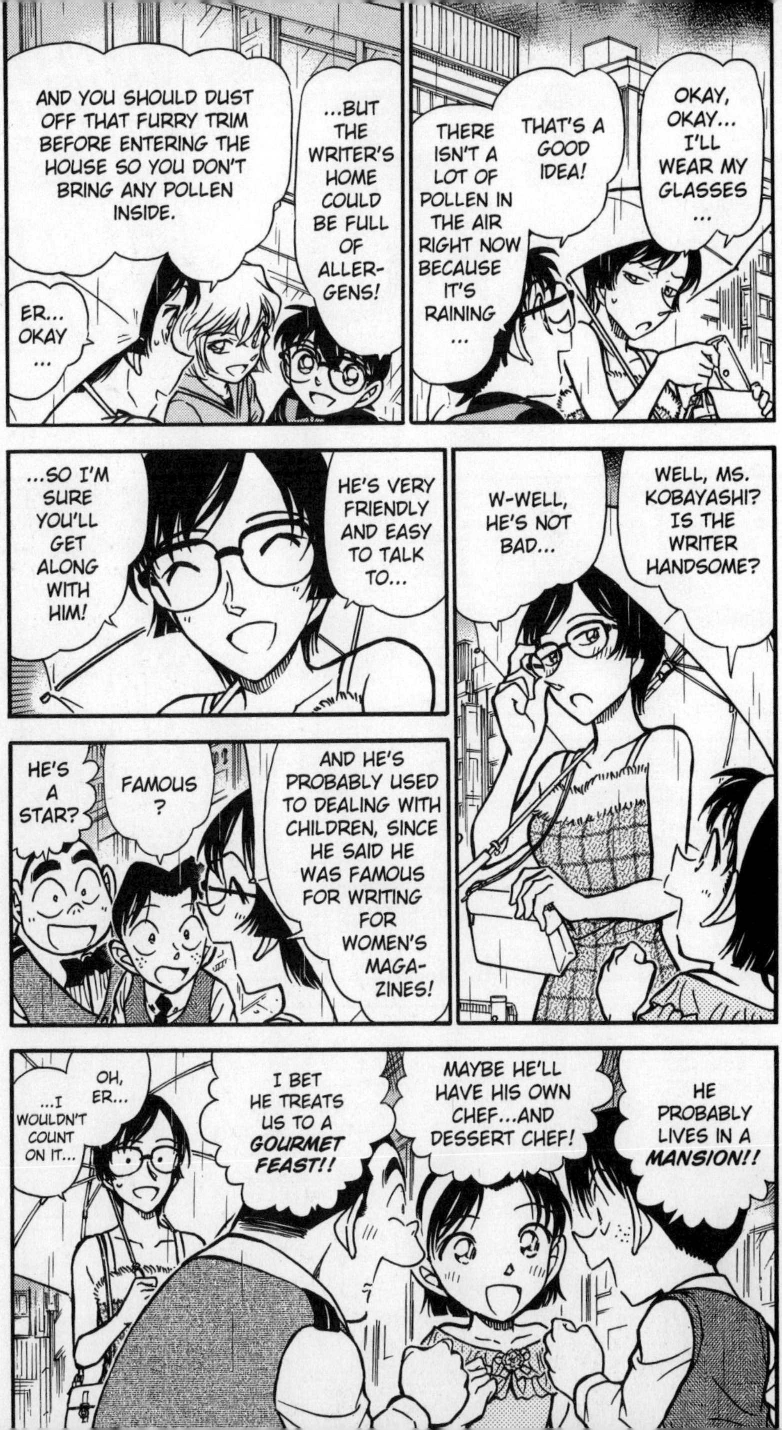
OKAY, OKAY... I'LL WEAR MY GLASSES...
THAT'S A GOOD IDEA!
THERE ISN'T A LOT OF POLLEN IN THE AIR RIGHT NOW BECAUSE IT'S RAINING...
...BUT THE WRITER'S HOME COULD BE FULL OF ALLER-GENS!
AND YOU SHOULD DUST OFF THAT FURRY TRIM BEFORE ENTERING THE HOUSE SO YOU DON'T BRING ANY POLLEN INSIDE.
ER... OKAY...
WELL, MS. KOBAYASHI? IS THE WRITER HANDSOME?
W-WELL, HE'S NOT BAD...
HE'S VERY FRIENDLY AND EASY TO TALK TO...
...SO I'M SURE YOU'LL GET ALONG WITH HIM!
AND HE'S PROBABLY USED TO DEALING WITH CHILDREN, SINCE HE SAID HE WAS FAMOUS FOR WRITING FOR WOMEN'S MAGA-ZINES!
FAMOUS?
HE'S A STAR?
HE PROBABLY LIVES IN A *MANSION!!*
MAYBE HE'LL HAVE HIS OWN CHEF...AND DESSERT CHEF!
I BET HE TREATS US TO A *GOURMET FEAST!!*
OH, ER...
...I WOULDN'T COUNT ON IT...

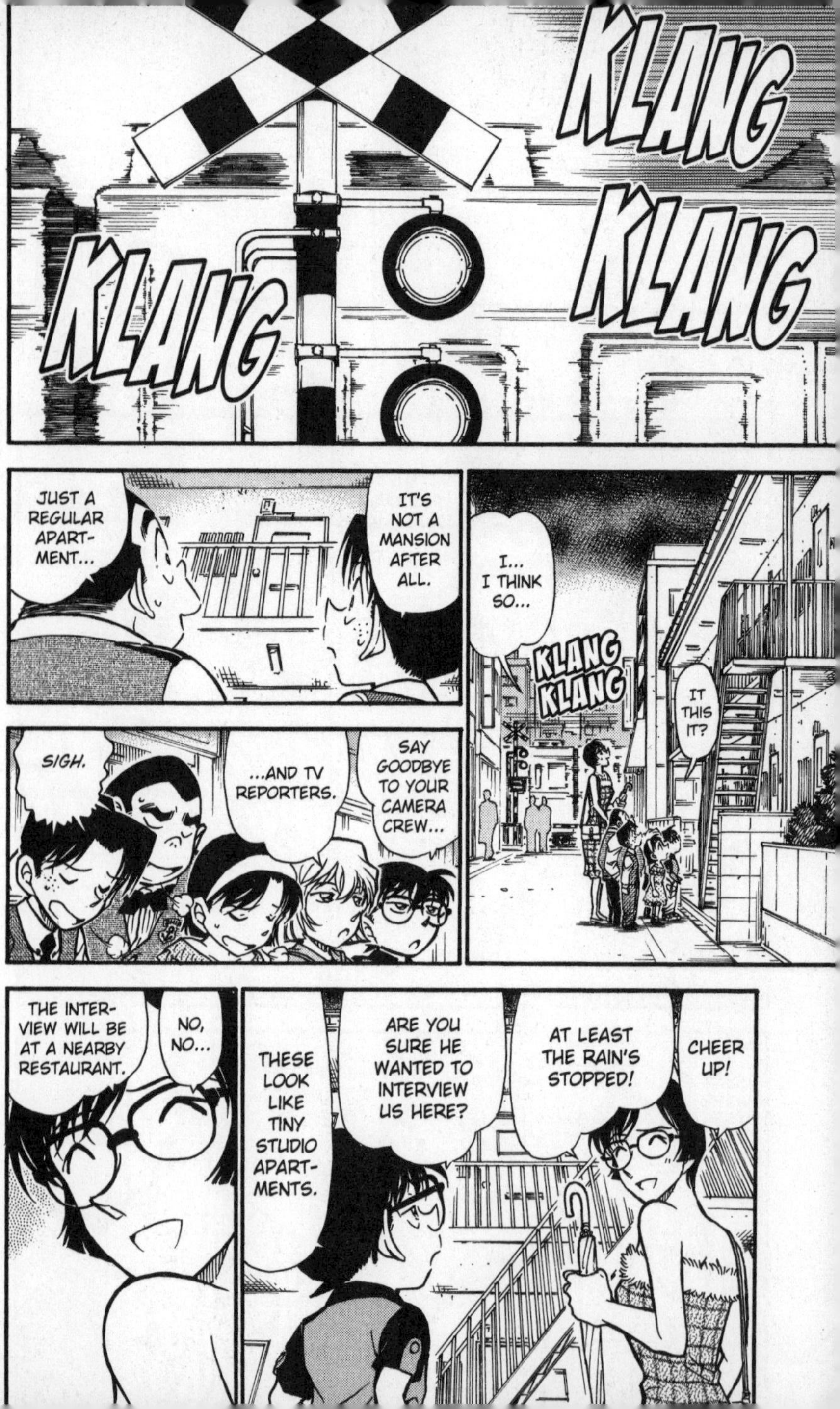
KLANG
KLANG
KLANG
IT THIS IT?
I... I THINK SO...
KLANG KLANG
IT'S NOT A MANSION AFTER ALL.
JUST A REGULAR APARTMENT...
SAY GOODBYE TO YOUR CAMERA CREW...
...AND TV REPORTERS.
SIGH.
CHEER UP!
AT LEAST THE RAIN'S STOPPED!
ARE YOU SURE HE WANTED TO INTERVIEW US HERE?
THESE LOOK LIKE TINY STUDIO APARTMENTS.
NO, NO...
THE INTERVIEW WILL BE AT A NEARBY RESTAURANT.

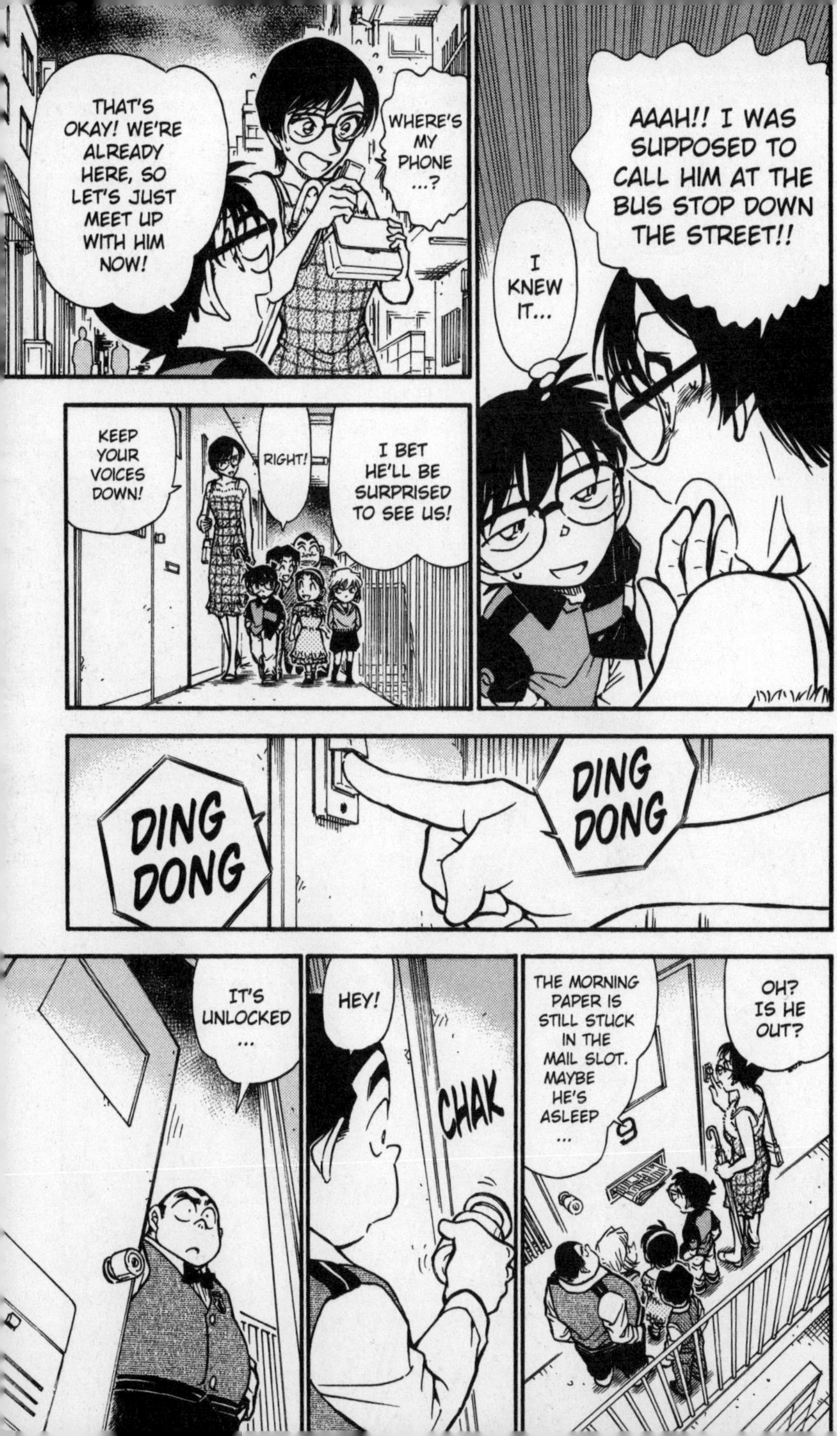
AAAH!! I WAS SUPPOSED TO CALL HIM AT THE BUS STOP DOWN THE STREET!!
I KNEW IT...
WHERE'S MY PHONE ...?
THAT'S OKAY! WE'RE ALREADY HERE, SO LET'S JUST MEET UP WITH HIM NOW!
I BET HE'LL BE SURPRISED TO SEE US!
RIGHT!
KEEP YOUR VOICES DOWN!
DING DONG
DING DONG
OH? IS HE OUT?
THE MORNING PAPER IS STILL STUCK IN THE MAIL SLOT. MAYBE HE'S ASLEEP ...
HEY!
CHAK
IT'S UNLOCKED ...

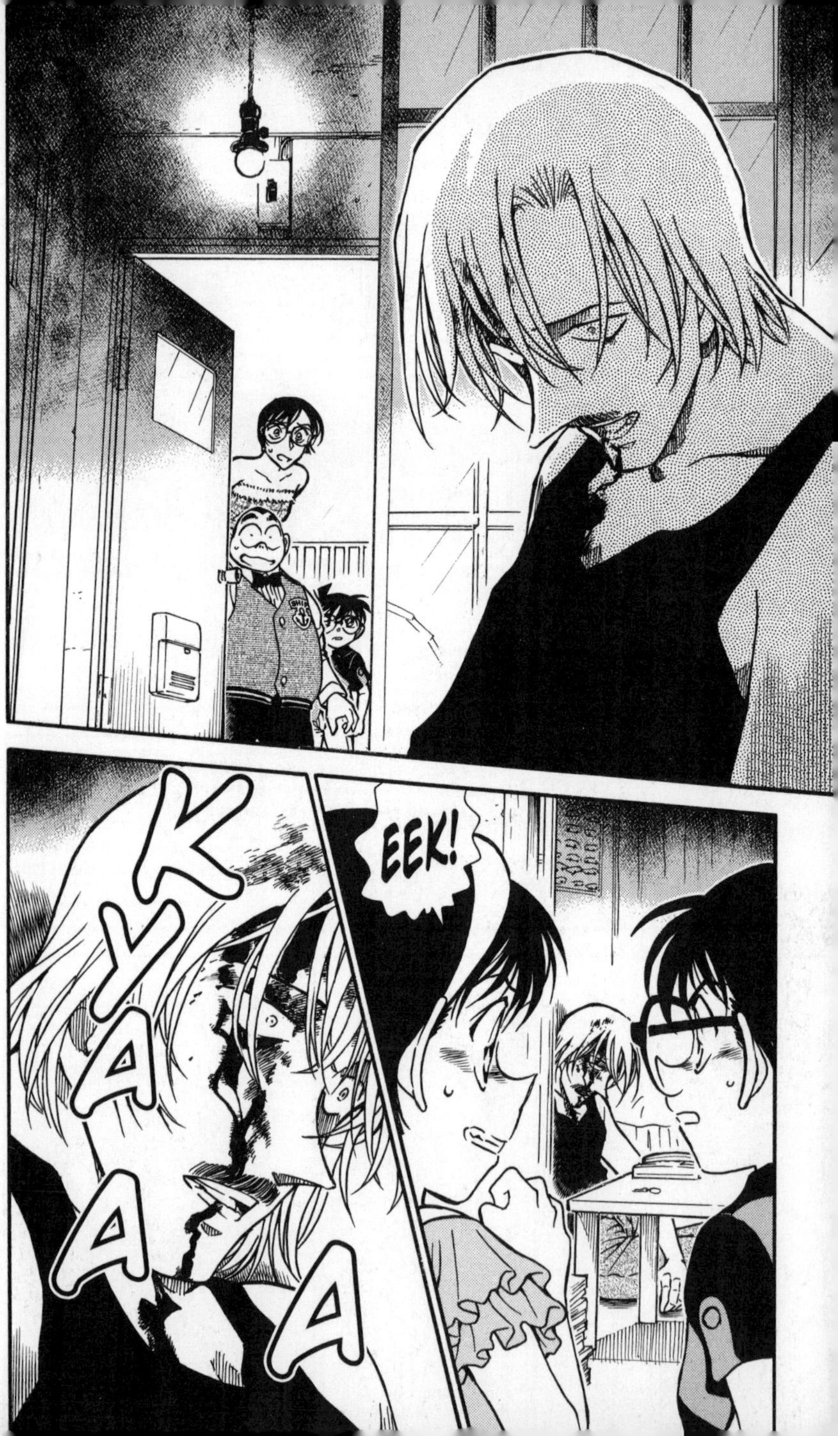
EEK!
KYAAAA

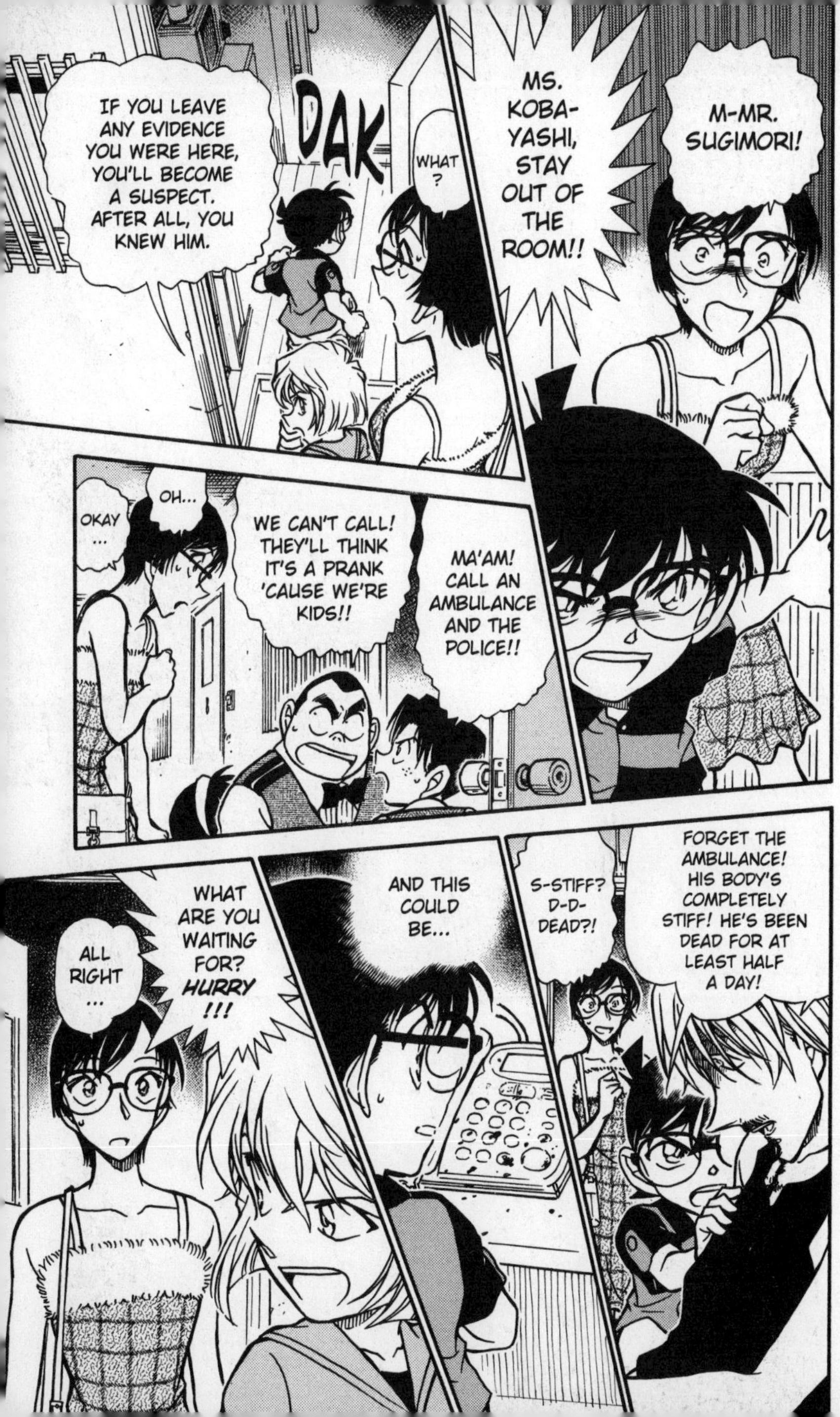
M-MR. SUGIMORI!
MS. KOBA-YASHI, STAY OUT OF THE ROOM!!
DAK
WHAT?
IF YOU LEAVE ANY EVIDENCE YOU WERE HERE, YOU'LL BECOME A SUSPECT. AFTER ALL, YOU KNEW HIM.
MA'AM! CALL AN AMBULANCE AND THE POLICE!!
WE CAN'T CALL! THEY'LL THINK IT'S A PRANK 'CAUSE WE'RE KIDS!!
OH...
OKAY...
FORGET THE AMBULANCE! HIS BODY'S COMPLETELY STIFF! HE'S BEEN DEAD FOR AT LEAST HALF A DAY!
S-STIFF? D-D-DEAD?!
AND THIS COULD BE...
WHAT ARE YOU WAITING FOR? HURRY!!!
ALL RIGHT...

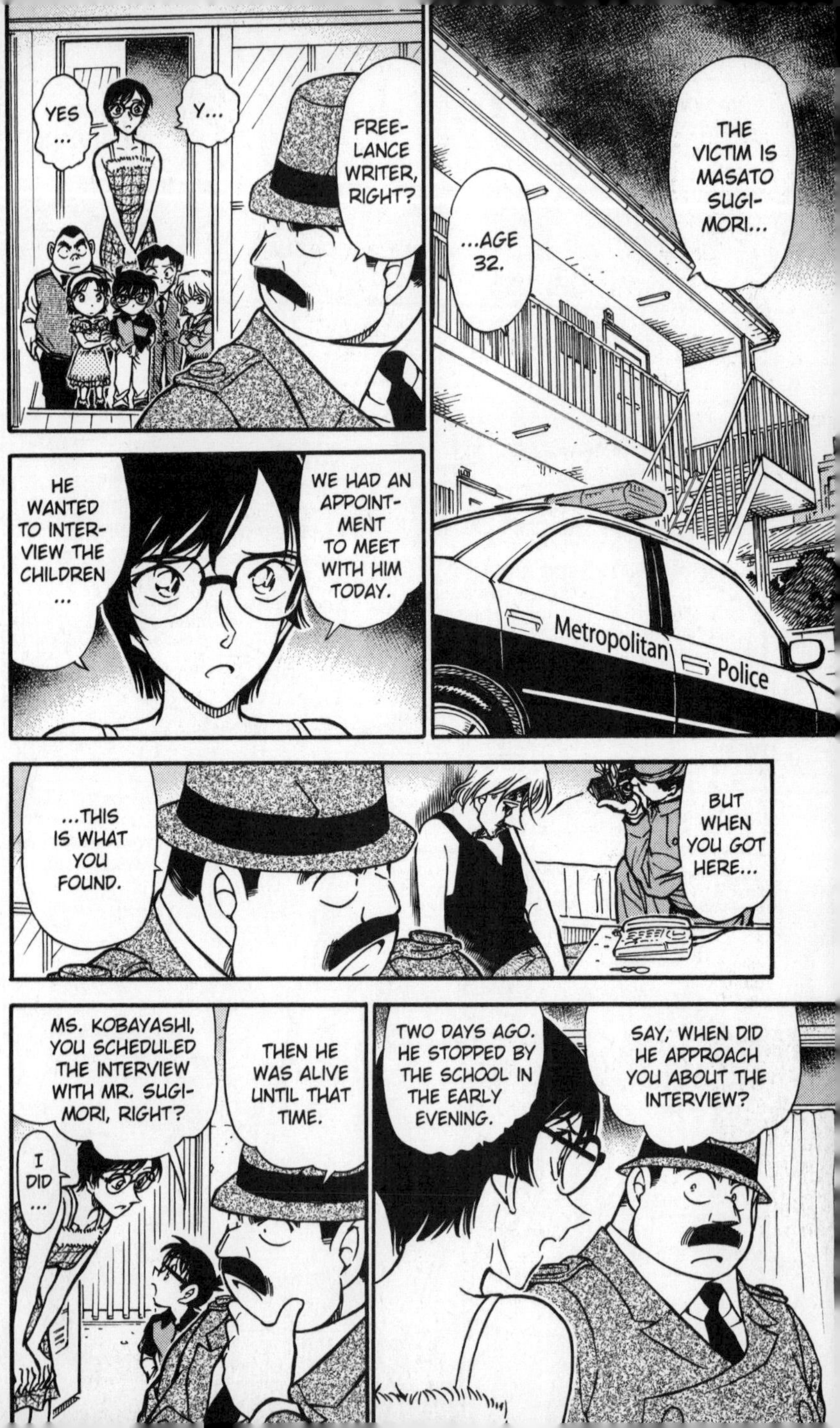
THE VICTIM IS MASATO SUGI-MORI...
...AGE 32.
Metropolitan Police
FREE-LANCE WRITER, RIGHT?
Y...
YES ...
WE HAD AN APPOINT-MENT TO MEET WITH HIM TODAY.
HE WANTED TO INTER-VIEW THE CHILDREN ...
BUT WHEN YOU GOT HERE...
...THIS IS WHAT YOU FOUND.
SAY, WHEN DID HE APPROACH YOU ABOUT THE INTERVIEW?
TWO DAYS AGO. HE STOPPED BY THE SCHOOL IN THE EARLY EVENING.
THEN HE WAS ALIVE UNTIL THAT TIME.
MS. KOBAYASHI, YOU SCHEDULED THE INTERVIEW WITH MR. SUGI-MORI, RIGHT?
I DID ...

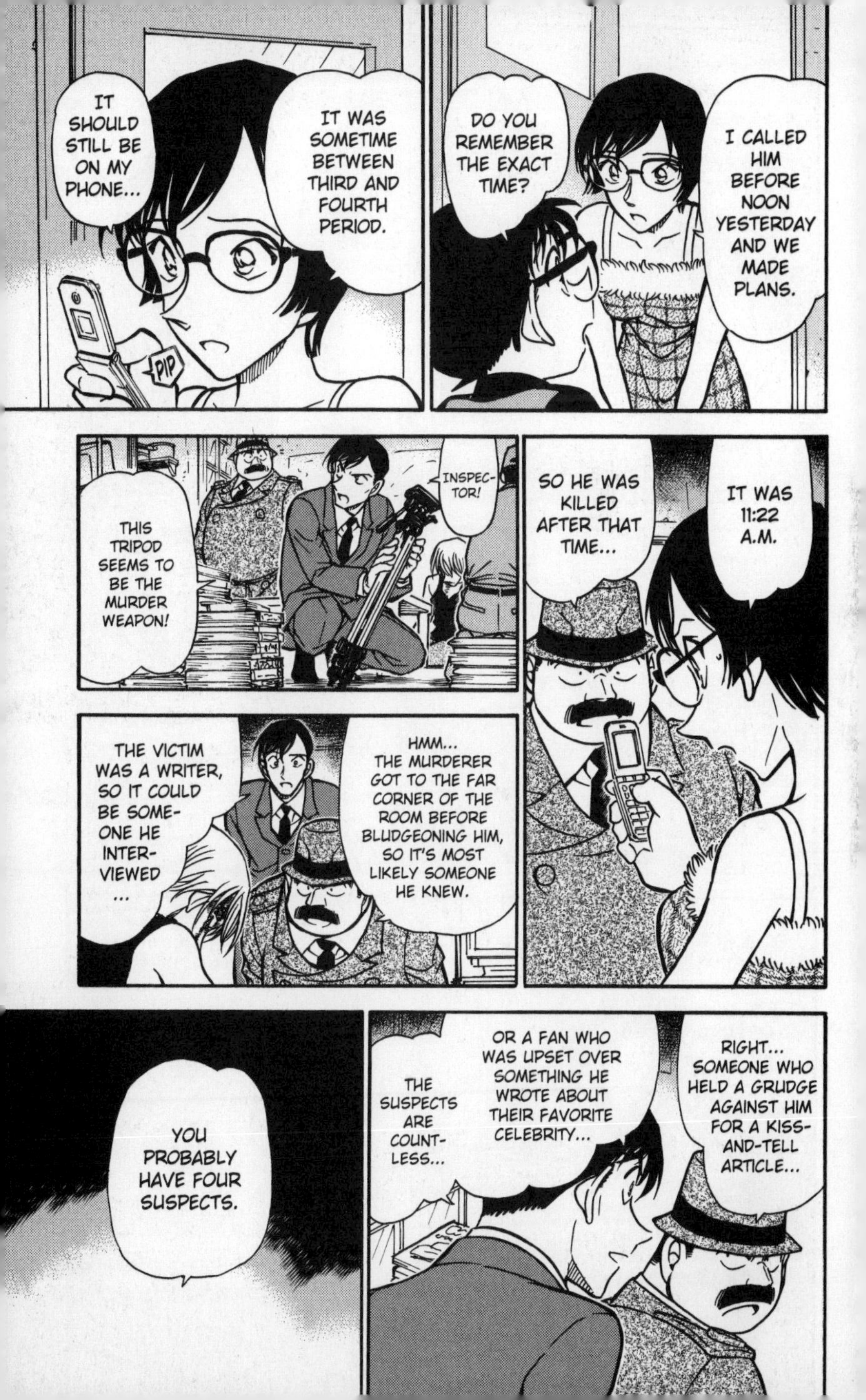
I CALLED HIM BEFORE NOON YESTERDAY AND WE MADE PLANS.
DO YOU REMEMBER THE EXACT TIME?
IT WAS SOMETIME BETWEEN THIRD AND FOURTH PERIOD.
IT SHOULD STILL BE ON MY PHONE...
PIP
IT WAS 11:22 A.M.
SO HE WAS KILLED AFTER THAT TIME...
INSPECTOR!
THIS TRIPOD SEEMS TO BE THE MURDER WEAPON!
HMM... THE MURDERER GOT TO THE FAR CORNER OF THE ROOM BEFORE BLUDGEONING HIM, SO IT'S MOST LIKELY SOMEONE HE KNEW.
THE VICTIM WAS A WRITER, SO IT COULD BE SOME-ONE HE INTER-VIEWED ...
RIGHT... SOMEONE WHO HELD A GRUDGE AGAINST HIM FOR A KISS-AND-TELL ARTICLE...
OR A FAN WHO WAS UPSET OVER SOMETHING HE WROTE ABOUT THEIR FAVORITE CELEBRITY...
THE SUSPECTS ARE COUNT-LESS...
YOU PROBABLY HAVE FOUR SUSPECTS.

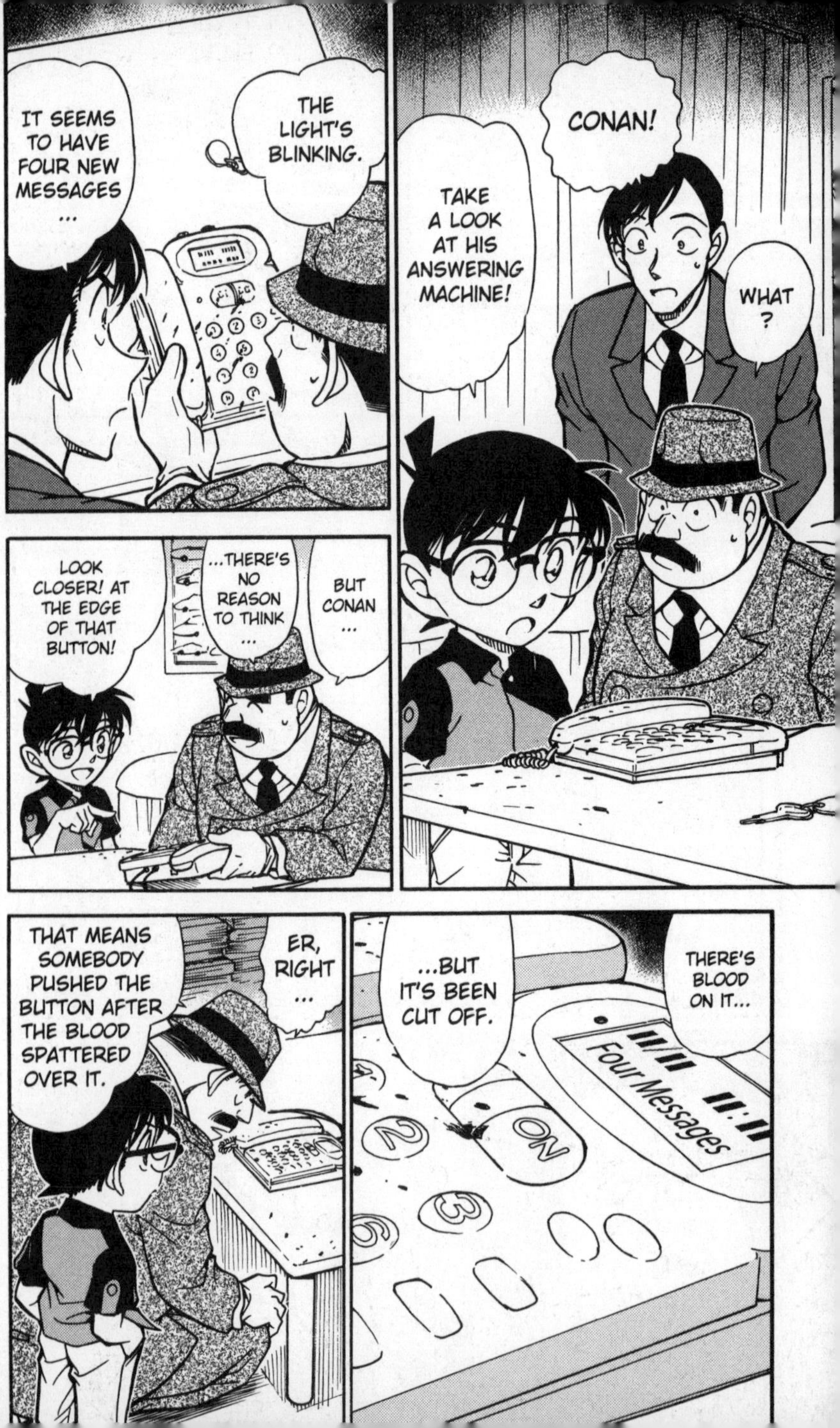
CONAN!
TAKE A LOOK AT HIS ANSWERING MACHINE!
WHAT?
THE LIGHT'S BLINKING.
IT SEEMS TO HAVE FOUR NEW MESSAGES ...
BUT CONAN ...
...THERE'S NO REASON TO THINK ...
LOOK CLOSER! AT THE EDGE OF THAT BUTTON!
THERE'S BLOOD ON IT...
...BUT IT'S BEEN CUT OFF.
Four Messages
ON
ER, RIGHT ...
THAT MEANS SOMEBODY PUSHED THE BUTTON AFTER THE BLOOD SPATTERED OVER IT.

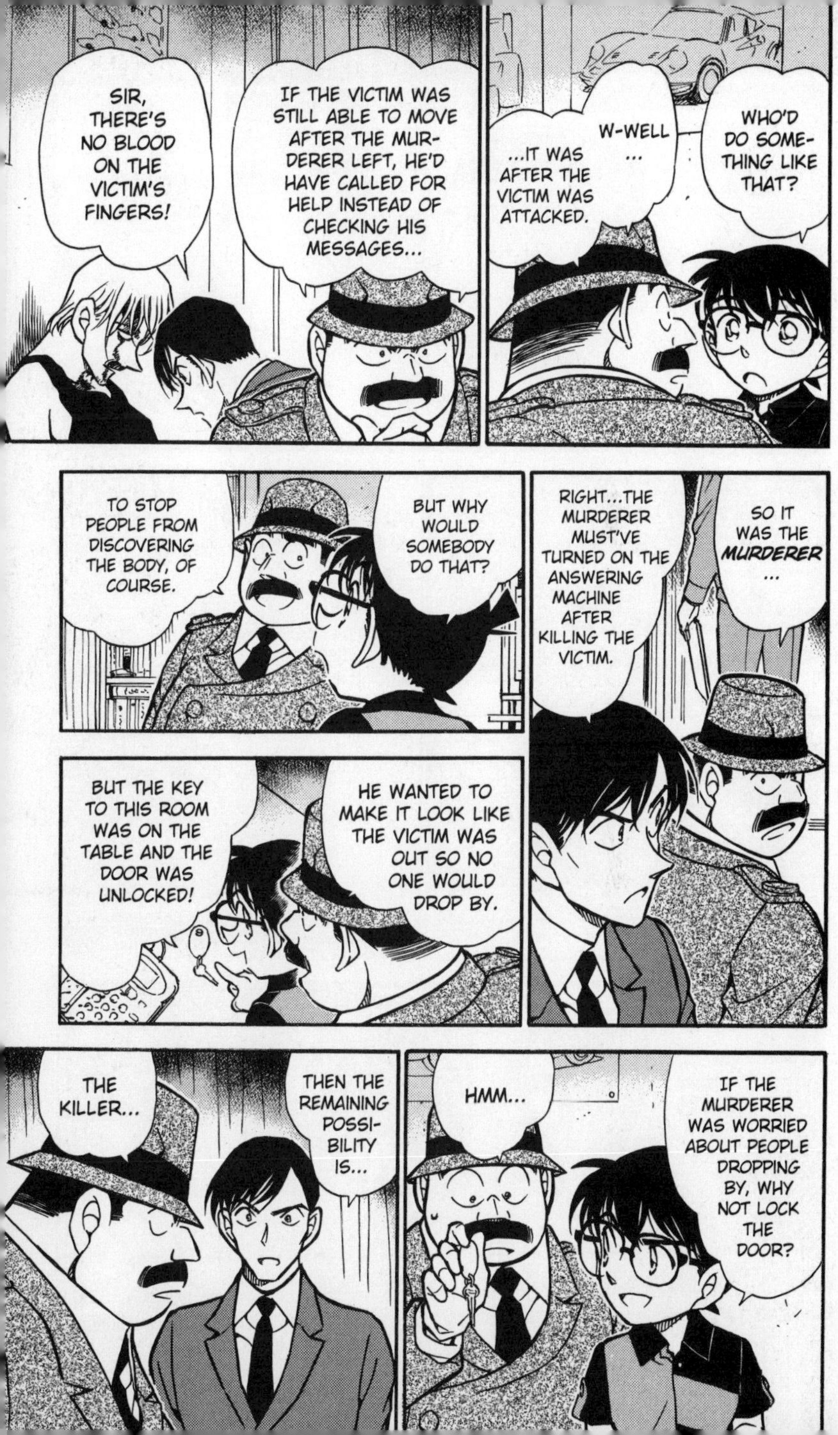
WHO'D DO SOME-THING LIKE THAT?
W-WELL ...
...IT WAS AFTER THE VICTIM WAS ATTACKED.
IF THE VICTIM WAS STILL ABLE TO MOVE AFTER THE MUR-DERER LEFT, HE'D HAVE CALLED FOR HELP INSTEAD OF CHECKING HIS MESSAGES...
SIR, THERE'S NO BLOOD ON THE VICTIM'S FINGERS!
SO IT WAS THE ***MURDERER*** ...
RIGHT...THE MURDERER MUST'VE TURNED ON THE ANSWERING MACHINE AFTER KILLING THE VICTIM.
BUT WHY WOULD SOMEBODY DO THAT?
TO STOP PEOPLE FROM DISCOVERING THE BODY, OF COURSE.
HE WANTED TO MAKE IT LOOK LIKE THE VICTIM WAS OUT SO NO ONE WOULD DROP BY.
BUT THE KEY TO THIS ROOM WAS ON THE TABLE AND THE DOOR WAS UNLOCKED!
IF THE MURDERER WAS WORRIED ABOUT PEOPLE DROPPING BY, WHY NOT LOCK THE DOOR?
HMM...
THEN THE REMAINING POSSI-BILITY IS...
THE KILLER...

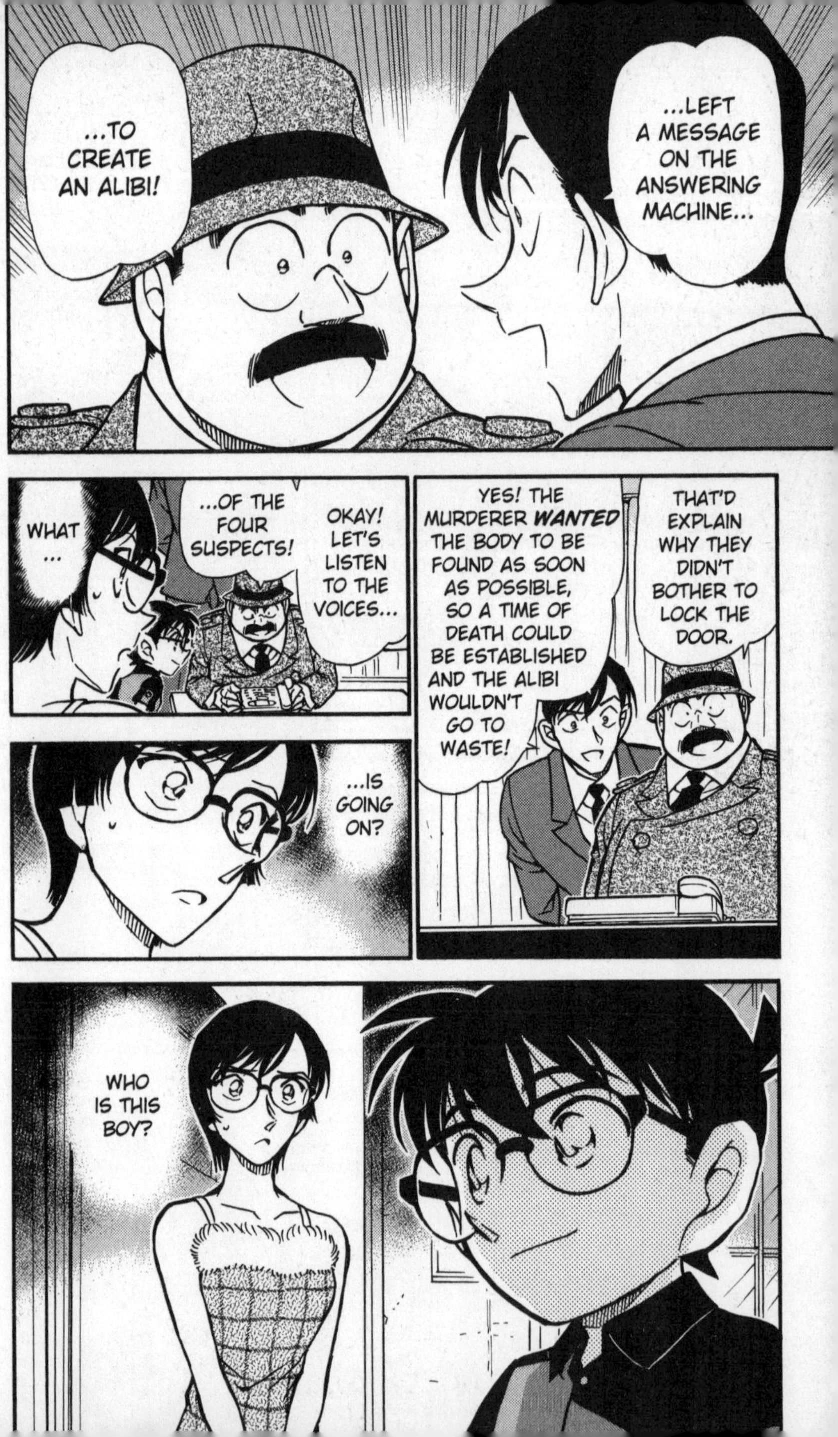
...LEFT A MESSAGE ON THE ANSWERING MACHINE...
...TO CREATE AN ALIBI!
THAT'D EXPLAIN WHY THEY DIDN'T BOTHER TO LOCK THE DOOR.
YES! THE MURDERER ***WANTED*** THE BODY TO BE FOUND AS SOON AS POSSIBLE, SO A TIME OF DEATH COULD BE ESTABLISHED AND THE ALIBI WOULDN'T GO TO WASTE!
OKAY! LET'S LISTEN TO THE VOICES...
...OF THE FOUR SUSPECTS!
WHAT ...
...IS GOING ON?
WHO IS THIS BOY?

FILE 6:
A MESSAGE FROM A MURDERER

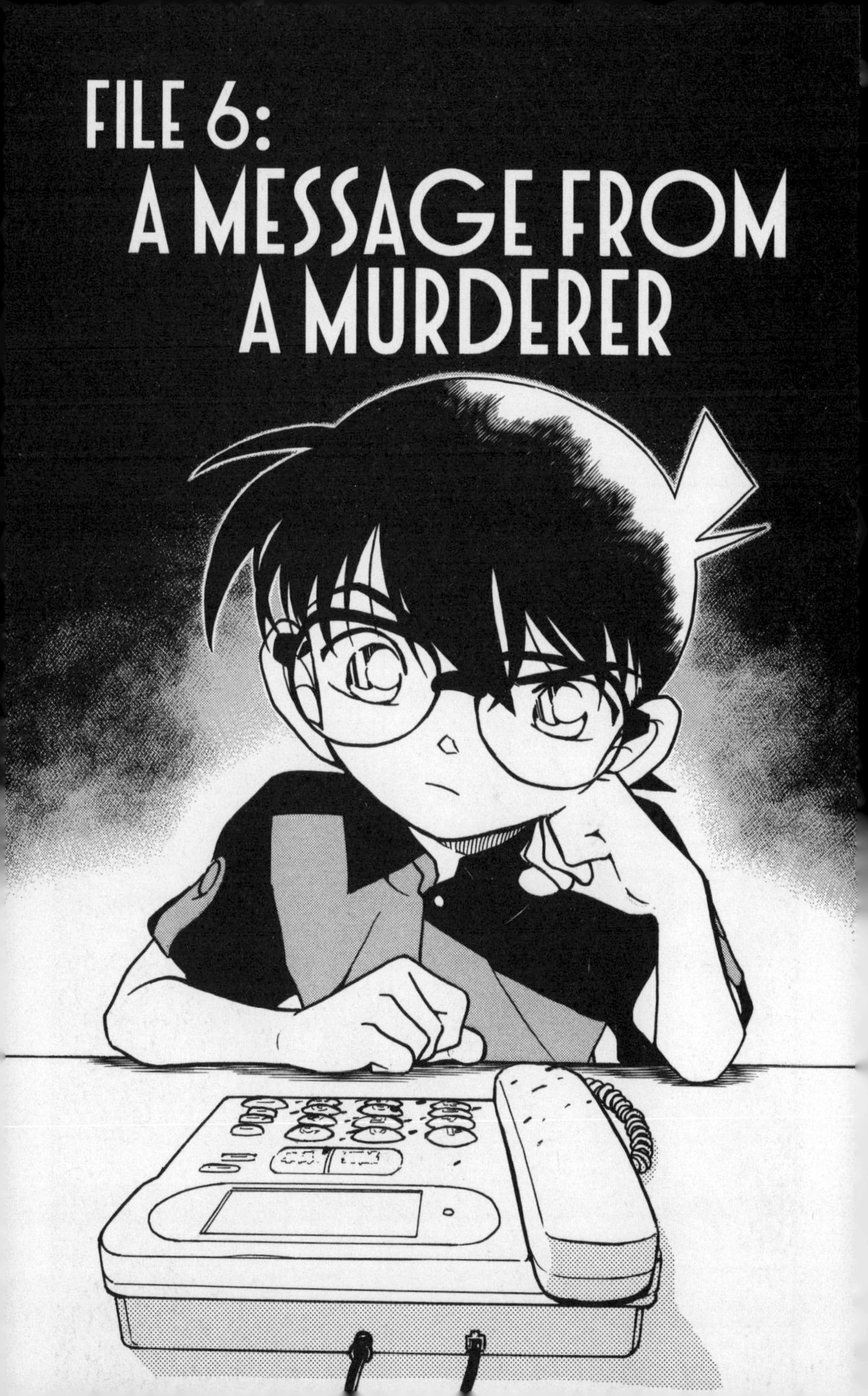

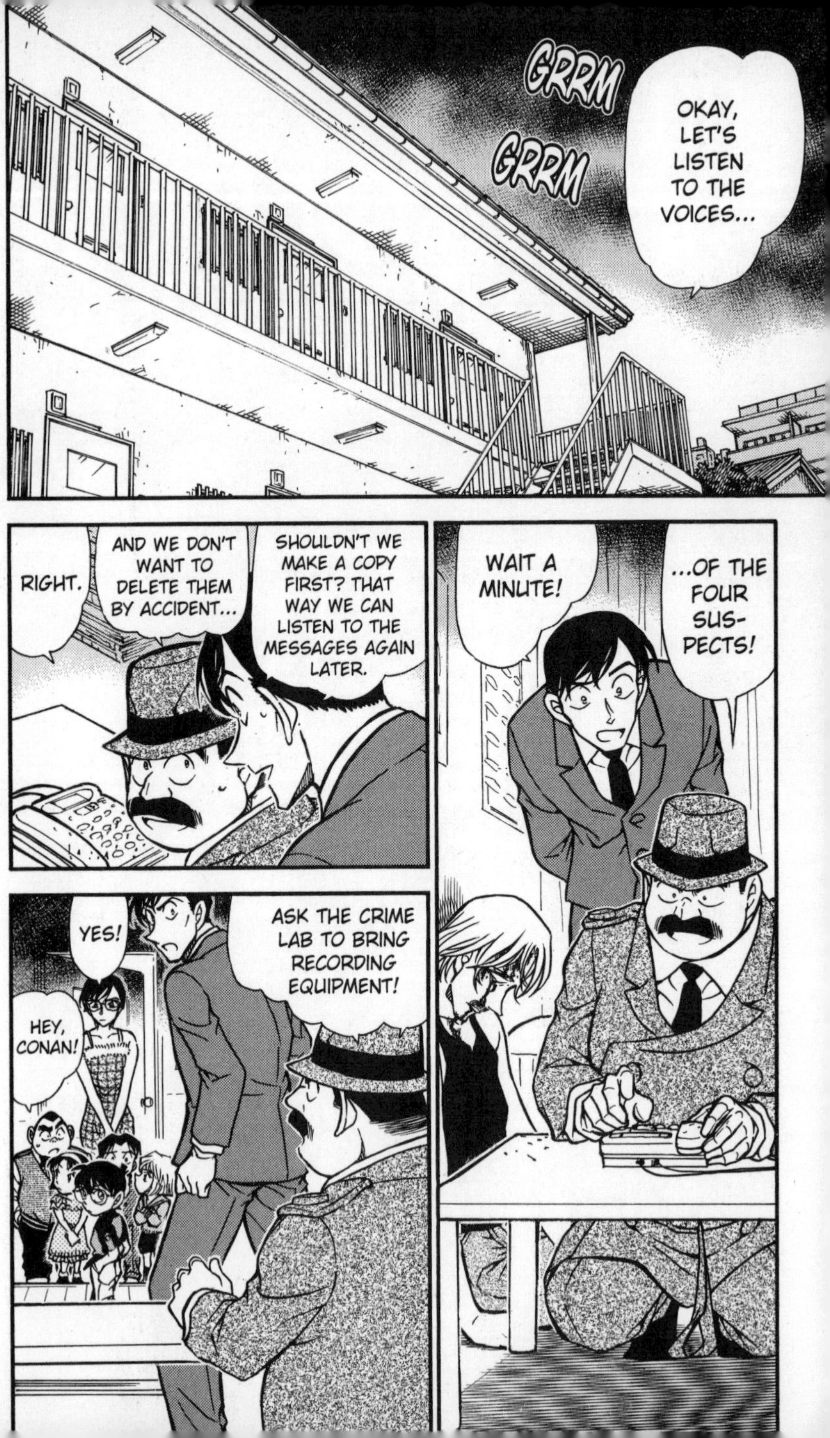
GRRM
GRRM
OKAY, LET'S LISTEN TO THE VOICES...
...OF THE FOUR SUS-PECTS!
WAIT A MINUTE!
SHOULDN'T WE MAKE A COPY FIRST? THAT WAY WE CAN LISTEN TO THE MESSAGES AGAIN LATER.
AND WE DON'T WANT TO DELETE THEM BY ACCIDENT...
RIGHT.
ASK THE CRIME LAB TO BRING RECORDING EQUIPMENT!
YES!
HEY, CONAN!

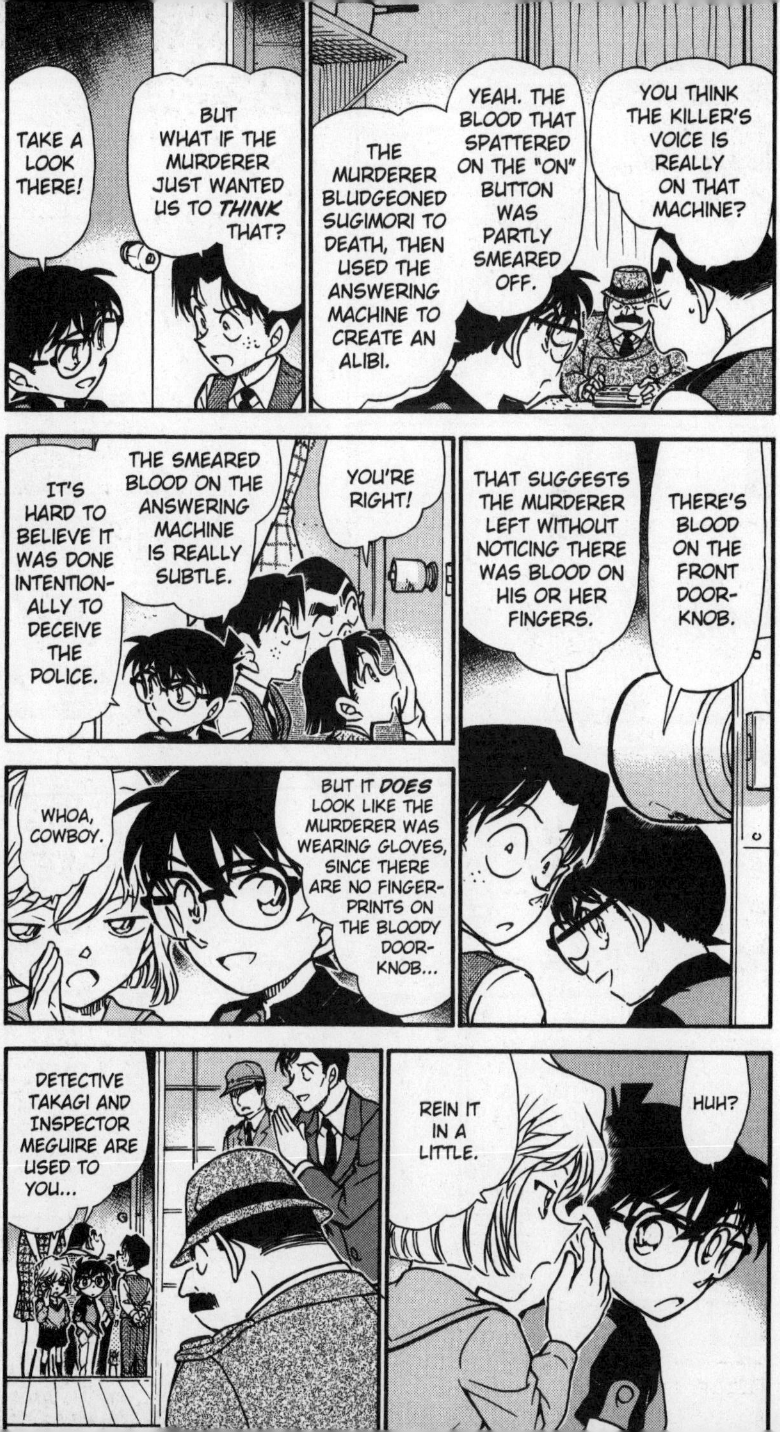
YOU THINK THE KILLER'S VOICE IS REALLY ON THAT MACHINE?
YEAH. THE BLOOD THAT SPATTERED ON THE "ON" BUTTON WAS PARTLY SMEARED OFF.
THE MURDERER BLUDGEONED SUGIMORI TO DEATH, THEN USED THE ANSWERING MACHINE TO CREATE AN ALIBI.
BUT WHAT IF THE MURDERER JUST WANTED US TO *THINK* THAT?
TAKE A LOOK THERE!
THERE'S BLOOD ON THE FRONT DOOR-KNOB.
THAT SUGGESTS THE MURDERER LEFT WITHOUT NOTICING THERE WAS BLOOD ON HIS OR HER FINGERS.
YOU'RE RIGHT!
THE SMEARED BLOOD ON THE ANSWERING MACHINE IS REALLY SUBTLE.
IT'S HARD TO BELIEVE IT WAS DONE INTENTION-ALLY TO DECEIVE THE POLICE.
BUT IT ***DOES*** LOOK LIKE THE MURDERER WAS WEARING GLOVES, SINCE THERE ARE NO FINGER-PRINTS ON THE BLOODY DOOR-KNOB...
WHOA, COWBOY.
HUH?
REIN IT IN A LITTLE.
DETECTIVE TAKAGI AND INSPECTOR MEGUIRE ARE USED TO YOU...

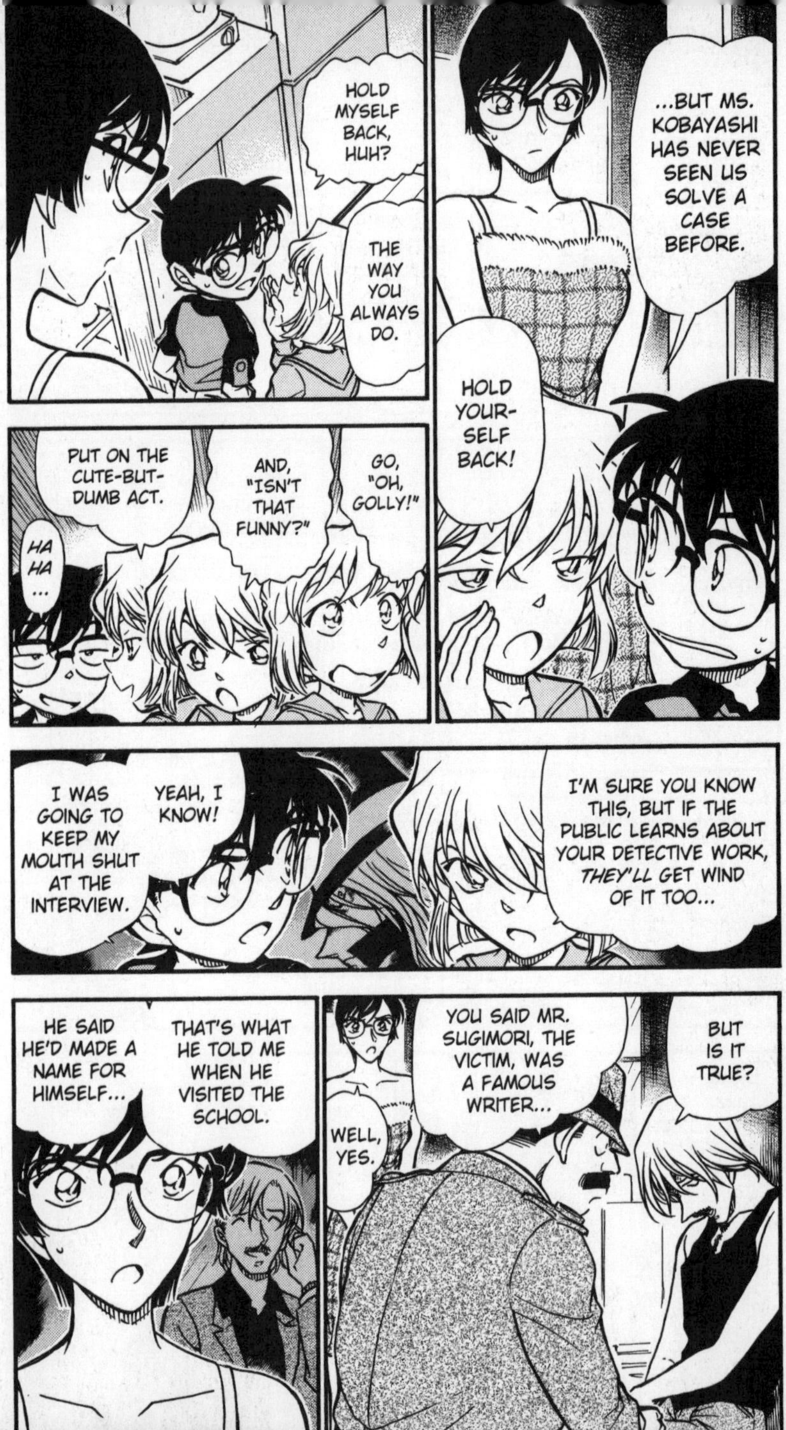
...BUT MS. KOBAYASHI HAS NEVER SEEN US SOLVE A CASE BEFORE.
HOLD YOURSELF BACK!
HOLD MYSELF BACK, HUH?
THE WAY YOU ALWAYS DO.
GO, "OH, GOLLY!"
AND, "ISN'T THAT FUNNY?"
PUT ON THE CUTE-BUT-DUMB ACT.
HA HA ...
I'M SURE YOU KNOW THIS, BUT IF THE PUBLIC LEARNS ABOUT YOUR DETECTIVE WORK, *THEY'LL* GET WIND OF IT TOO...
YEAH, I KNOW!
I WAS GOING TO KEEP MY MOUTH SHUT AT THE INTERVIEW.
BUT IS IT TRUE?
YOU SAID MR. SUGIMORI, THE VICTIM, WAS A FAMOUS WRITER...
WELL, YES.
THAT'S WHAT HE TOLD ME WHEN HE VISITED THE SCHOOL.
HE SAID HE'D MADE A NAME FOR HIMSELF...

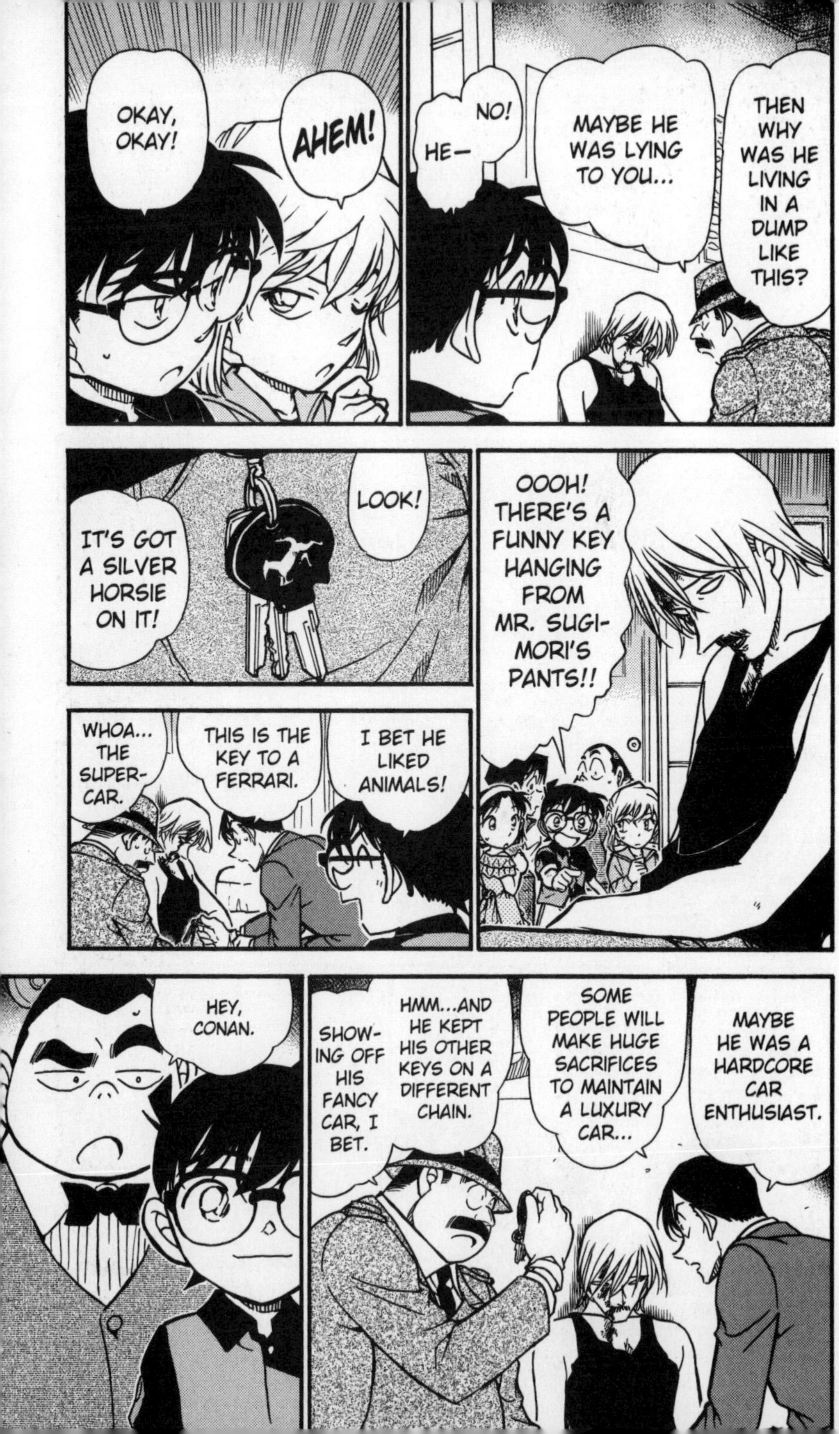
THEN WHY WAS HE LIVING IN A DUMP LIKE THIS?
MAYBE HE WAS LYING TO YOU...
NO!
HE—
AHEM!
OKAY, OKAY!
OOOH! THERE'S A FUNNY KEY HANGING FROM MR. SUGI-MORI'S PANTS!!
LOOK!
IT'S GOT A SILVER HORSIE ON IT!
I BET HE LIKED ANIMALS!
THIS IS THE KEY TO A FERRARI.
WHOA... THE SUPER-CAR.
MAYBE HE WAS A HARDCORE CAR ENTHUSIAST.
SOME PEOPLE WILL MAKE HUGE SACRIFICES TO MAINTAIN A LUXURY CAR...
HMM...AND HE KEPT HIS OTHER KEYS ON A DIFFERENT CHAIN.
SHOW-ING OFF HIS FANCY CAR, I BET.
HEY, CONAN.

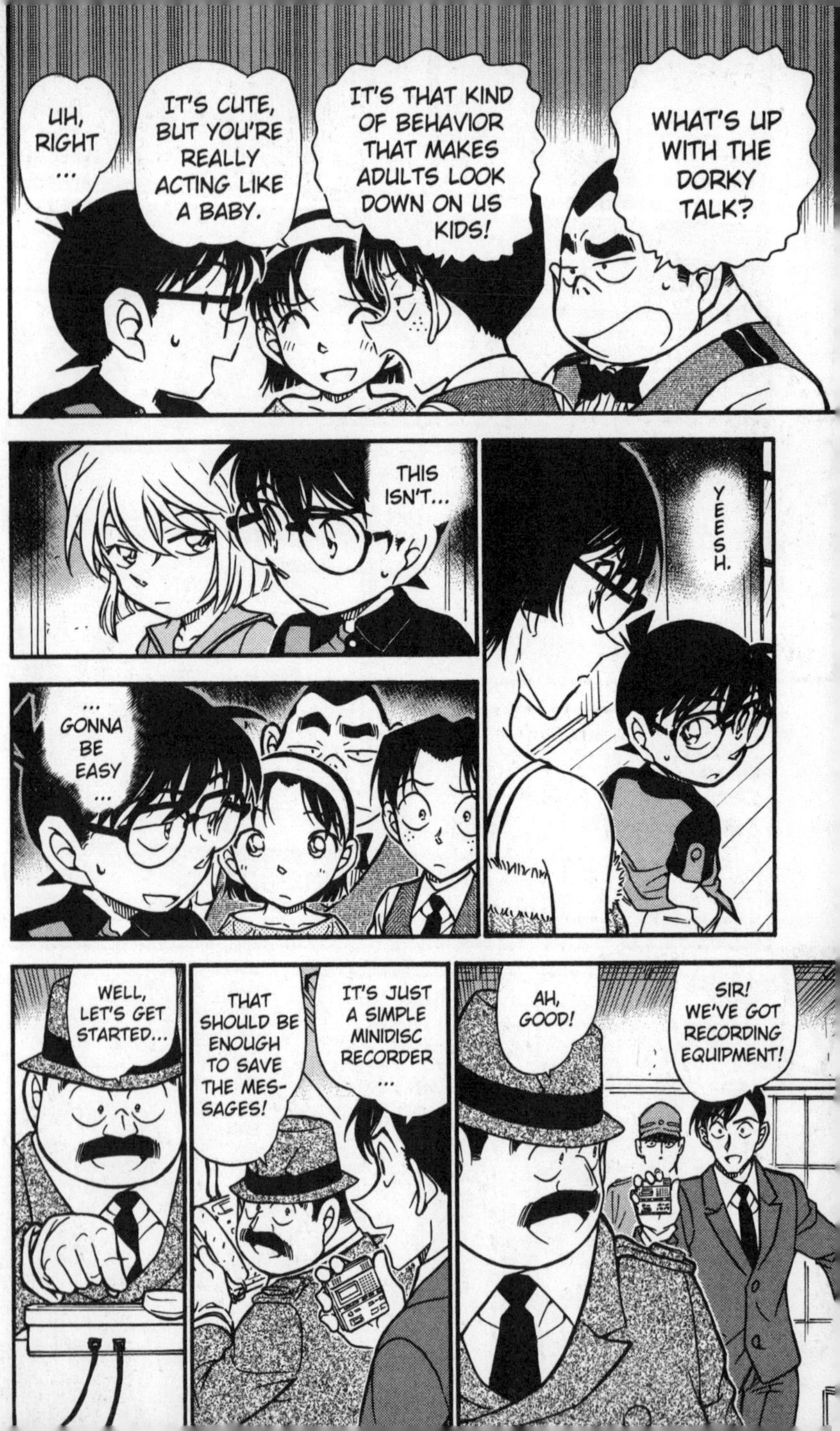
WHAT'S UP WITH THE DORKY TALK?
IT'S THAT KIND OF BEHAVIOR THAT MAKES ADULTS LOOK DOWN ON US KIDS!
IT'S CUTE, BUT YOU'RE REALLY ACTING LIKE A BABY.
UH, RIGHT ...
YEESH.
THIS ISN'T...
... GONNA BE EASY ...
SIR! WE'VE GOT RECORDING EQUIPMENT!
AH, GOOD!
IT'S JUST A SIMPLE MINIDISC RECORDER ...
THAT SHOULD BE ENOUGH TO SAVE THE MES-SAGES!
WELL, LET'S GET STARTED...

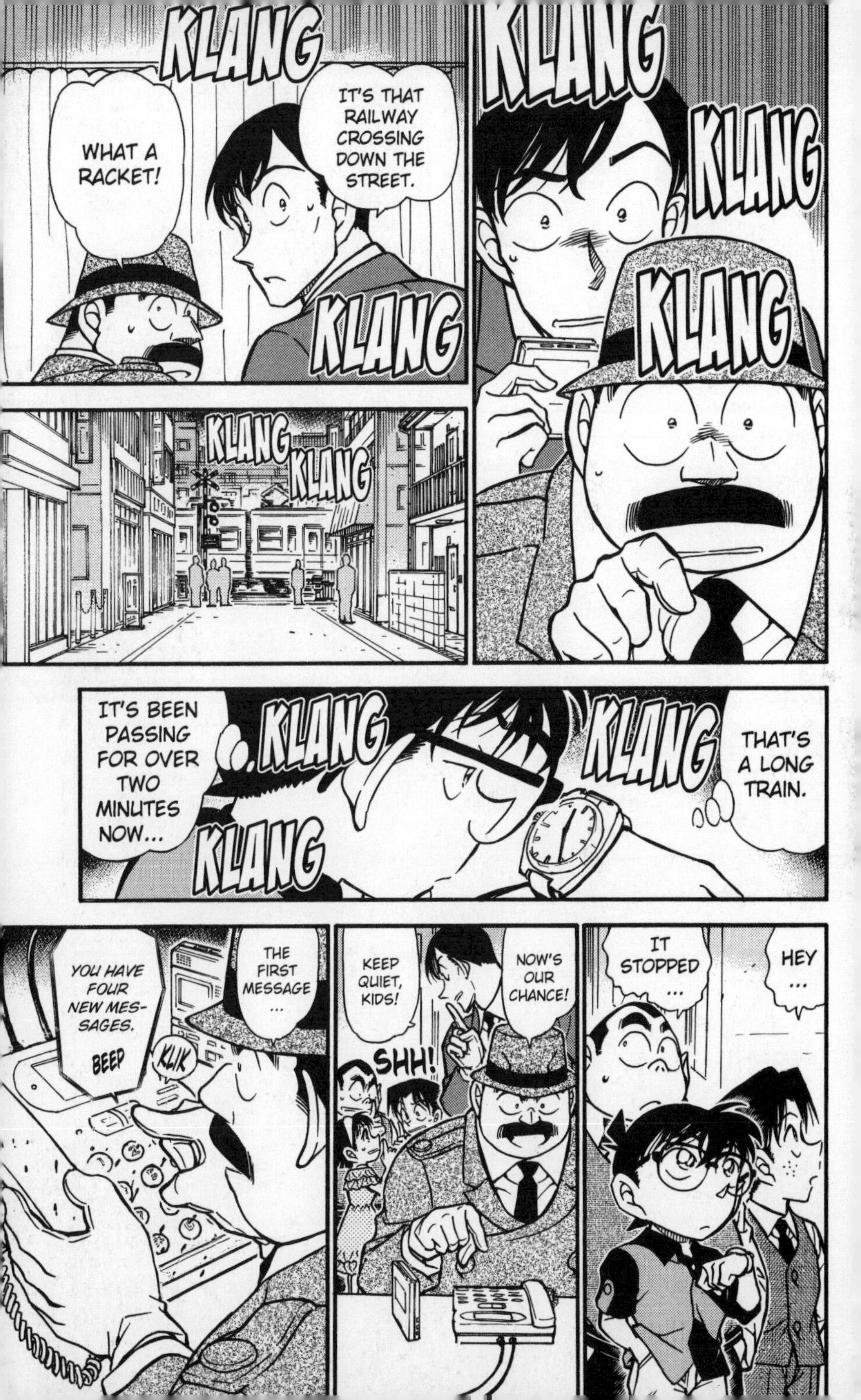
KLANG
KLANG
KLANG
KLANG
IT'S THAT RAILWAY CROSSING DOWN THE STREET.
WHAT A RACKET!
KLANG
KLANG KLANG
THAT'S A LONG TRAIN.
KLANG
KLANG
IT'S BEEN PASSING FOR OVER TWO MINUTES NOW...
KLANG
HEY...
IT STOPPED...
NOW'S OUR CHANCE!
KEEP QUIET, KIDS!
SHH!
THE FIRST MESSAGE...
YOU HAVE FOUR NEW MES-SAGES.
KLIK
BEEP

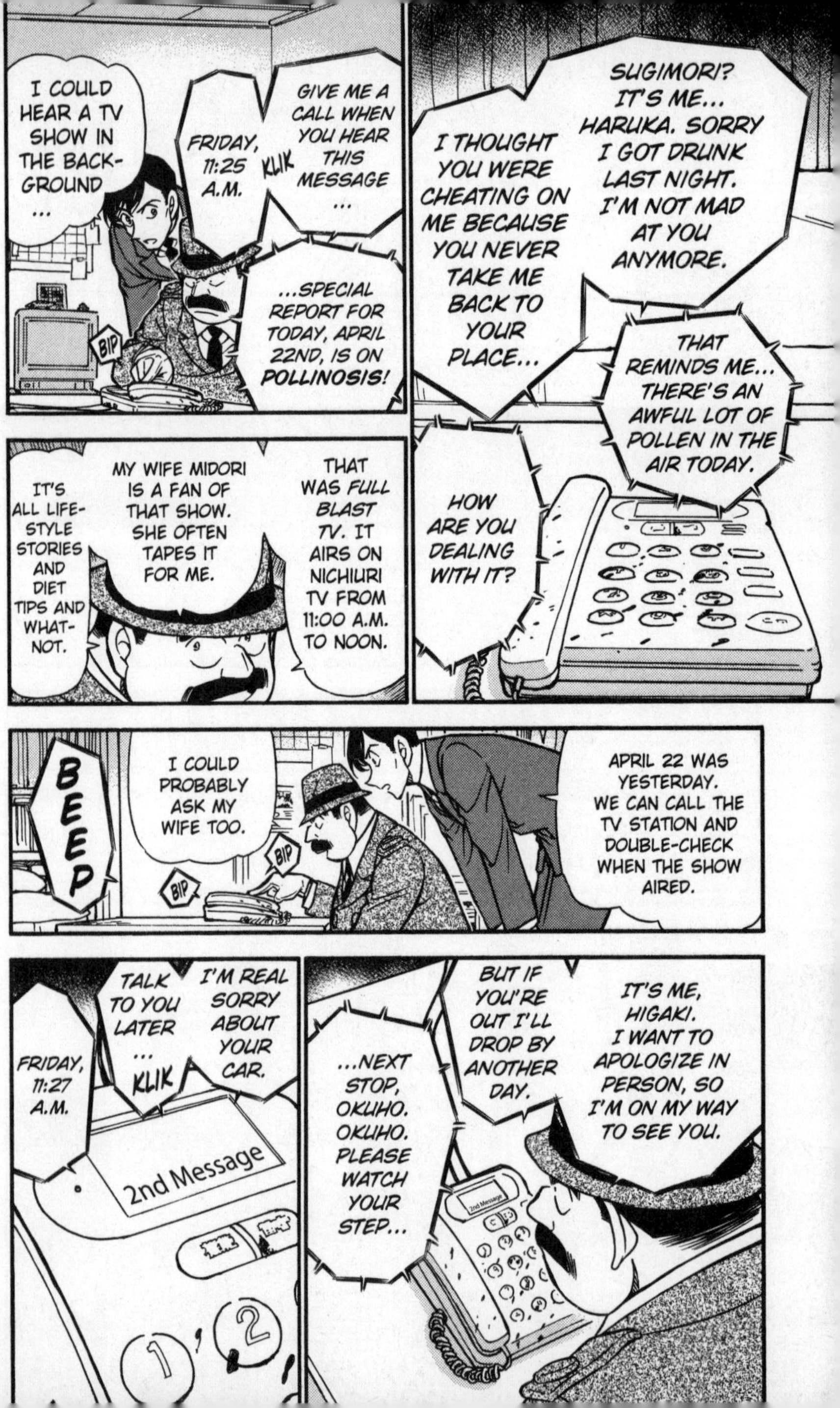
SUGIMORI? IT'S ME... HARUKA. SORRY I GOT DRUNK LAST NIGHT. I'M NOT MAD AT YOU ANYMORE.
I THOUGHT YOU WERE CHEATING ON ME BECAUSE YOU NEVER TAKE ME BACK TO YOUR PLACE...
THAT REMINDS ME... THERE'S AN AWFUL LOT OF POLLEN IN THE AIR TODAY.
HOW ARE YOU DEALING WITH IT?
GIVE ME A CALL WHEN YOU HEAR THIS MESSAGE ...
KLIK
FRIDAY, 11:25 A.M.
...SPECIAL REPORT FOR TODAY, APRIL 22ND, IS ON POLLINOSIS!
I COULD HEAR A TV SHOW IN THE BACKGROUND ...
BIP
THAT WAS FULL BLAST TV. IT AIRS ON NICHIURI TV FROM 11:00 A.M. TO NOON.
MY WIFE MIDORI IS A FAN OF THAT SHOW. SHE OFTEN TAPES IT FOR ME.
IT'S ALL LIFESTYLE STORIES AND DIET TIPS AND WHATNOT.
APRIL 22 WAS YESTERDAY. WE CAN CALL THE TV STATION AND DOUBLE-CHECK WHEN THE SHOW AIRED.
BIP
BIP
I COULD PROBABLY ASK MY WIFE TOO.
BEEP
IT'S ME, HIGAKI. I WANT TO APOLOGIZE IN PERSON, SO I'M ON MY WAY TO SEE YOU.
BUT IF YOU'RE OUT I'LL DROP BY ANOTHER DAY.
...NEXT STOP, OKUHO. OKUHO. PLEASE WATCH YOUR STEP...
2nd Message
I'M REAL SORRY ABOUT YOUR CAR.
TALK TO YOU LATER ...
KLIK
FRIDAY, 11:27 A.M.
2nd Message
1
2

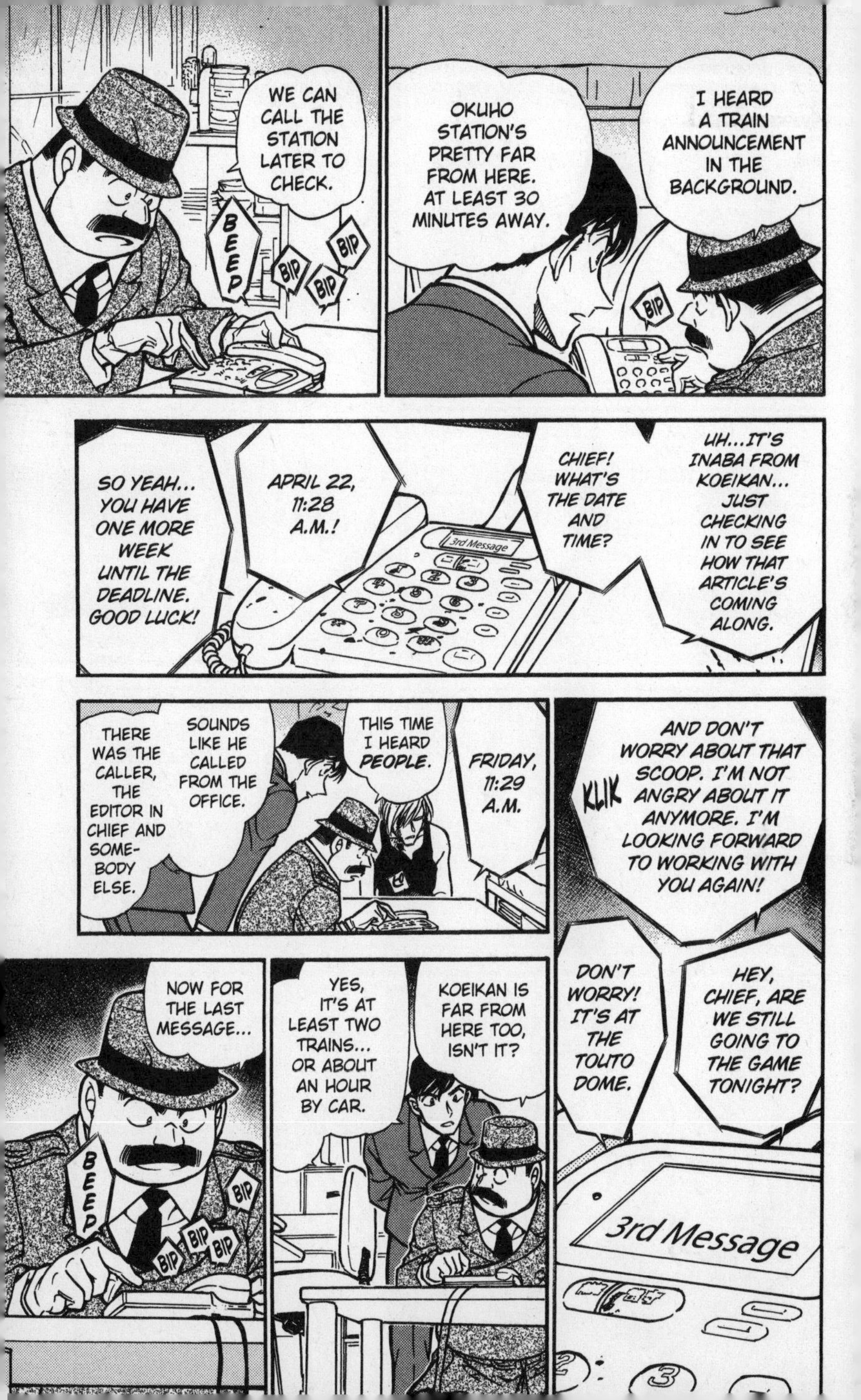
I HEARD A TRAIN ANNOUNCEMENT IN THE BACKGROUND.
OKUHO STATION'S PRETTY FAR FROM HERE. AT LEAST 30 MINUTES AWAY.
BIP
WE CAN CALL THE STATION LATER TO CHECK.
BEEP
BIP
BIP
BIP
UH...IT'S INABA FROM KOEIKAN... JUST CHECKING IN TO SEE HOW THAT ARTICLE'S COMING ALONG.
CHIEF! WHAT'S THE DATE AND TIME?
3rd Message
APRIL 22, 11:28 A.M.!
SO YEAH... YOU HAVE ONE MORE WEEK UNTIL THE DEADLINE. GOOD LUCK!
AND DON'T WORRY ABOUT THAT SCOOP. I'M NOT ANGRY ABOUT IT ANYMORE. I'M LOOKING FORWARD TO WORKING WITH YOU AGAIN!
KLIK
HEY, CHIEF, ARE WE STILL GOING TO THE GAME TONIGHT?
DON'T WORRY! IT'S AT THE TOUTO DOME.
3rd Message
FRIDAY, 11:29 A.M.
THIS TIME I HEARD PEOPLE.
SOUNDS LIKE HE CALLED FROM THE OFFICE.
THERE WAS THE CALLER, THE EDITOR IN CHIEF AND SOMEBODY ELSE.
KOEIKAN IS FAR FROM HERE TOO, ISN'T IT?
YES, IT'S AT LEAST TWO TRAINS... OR ABOUT AN HOUR BY CAR.
NOW FOR THE LAST MESSAGE...
BEEP
BIP
BIP
BIP
BIP

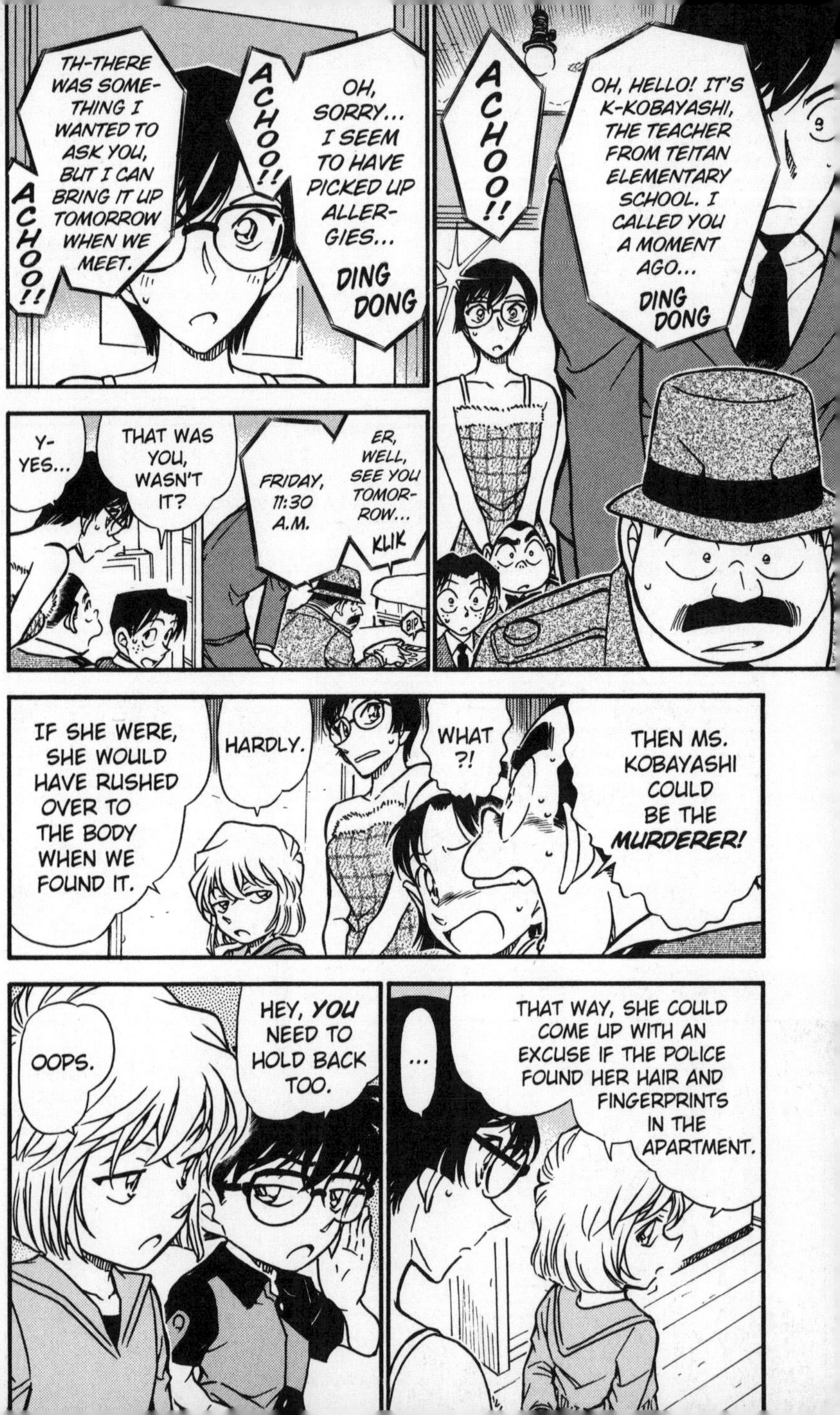
OH, HELLO! IT'S K-KOBAYASHI, THE TEACHER FROM TEITAN ELEMENTARY SCHOOL. I CALLED YOU A MOMENT AGO...
DING DONG
ACHOO!!
OH, SORRY... I SEEM TO HAVE PICKED UP ALLERGIES...
DING DONG
ACHOO!!
TH-THERE WAS SOMETHING I WANTED TO ASK YOU, BUT I CAN BRING IT UP TOMORROW WHEN WE MEET.
ACHOO!!
ER, WELL, SEE YOU TOMORROW...
KLIK
BIP
FRIDAY, 11:30 A.M.
THAT WAS YOU, WASN'T IT?
Y-YES...
THEN MS. KOBAYASHI COULD BE THE *MURDERER!*
WHAT?!
HARDLY.
IF SHE WERE, SHE WOULD HAVE RUSHED OVER TO THE BODY WHEN WE FOUND IT.
THAT WAY, SHE COULD COME UP WITH AN EXCUSE IF THE POLICE FOUND HER HAIR AND FINGERPRINTS IN THE APARTMENT.
...
HEY, *YOU* NEED TO HOLD BACK TOO.
OOPS.

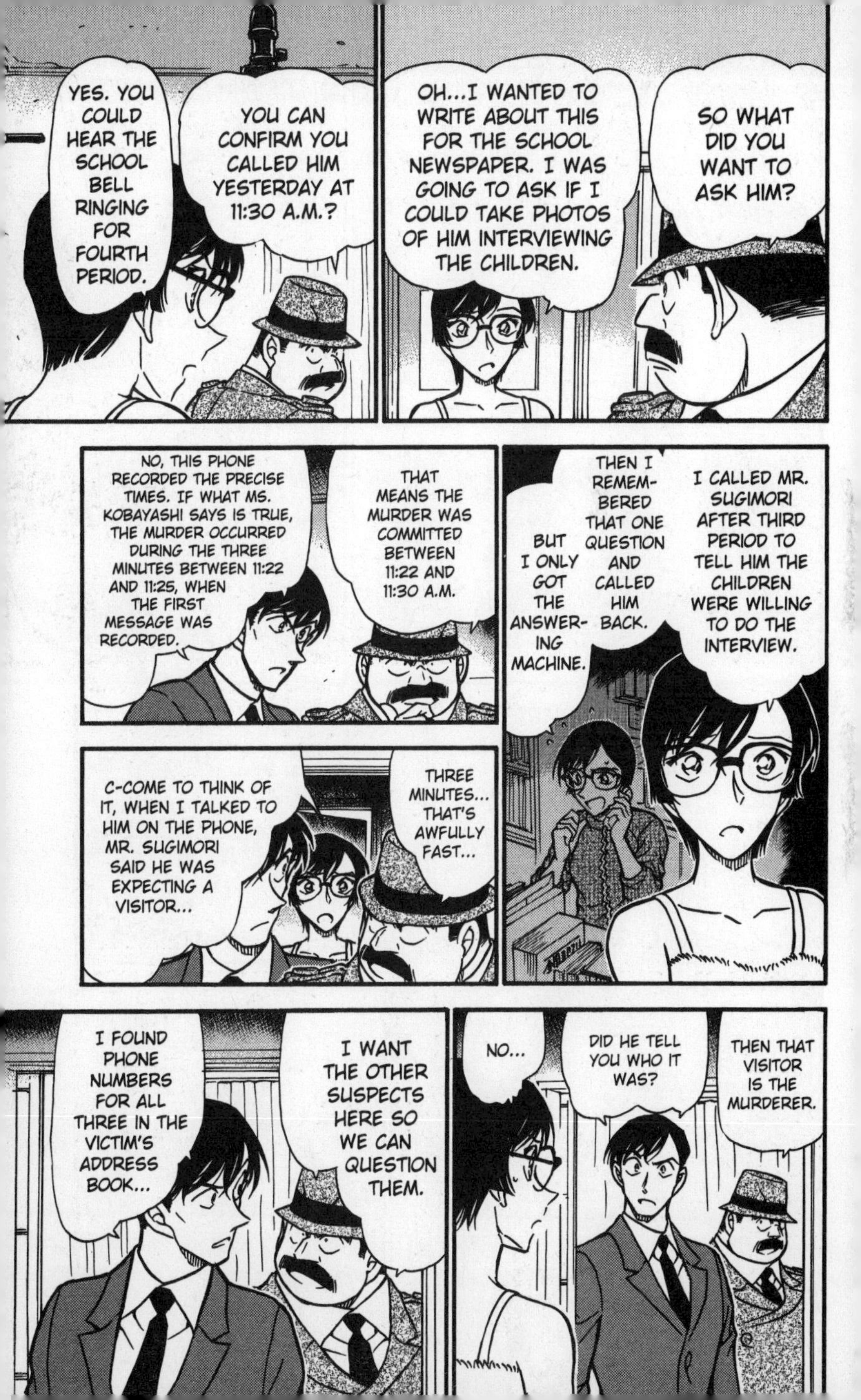
SO WHAT DID YOU WANT TO ASK HIM?
OH...I WANTED TO WRITE ABOUT THIS FOR THE SCHOOL NEWSPAPER. I WAS GOING TO ASK IF I COULD TAKE PHOTOS OF HIM INTERVIEWING THE CHILDREN.
YOU CAN CONFIRM YOU CALLED HIM YESTERDAY AT 11:30 A.M.?
YES. YOU COULD HEAR THE SCHOOL BELL RINGING FOR FOURTH PERIOD.
I CALLED MR. SUGIMORI AFTER THIRD PERIOD TO TELL HIM THE CHILDREN WERE WILLING TO DO THE INTERVIEW.
THEN I REMEMBERED THAT ONE QUESTION AND CALLED HIM BACK.
BUT I ONLY GOT THE ANSWERING MACHINE.
THAT MEANS THE MURDER WAS COMMITTED BETWEEN 11:22 AND 11:30 A.M.
NO, THIS PHONE RECORDED THE PRECISE TIMES. IF WHAT MS. KOBAYASHI SAYS IS TRUE, THE MURDER OCCURRED DURING THE THREE MINUTES BETWEEN 11:22 AND 11:25, WHEN THE FIRST MESSAGE WAS RECORDED.
THREE MINUTES... THAT'S AWFULLY FAST...
C-COME TO THINK OF IT, WHEN I TALKED TO HIM ON THE PHONE, MR. SUGIMORI SAID HE WAS EXPECTING A VISITOR...
THEN THAT VISITOR IS THE MURDERER.
DID HE TELL YOU WHO IT WAS?
NO...
I WANT THE OTHER SUSPECTS HERE SO WE CAN QUESTION THEM.
I FOUND PHONE NUMBERS FOR ALL THREE IN THE VICTIM'S ADDRESS BOOK...

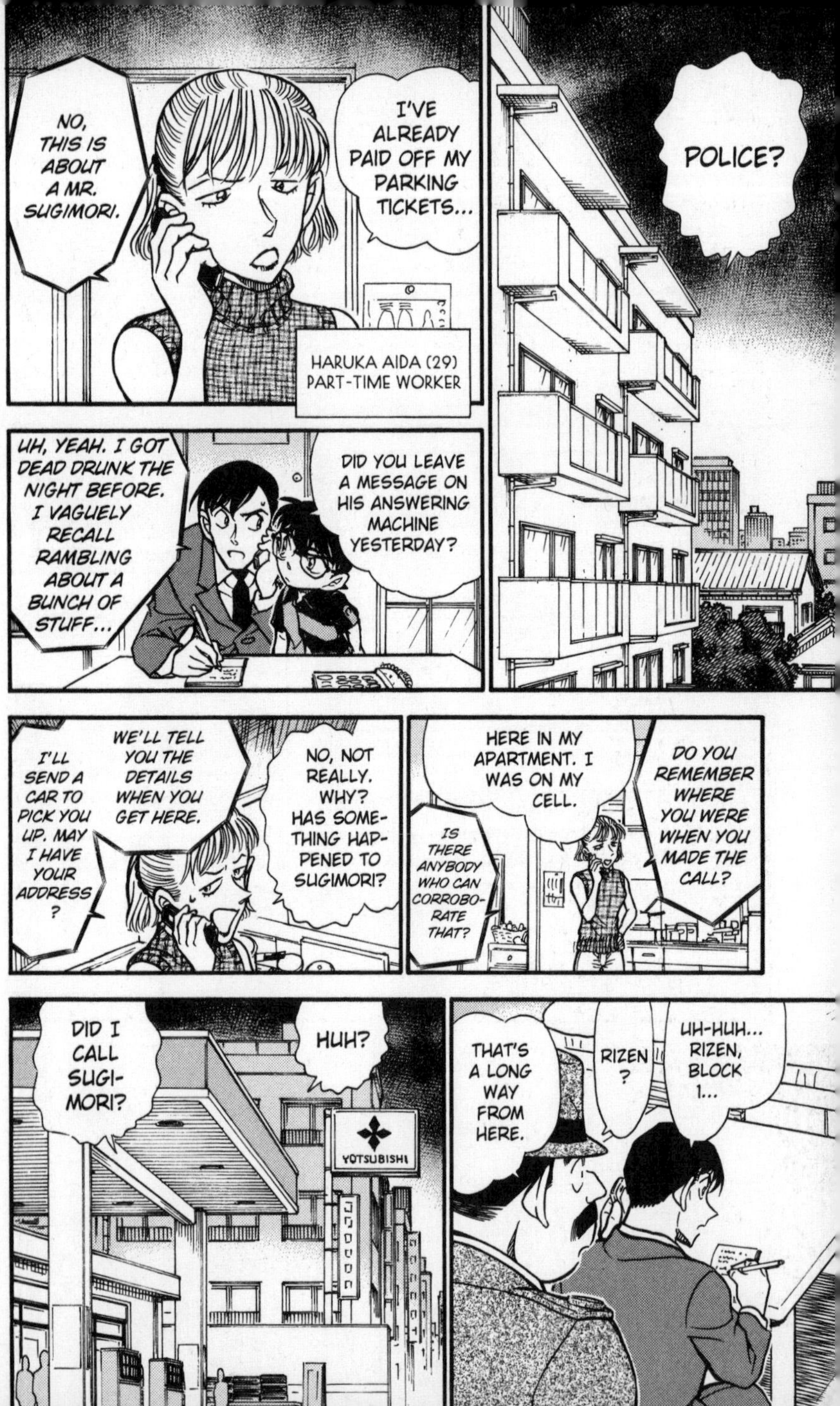

POLICE?
I'VE ALREADY PAID OFF MY PARKING TICKETS...
NO, THIS IS ABOUT A MR. SUGIMORI.
HARUKA AIDA (29) PART-TIME WORKER
DID YOU LEAVE A MESSAGE ON HIS ANSWERING MACHINE YESTERDAY?
UH, YEAH. I GOT DEAD DRUNK THE NIGHT BEFORE. I VAGUELY RECALL RAMBLING ABOUT A BUNCH OF STUFF...
DO YOU REMEMBER WHERE YOU WERE WHEN YOU MADE THE CALL?
HERE IN MY APARTMENT. I WAS ON MY CELL.
IS THERE ANYBODY WHO CAN CORROBORATE THAT?
NO, NOT REALLY. WHY? HAS SOMETHING HAPPENED TO SUGIMORI?
WE'LL TELL YOU THE DETAILS WHEN YOU GET HERE.
I'LL SEND A CAR TO PICK YOU UP. MAY I HAVE YOUR ADDRESS?
UH-HUH... RIZEN, BLOCK 1...
RIZEN?
THAT'S A LONG WAY FROM HERE.
HUH?
DID I CALL SUGIMORI?
YOTSUBISHI

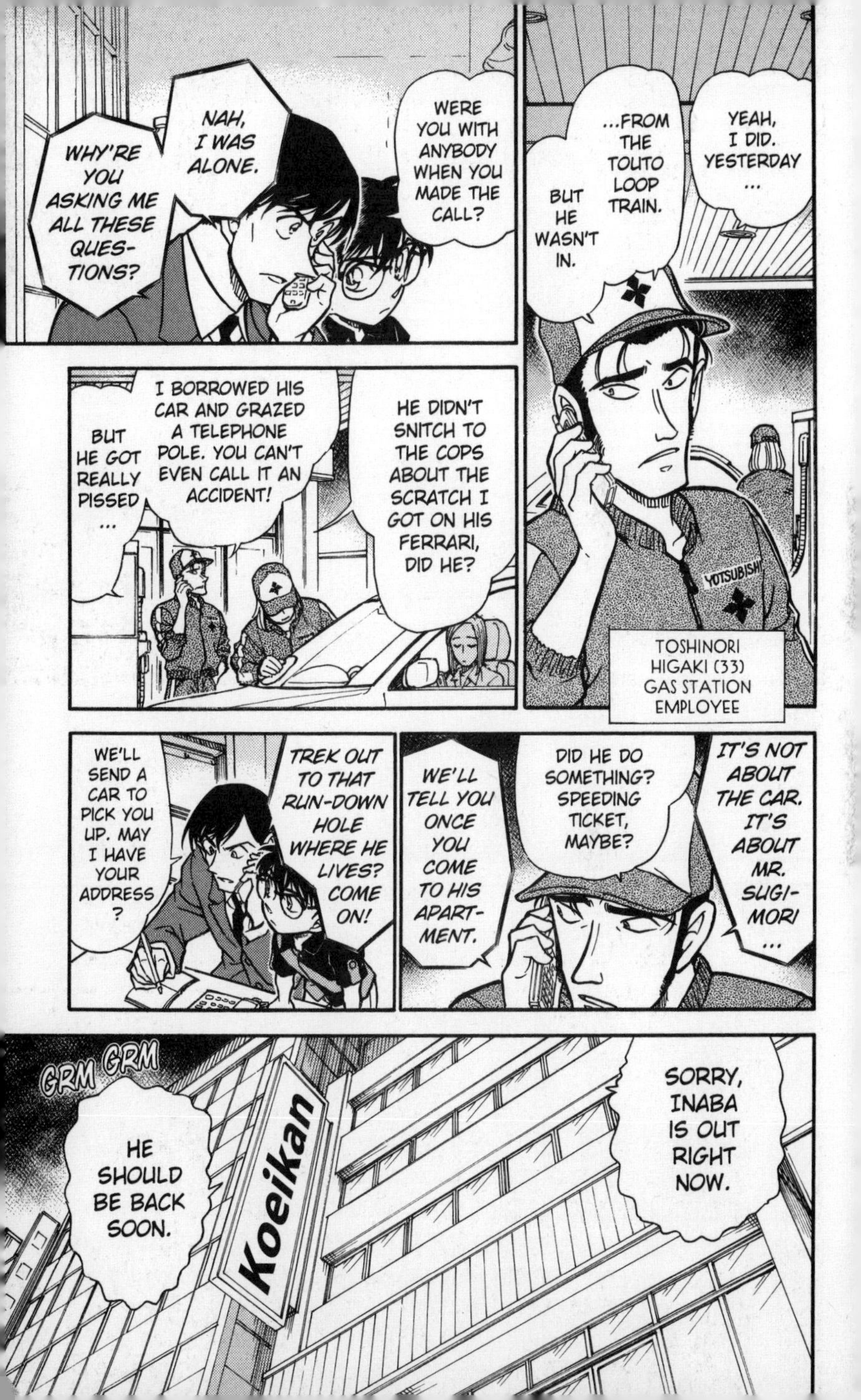
YEAH, I DID. YESTERDAY ...
...FROM THE TOUTO LOOP TRAIN.
BUT HE WASN'T IN.
YOTSUBISHI
TOSHINORI HIGAKI (33) GAS STATION EMPLOYEE
WERE YOU WITH ANYBODY WHEN YOU MADE THE CALL?
NAH, I WAS ALONE.
WHY'RE YOU ASKING ME ALL THESE QUES-TIONS?
HE DIDN'T SNITCH TO THE COPS ABOUT THE SCRATCH I GOT ON HIS FERRARI, DID HE?
I BORROWED HIS CAR AND GRAZED A TELEPHONE POLE. YOU CAN'T EVEN CALL IT AN ACCIDENT!
BUT HE GOT REALLY PISSED ...
IT'S NOT ABOUT THE CAR. IT'S ABOUT MR. SUGI-MORI ...
DID HE DO SOMETHING? SPEEDING TICKET, MAYBE?
WE'LL TELL YOU ONCE YOU COME TO HIS APART-MENT.
TREK OUT TO THAT RUN-DOWN HOLE WHERE HE LIVES? COME ON!
WE'LL SEND A CAR TO PICK YOU UP. MAY I HAVE YOUR ADDRESS ?
SORRY, INABA IS OUT RIGHT NOW.
GRM GRM
HE SHOULD BE BACK SOON.
Koeikan

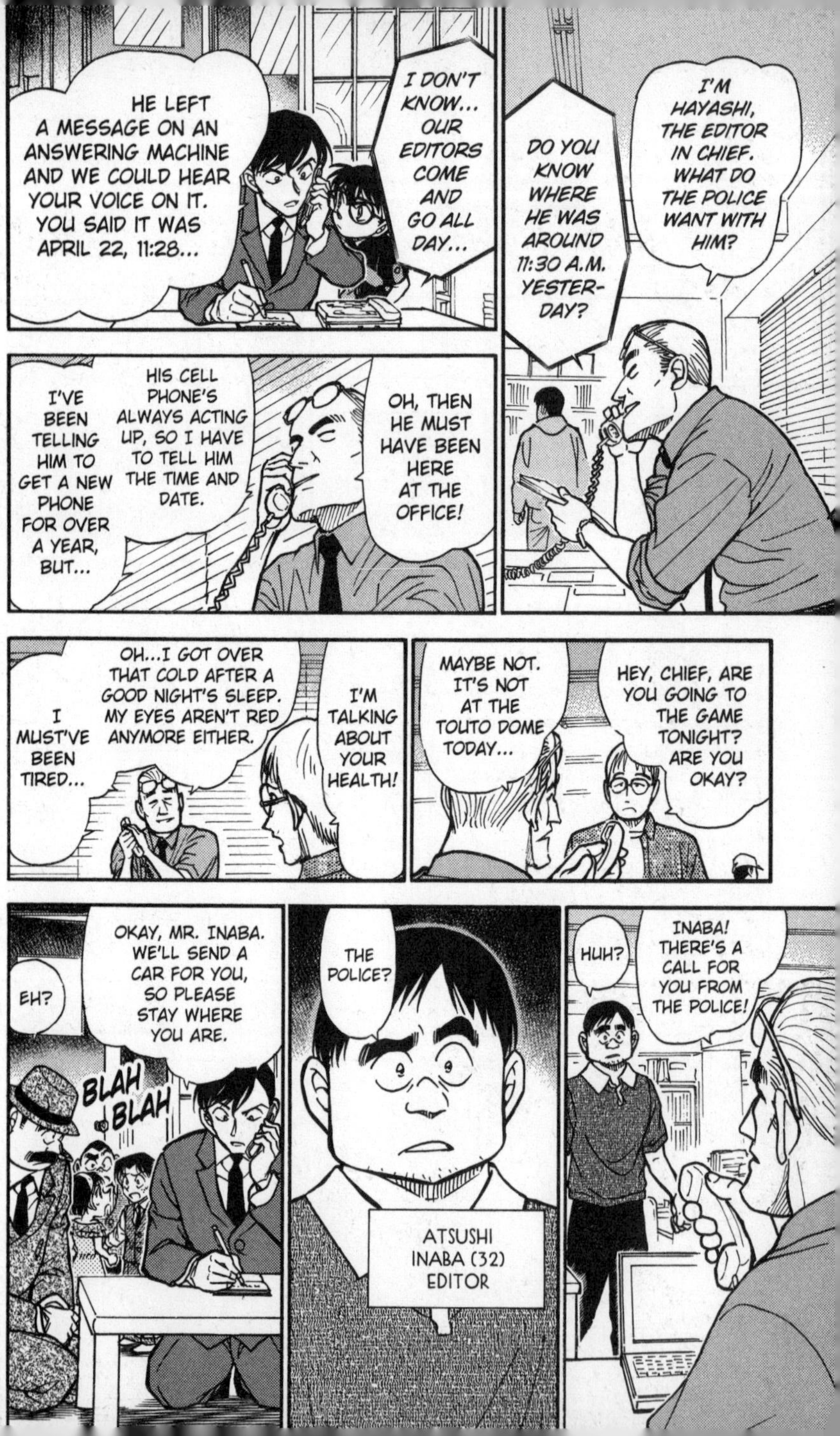
I'M HAYASHI, THE EDITOR IN CHIEF. WHAT DO THE POLICE WANT WITH HIM?
DO YOU KNOW WHERE HE WAS AROUND 11:30 A.M. YESTERDAY?
I DON'T KNOW... OUR EDITORS COME AND GO ALL DAY...
HE LEFT A MESSAGE ON AN ANSWERING MACHINE AND WE COULD HEAR YOUR VOICE ON IT. YOU SAID IT WAS APRIL 22, 11:28...
OH, THEN HE MUST HAVE BEEN HERE AT THE OFFICE!
HIS CELL PHONE'S ALWAYS ACTING UP, SO I HAVE TO TELL HIM THE TIME AND DATE.
I'VE BEEN TELLING HIM TO GET A NEW PHONE FOR OVER A YEAR, BUT...
HEY, CHIEF, ARE YOU GOING TO THE GAME TONIGHT? ARE YOU OKAY?
MAYBE NOT. IT'S NOT AT THE TOUTO DOME TODAY...
I'M TALKING ABOUT YOUR HEALTH!
OH...I GOT OVER THAT COLD AFTER A GOOD NIGHT'S SLEEP. MY EYES AREN'T RED ANYMORE EITHER.
I MUST'VE BEEN TIRED...
INABA! THERE'S A CALL FOR YOU FROM THE POLICE!
HUH?
THE POLICE?
ATSUSHI INABA (32) EDITOR
OKAY, MR. INABA. WE'LL SEND A CAR FOR YOU, SO PLEASE STAY WHERE YOU ARE.
EH?
BLAH BLAH

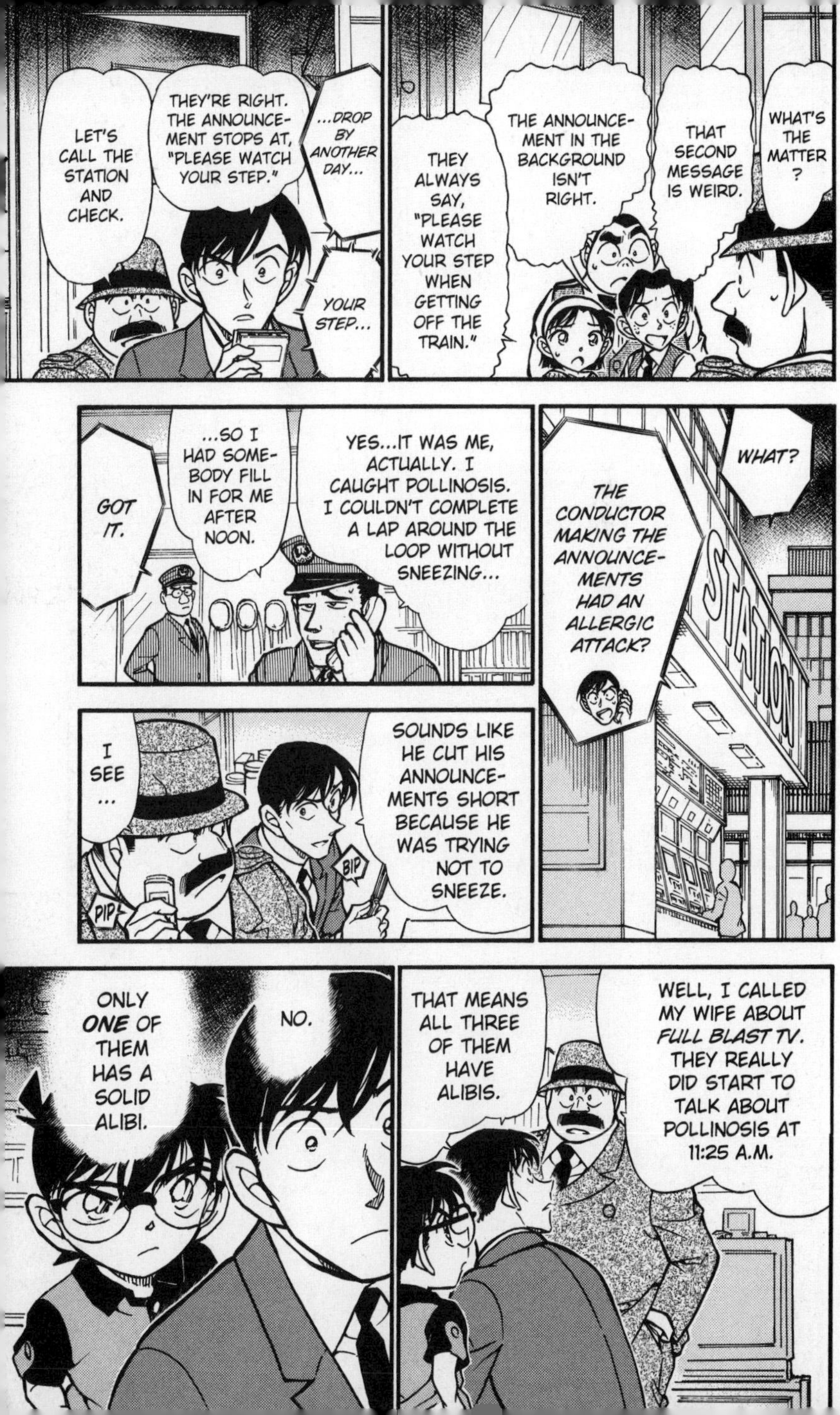
WHAT'S THE MATTER?
THAT SECOND MESSAGE IS WEIRD.
THE ANNOUNCEMENT IN THE BACKGROUND ISN'T RIGHT.
THEY ALWAYS SAY, "PLEASE WATCH YOUR STEP WHEN GETTING OFF THE TRAIN."
...DROP BY ANOTHER DAY...
YOUR STEP...
THEY'RE RIGHT. THE ANNOUNCEMENT STOPS AT, "PLEASE WATCH YOUR STEP."
LET'S CALL THE STATION AND CHECK.
WHAT?
THE CONDUCTOR MAKING THE ANNOUNCEMENTS HAD AN ALLERGIC ATTACK?
STATION
YES...IT WAS ME, ACTUALLY. I CAUGHT POLLINOSIS. I COULDN'T COMPLETE A LAP AROUND THE LOOP WITHOUT SNEEZING...
...SO I HAD SOMEBODY FILL IN FOR ME AFTER NOON.
GOT IT.
SOUNDS LIKE HE CUT HIS ANNOUNCEMENTS SHORT BECAUSE HE WAS TRYING NOT TO SNEEZE.
BIP
I SEE...
PIP
WELL, I CALLED MY WIFE ABOUT *FULL BLAST TV*. THEY REALLY DID START TO TALK ABOUT POLLINOSIS AT 11:25 A.M.
THAT MEANS ALL THREE OF THEM HAVE ALIBIS.
NO.
ONLY *ONE* OF THEM HAS A SOLID ALIBI.

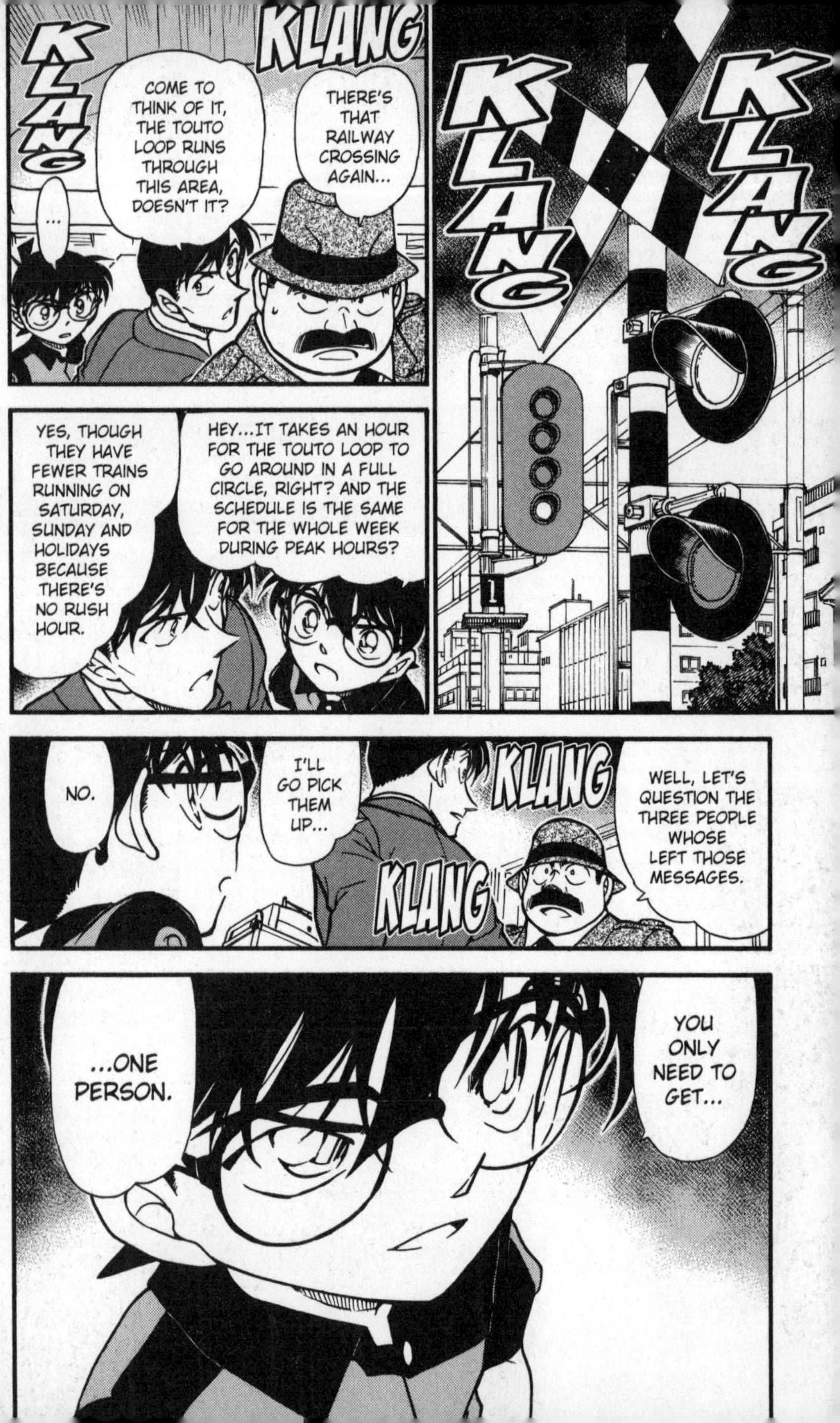
KLANG
KLANG
KLANG
THERE'S THAT RAILWAY CROSSING AGAIN...
COME TO THINK OF IT, THE TOUTO LOOP RUNS THROUGH THIS AREA, DOESN'T IT?
KLANG
...
HEY...IT TAKES AN HOUR FOR THE TOUTO LOOP TO GO AROUND IN A FULL CIRCLE, RIGHT? AND THE SCHEDULE IS THE SAME FOR THE WHOLE WEEK DURING PEAK HOURS?
YES, THOUGH THEY HAVE FEWER TRAINS RUNNING ON SATURDAY, SUNDAY AND HOLIDAYS BECAUSE THERE'S NO RUSH HOUR.
WELL, LET'S QUESTION THE THREE PEOPLE WHOSE LEFT THOSE MESSAGES.
KLANG
KLANG
I'LL GO PICK THEM UP...
NO.
YOU ONLY NEED TO GET...
...ONE PERSON.

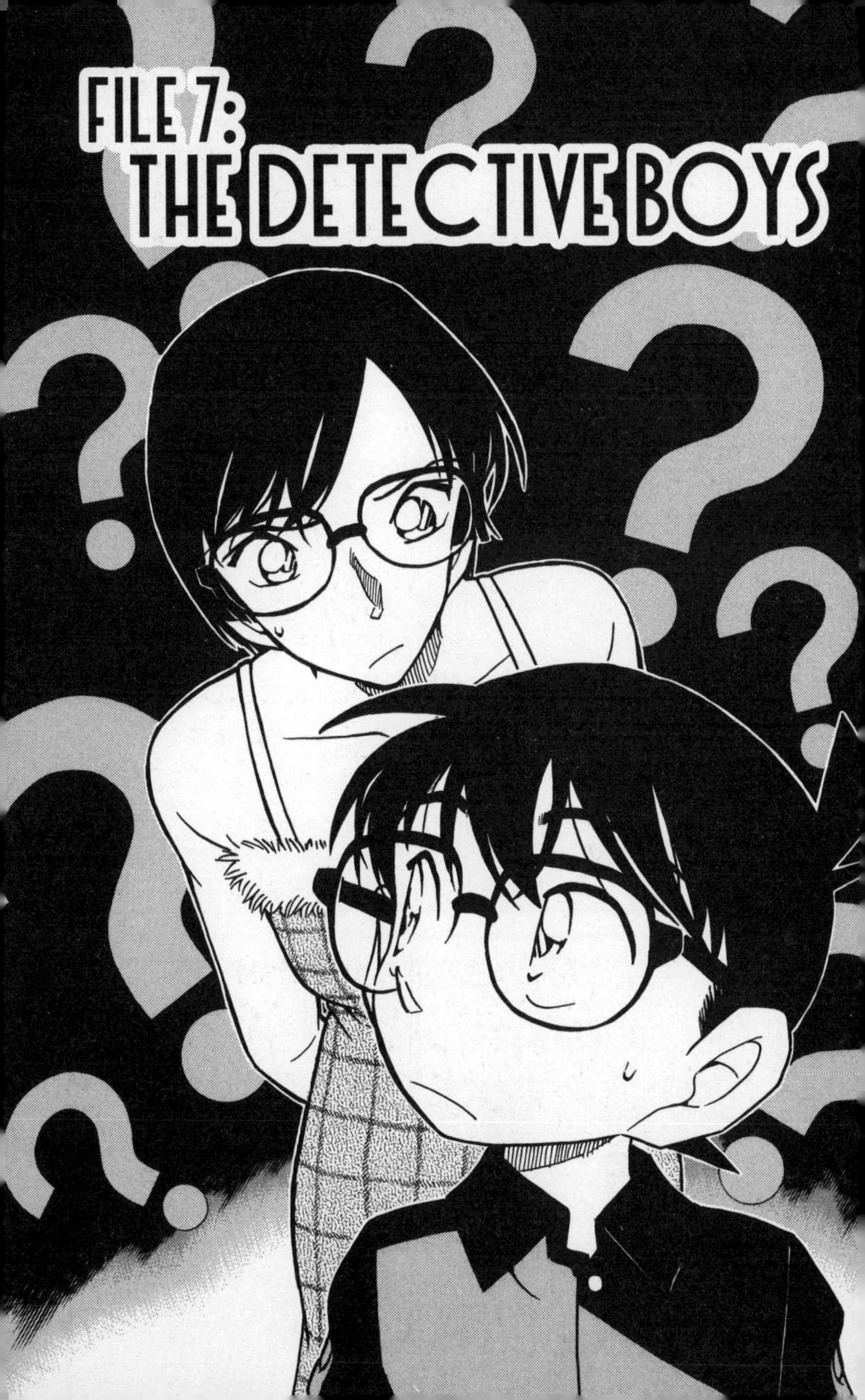
FILE 7:
THE DETECTIVE BOYS

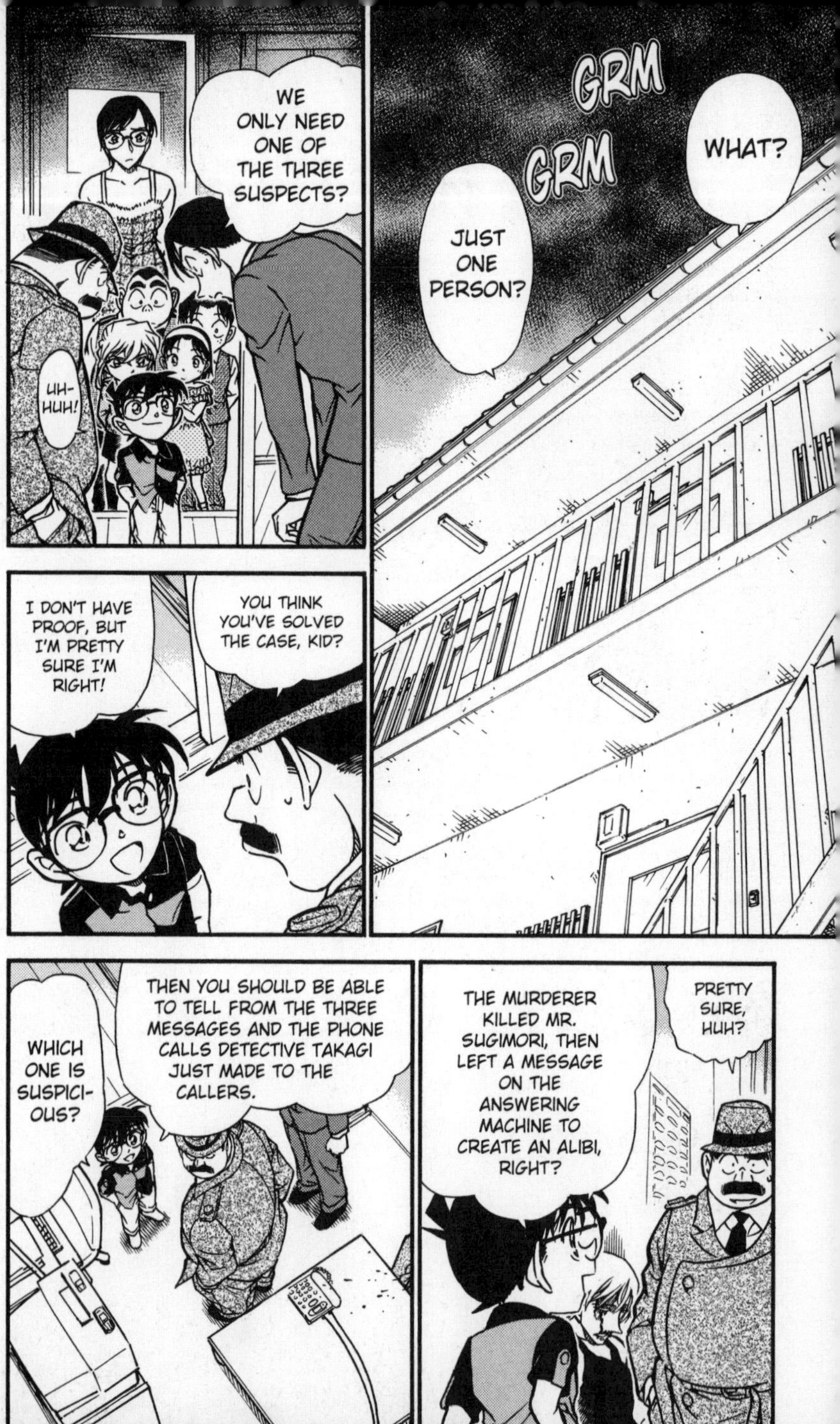
WHAT?
GRM GRM
JUST ONE PERSON?
WE ONLY NEED ONE OF THE THREE SUSPECTS?
UH-HUH!
YOU THINK YOU'VE SOLVED THE CASE, KID?
I DON'T HAVE PROOF, BUT I'M PRETTY SURE I'M RIGHT!
PRETTY SURE, HUH?
THE MURDERER KILLED MR. SUGIMORI, THEN LEFT A MESSAGE ON THE ANSWERING MACHINE TO CREATE AN ALIBI, RIGHT?
THEN YOU SHOULD BE ABLE TO TELL FROM THE THREE MESSAGES AND THE PHONE CALLS DETECTIVE TAKAGI JUST MADE TO THE CALLERS.
WHICH ONE IS SUSPICI-OUS?

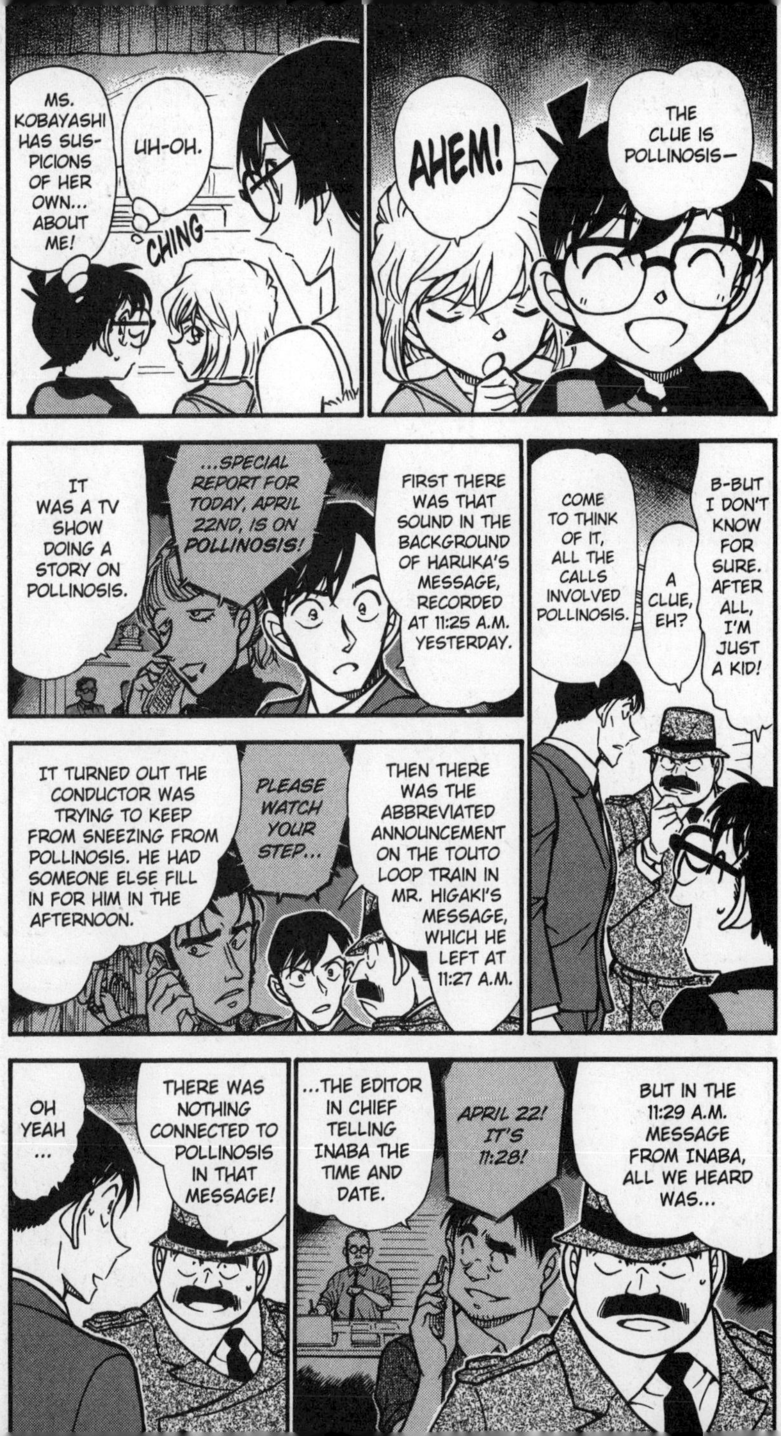
THE CLUE IS POLLINOSIS—
AHEM!
UH-OH.
MS. KOBAYASHI HAS SUSPICIONS OF HER OWN... ABOUT ME!
CHING
B-BUT I DON'T KNOW FOR SURE. AFTER ALL, I'M JUST A KID!
A CLUE, EH?
COME TO THINK OF IT, ALL THE CALLS INVOLVED POLLINOSIS.
FIRST THERE WAS THAT SOUND IN THE BACKGROUND OF HARUKA'S MESSAGE, RECORDED AT 11:25 A.M. YESTERDAY.
...SPECIAL REPORT FOR TODAY, APRIL 22ND, IS ON POLLINOSIS!
IT WAS A TV SHOW DOING A STORY ON POLLINOSIS.
THEN THERE WAS THE ABBREVIATED ANNOUNCEMENT ON THE TOUTO LOOP TRAIN IN MR. HIGAKI'S MESSAGE, WHICH HE LEFT AT 11:27 A.M.
PLEASE WATCH YOUR STEP...
IT TURNED OUT THE CONDUCTOR WAS TRYING TO KEEP FROM SNEEZING FROM POLLINOSIS. HE HAD SOMEONE ELSE FILL IN FOR HIM IN THE AFTERNOON.
BUT IN THE 11:29 A.M. MESSAGE FROM INABA, ALL WE HEARD WAS...
APRIL 22! IT'S 11:28!
...THE EDITOR IN CHIEF TELLING INABA THE TIME AND DATE.
THERE WAS NOTHING CONNECTED TO POLLINOSIS IN THAT MESSAGE!
OH YEAH ...

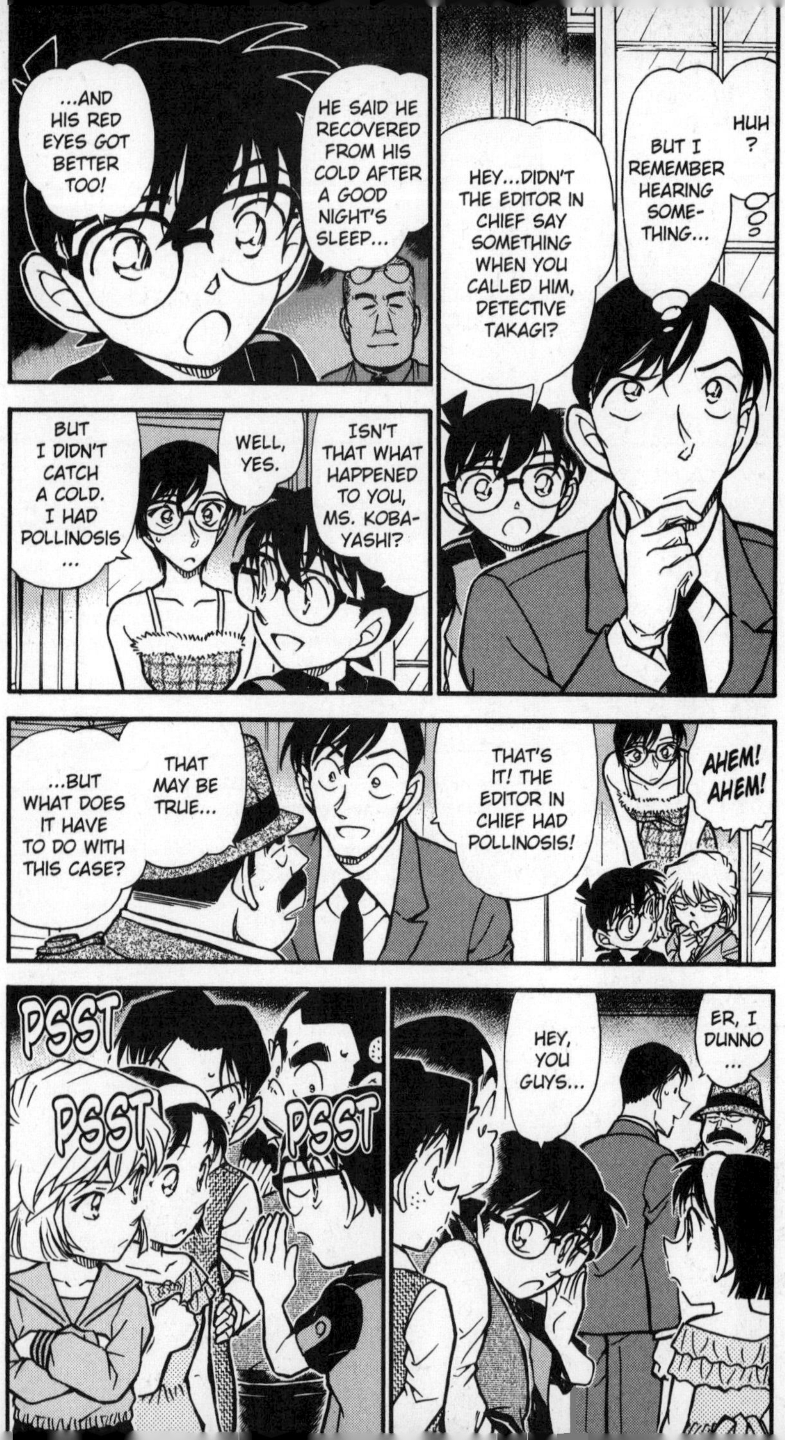
HUH ?
BUT I REMEMBER HEARING SOME-THING...
HEY...DIDN'T THE EDITOR IN CHIEF SAY SOMETHING WHEN YOU CALLED HIM, DETECTIVE TAKAGI?
HE SAID HE RECOVERED FROM HIS COLD AFTER A GOOD NIGHT'S SLEEP...
...AND HIS RED EYES GOT BETTER TOO!
ISN'T THAT WHAT HAPPENED TO YOU, MS. KOBA-YASHI?
WELL, YES.
BUT I DIDN'T CATCH A COLD. I HAD POLLINOSIS ...
AHEM! AHEM!
THAT'S IT! THE EDITOR IN CHIEF HAD POLLINOSIS!
THAT MAY BE TRUE...
...BUT WHAT DOES IT HAVE TO DO WITH THIS CASE?
ER, I DUNNO ...
HEY, YOU GUYS...
PSST
PSST
PSST

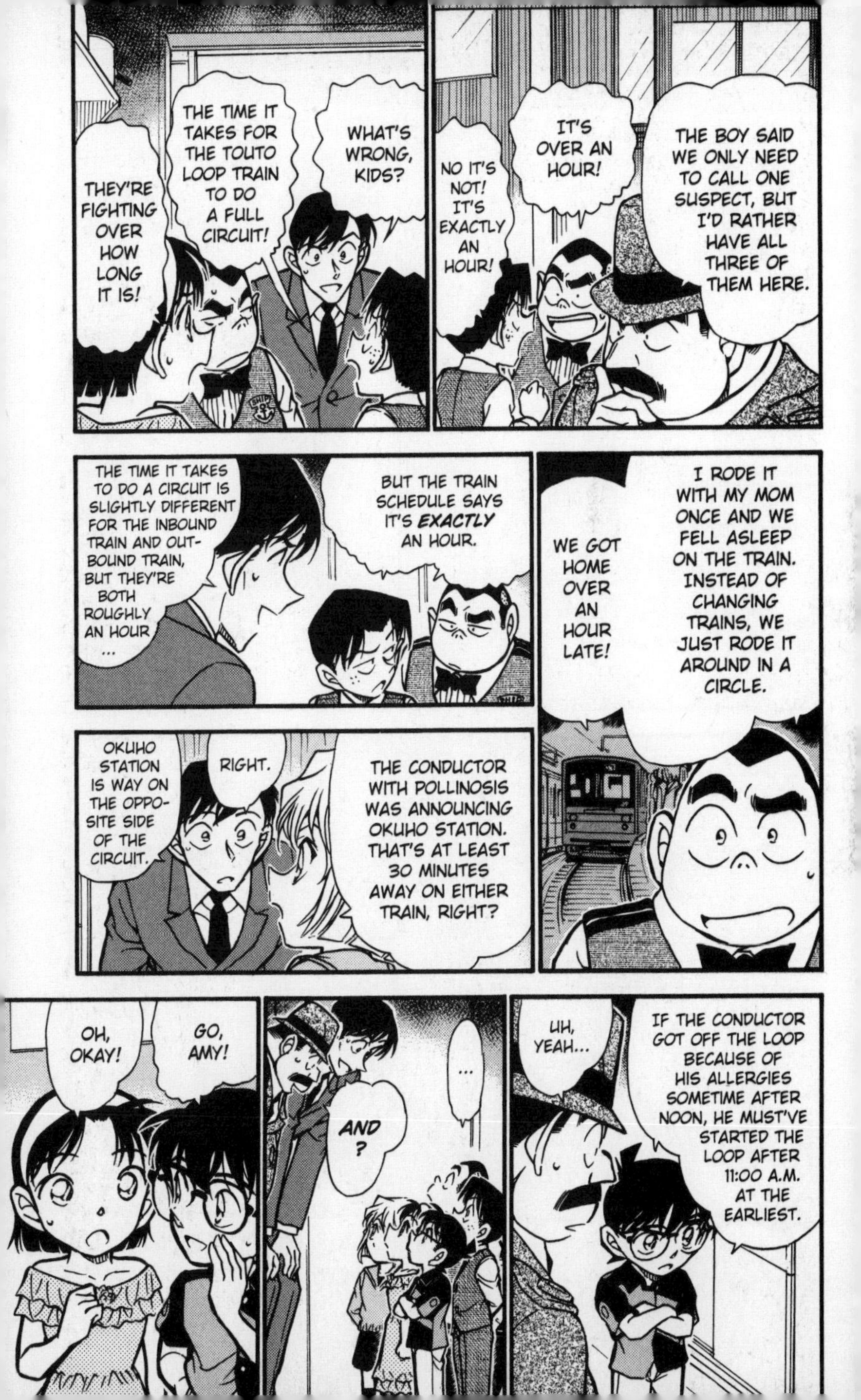
THE BOY SAID WE ONLY NEED TO CALL ONE SUSPECT, BUT I'D RATHER HAVE ALL THREE OF THEM HERE.
IT'S OVER AN HOUR!
NO IT'S NOT! IT'S EXACTLY AN HOUR!
WHAT'S WRONG, KIDS?
THE TIME IT TAKES FOR THE TOUTO LOOP TRAIN TO DO A FULL CIRCUIT!
THEY'RE FIGHTING OVER HOW LONG IT IS!
I RODE IT WITH MY MOM ONCE AND WE FELL ASLEEP ON THE TRAIN. INSTEAD OF CHANGING TRAINS, WE JUST RODE IT AROUND IN A CIRCLE.
WE GOT HOME OVER AN HOUR LATE!
BUT THE TRAIN SCHEDULE SAYS IT'S *EXACTLY* AN HOUR.
THE TIME IT TAKES TO DO A CIRCUIT IS SLIGHTLY DIFFERENT FOR THE INBOUND TRAIN AND OUT-BOUND TRAIN, BUT THEY'RE BOTH ROUGHLY AN HOUR ...
THE CONDUCTOR WITH POLLINOSIS WAS ANNOUNCING OKUHO STATION. THAT'S AT LEAST 30 MINUTES AWAY ON EITHER TRAIN, RIGHT?
RIGHT.
OKUHO STATION IS WAY ON THE OPPO-SITE SIDE OF THE CIRCUIT.
IF THE CONDUCTOR GOT OFF THE LOOP BECAUSE OF HIS ALLERGIES SOMETIME AFTER NOON, HE MUST'VE STARTED THE LOOP AFTER 11:00 A.M. AT THE EARLIEST.
UH, YEAH...
...
AND ?
GO, AMY!
OH, OKAY!

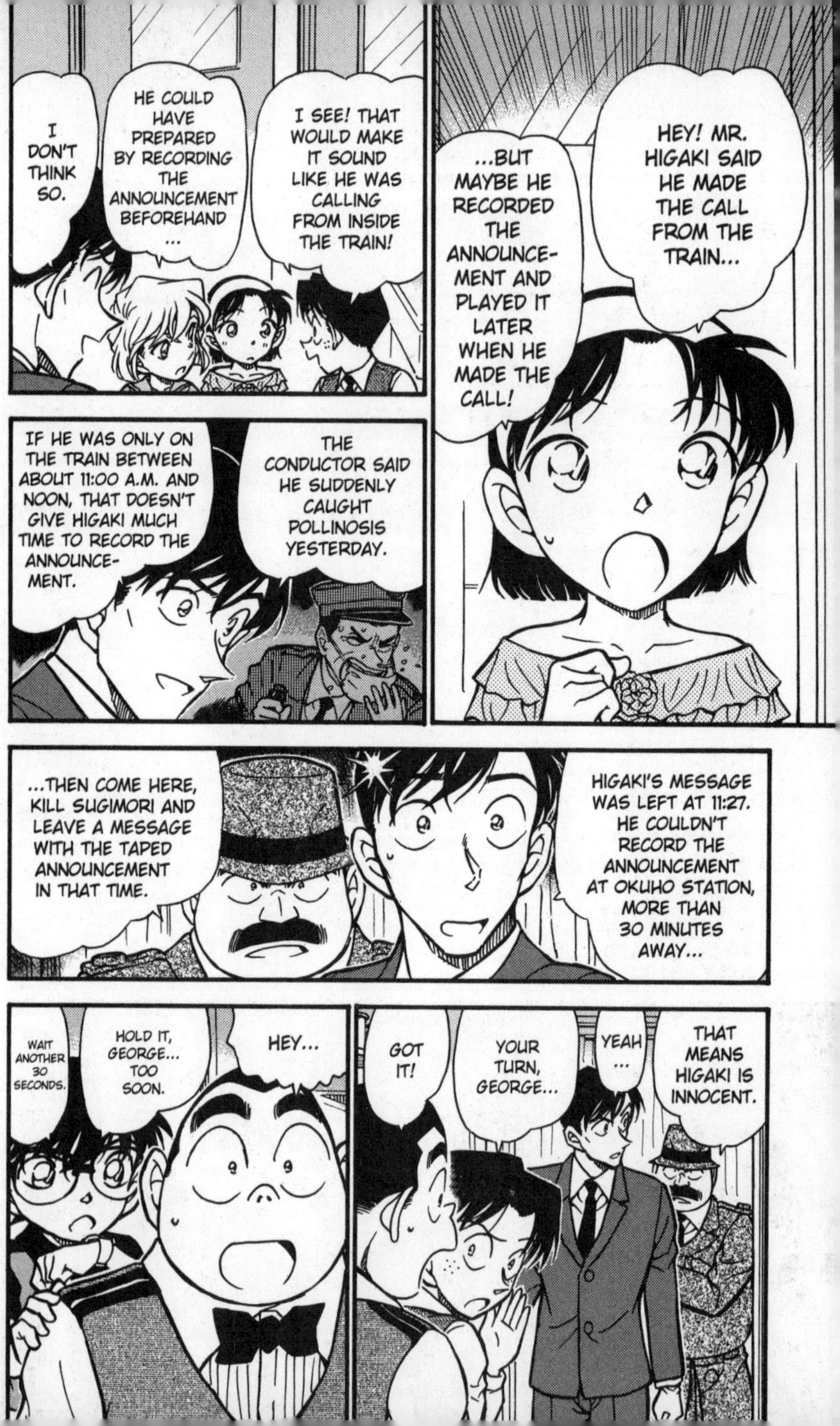
HEY! MR. HIGAKI SAID HE MADE THE CALL FROM THE TRAIN...
...BUT MAYBE HE RECORDED THE ANNOUNCE-MENT AND PLAYED IT LATER WHEN HE MADE THE CALL!
I SEE! THAT WOULD MAKE IT SOUND LIKE HE WAS CALLING FROM INSIDE THE TRAIN!
HE COULD HAVE PREPARED BY RECORDING THE ANNOUNCEMENT BEFOREHAND ...
I DON'T THINK SO.
THE CONDUCTOR SAID HE SUDDENLY CAUGHT POLLINOSIS YESTERDAY.
IF HE WAS ONLY ON THE TRAIN BETWEEN ABOUT 11:00 A.M. AND NOON, THAT DOESN'T GIVE HIGAKI MUCH TIME TO RECORD THE ANNOUNCE-MENT.
HIGAKI'S MESSAGE WAS LEFT AT 11:27. HE COULDN'T RECORD THE ANNOUNCEMENT AT OKUHO STATION, MORE THAN 30 MINUTES AWAY...
...THEN COME HERE, KILL SUGIMORI AND LEAVE A MESSAGE WITH THE TAPED ANNOUNCEMENT IN THAT TIME.
THAT MEANS HIGAKI IS INNOCENT.
YEAH ...
YOUR TURN, GEORGE...
GOT IT!
HEY...
HOLD IT, GEORGE... TOO SOON.
WAIT ANOTHER 30 SECONDS.

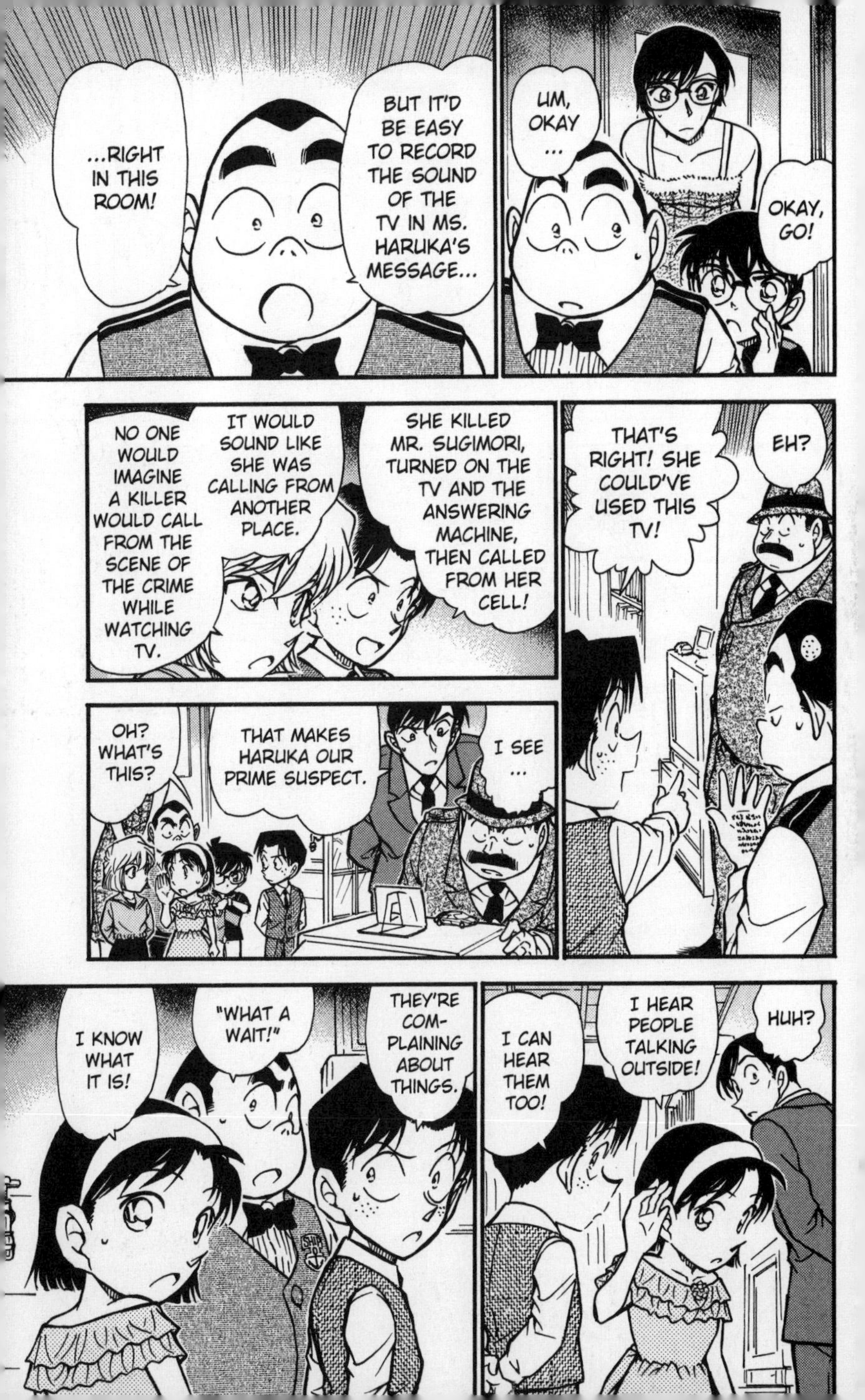
OKAY, GO!
UM, OKAY ...
BUT IT'D BE EASY TO RECORD THE SOUND OF THE TV IN MS. HARUKA'S MESSAGE...
...RIGHT IN THIS ROOM!
EH?
THAT'S RIGHT! SHE COULD'VE USED THIS TV!
SHE KILLED MR. SUGIMORI, TURNED ON THE TV AND THE ANSWERING MACHINE, THEN CALLED FROM HER CELL!
IT WOULD SOUND LIKE SHE WAS CALLING FROM ANOTHER PLACE.
NO ONE WOULD IMAGINE A KILLER WOULD CALL FROM THE SCENE OF THE CRIME WHILE WATCHING TV.
I SEE ...
THAT MAKES HARUKA OUR PRIME SUSPECT.
OH? WHAT'S THIS?
HUH?
I HEAR PEOPLE TALKING OUTSIDE!
I CAN HEAR THEM TOO!
THEY'RE COM-PLAINING ABOUT THINGS.
"WHAT A WAIT!"
I KNOW WHAT IT IS!

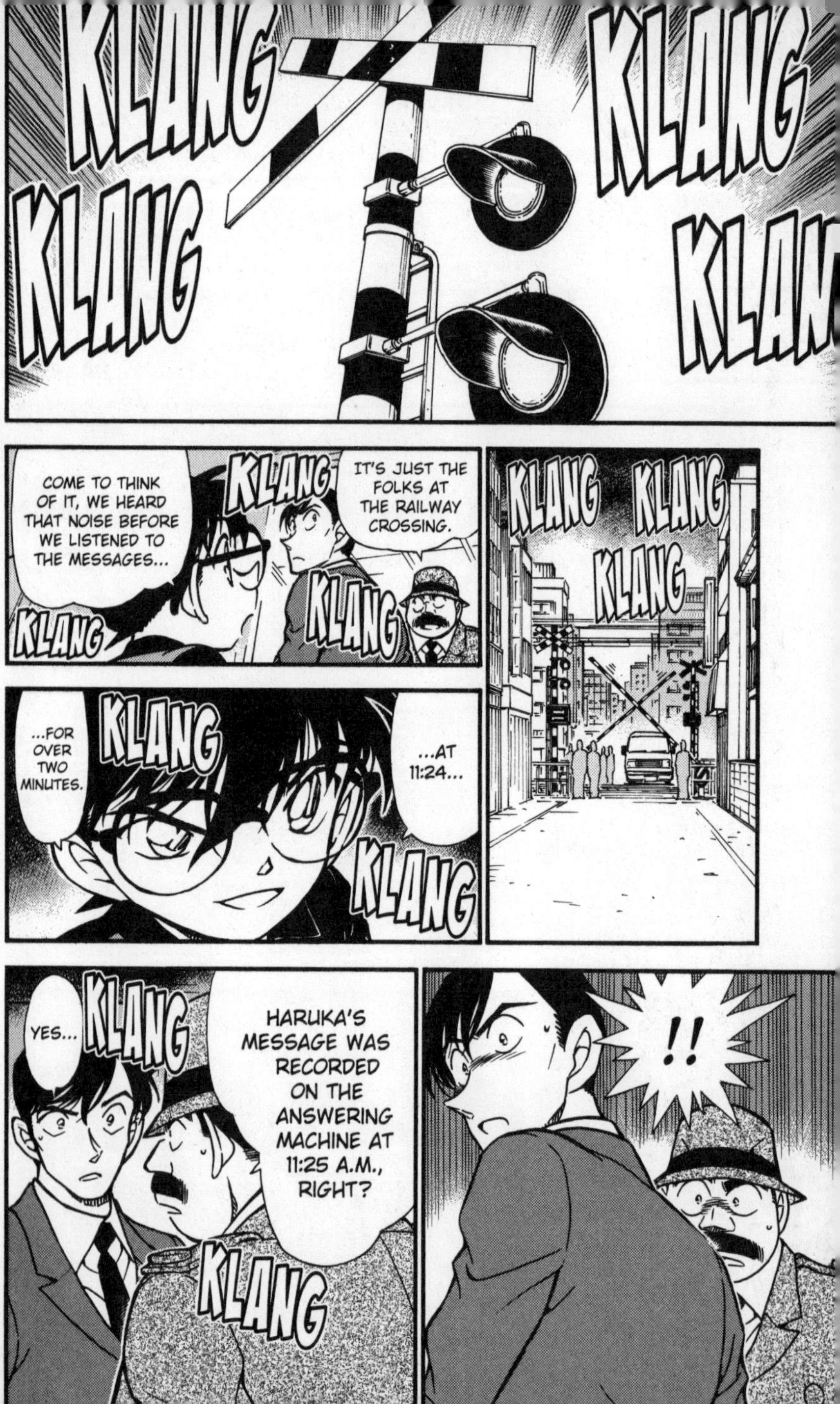
KLANG
KLANG
KLAN
KLANG
KLANG
KLANG
KLANG
KLANG
IT'S JUST THE FOLKS AT THE RAILWAY CROSSING.
KLANG
COME TO THINK OF IT, WE HEARD THAT NOISE BEFORE WE LISTENED TO THE MESSAGES...
KLANG
KLANG
...AT 11:24...
KLANG
...FOR OVER TWO MINUTES.
KLANG
!!
HARUKA'S MESSAGE WAS RECORDED ON THE ANSWERING MACHINE AT 11:25 A.M., RIGHT?
KLANG
YES...
KLANG

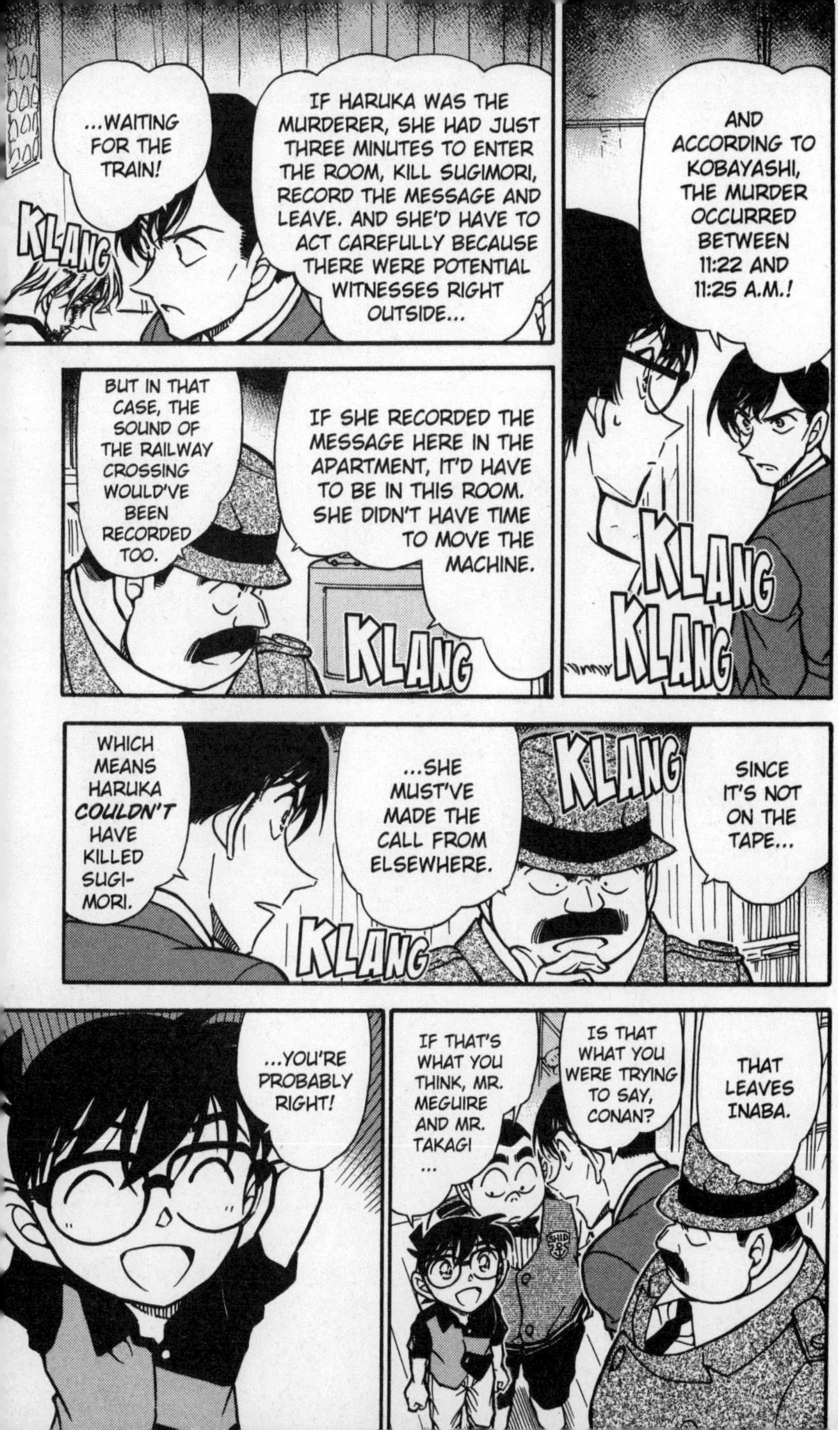
AND ACCORDING TO KOBAYASHI, THE MURDER OCCURRED BETWEEN 11:22 AND 11:25 A.M.!
KLANG
KLANG
IF HARUKA WAS THE MURDERER, SHE HAD JUST THREE MINUTES TO ENTER THE ROOM, KILL SUGIMORI, RECORD THE MESSAGE AND LEAVE. AND SHE'D HAVE TO ACT CAREFULLY BECAUSE THERE WERE POTENTIAL WITNESSES RIGHT OUTSIDE...
...WAITING FOR THE TRAIN!
KLANG
IF SHE RECORDED THE MESSAGE HERE IN THE APARTMENT, IT'D HAVE TO BE IN THIS ROOM. SHE DIDN'T HAVE TIME TO MOVE THE MACHINE.
BUT IN THAT CASE, THE SOUND OF THE RAILWAY CROSSING WOULD'VE BEEN RECORDED TOO.
KLANG
SINCE IT'S NOT ON THE TAPE...
KLANG
...SHE MUST'VE MADE THE CALL FROM ELSEWHERE.
KLANG
WHICH MEANS HARUKA *COULDN'T* HAVE KILLED SUGI-MORI.
THAT LEAVES INABA.
IS THAT WHAT YOU WERE TRYING TO SAY, CONAN?
IF THAT'S WHAT YOU THINK, MR. MEGUIRE AND MR. TAKAGI ...
...YOU'RE PROBABLY RIGHT!

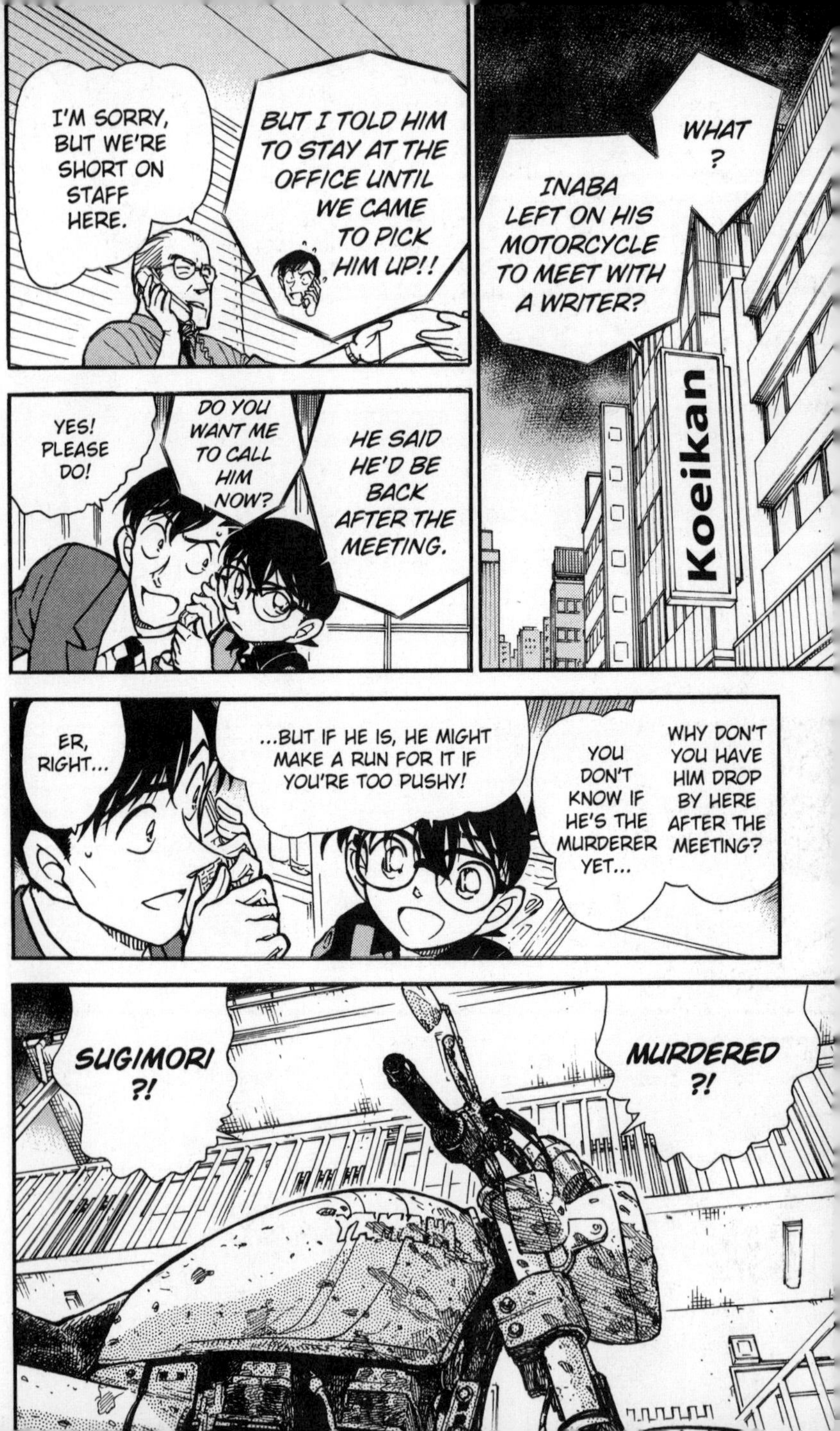
WHAT?
INABA LEFT ON HIS MOTORCYCLE TO MEET WITH A WRITER?
Koeikan
BUT I TOLD HIM TO STAY AT THE OFFICE UNTIL WE CAME TO PICK HIM UP!!
I'M SORRY, BUT WE'RE SHORT ON STAFF HERE.
HE SAID HE'D BE BACK AFTER THE MEETING.
DO YOU WANT ME TO CALL HIM NOW?
YES! PLEASE DO!
WHY DON'T YOU HAVE HIM DROP BY HERE AFTER THE MEETING?
YOU DON'T KNOW IF HE'S THE MURDERER YET...
...BUT IF HE IS, HE MIGHT MAKE A RUN FOR IT IF YOU'RE TOO PUSHY!
ER, RIGHT...
MURDERED?!
SUGIMORI?!

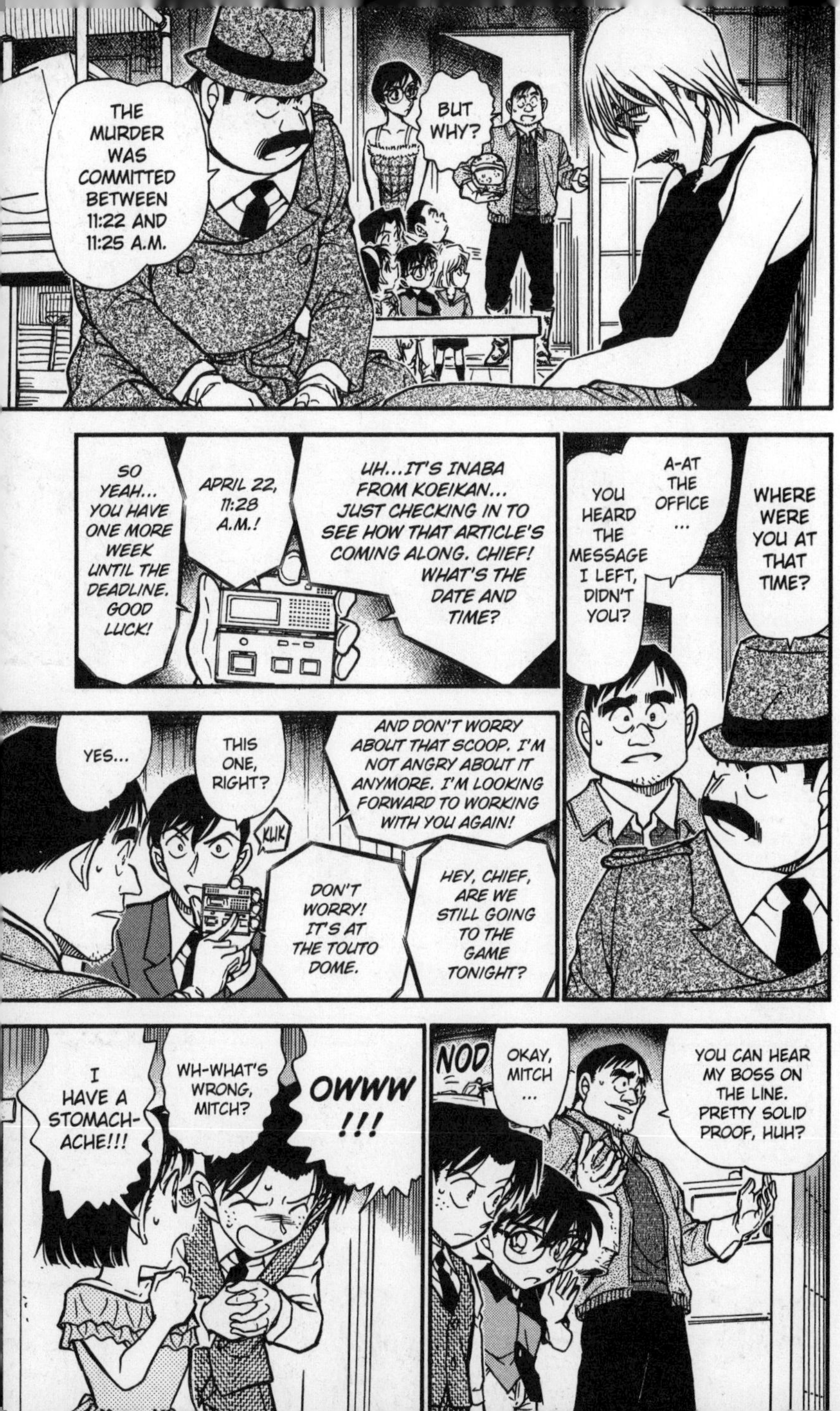
BUT WHY?
THE MURDER WAS COMMITTED BETWEEN 11:22 AND 11:25 A.M.
WHERE WERE YOU AT THAT TIME?
A-AT THE OFFICE ...
YOU HEARD THE MESSAGE I LEFT, DIDN'T YOU?
UH...IT'S INABA FROM KOEIKAN... JUST CHECKING IN TO SEE HOW THAT ARTICLE'S COMING ALONG. CHIEF! WHAT'S THE DATE AND TIME?
APRIL 22, 11:28 A.M.!
SO YEAH... YOU HAVE ONE MORE WEEK UNTIL THE DEADLINE. GOOD LUCK!
AND DON'T WORRY ABOUT THAT SCOOP. I'M NOT ANGRY ABOUT IT ANYMORE. I'M LOOKING FORWARD TO WORKING WITH YOU AGAIN!
KLIK
HEY, CHIEF, ARE WE STILL GOING TO THE GAME TONIGHT?
DON'T WORRY! IT'S AT THE TOUTO DOME.
THIS ONE, RIGHT?
YES...
YOU CAN HEAR MY BOSS ON THE LINE. PRETTY SOLID PROOF, HUH?
OKAY, MITCH ...
NOD
OWWW !!!
WH-WHAT'S WRONG, MITCH?
I HAVE A STOMACH-ACHE!!!

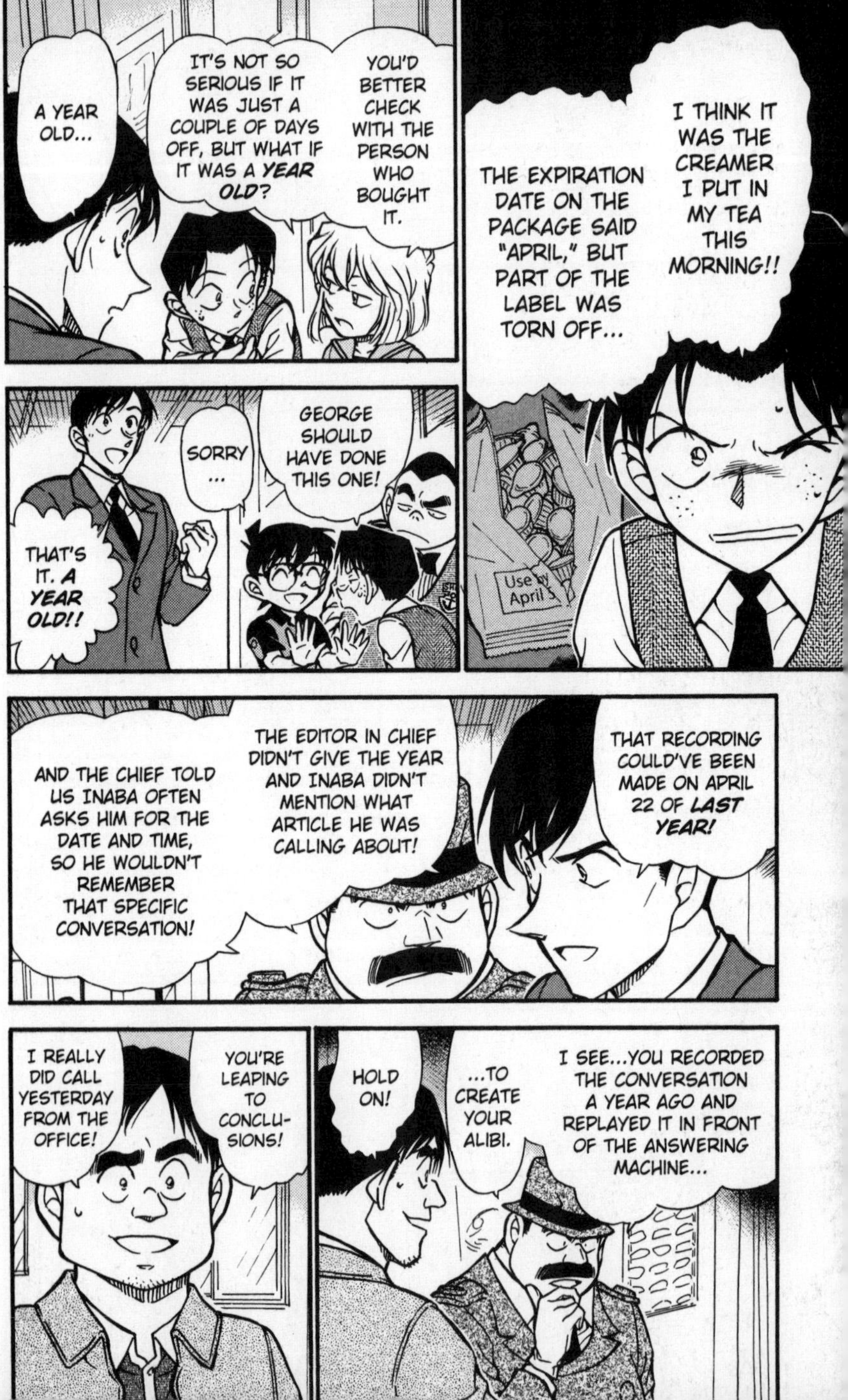
I THINK IT WAS THE CREAMER I PUT IN MY TEA THIS MORNING!!
THE EXPIRATION DATE ON THE PACKAGE SAID "APRIL," BUT PART OF THE LABEL WAS TORN OFF...
Use by April 5
YOU'D BETTER CHECK WITH THE PERSON WHO BOUGHT IT.
IT'S NOT SO SERIOUS IF IT WAS JUST A COUPLE OF DAYS OFF, BUT WHAT IF IT WAS A *YEAR OLD*?
A YEAR OLD...
GEORGE SHOULD HAVE DONE THIS ONE!
SORRY...
THAT'S IT. *A YEAR OLD!!*
THAT RECORDING COULD'VE BEEN MADE ON APRIL 22 OF *LAST YEAR!*
THE EDITOR IN CHIEF DIDN'T GIVE THE YEAR AND INABA DIDN'T MENTION WHAT ARTICLE HE WAS CALLING ABOUT!
AND THE CHIEF TOLD US INABA OFTEN ASKS HIM FOR THE DATE AND TIME, SO HE WOULDN'T REMEMBER THAT SPECIFIC CONVERSATION!
I SEE...YOU RECORDED THE CONVERSATION A YEAR AGO AND REPLAYED IT IN FRONT OF THE ANSWERING MACHINE...
...TO CREATE YOUR ALIBI.
HOLD ON!
YOU'RE LEAPING TO CONCLUSIONS!
I REALLY DID CALL YESTERDAY FROM THE OFFICE!

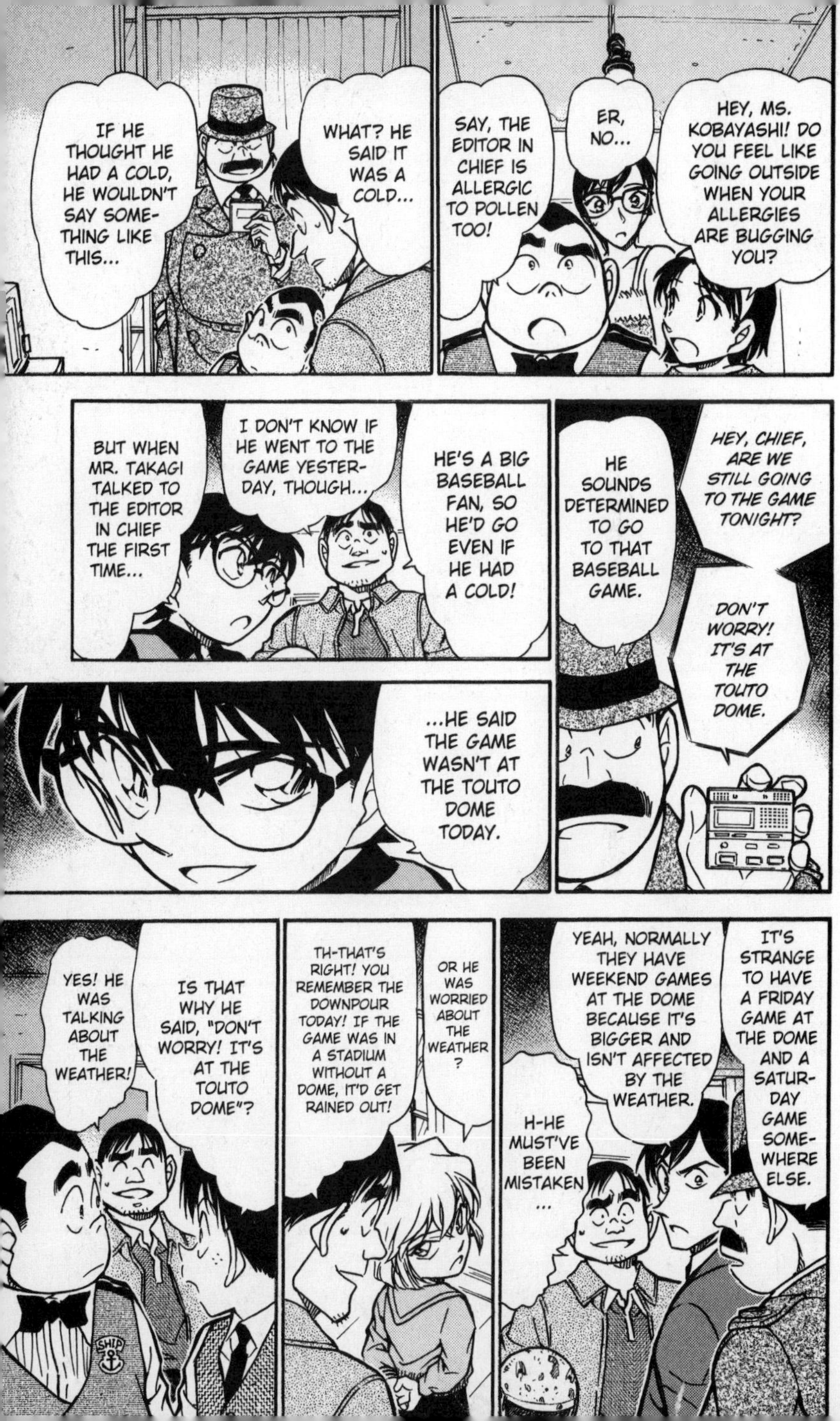
HEY, MS. KOBAYASHI! DO YOU FEEL LIKE GOING OUTSIDE WHEN YOUR ALLERGIES ARE BUGGING YOU?
ER, NO...
SAY, THE EDITOR IN CHIEF IS ALLERGIC TO POLLEN TOO!
WHAT? HE SAID IT WAS A COLD...
IF HE THOUGHT HE HAD A COLD, HE WOULDN'T SAY SOME-THING LIKE THIS...
HEY, CHIEF, ARE WE STILL GOING TO THE GAME TONIGHT?
HE SOUNDS DETERMINED TO GO TO THAT BASEBALL GAME.
DON'T WORRY! IT'S AT THE TOUTO DOME.
HE'S A BIG BASEBALL FAN, SO HE'D GO EVEN IF HE HAD A COLD!
I DON'T KNOW IF HE WENT TO THE GAME YESTER-DAY, THOUGH...
BUT WHEN MR. TAKAGI TALKED TO THE EDITOR IN CHIEF THE FIRST TIME...
...HE SAID THE GAME WASN'T AT THE TOUTO DOME TODAY.
IT'S STRANGE TO HAVE A FRIDAY GAME AT THE DOME AND A SATUR-DAY GAME SOME-WHERE ELSE.
YEAH, NORMALLY THEY HAVE WEEKEND GAMES AT THE DOME BECAUSE IT'S BIGGER AND ISN'T AFFECTED BY THE WEATHER.
H-HE MUST'VE BEEN MISTAKEN...
OR HE WAS WORRIED ABOUT THE WEATHER?
TH-THAT'S RIGHT! YOU REMEMBER THE DOWNPOUR TODAY! IF THE GAME WAS IN A STADIUM WITHOUT A DOME, IT'D GET RAINED OUT!
IS THAT WHY HE SAID, "DON'T WORRY! IT'S AT THE TOUTO DOME"?
YES! HE WAS TALKING ABOUT THE WEATHER!

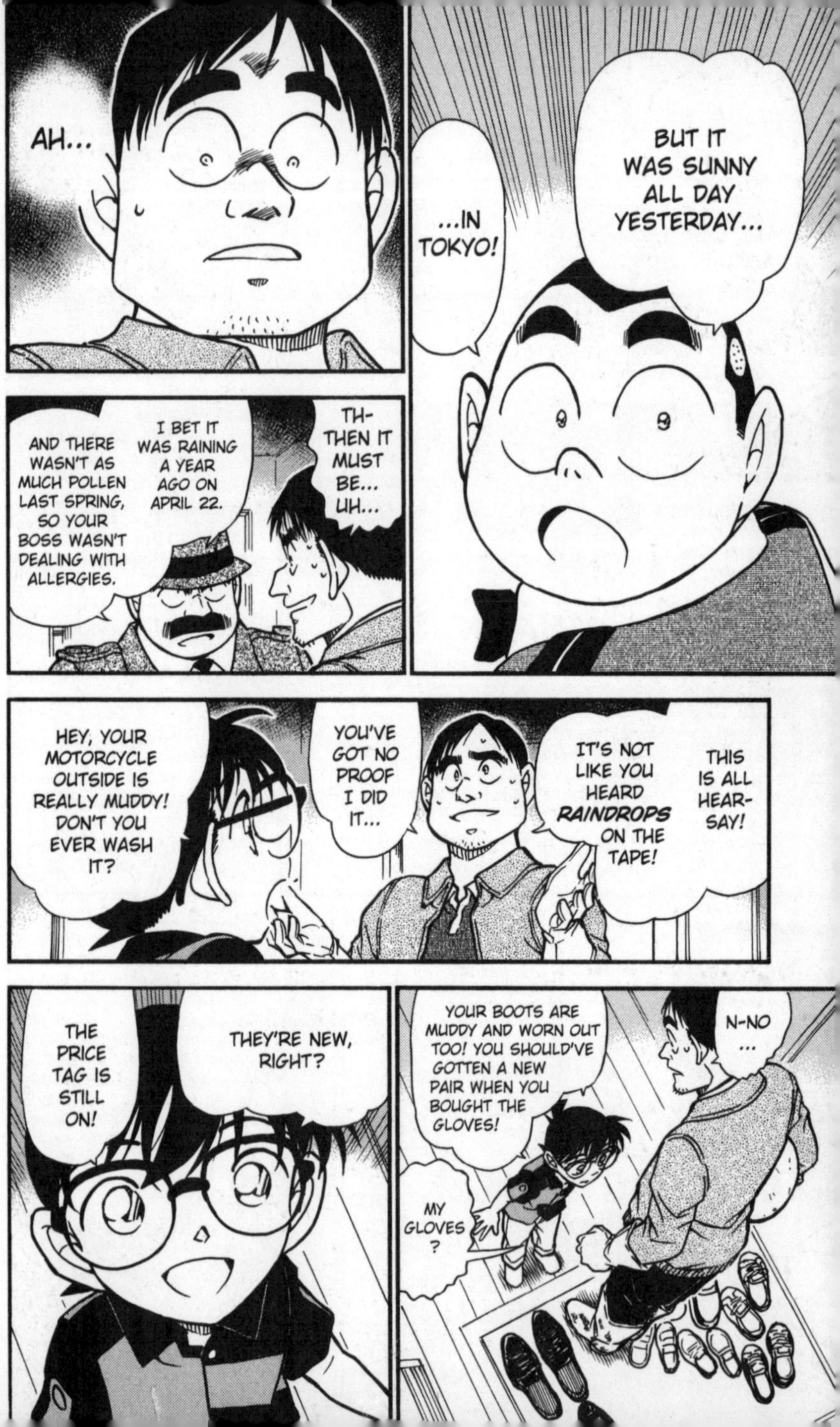
BUT IT WAS SUNNY ALL DAY YESTERDAY...
...IN TOKYO!
AH...
TH- THEN IT MUST BE... UH...
I BET IT WAS RAINING A YEAR AGO ON APRIL 22.
AND THERE WASN'T AS MUCH POLLEN LAST SPRING, SO YOUR BOSS WASN'T DEALING WITH ALLERGIES.
THIS IS ALL HEAR-SAY!
IT'S NOT LIKE YOU HEARD ***RAINDROPS*** ON THE TAPE!
YOU'VE GOT NO PROOF I DID IT...
HEY, YOUR MOTORCYCLE OUTSIDE IS REALLY MUDDY! DON'T YOU EVER WASH IT?
N-NO ...
YOUR BOOTS ARE MUDDY AND WORN OUT TOO! YOU SHOULD'VE GOTTEN A NEW PAIR WHEN YOU BOUGHT THE GLOVES!
MY GLOVES ?
THEY'RE NEW, RIGHT?
THE PRICE TAG IS STILL ON!

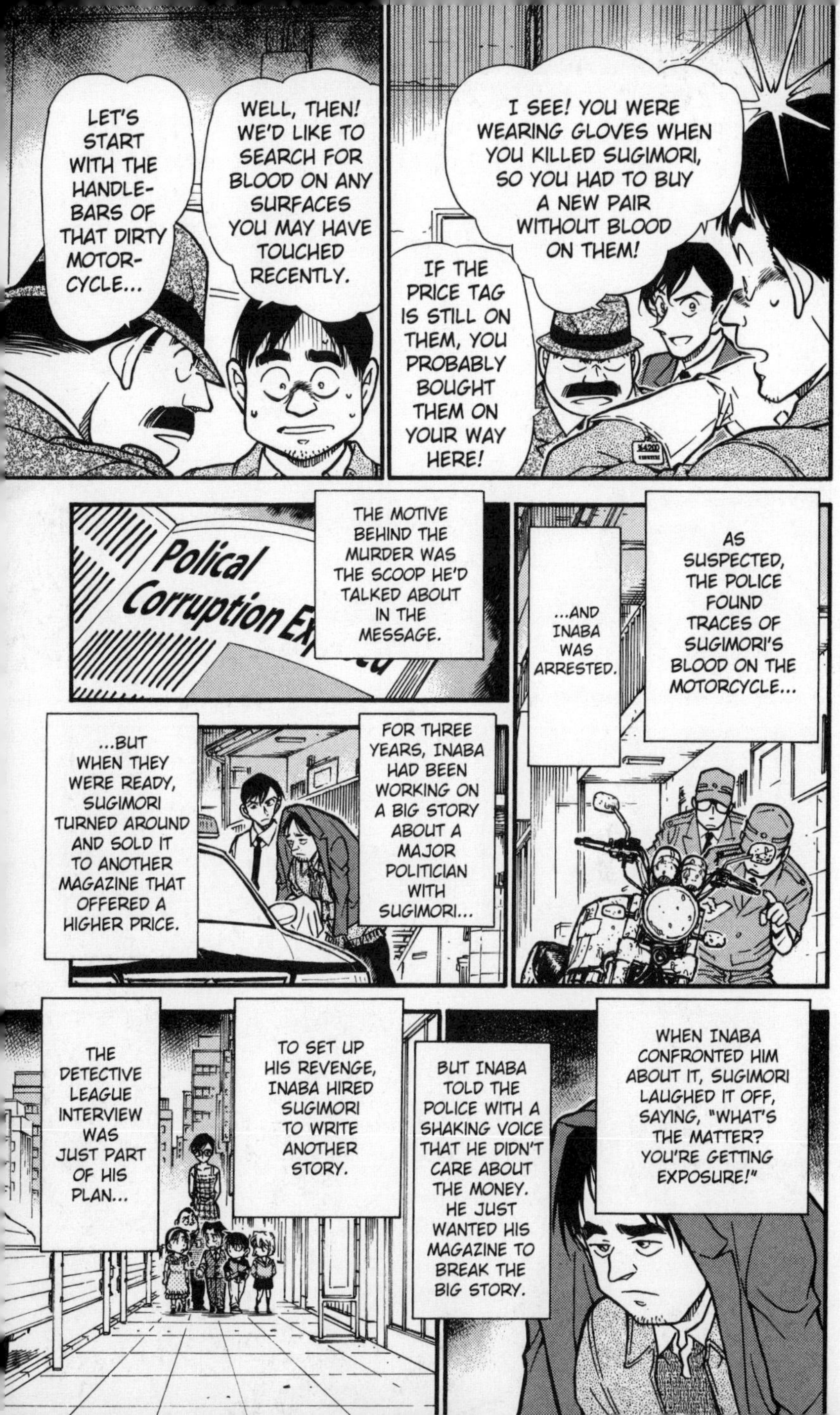
I SEE! YOU WERE WEARING GLOVES WHEN YOU KILLED SUGIMORI, SO YOU HAD TO BUY A NEW PAIR WITHOUT BLOOD ON THEM!
IF THE PRICE TAG IS STILL ON THEM, YOU PROBABLY BOUGHT THEM ON YOUR WAY HERE!
WELL, THEN! WE'D LIKE TO SEARCH FOR BLOOD ON ANY SURFACES YOU MAY HAVE TOUCHED RECENTLY.
LET'S START WITH THE HANDLE-BARS OF THAT DIRTY MOTOR-CYCLE...
AS SUSPECTED, THE POLICE FOUND TRACES OF SUGIMORI'S BLOOD ON THE MOTORCYCLE...
...AND INABA WAS ARRESTED.
THE MOTIVE BEHIND THE MURDER WAS THE SCOOP HE'D TALKED ABOUT IN THE MESSAGE.
Polical Corruption Ex
FOR THREE YEARS, INABA HAD BEEN WORKING ON A BIG STORY ABOUT A MAJOR POLITICIAN WITH SUGIMORI...
...BUT WHEN THEY WERE READY, SUGIMORI TURNED AROUND AND SOLD IT TO ANOTHER MAGAZINE THAT OFFERED A HIGHER PRICE.
WHEN INABA CONFRONTED HIM ABOUT IT, SUGIMORI LAUGHED IT OFF, SAYING, "WHAT'S THE MATTER? YOU'RE GETTING EXPOSURE!"
BUT INABA TOLD THE POLICE WITH A SHAKING VOICE THAT HE DIDN'T CARE ABOUT THE MONEY. HE JUST WANTED HIS MAGAZINE TO BREAK THE BIG STORY.
TO SET UP HIS REVENGE, INABA HIRED SUGIMORI TO WRITE ANOTHER STORY.
THE DETECTIVE LEAGUE INTERVIEW WAS JUST PART OF HIS PLAN...

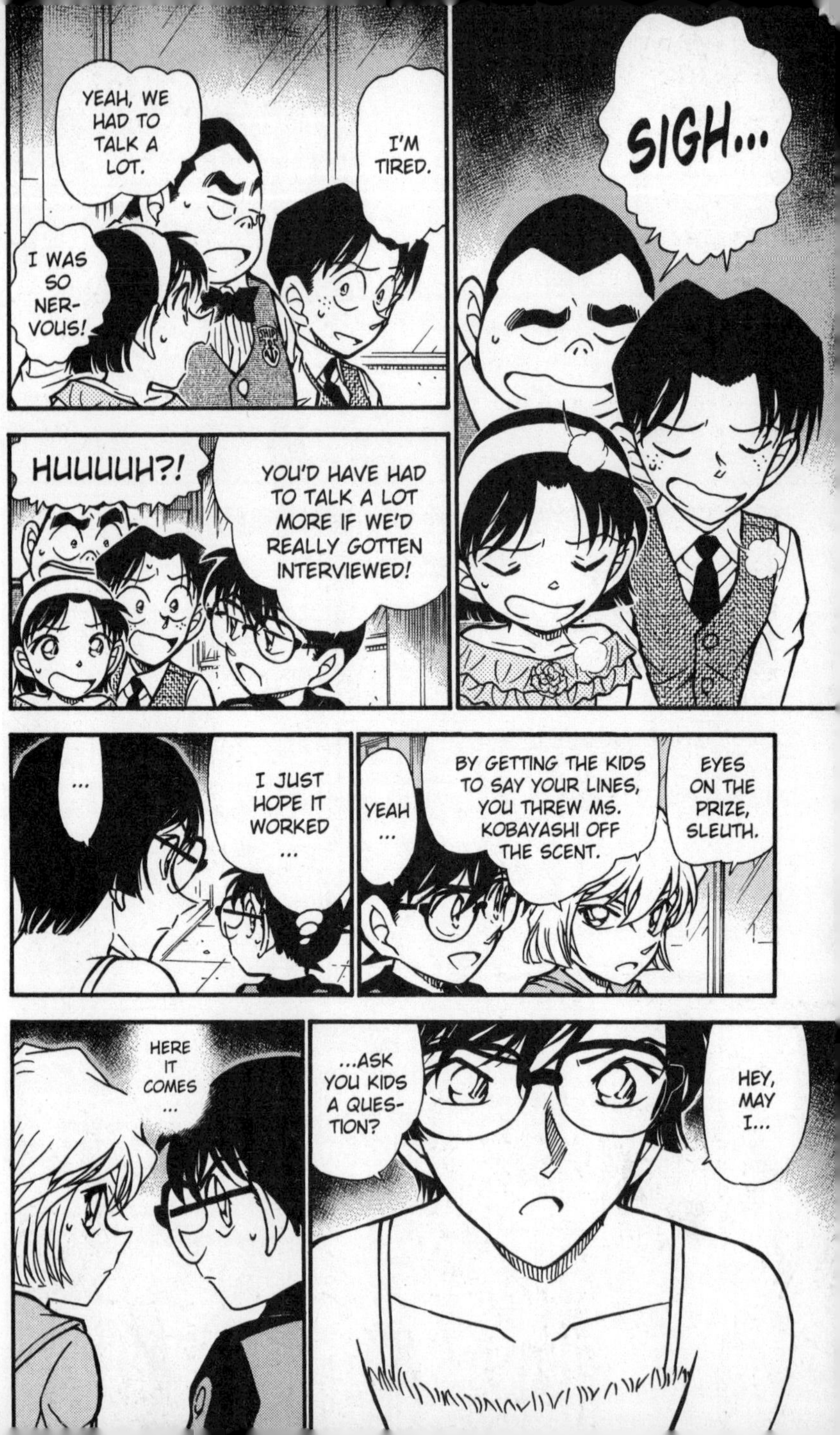
SIGH...
I'M TIRED.
YEAH, WE HAD TO TALK A LOT.
I WAS SO NERVOUS!
YOU'D HAVE HAD TO TALK A LOT MORE IF WE'D REALLY GOTTEN INTERVIEWED!
HUUUUH?!
EYES ON THE PRIZE, SLEUTH.
BY GETTING THE KIDS TO SAY YOUR LINES, YOU THREW MS. KOBAYASHI OFF THE SCENT.
YEAH...
I JUST HOPE IT WORKED...
...
HEY, MAY I...
...ASK YOU KIDS A QUESTION?
HERE IT COMES...

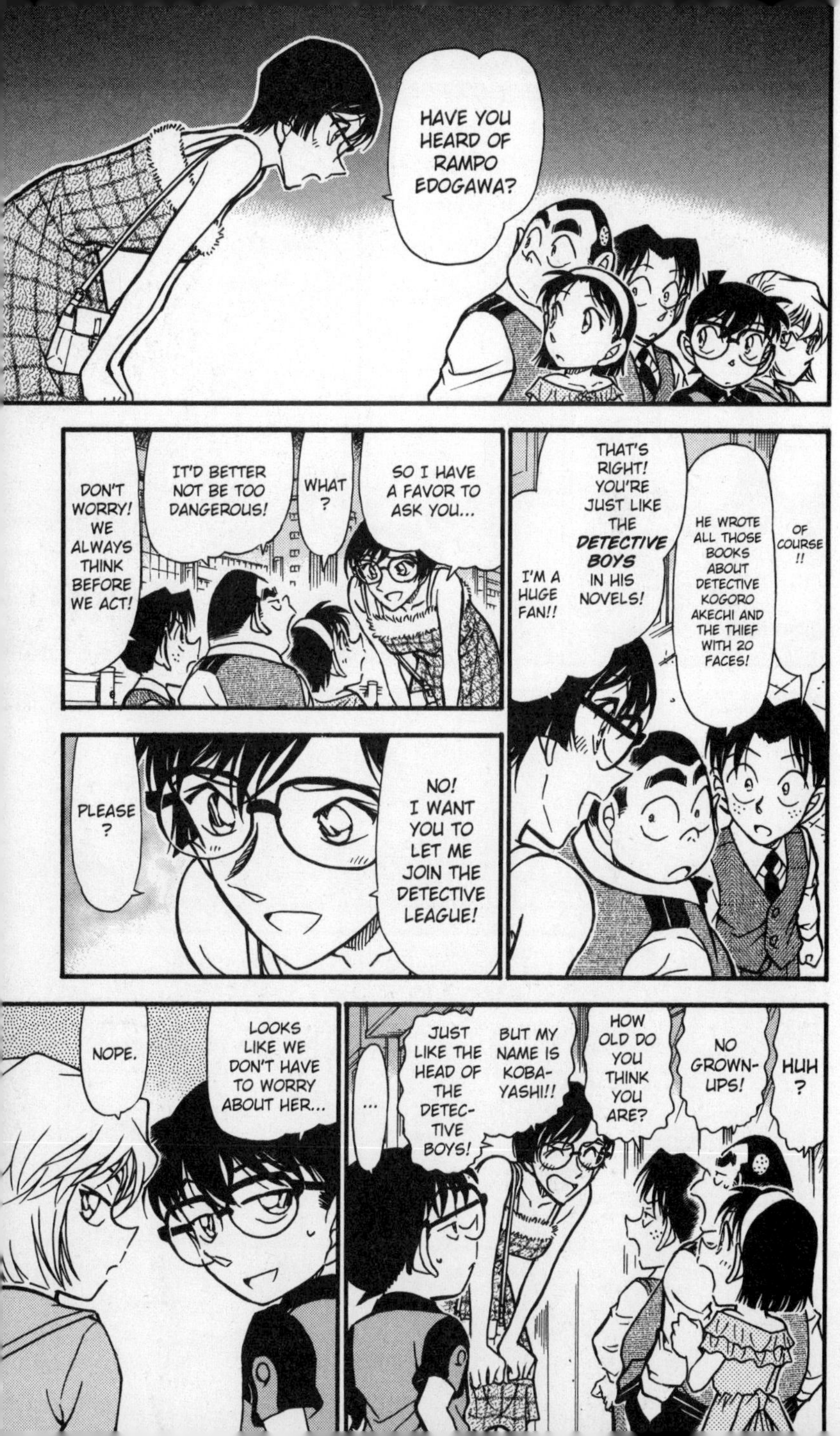
HAVE YOU HEARD OF RAMPO EDOGAWA?
OF COURSE!!
HE WROTE ALL THOSE BOOKS ABOUT DETECTIVE KOGORO AKECHI AND THE THIEF WITH 20 FACES!
THAT'S RIGHT! YOU'RE JUST LIKE THE DETECTIVE BOYS IN HIS NOVELS!
I'M A HUGE FAN!!
SO I HAVE A FAVOR TO ASK YOU...
WHAT?
IT'D BETTER NOT BE TOO DANGEROUS!
DON'T WORRY! WE ALWAYS THINK BEFORE WE ACT!
NO! I WANT YOU TO LET ME JOIN THE DETECTIVE LEAGUE!
PLEASE?
HUH?
NO GROWN-UPS!
HOW OLD DO YOU THINK YOU ARE?
BUT MY NAME IS KOBA-YASHI!!
JUST LIKE THE HEAD OF THE DETEC-TIVE BOYS!
...
LOOKS LIKE WE DON'T HAVE TO WORRY ABOUT HER...
NOPE.

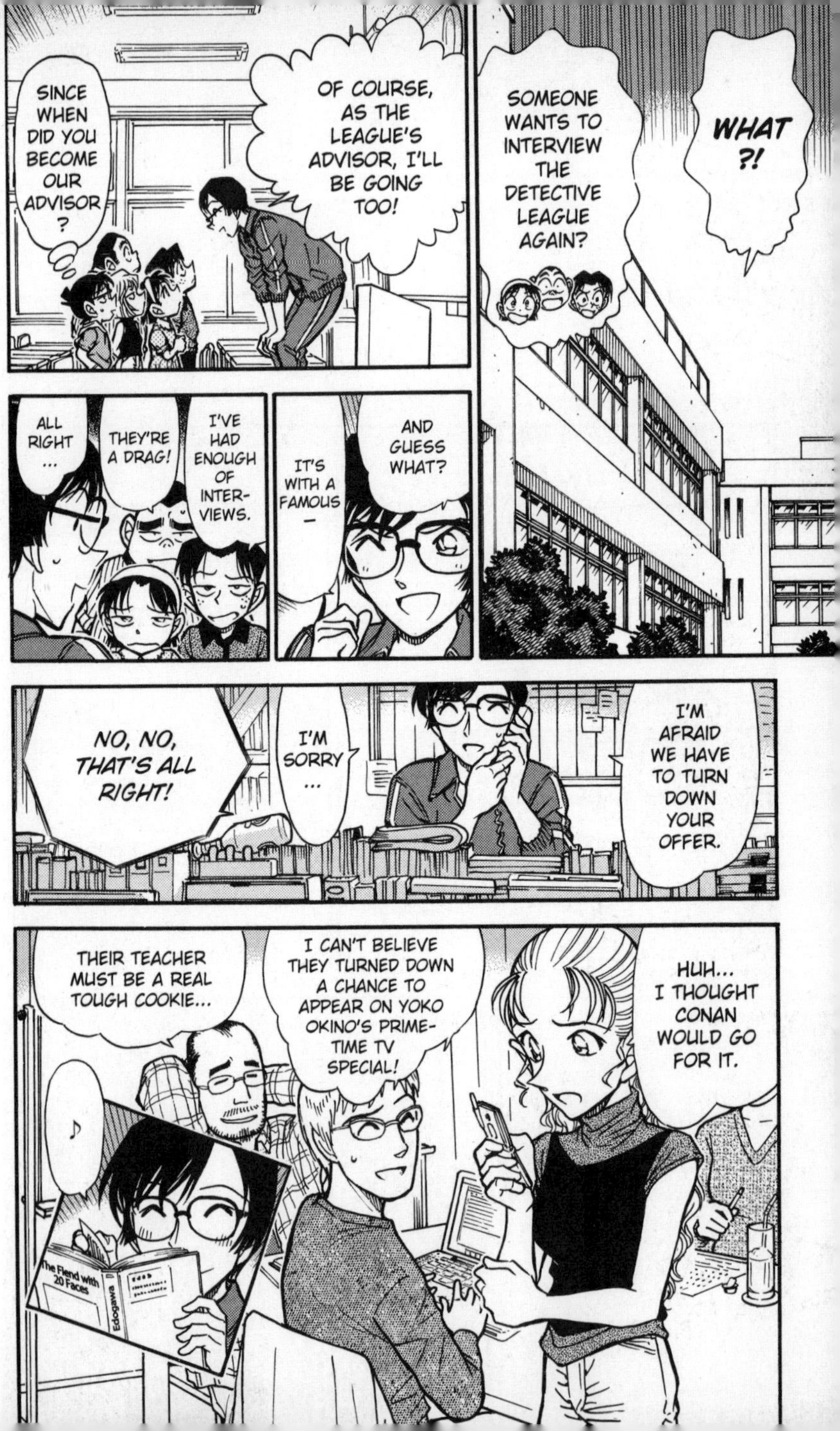
WHAT ?!
SOMEONE WANTS TO INTERVIEW THE DETECTIVE LEAGUE AGAIN?
OF COURSE, AS THE LEAGUE'S ADVISOR, I'LL BE GOING TOO!
SINCE WHEN DID YOU BECOME OUR ADVISOR ?
AND GUESS WHAT?
IT'S WITH A FAMOUS —
I'VE HAD ENOUGH OF INTER-VIEWS.
THEY'RE A DRAG!
ALL RIGHT ...
I'M AFRAID WE HAVE TO TURN DOWN YOUR OFFER.
I'M SORRY ...
NO, NO, THAT'S ALL RIGHT!
HUH... I THOUGHT CONAN WOULD GO FOR IT.
I CAN'T BELIEVE THEY TURNED DOWN A CHANCE TO APPEAR ON YOKO OKINO'S PRIME-TIME TV SPECIAL!
THEIR TEACHER MUST BE A REAL TOUGH COOKIE...
♪
The Fiend with 20 Faces
Edogawa

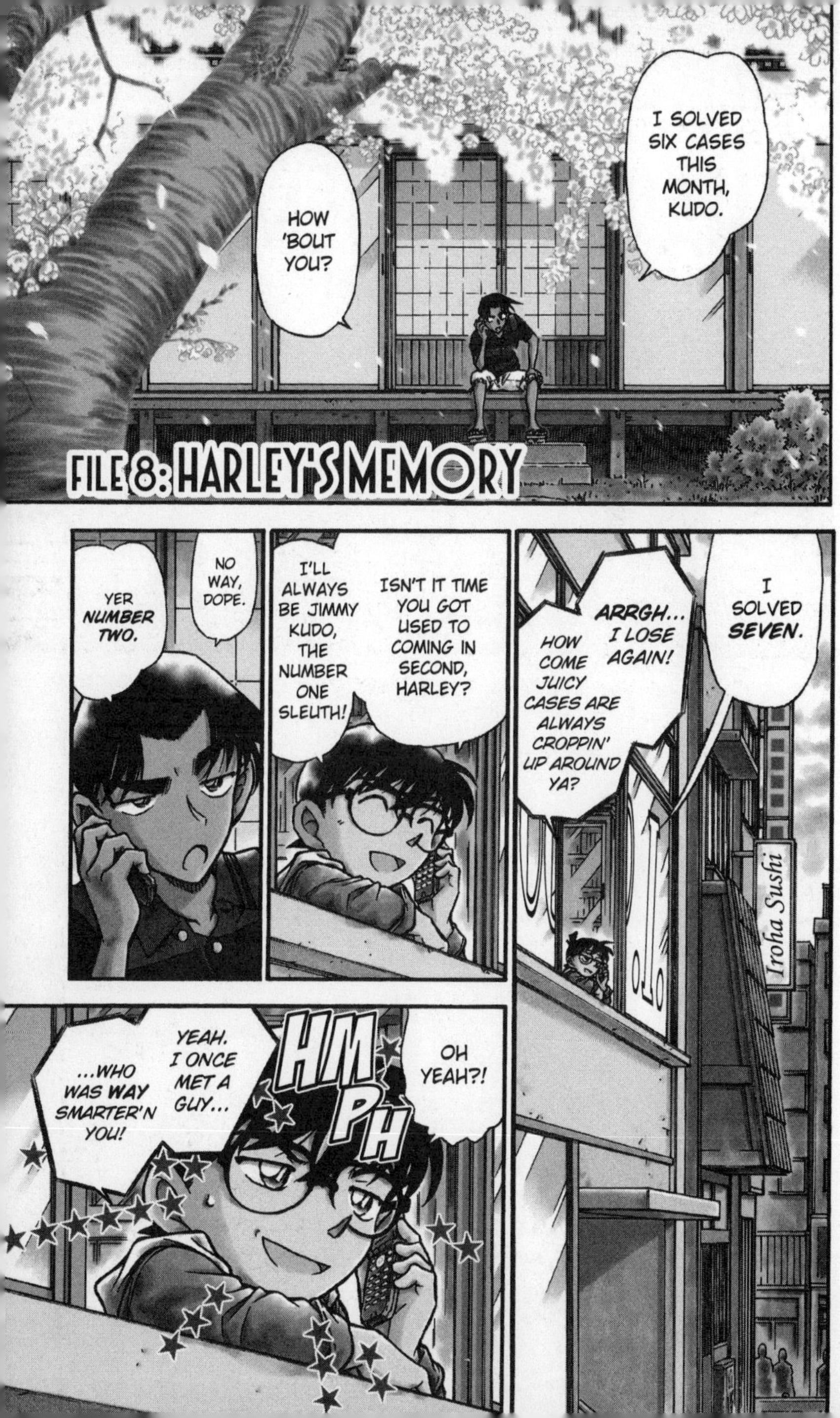
I SOLVED SIX CASES THIS MONTH, KUDO.
HOW 'BOUT YOU?
FILE 8: HARLEY'S MEMORY
I SOLVED **SEVEN**.
ARRGH... I LOSE AGAIN!
HOW COME JUICY CASES ARE ALWAYS CROPPIN' UP AROUND YA?
Iroha Sushi
ISN'T IT TIME YOU GOT USED TO COMING IN SECOND, HARLEY?
I'LL ALWAYS BE JIMMY KUDO, THE NUMBER ONE SLEUTH!
NO WAY, DOPE.
YER **NUMBER TWO.**
OH YEAH?!
HMPH
YEAH. I ONCE MET A GUY...
...WHO WAS **WAY** SMARTER'N YOU!

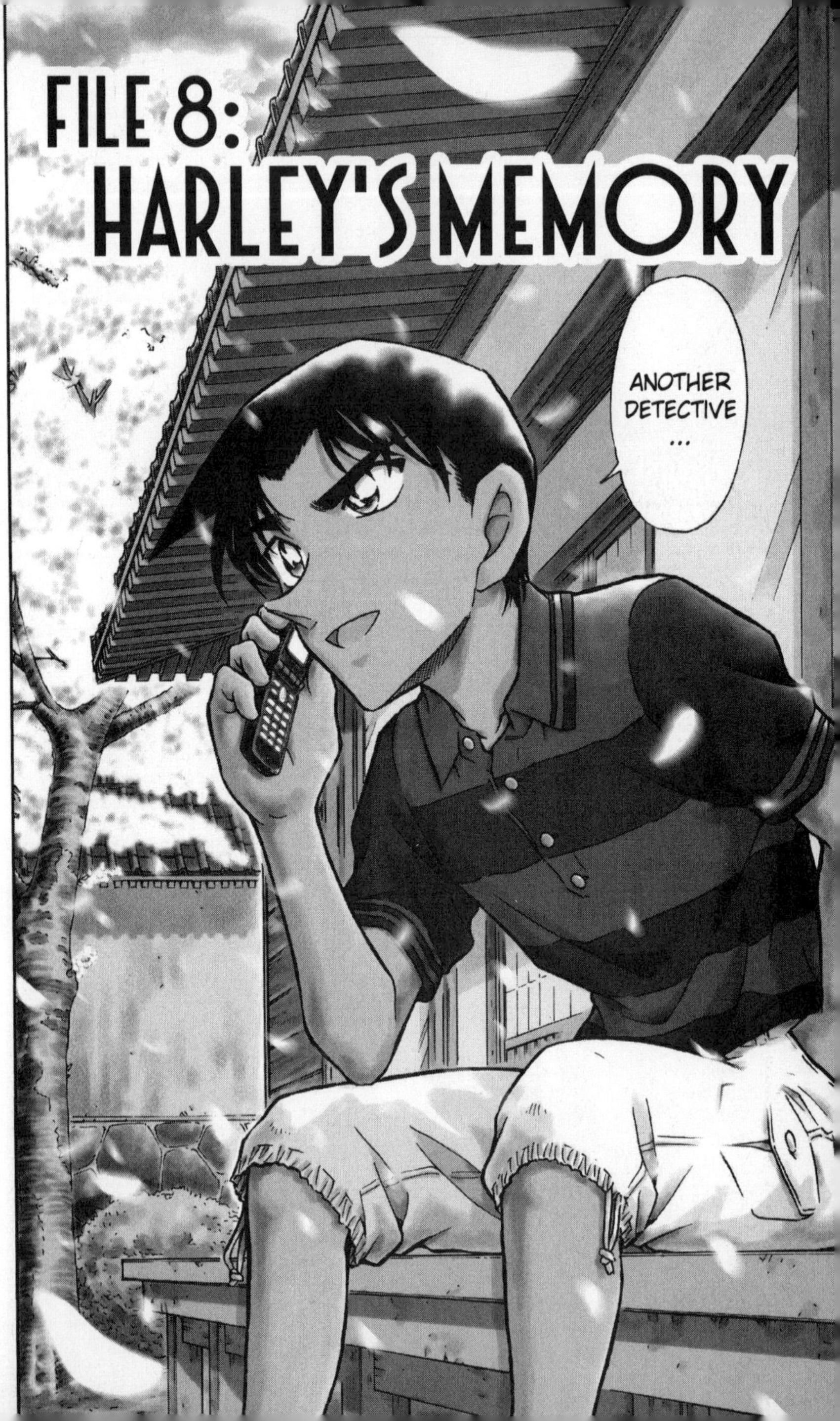
FILE 8:
HARLEY'S MEMORY
ANOTHER DETECTIVE ...

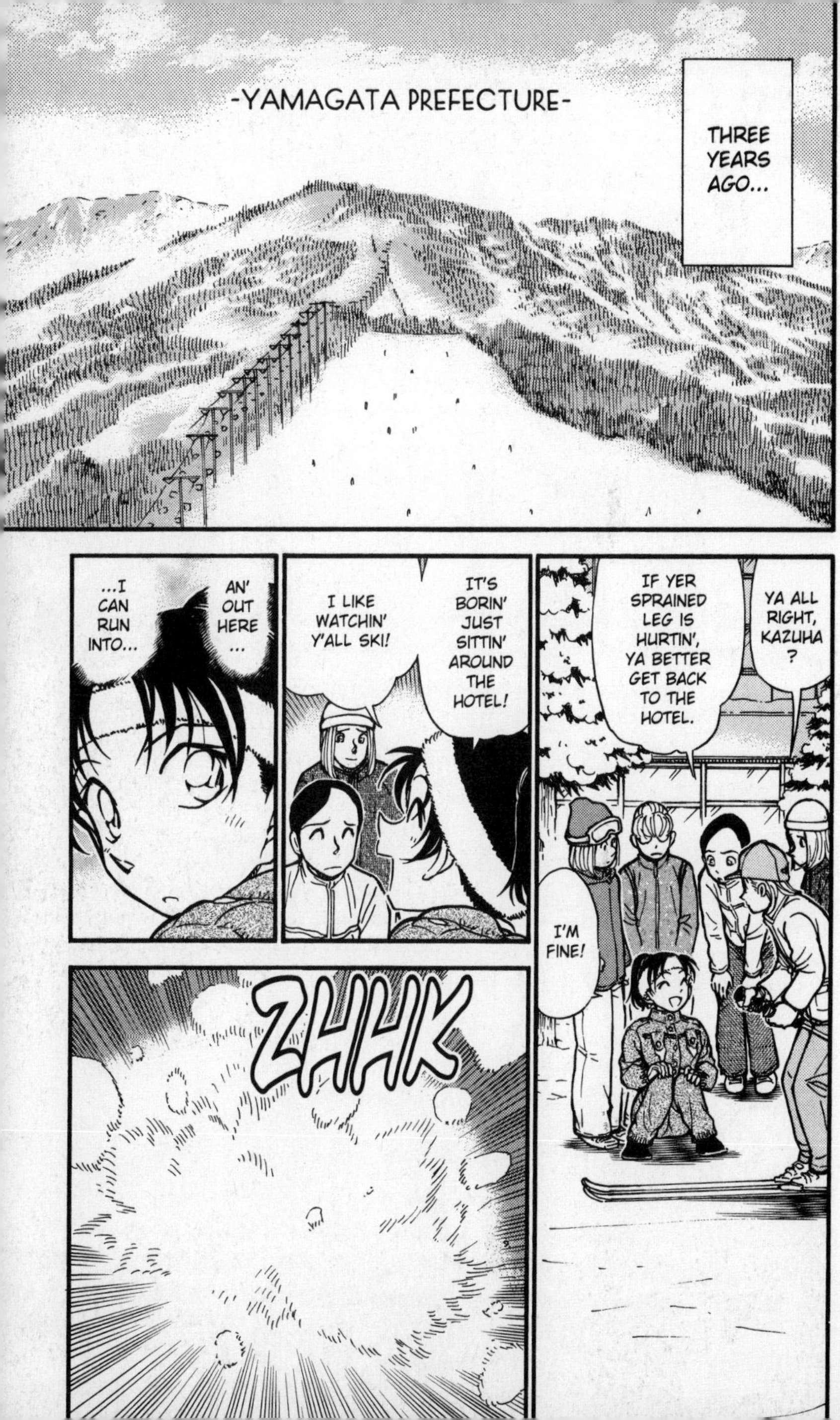
THREE YEARS AGO...
-YAMAGATA PREFECTURE-
YA ALL RIGHT, KAZUHA?
IF YER SPRAINED LEG IS HURTIN', YA BETTER GET BACK TO THE HOTEL.
I'M FINE!
IT'S BORIN' JUST SITTIN' AROUND THE HOTEL!
I LIKE WATCHIN' Y'ALL SKI!
AN' OUT HERE...
...I CAN RUN INTO...
ZHHK

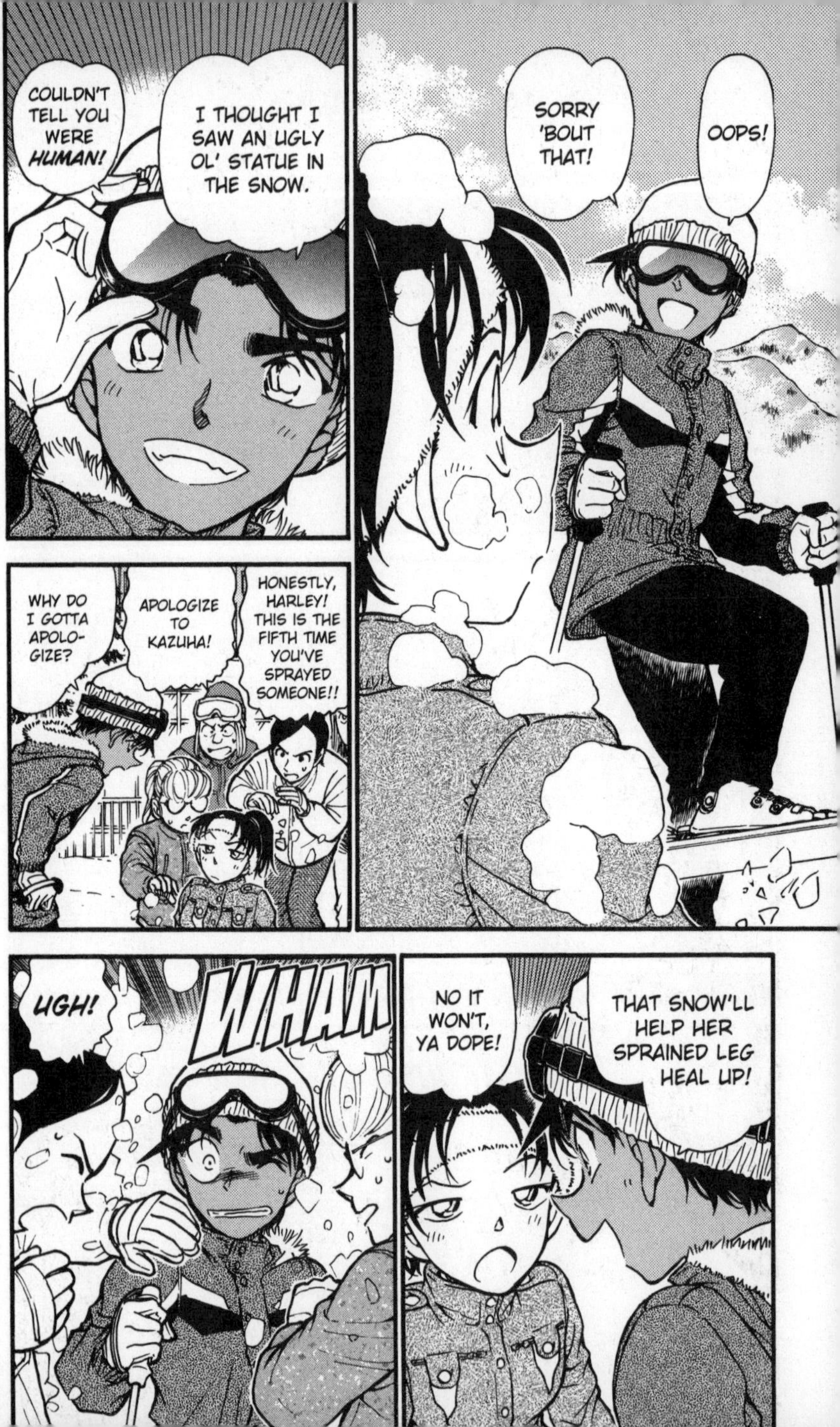
OOPS!
SORRY 'BOUT THAT!
I THOUGHT I SAW AN UGLY OL' STATUE IN THE SNOW.
COULDN'T TELL YOU WERE *HUMAN!*
HONESTLY, HARLEY! THIS IS THE FIFTH TIME YOU'VE SPRAYED SOMEONE!!
APOLOGIZE TO KAZUHA!
WHY DO I GOTTA APOLOGIZE?
THAT SNOW'LL HELP HER SPRAINED LEG HEAL UP!
NO IT WON'T, YA DOPE!
WHAM
UGH!

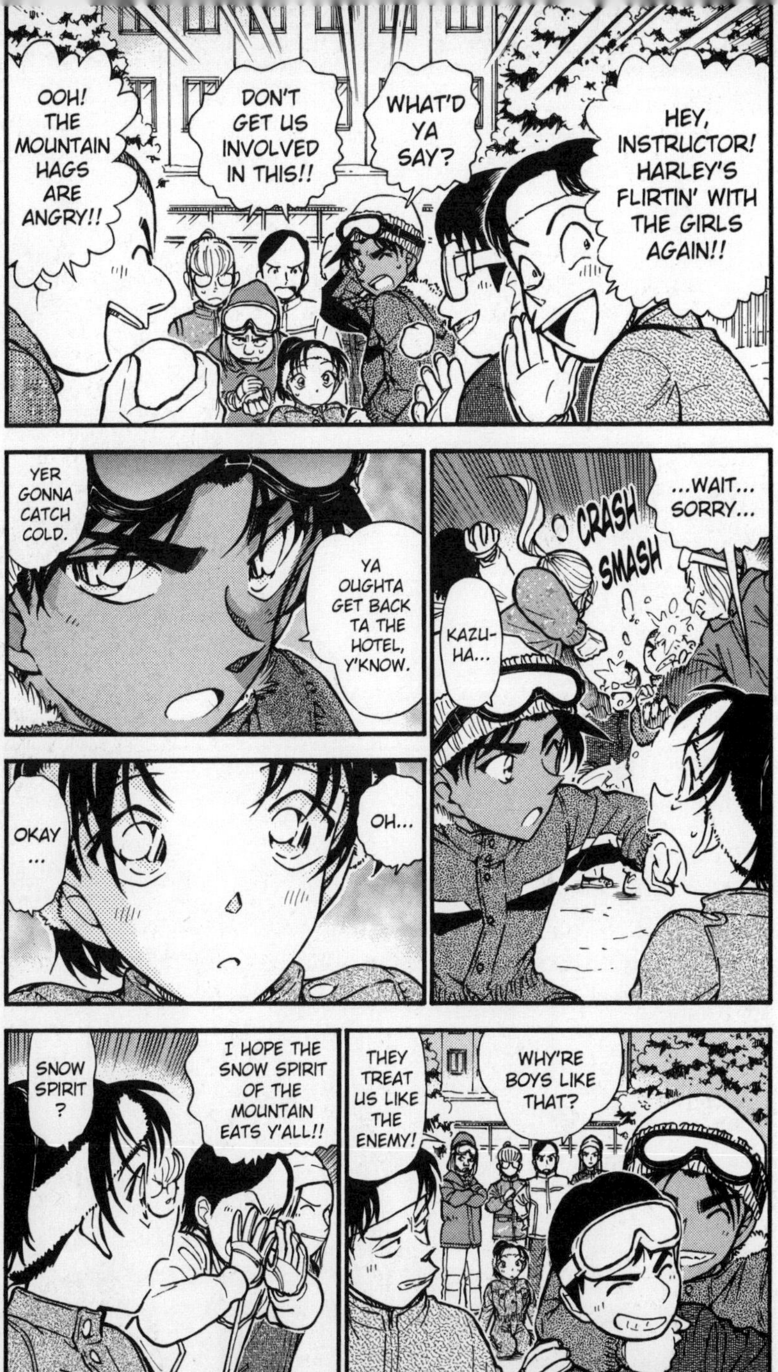
HEY, INSTRUCTOR! HARLEY'S FLIRTIN' WITH THE GIRLS AGAIN!!
WHAT'D YA SAY?
DON'T GET US INVOLVED IN THIS!!
OOH! THE MOUNTAIN HAGS ARE ANGRY!!
...WAIT... SORRY...
CRASH
SMASH
KAZU-HA...
YER GONNA CATCH COLD.
YA OUGHTA GET BACK TA THE HOTEL, Y'KNOW.
OH...
OKAY...
WHY'RE BOYS LIKE THAT?
THEY TREAT US LIKE THE ENEMY!
I HOPE THE SNOW SPIRIT OF THE MOUNTAIN EATS Y'ALL!!
SNOW SPIRIT?

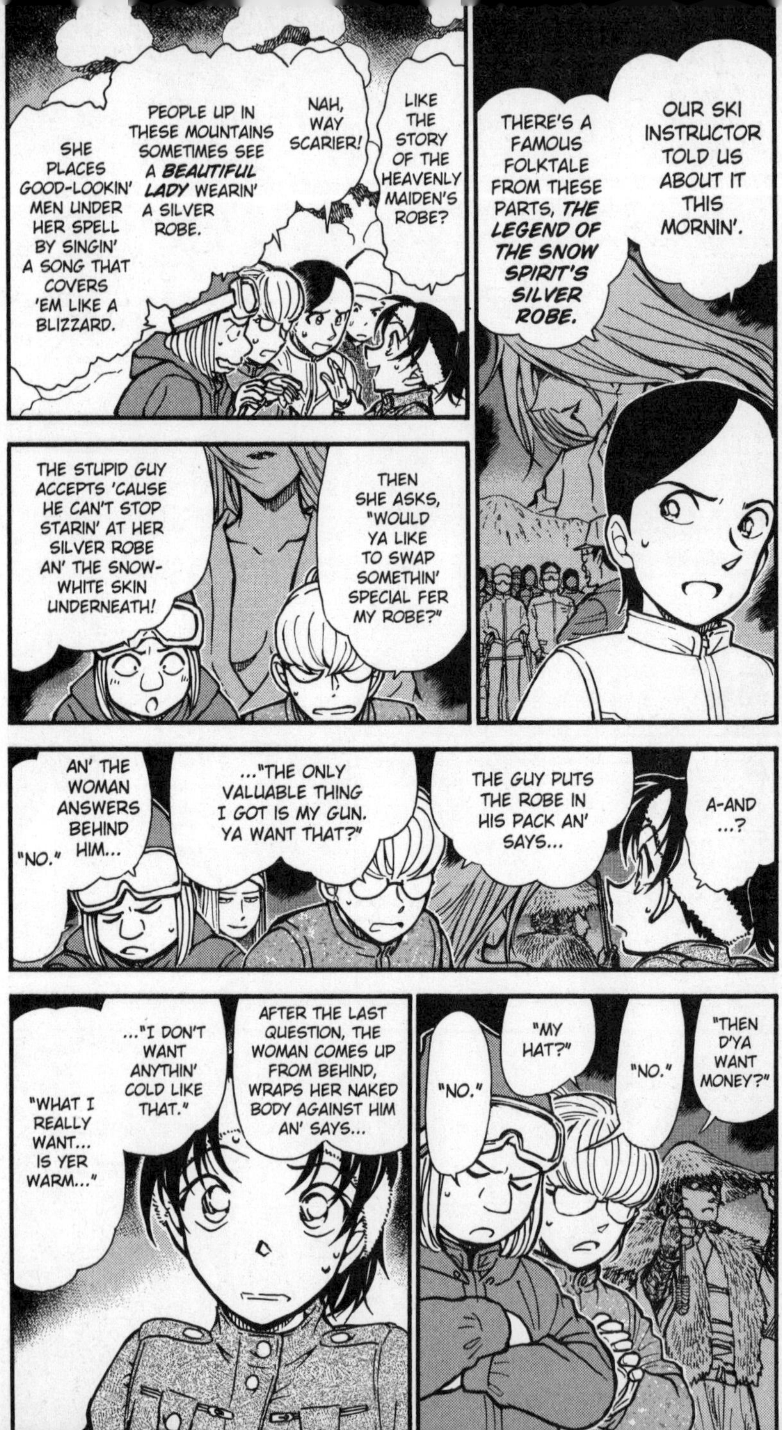
OUR SKI INSTRUCTOR TOLD US ABOUT IT THIS MORNIN'.
THERE'S A FAMOUS FOLKTALE FROM THESE PARTS, ***THE LEGEND OF THE SNOW SPIRIT'S SILVER ROBE.***
LIKE THE STORY OF THE HEAVENLY MAIDEN'S ROBE?
NAH, WAY SCARIER!
PEOPLE UP IN THESE MOUNTAINS SOMETIMES SEE A ***BEAUTIFUL LADY*** WEARIN' A SILVER ROBE.
SHE PLACES GOOD-LOOKIN' MEN UNDER HER SPELL BY SINGIN' A SONG THAT COVERS 'EM LIKE A BLIZZARD.
THEN SHE ASKS, "WOULD YA LIKE TO SWAP SOMETHIN' SPECIAL FER MY ROBE?"
THE STUPID GUY ACCEPTS 'CAUSE HE CAN'T STOP STARIN' AT HER SILVER ROBE AN' THE SNOW-WHITE SKIN UNDERNEATH!
A-AND ...?
THE GUY PUTS THE ROBE IN HIS PACK AN' SAYS...
..."THE ONLY VALUABLE THING I GOT IS MY GUN. YA WANT THAT?"
AN' THE WOMAN ANSWERS BEHIND HIM...
"NO."
"THEN D'YA WANT MONEY?"
"NO."
"MY HAT?"
"NO."
AFTER THE LAST QUESTION, THE WOMAN COMES UP FROM BEHIND, WRAPS HER NAKED BODY AGAINST HIM AN' SAYS...
..."I DON'T WANT ANYTHIN' COLD LIKE THAT."
"WHAT I REALLY WANT... IS YER WARM..."

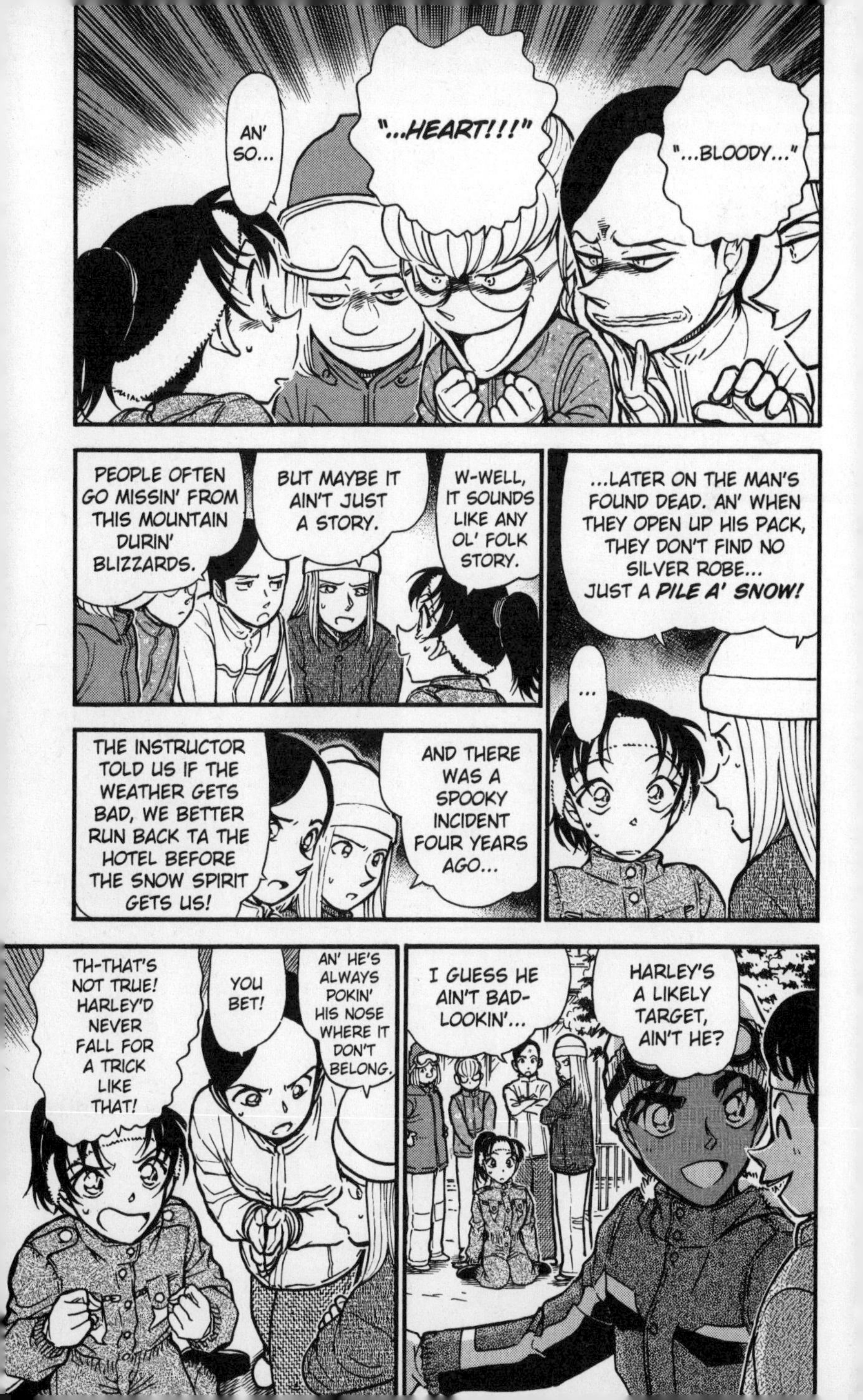
"...BLOODY..."
"...HEART!!!"
AN' SO...
...LATER ON THE MAN'S FOUND DEAD. AN' WHEN THEY OPEN UP HIS PACK, THEY DON'T FIND NO SILVER ROBE... JUST A *PILE A' SNOW!*
...
W-WELL, IT SOUNDS LIKE ANY OL' FOLK STORY.
BUT MAYBE IT AIN'T JUST A STORY.
PEOPLE OFTEN GO MISSIN' FROM THIS MOUNTAIN DURIN' BLIZZARDS.
AND THERE WAS A SPOOKY INCIDENT FOUR YEARS AGO...
THE INSTRUCTOR TOLD US IF THE WEATHER GETS BAD, WE BETTER RUN BACK TA THE HOTEL BEFORE THE SNOW SPIRIT GETS US!
HARLEY'S A LIKELY TARGET, AIN'T HE?
I GUESS HE AIN'T BAD-LOOKIN'...
AN' HE'S ALWAYS POKIN' HIS NOSE WHERE IT DON'T BELONG.
YOU BET!
TH-THAT'S NOT TRUE! HARLEY'D NEVER FALL FOR A TRICK LIKE THAT!

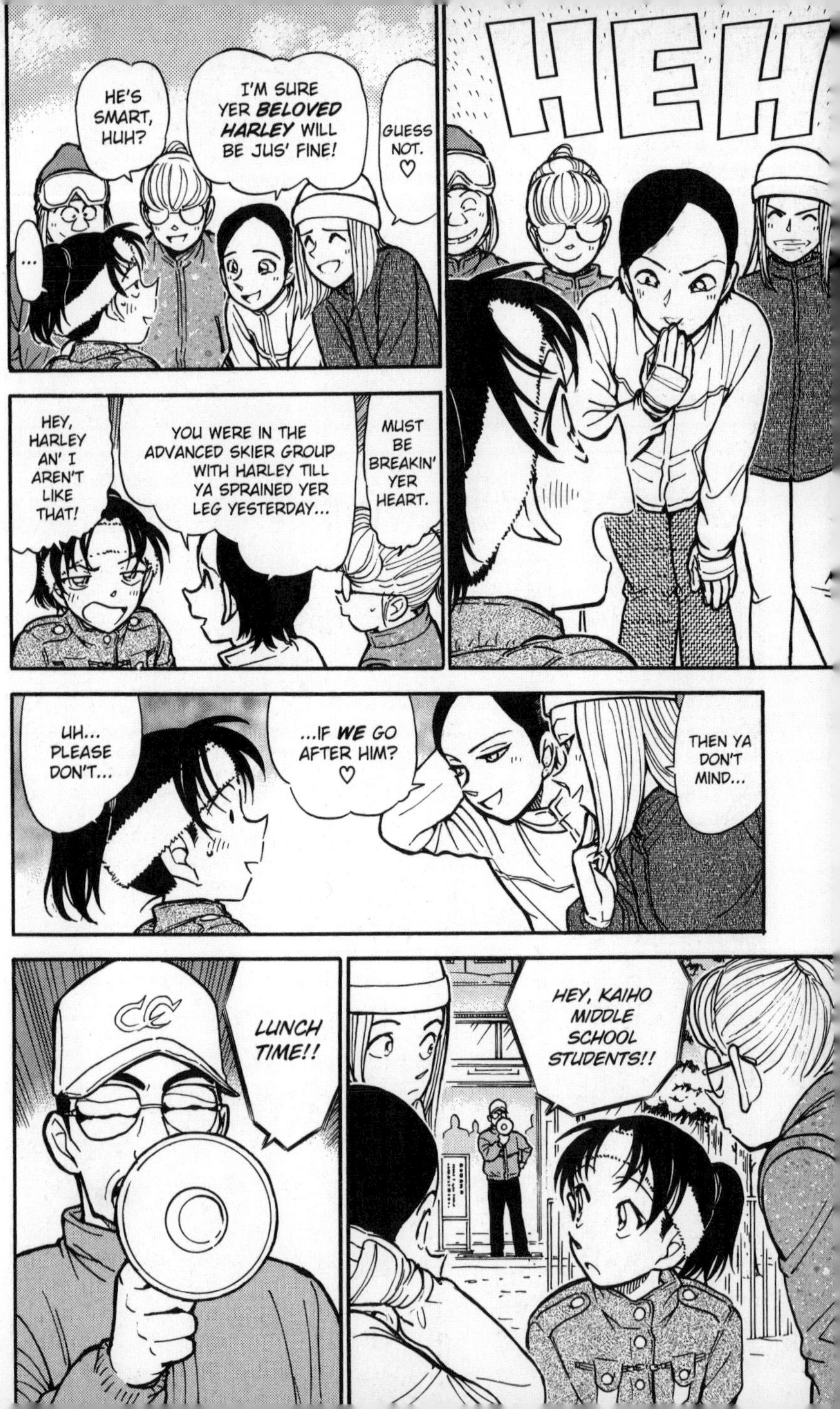
HEH
GUESS NOT. ♥
I'M SURE YER BELOVED HARLEY WILL BE JUS' FINE!
HE'S SMART, HUH?
...
MUST BE BREAKIN' YER HEART.
YOU WERE IN THE ADVANCED SKIER GROUP WITH HARLEY TILL YA SPRAINED YER LEG YESTERDAY...
HEY, HARLEY AN' I AREN'T LIKE THAT!
THEN YA DON'T MIND...
...IF WE GO AFTER HIM? ♥
UH... PLEASE DON'T...
HEY, KAIHO MIDDLE SCHOOL STUDENTS!!
LUNCH TIME!!

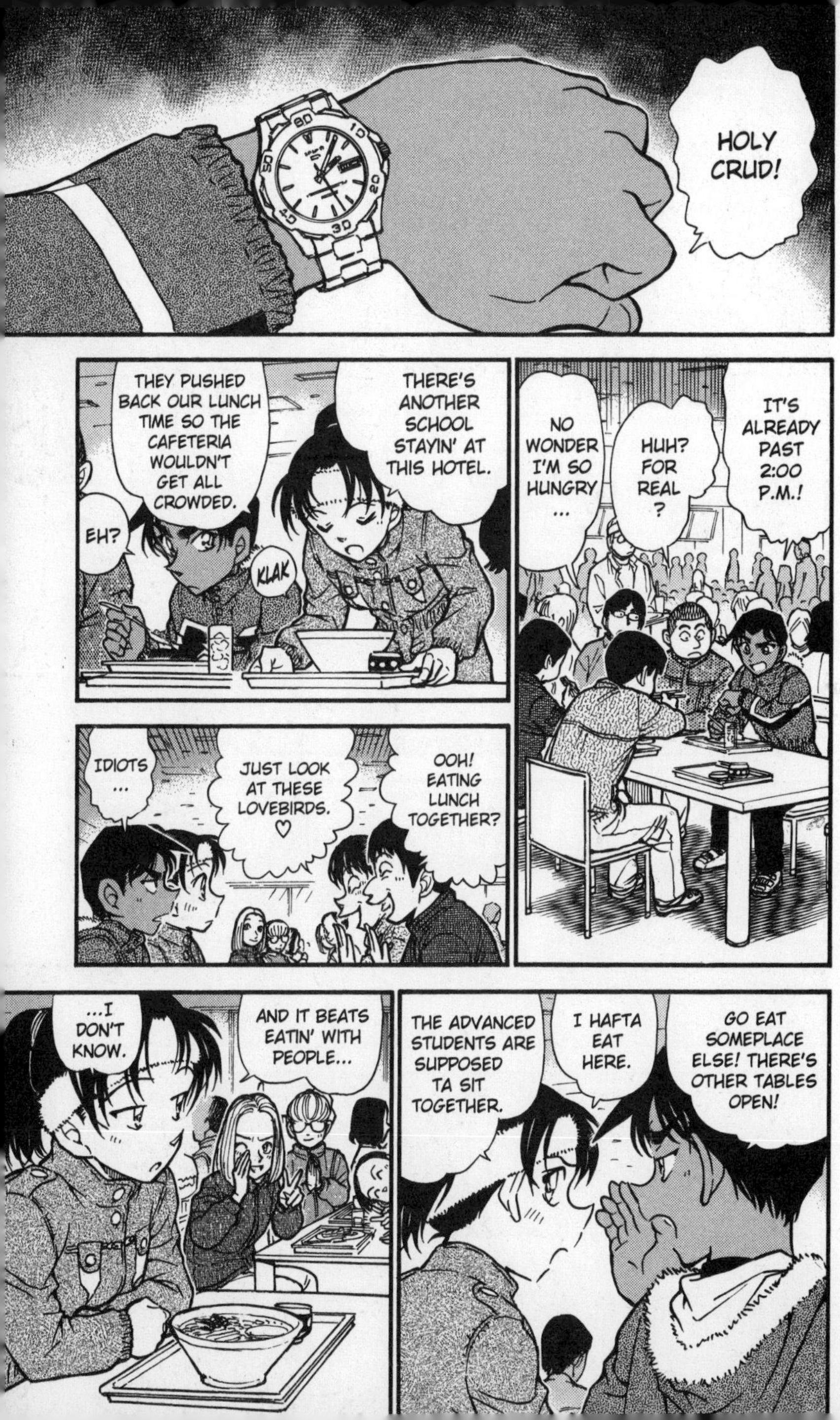
HOLY CRUD!
IT'S ALREADY PAST 2:00 P.M.!
HUH? FOR REAL?
NO WONDER I'M SO HUNGRY...
THERE'S ANOTHER SCHOOL STAYIN' AT THIS HOTEL.
THEY PUSHED BACK OUR LUNCH TIME SO THE CAFETERIA WOULDN'T GET ALL CROWDED.
KLAK
EH?
OOH! EATING LUNCH TOGETHER?
JUST LOOK AT THESE LOVEBIRDS. ♡
IDIOTS...
GO EAT SOMEPLACE ELSE! THERE'S OTHER TABLES OPEN!
I HAFTA EAT HERE.
THE ADVANCED STUDENTS ARE SUPPOSED TA SIT TOGETHER.
AND IT BEATS EATIN' WITH PEOPLE...
...I DON'T KNOW.

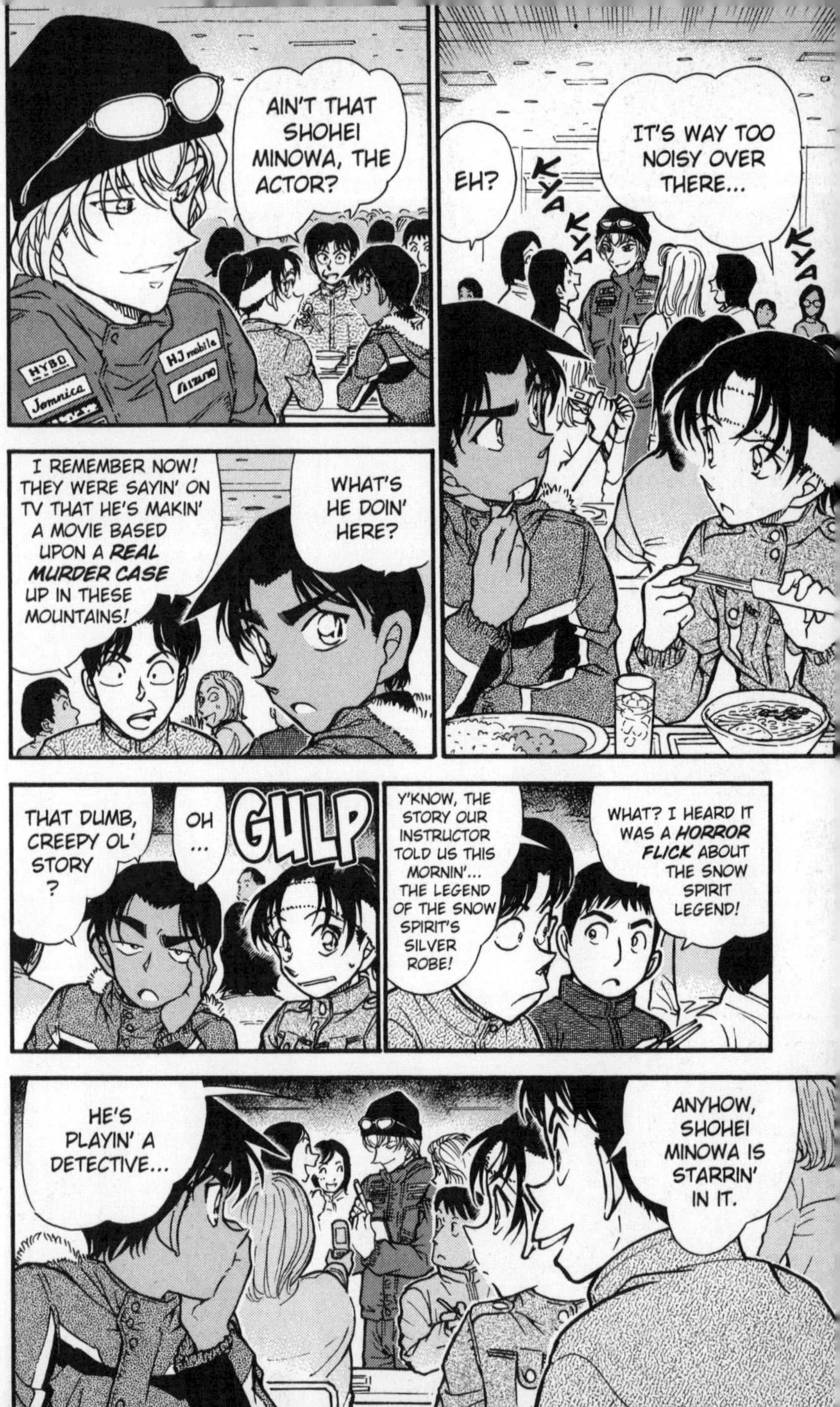
IT'S WAY TOO NOISY OVER THERE...
KYA KYA KYA
EH?
AIN'T THAT SHOHEI MINOWA, THE ACTOR?
WHAT'S HE DOIN' HERE?
I REMEMBER NOW! THEY WERE SAYIN' ON TV THAT HE'S MAKIN' A MOVIE BASED UPON A **REAL MURDER CASE** UP IN THESE MOUNTAINS!
WHAT? I HEARD IT WAS A **HORROR FLICK** ABOUT THE SNOW SPIRIT LEGEND!
Y'KNOW, THE STORY OUR INSTRUCTOR TOLD US THIS MORNIN'... THE LEGEND OF THE SNOW SPIRIT'S SILVER ROBE!
GULP
OH ...
THAT DUMB, CREEPY OL' STORY ?
ANYHOW, SHOHEI MINOWA IS STARRIN' IN IT.
HE'S PLAYIN' A DETECTIVE...

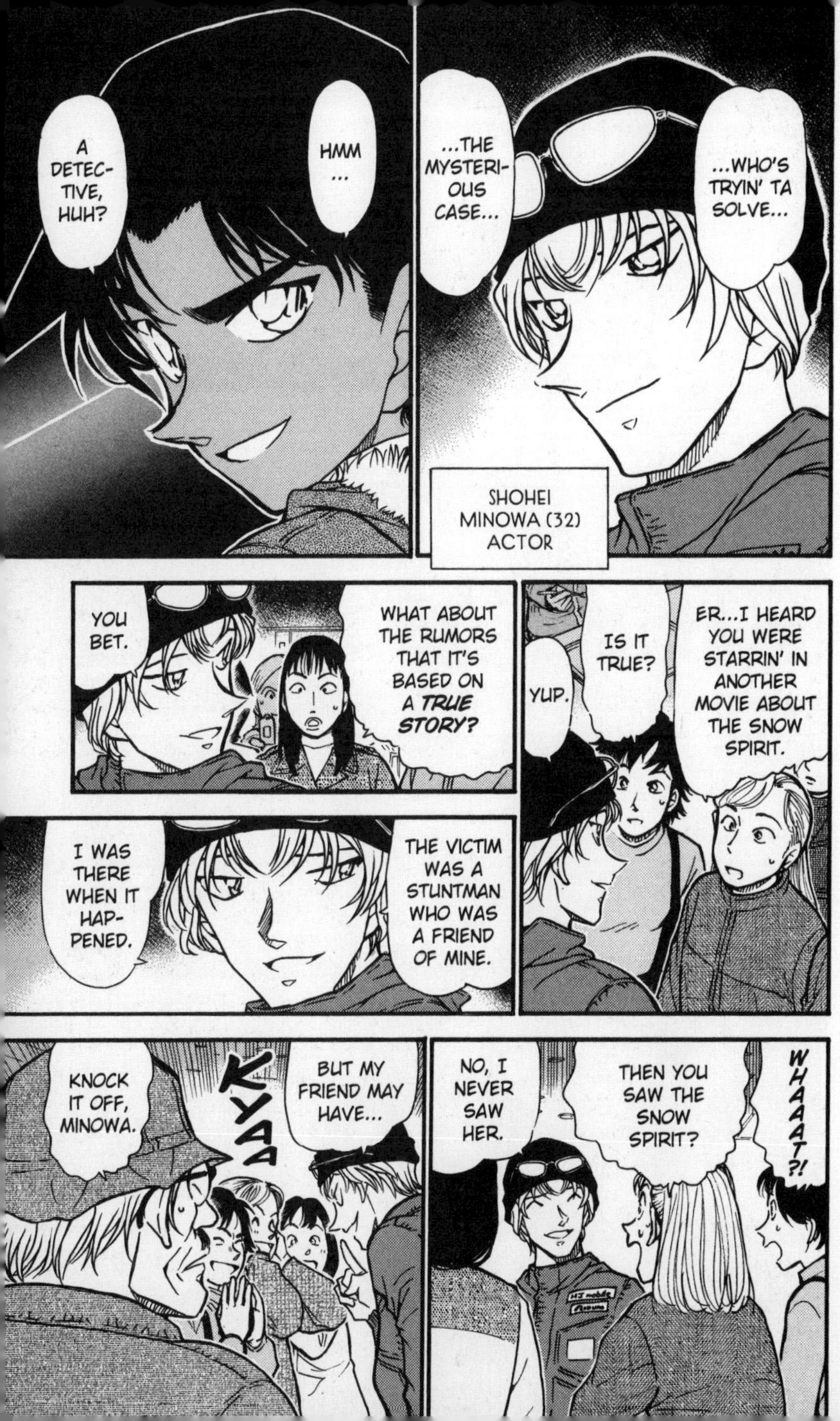
...WHO'S TRYIN' TA SOLVE...
...THE MYSTERIOUS CASE...
SHOHEI MINOWA (32) ACTOR
HMM ...
A DETECTIVE, HUH?
ER...I HEARD YOU WERE STARRIN' IN ANOTHER MOVIE ABOUT THE SNOW SPIRIT.
IS IT TRUE?
YUP.
WHAT ABOUT THE RUMORS THAT IT'S BASED ON A TRUE STORY?
YOU BET.
THE VICTIM WAS A STUNTMAN WHO WAS A FRIEND OF MINE.
I WAS THERE WHEN IT HAPPENED.
WHAAAT?!
THEN YOU SAW THE SNOW SPIRIT?
NO, I NEVER SAW HER.
BUT MY FRIEND MAY HAVE...
KYAA
KNOCK IT OFF, MINOWA.

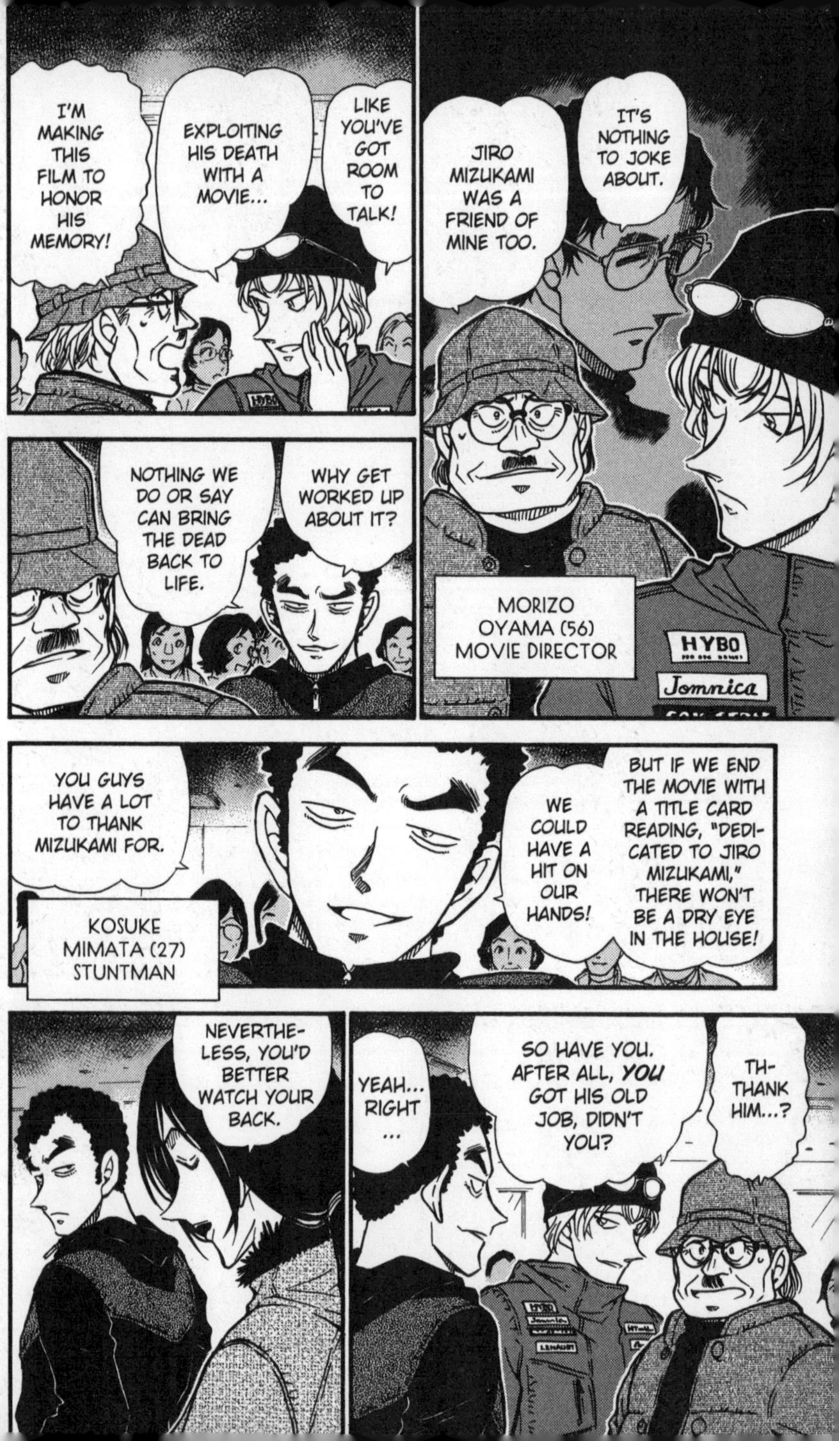
IT'S NOTHING TO JOKE ABOUT.
JIRO MIZUKAMI WAS A FRIEND OF MINE TOO.
HYBO
Jomnica
MORIZO OYAMA (56) MOVIE DIRECTOR
LIKE YOU'VE GOT ROOM TO TALK!
EXPLOITING HIS DEATH WITH A MOVIE...
I'M MAKING THIS FILM TO HONOR HIS MEMORY!
WHY GET WORKED UP ABOUT IT?
NOTHING WE DO OR SAY CAN BRING THE DEAD BACK TO LIFE.
BUT IF WE END THE MOVIE WITH A TITLE CARD READING, "DEDI-CATED TO JIRO MIZUKAMI," THERE WON'T BE A DRY EYE IN THE HOUSE!
WE COULD HAVE A HIT ON OUR HANDS!
YOU GUYS HAVE A LOT TO THANK MIZUKAMI FOR.
KOSUKE MIMATA (27) STUNTMAN
TH-THANK HIM...?
SO HAVE YOU. AFTER ALL, *YOU* GOT HIS OLD JOB, DIDN'T YOU?
YEAH... RIGHT...
NEVERTHE-LESS, YOU'D BETTER WATCH YOUR BACK.

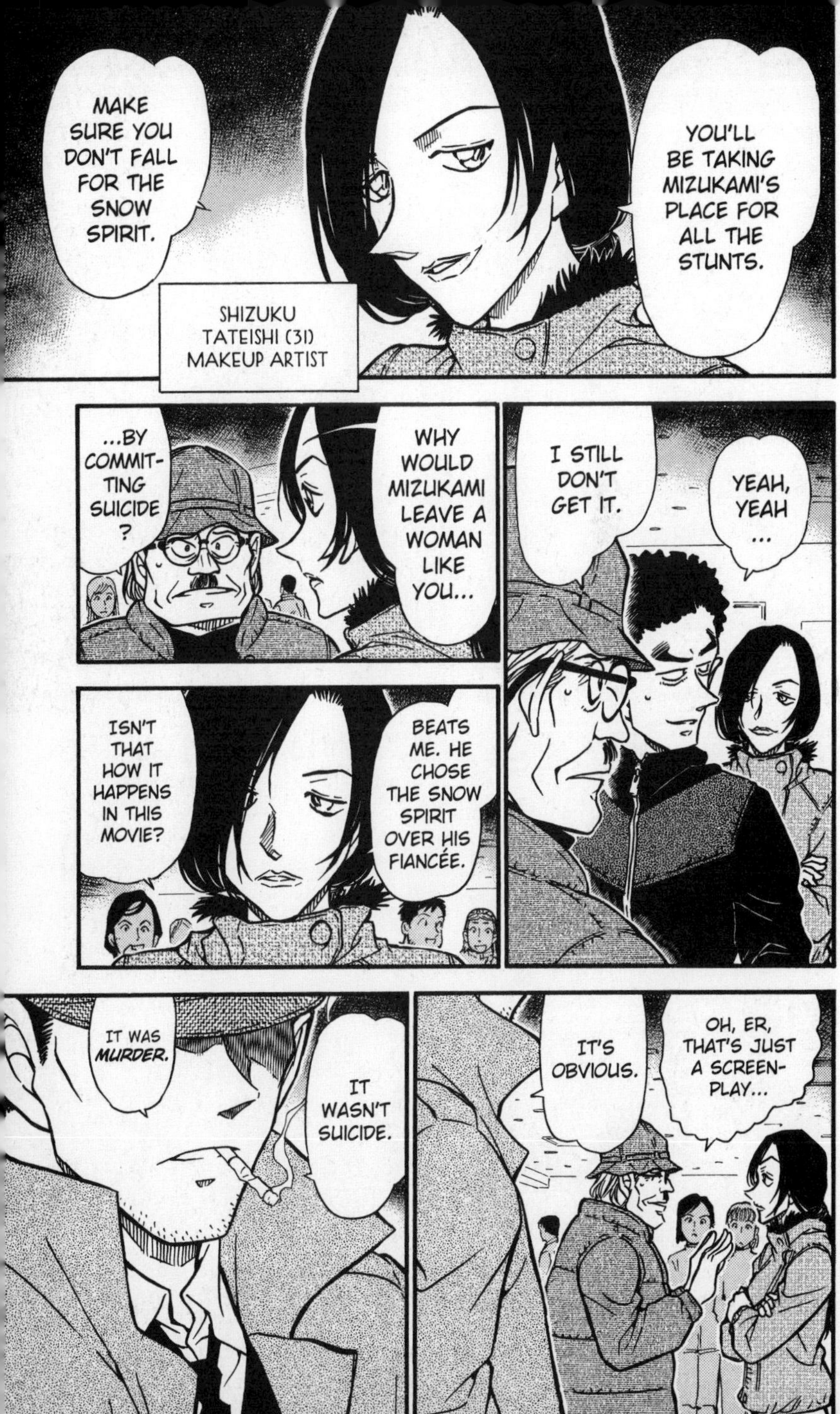
YOU'LL BE TAKING MIZUKAMI'S PLACE FOR ALL THE STUNTS.
MAKE SURE YOU DON'T FALL FOR THE SNOW SPIRIT.
SHIZUKU TATEISHI (31) MAKEUP ARTIST
I STILL DON'T GET IT.
YEAH, YEAH...
WHY WOULD MIZUKAMI LEAVE A WOMAN LIKE YOU...
...BY COMMITTING SUICIDE?
BEATS ME. HE CHOSE THE SNOW SPIRIT OVER HIS FIANCÉE.
ISN'T THAT HOW IT HAPPENS IN THIS MOVIE?
OH, ER, THAT'S JUST A SCREENPLAY...
IT'S OBVIOUS.
IT WASN'T SUICIDE.
IT WAS *MURDER.*

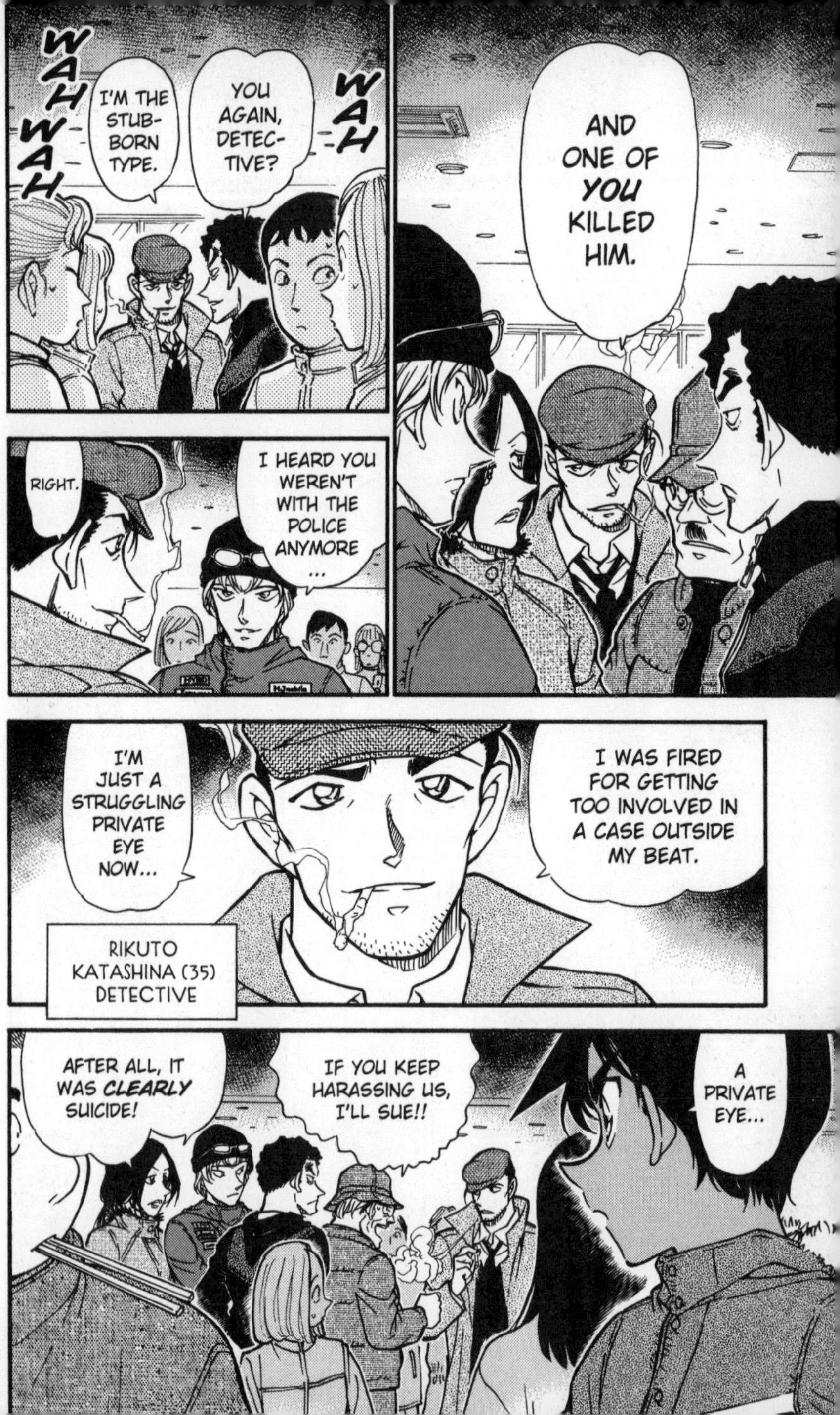
AND ONE OF YOU KILLED HIM.
WAH WAH
YOU AGAIN, DETECTIVE?
I'M THE STUBBORN TYPE.
WAH WAH
I HEARD YOU WEREN'T WITH THE POLICE ANYMORE ...
RIGHT.
I WAS FIRED FOR GETTING TOO INVOLVED IN A CASE OUTSIDE MY BEAT.
I'M JUST A STRUGGLING PRIVATE EYE NOW...
RIKUTO KATASHINA (35) DETECTIVE
A PRIVATE EYE...
IF YOU KEEP HARASSING US, I'LL SUE!!
AFTER ALL, IT WAS CLEARLY SUICIDE!

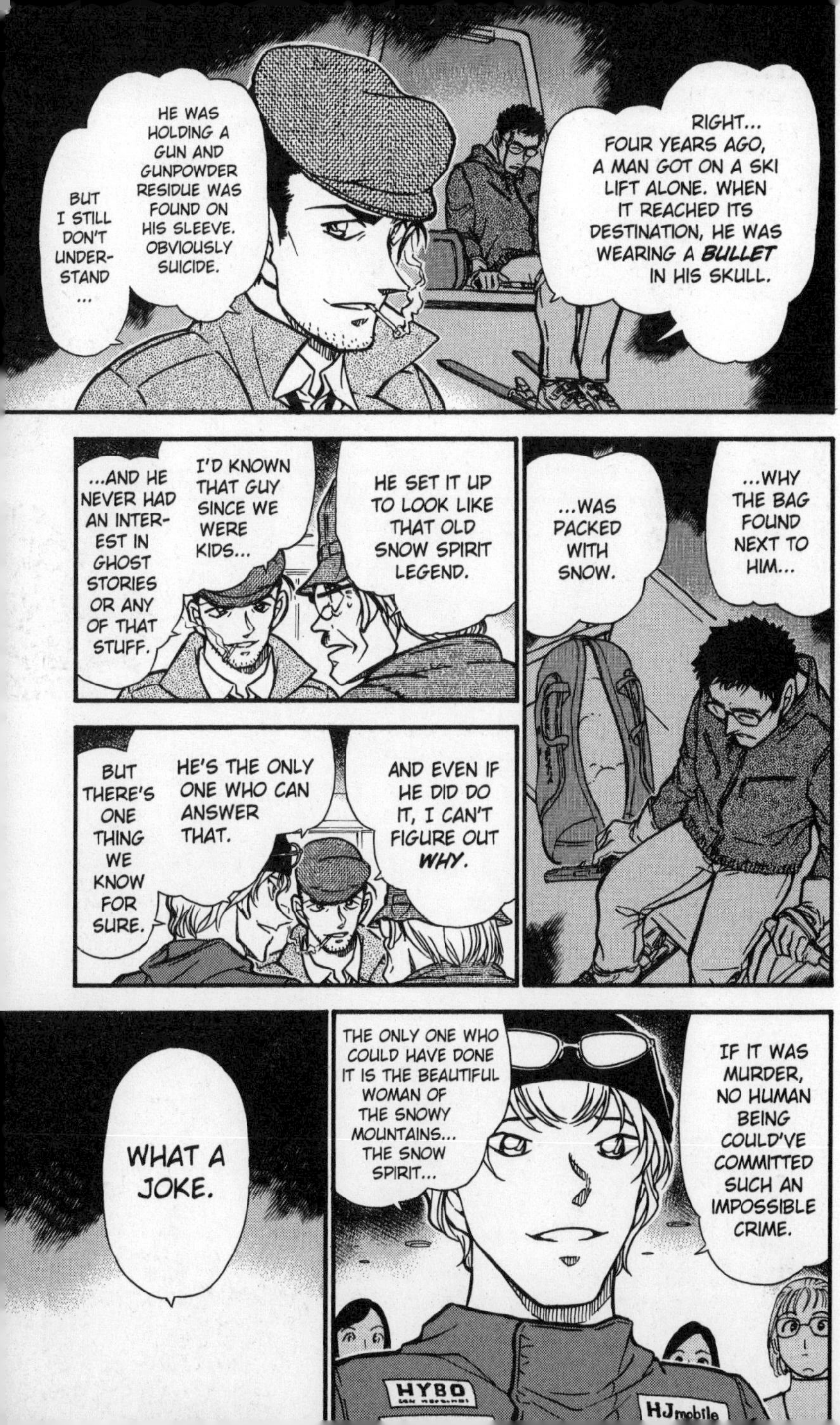
RIGHT... FOUR YEARS AGO, A MAN GOT ON A SKI LIFT ALONE. WHEN IT REACHED ITS DESTINATION, HE WAS WEARING A ***BULLET*** IN HIS SKULL.
HE WAS HOLDING A GUN AND GUNPOWDER RESIDUE WAS FOUND ON HIS SLEEVE. OBVIOUSLY SUICIDE.
BUT I STILL DON'T UNDER-STAND ...
...WHY THE BAG FOUND NEXT TO HIM...
...WAS PACKED WITH SNOW.
HE SET IT UP TO LOOK LIKE THAT OLD SNOW SPIRIT LEGEND.
I'D KNOWN THAT GUY SINCE WE WERE KIDS...
...AND HE NEVER HAD AN INTER-EST IN GHOST STORIES OR ANY OF THAT STUFF.
AND EVEN IF HE DID DO IT, I CAN'T FIGURE OUT ***WHY***.
HE'S THE ONLY ONE WHO CAN ANSWER THAT.
BUT THERE'S ONE THING WE KNOW FOR SURE.
IF IT WAS MURDER, NO HUMAN BEING COULD'VE COMMITTED SUCH AN IMPOSSIBLE CRIME.
THE ONLY ONE WHO COULD HAVE DONE IT IS THE BEAUTIFUL WOMAN OF THE SNOWY MOUNTAINS... THE SNOW SPIRIT...
WHAT A JOKE.
HYBO
HJmobile

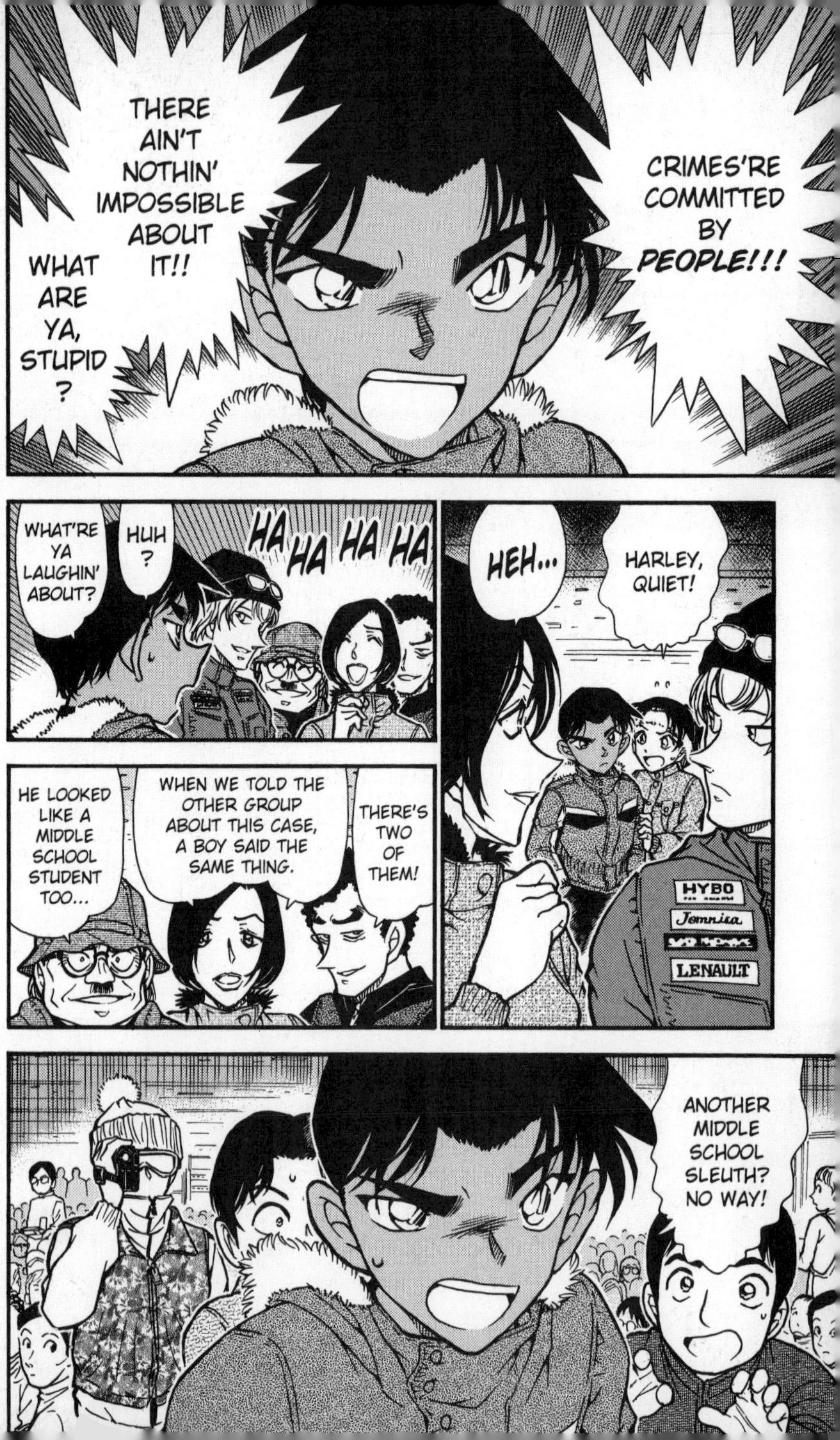
CRIMES'RE COMMITTED BY PEOPLE!!!
THERE AIN'T NOTHIN' IMPOSSIBLE ABOUT IT!!
WHAT ARE YA, STUPID?
HARLEY, QUIET!
HEH...
HYBO
LENAULT
HA HA HA HA
HUH?
WHAT'RE YA LAUGHIN' ABOUT?
THERE'S TWO OF THEM!
WHEN WE TOLD THE OTHER GROUP ABOUT THIS CASE, A BOY SAID THE SAME THING.
HE LOOKED LIKE A MIDDLE SCHOOL STUDENT TOO...
ANOTHER MIDDLE SCHOOL SLEUTH? NO WAY!

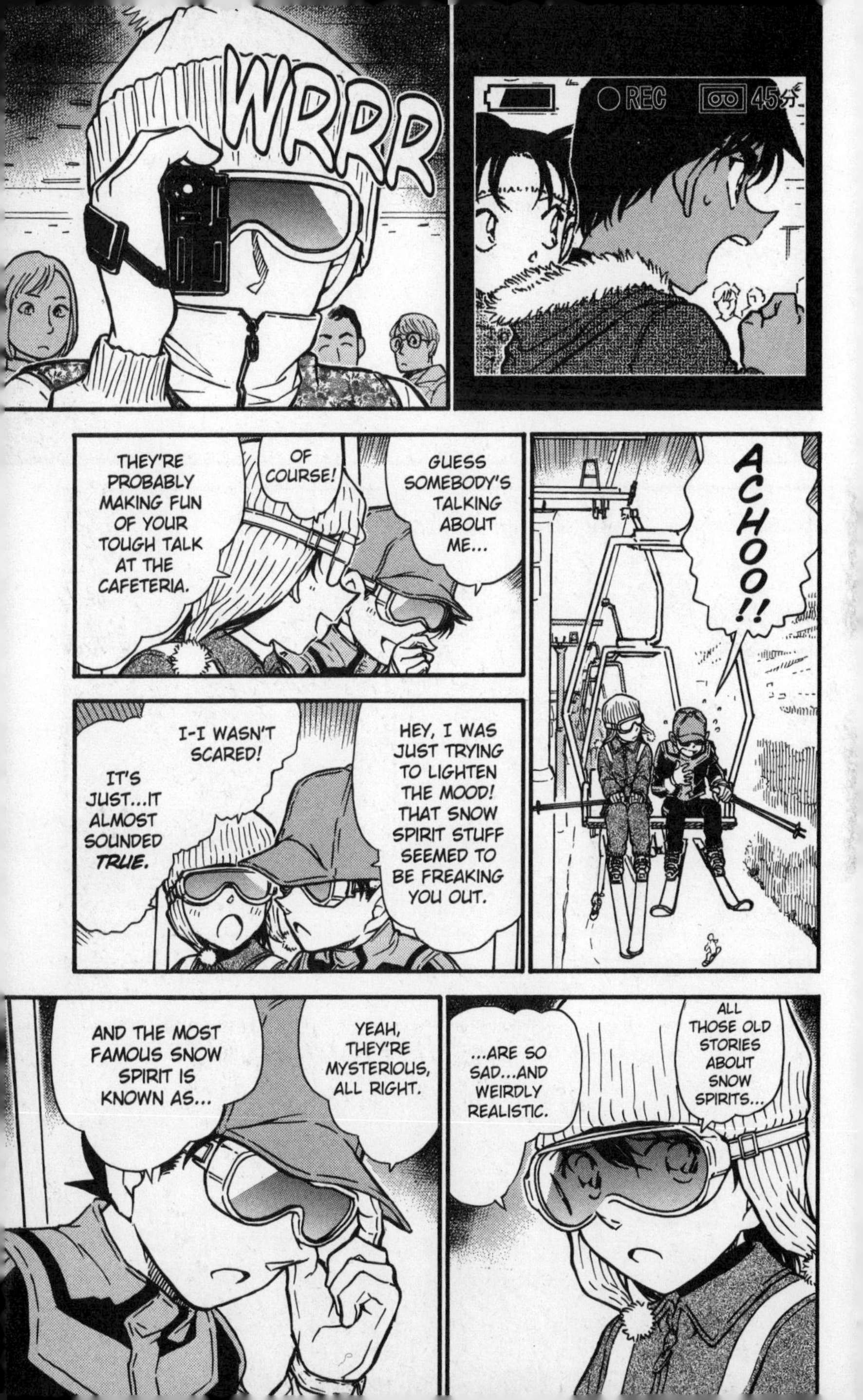
REC
45分
WRRR
ACHOO!!
GUESS SOMEBODY'S TALKING ABOUT ME...
OF COURSE!
THEY'RE PROBABLY MAKING FUN OF YOUR TOUGH TALK AT THE CAFETERIA.
HEY, I WAS JUST TRYING TO LIGHTEN THE MOOD! THAT SNOW SPIRIT STUFF SEEMED TO BE FREAKING YOU OUT.
I-I WASN'T SCARED!
IT'S JUST...IT ALMOST SOUNDED *TRUE*.
ALL THOSE OLD STORIES ABOUT SNOW SPIRITS...
...ARE SO SAD...AND WEIRDLY REALISTIC.
YEAH, THEY'RE MYSTERIOUS, ALL RIGHT.
AND THE MOST FAMOUS SNOW SPIRIT IS KNOWN AS...

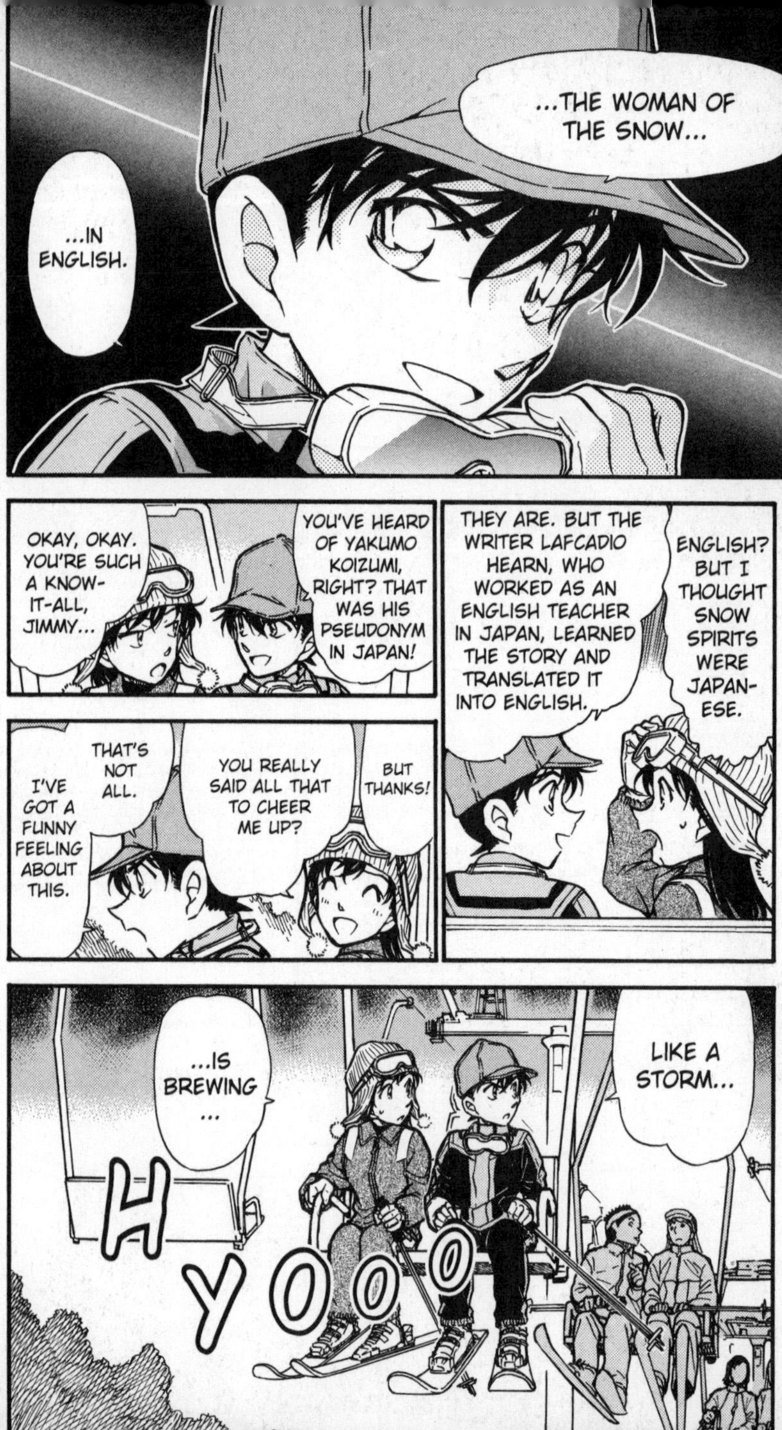
...THE WOMAN OF THE SNOW...
...IN ENGLISH.
ENGLISH? BUT I THOUGHT SNOW SPIRITS WERE JAPANESE.
THEY ARE. BUT THE WRITER LAFCADIO HEARN, WHO WORKED AS AN ENGLISH TEACHER IN JAPAN, LEARNED THE STORY AND TRANSLATED IT INTO ENGLISH.
YOU'VE HEARD OF YAKUMO KOIZUMI, RIGHT? THAT WAS HIS PSEUDONYM IN JAPAN!
OKAY, OKAY. YOU'RE SUCH A KNOW-IT-ALL, JIMMY...
BUT THANKS!
YOU REALLY SAID ALL THAT TO CHEER ME UP?
THAT'S NOT ALL.
I'VE GOT A FUNNY FEELING ABOUT THIS.
LIKE A STORM...
...IS BREWING...
HYOOO

FILE 9: SCHEME OF THE SNOW SPIRIT

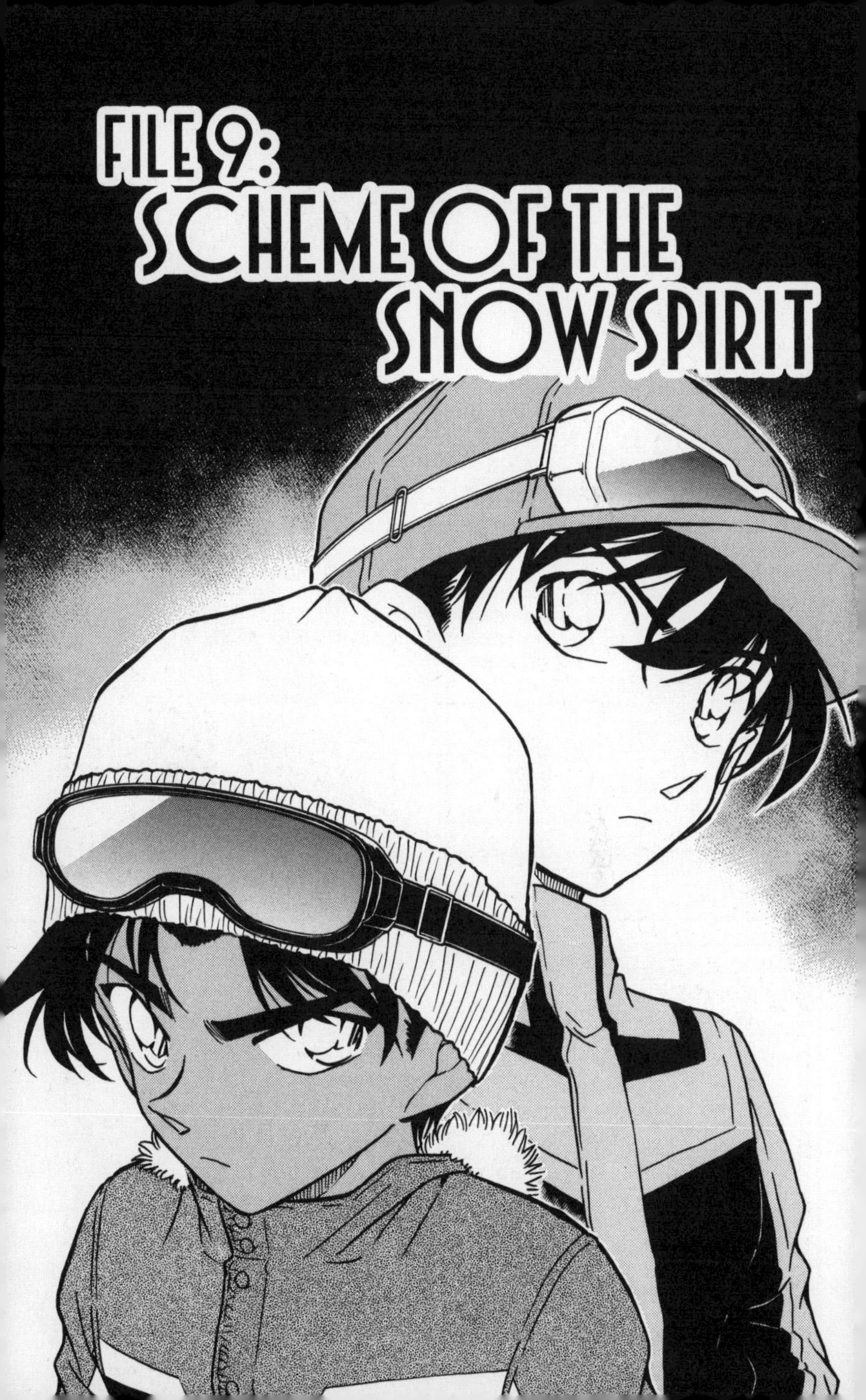

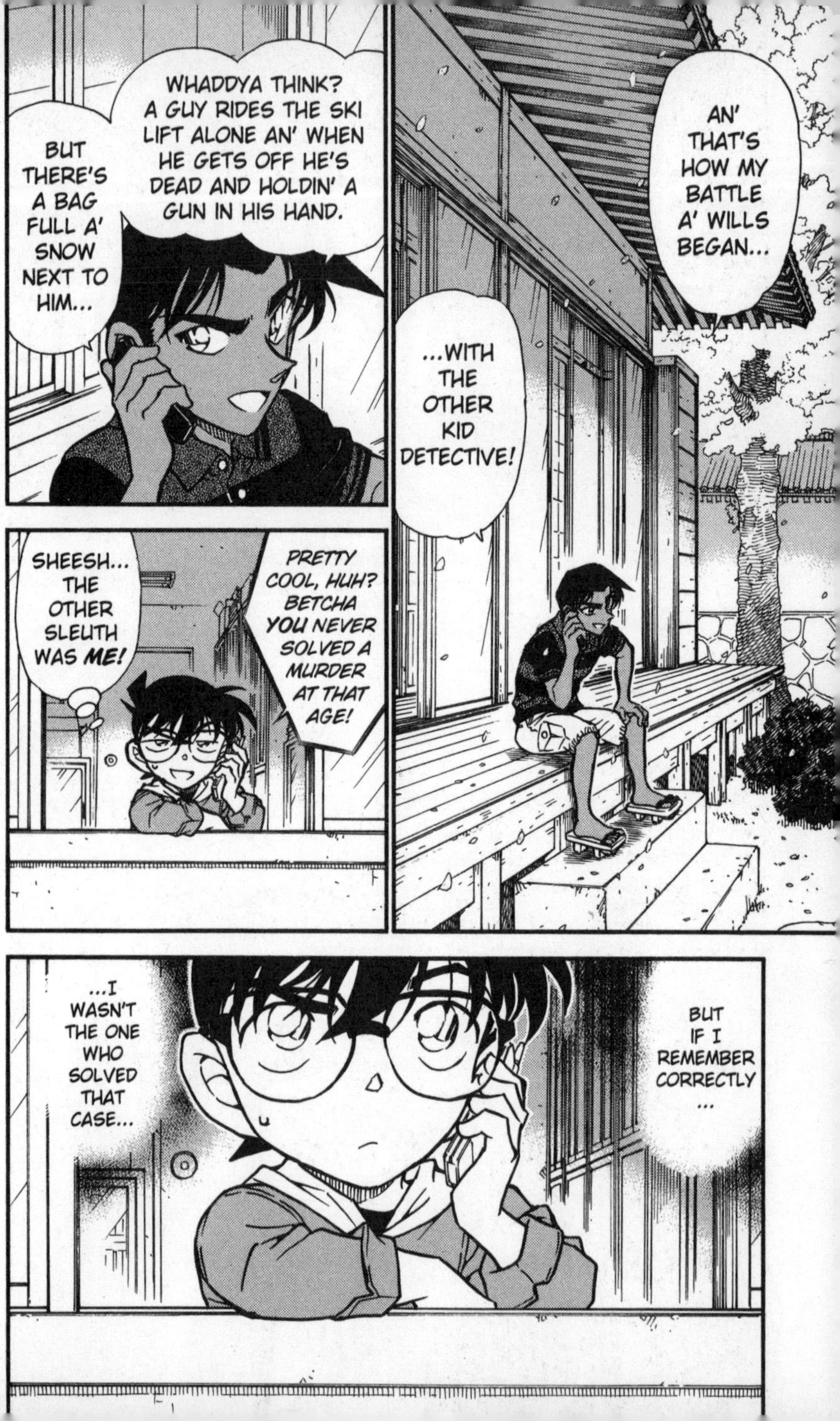
AN' THAT'S HOW MY BATTLE A' WILLS BEGAN...
...WITH THE OTHER KID DETECTIVE!
WHADDYA THINK? A GUY RIDES THE SKI LIFT ALONE AN' WHEN HE GETS OFF HE'S DEAD AND HOLDIN' A GUN IN HIS HAND.
BUT THERE'S A BAG FULL A' SNOW NEXT TO HIM...
PRETTY COOL, HUH? BETCHA YOU NEVER SOLVED A MURDER AT THAT AGE!
SHEESH... THE OTHER SLEUTH WAS ME!
BUT IF I REMEMBER CORRECTLY...
...I WASN'T THE ONE WHO SOLVED THAT CASE...

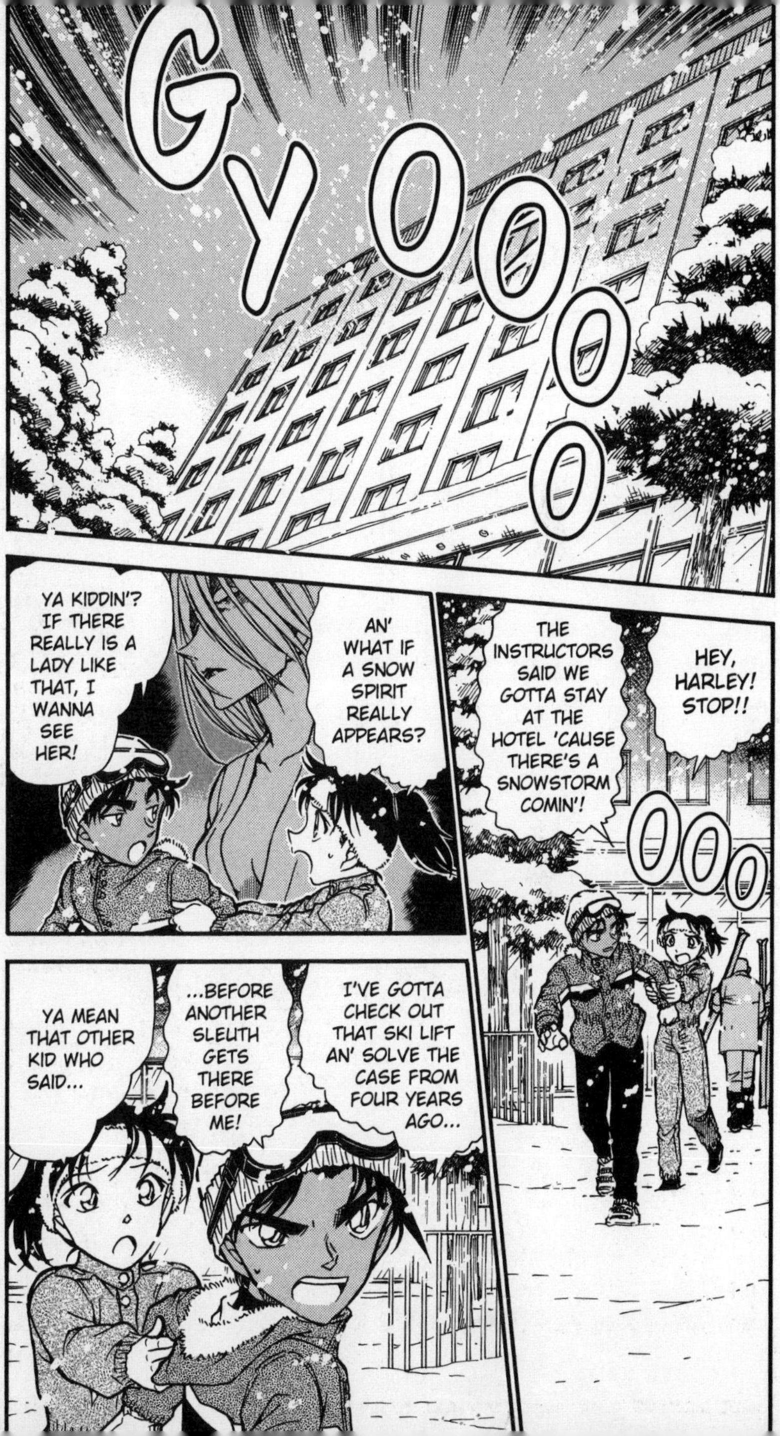
GYOOOOO
HEY, HARLEY! STOP!!
THE INSTRUCTORS SAID WE GOTTA STAY AT THE HOTEL 'CAUSE THERE'S A SNOWSTORM COMIN'!
OOO
AN' WHAT IF A SNOW SPIRIT REALLY APPEARS?
YA KIDDIN'? IF THERE REALLY IS A LADY LIKE THAT, I WANNA SEE HER!
I'VE GOTTA CHECK OUT THAT SKI LIFT AN' SOLVE THE CASE FROM FOUR YEARS AGO...
...BEFORE ANOTHER SLEUTH GETS THERE BEFORE ME!
YA MEAN THAT OTHER KID WHO SAID...

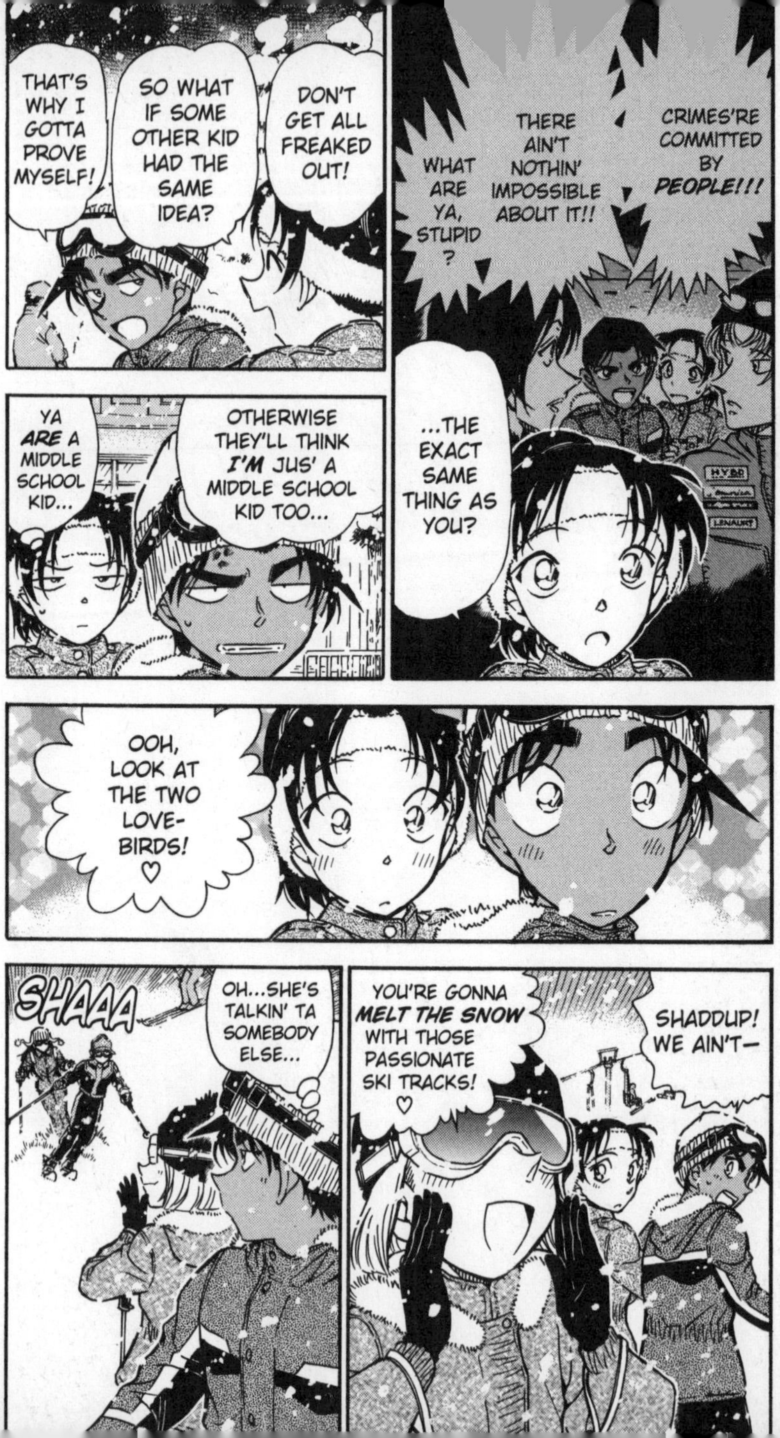
CRIMES'RE COMMITTED BY PEOPLE!!!
THERE AIN'T NOTHIN' IMPOSSIBLE ABOUT IT!!
WHAT ARE YA, STUPID?
...THE EXACT SAME THING AS YOU?
DON'T GET ALL FREAKED OUT!
SO WHAT IF SOME OTHER KID HAD THE SAME IDEA?
THAT'S WHY I GOTTA PROVE MYSELF!
OTHERWISE THEY'LL THINK I'M JUS' A MIDDLE SCHOOL KID TOO...
YA ARE A MIDDLE SCHOOL KID...
OOH, LOOK AT THE TWO LOVE-BIRDS! ♡
SHADDUP! WE AIN'T—
YOU'RE GONNA MELT THE SNOW WITH THOSE PASSIONATE SKI TRACKS! ♡
OH...SHE'S TALKIN' TA SOMEBODY ELSE...
SHAAA

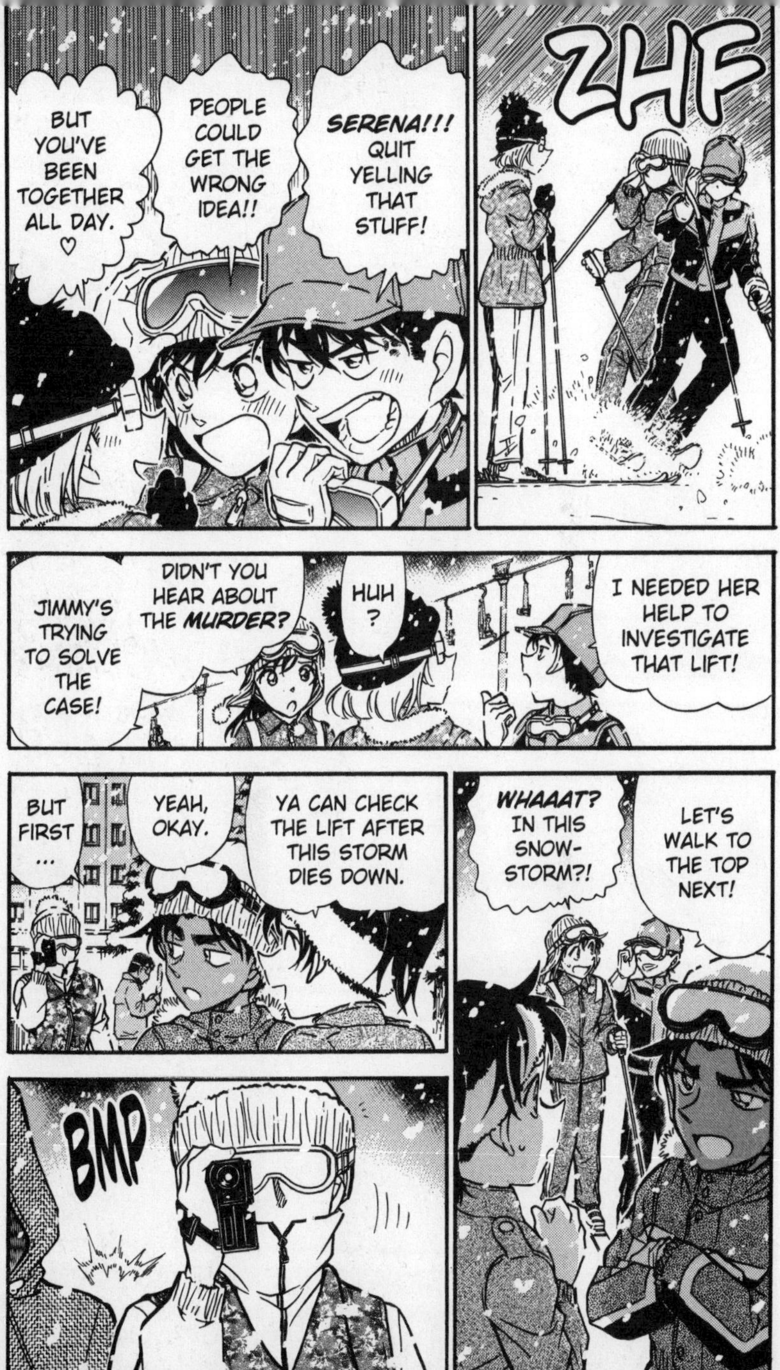
ZHF
SERENA!!! QUIT YELLING THAT STUFF!
PEOPLE COULD GET THE WRONG IDEA!!
BUT YOU'VE BEEN TOGETHER ALL DAY. ♡
I NEEDED HER HELP TO INVESTIGATE THAT LIFT!
HUH?
DIDN'T YOU HEAR ABOUT THE MURDER?
JIMMY'S TRYING TO SOLVE THE CASE!
LET'S WALK TO THE TOP NEXT!
WHAAAT? IN THIS SNOW-STORM?!
YA CAN CHECK THE LIFT AFTER THIS STORM DIES DOWN.
YEAH, OKAY.
BUT FIRST ...
BMP

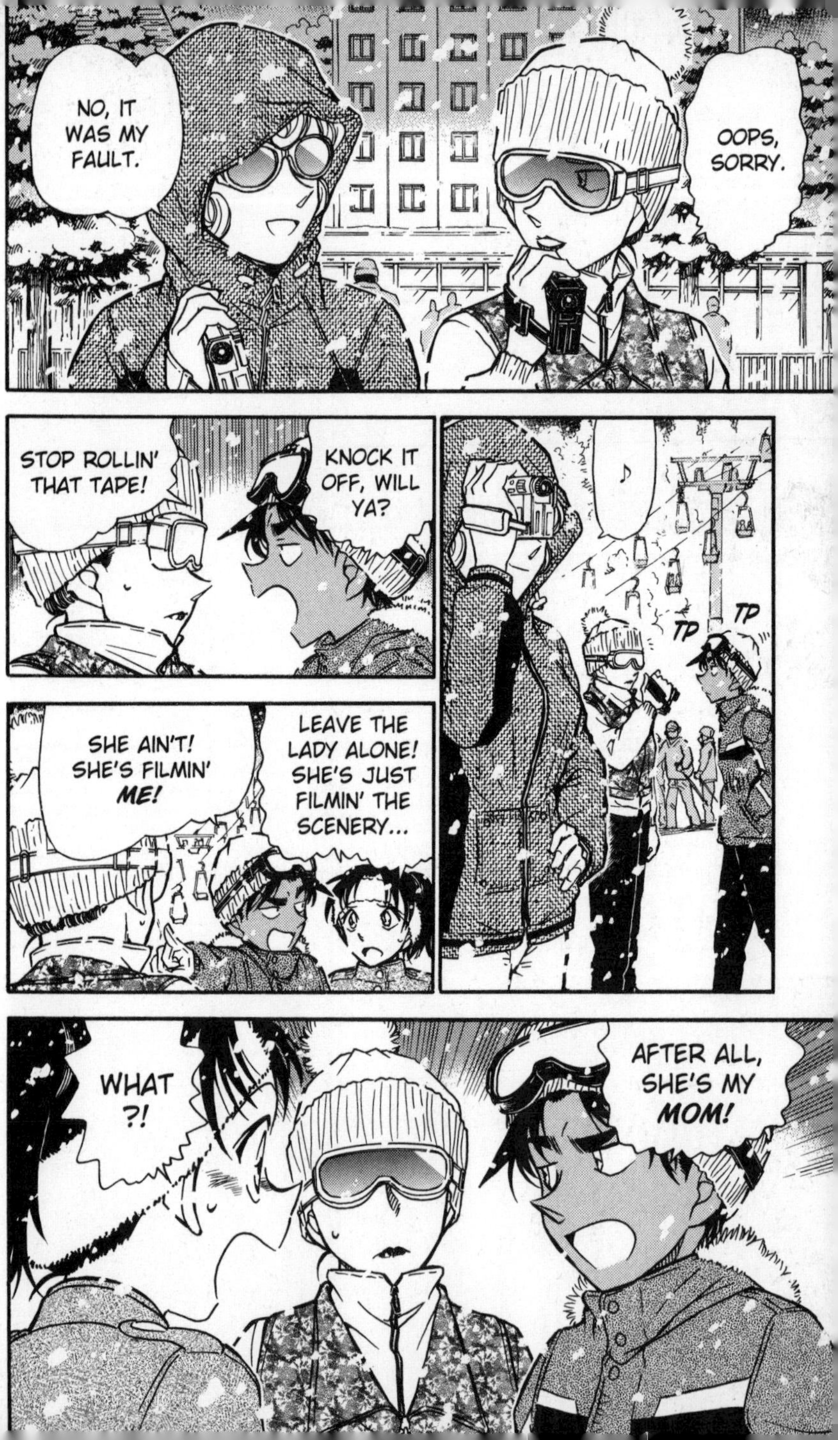
OOPS, SORRY.
NO, IT WAS MY FAULT.
♪
TP
TP
KNOCK IT OFF, WILL YA?
STOP ROLLIN' THAT TAPE!
LEAVE THE LADY ALONE! SHE'S JUST FILMIN' THE SCENERY...
SHE AIN'T! SHE'S FILMIN' *ME!*
AFTER ALL, SHE'S MY *MOM!*
WHAT ?!

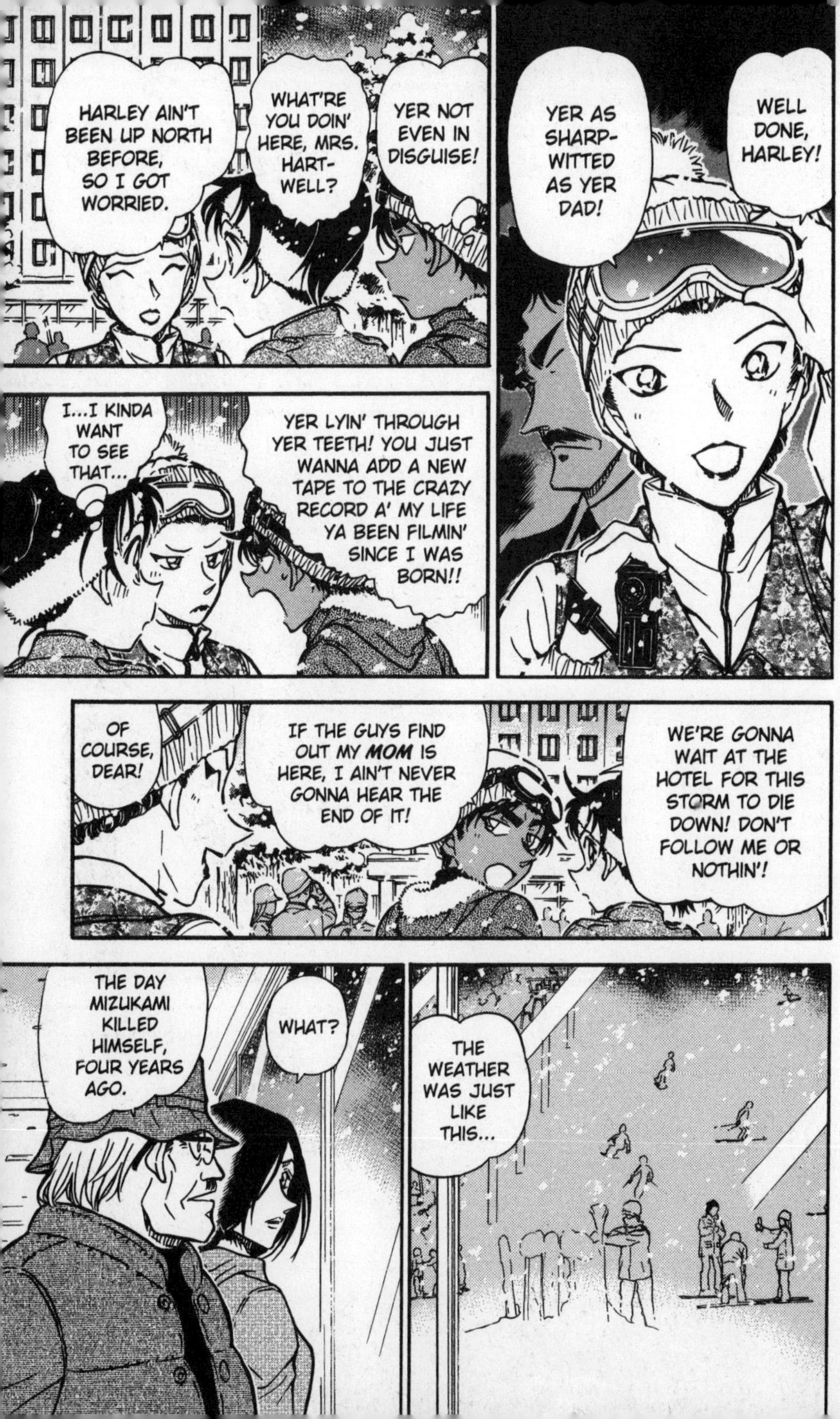
WELL DONE, HARLEY!
YER AS SHARP-WITTED AS YER DAD!
YER NOT EVEN IN DISGUISE!
WHAT'RE YOU DOIN' HERE, MRS. HARTWELL?
HARLEY AIN'T BEEN UP NORTH BEFORE, SO I GOT WORRIED.
YER LYIN' THROUGH YER TEETH! YOU JUST WANNA ADD A NEW TAPE TO THE CRAZY RECORD A' MY LIFE YA BEEN FILMIN' SINCE I WAS BORN!!
I...I KINDA WANT TO SEE THAT...
WE'RE GONNA WAIT AT THE HOTEL FOR THIS STORM TO DIE DOWN! DON'T FOLLOW ME OR NOTHIN'!
IF THE GUYS FIND OUT MY ***MOM*** IS HERE, I AIN'T NEVER GONNA HEAR THE END OF IT!
OF COURSE, DEAR!
THE WEATHER WAS JUST LIKE THIS...
WHAT?
THE DAY MIZUKAMI KILLED HIMSELF, FOUR YEARS AGO.

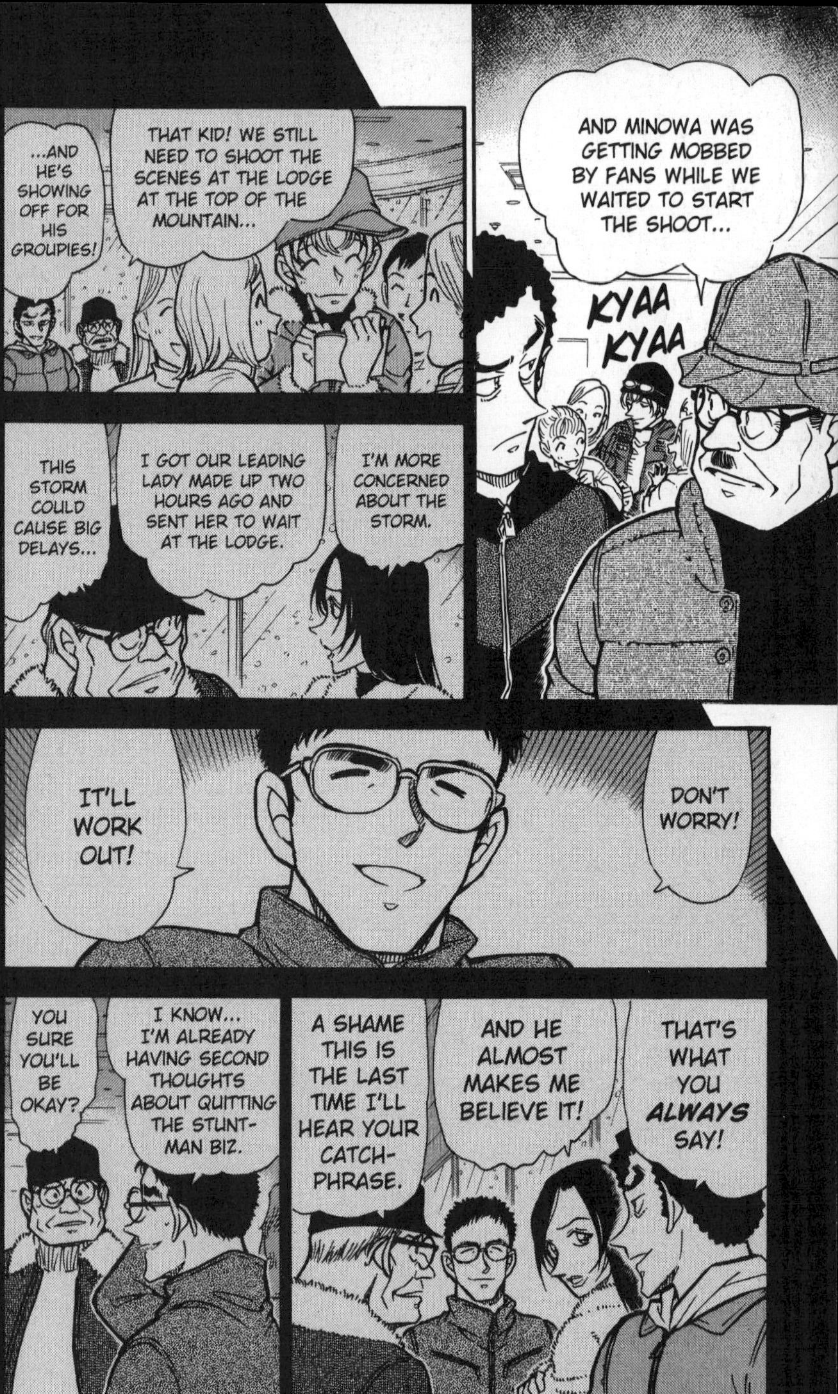
AND MINOWA WAS GETTING MOBBED BY FANS WHILE WE WAITED TO START THE SHOOT...
KYAA KYAA
THAT KID! WE STILL NEED TO SHOOT THE SCENES AT THE LODGE AT THE TOP OF THE MOUNTAIN...
...AND HE'S SHOWING OFF FOR HIS GROUPIES!
I'M MORE CONCERNED ABOUT THE STORM.
I GOT OUR LEADING LADY MADE UP TWO HOURS AGO AND SENT HER TO WAIT AT THE LODGE.
THIS STORM COULD CAUSE BIG DELAYS...
DON'T WORRY!
IT'LL WORK OUT!
THAT'S WHAT YOU ALWAYS SAY!
AND HE ALMOST MAKES ME BELIEVE IT!
A SHAME THIS IS THE LAST TIME I'LL HEAR YOUR CATCH-PHRASE.
I KNOW... I'M ALREADY HAVING SECOND THOUGHTS ABOUT QUITTING THE STUNT-MAN BIZ.
YOU SURE YOU'LL BE OKAY?

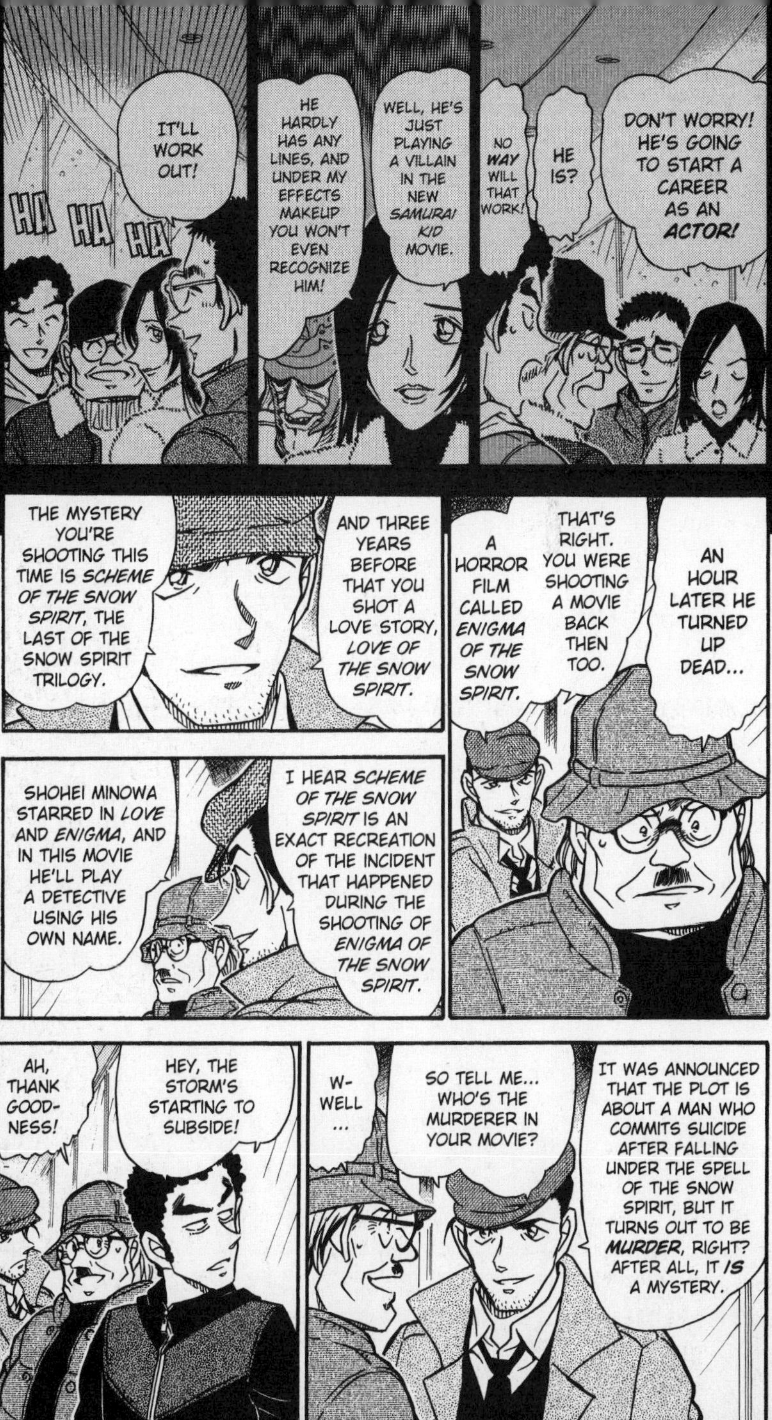
DON'T WORRY! HE'S GOING TO START A CAREER AS AN *ACTOR!*
HE IS?
NO *WAY* WILL THAT WORK!
WELL, HE'S JUST PLAYING A VILLAIN IN THE NEW *SAMURAI KID* MOVIE.
HE HARDLY HAS ANY LINES, AND UNDER MY EFFECTS MAKEUP YOU WON'T EVEN RECOGNIZE HIM!
IT'LL WORK OUT!
HA HA HA
AN HOUR LATER HE TURNED UP DEAD...
THAT'S RIGHT. YOU WERE SHOOTING A MOVIE BACK THEN TOO.
A HORROR FILM CALLED *ENIGMA OF THE SNOW SPIRIT.*
AND THREE YEARS BEFORE THAT YOU SHOT A LOVE STORY, *LOVE OF THE SNOW SPIRIT.*
THE MYSTERY YOU'RE SHOOTING THIS TIME IS *SCHEME OF THE SNOW SPIRIT*, THE LAST OF THE SNOW SPIRIT TRILOGY.
I HEAR *SCHEME OF THE SNOW SPIRIT* IS AN EXACT RECREATION OF THE INCIDENT THAT HAPPENED DURING THE SHOOTING OF *ENIGMA OF THE SNOW SPIRIT.*
SHOHEI MINOWA STARRED IN *LOVE* AND *ENIGMA*, AND IN THIS MOVIE HE'LL PLAY A DETECTIVE USING HIS OWN NAME.
IT WAS ANNOUNCED THAT THE PLOT IS ABOUT A MAN WHO COMMITS SUICIDE AFTER FALLING UNDER THE SPELL OF THE SNOW SPIRIT, BUT IT TURNS OUT TO BE ***MURDER***, RIGHT? AFTER ALL, IT *IS* A MYSTERY.
SO TELL ME... WHO'S THE MURDERER IN YOUR MOVIE?
W-WELL ...
HEY, THE STORM'S STARTING TO SUBSIDE!
AH, THANK GOOD-NESS!

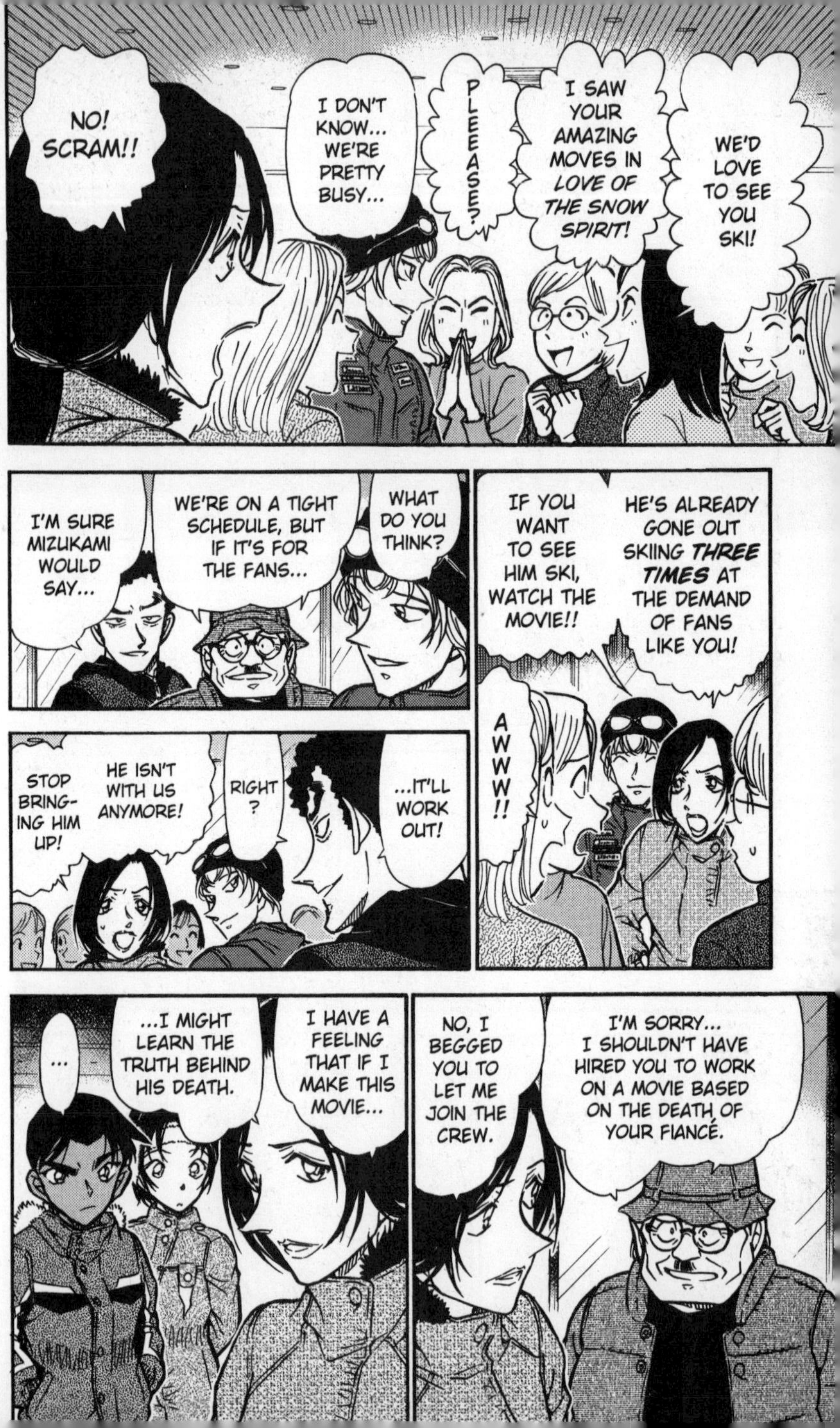
WE'D LOVE TO SEE YOU SKI!
I SAW YOUR AMAZING MOVES IN *LOVE OF THE SNOW SPIRIT!*
PLEEASE?
I DON'T KNOW... WE'RE PRETTY BUSY...
NO! SCRAM!!
HE'S ALREADY GONE OUT SKIING ***THREE TIMES*** AT THE DEMAND OF FANS LIKE YOU!
IF YOU WANT TO SEE HIM SKI, WATCH THE MOVIE!!
AWWWW!!
WHAT DO YOU THINK?
WE'RE ON A TIGHT SCHEDULE, BUT IF IT'S FOR THE FANS...
I'M SURE MIZUKAMI WOULD SAY...
...IT'LL WORK OUT!
RIGHT?
HE ISN'T WITH US ANYMORE!
STOP BRING-ING HIM UP!
I'M SORRY... I SHOULDN'T HAVE HIRED YOU TO WORK ON A MOVIE BASED ON THE DEATH OF YOUR FIANCÉ.
NO, I BEGGED YOU TO LET ME JOIN THE CREW.
I HAVE A FEELING THAT IF I MAKE THIS MOVIE...
...I MIGHT LEARN THE TRUTH BEHIND HIS DEATH.
...

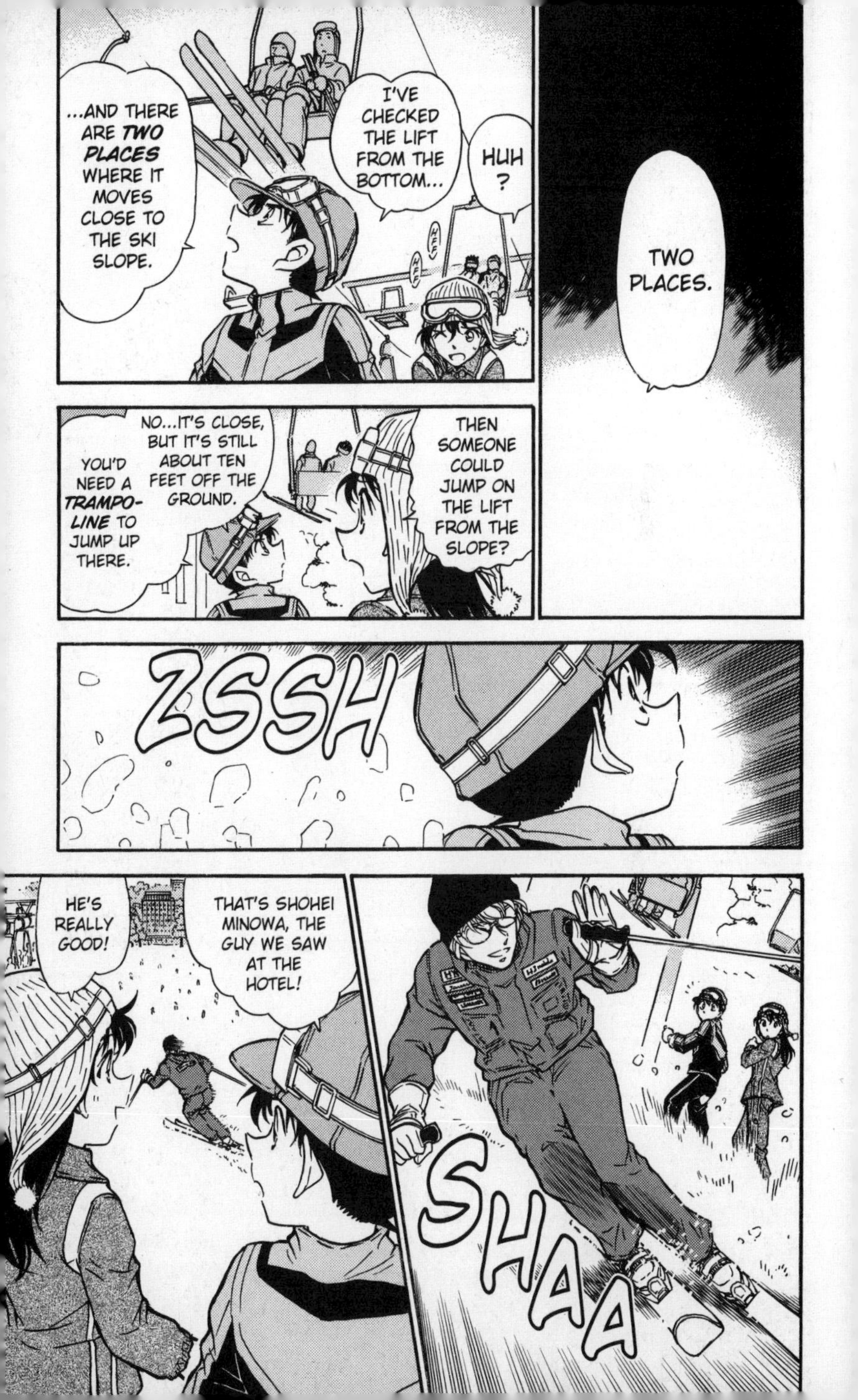
TWO PLACES.
HUH?
I'VE CHECKED THE LIFT FROM THE BOTTOM...
...AND THERE ARE *TWO PLACES* WHERE IT MOVES CLOSE TO THE SKI SLOPE.
THEN SOMEONE COULD JUMP ON THE LIFT FROM THE SLOPE?
NO...IT'S CLOSE, BUT IT'S STILL ABOUT TEN FEET OFF THE GROUND.
YOU'D NEED A *TRAMPOLINE* TO JUMP UP THERE.
ZSSH
SHAA
THAT'S SHOHEI MINOWA, THE GUY WE SAW AT THE HOTEL!
HE'S REALLY GOOD!

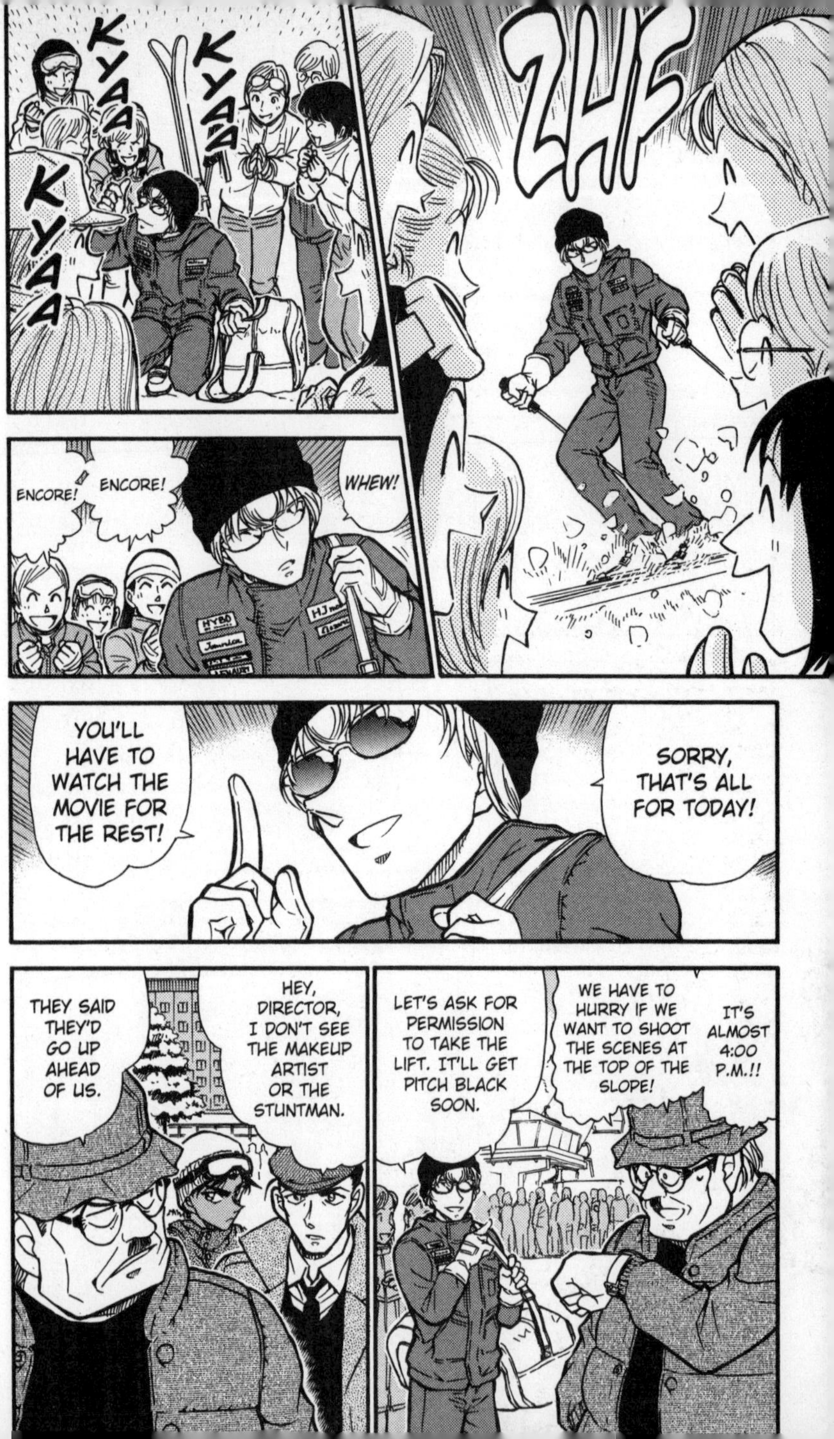
ZHF
KYAA
KYAA
KYAA
WHEW!
ENCORE!
ENCORE!
SORRY, THAT'S ALL FOR TODAY!
YOU'LL HAVE TO WATCH THE MOVIE FOR THE REST!
IT'S ALMOST 4:00 P.M.!!
WE HAVE TO HURRY IF WE WANT TO SHOOT THE SCENES AT THE TOP OF THE SLOPE!
LET'S ASK FOR PERMISSION TO TAKE THE LIFT. IT'LL GET PITCH BLACK SOON.
HEY, DIRECTOR, I DON'T SEE THE MAKEUP ARTIST OR THE STUNTMAN.
THEY SAID THEY'D GO UP AHEAD OF US.

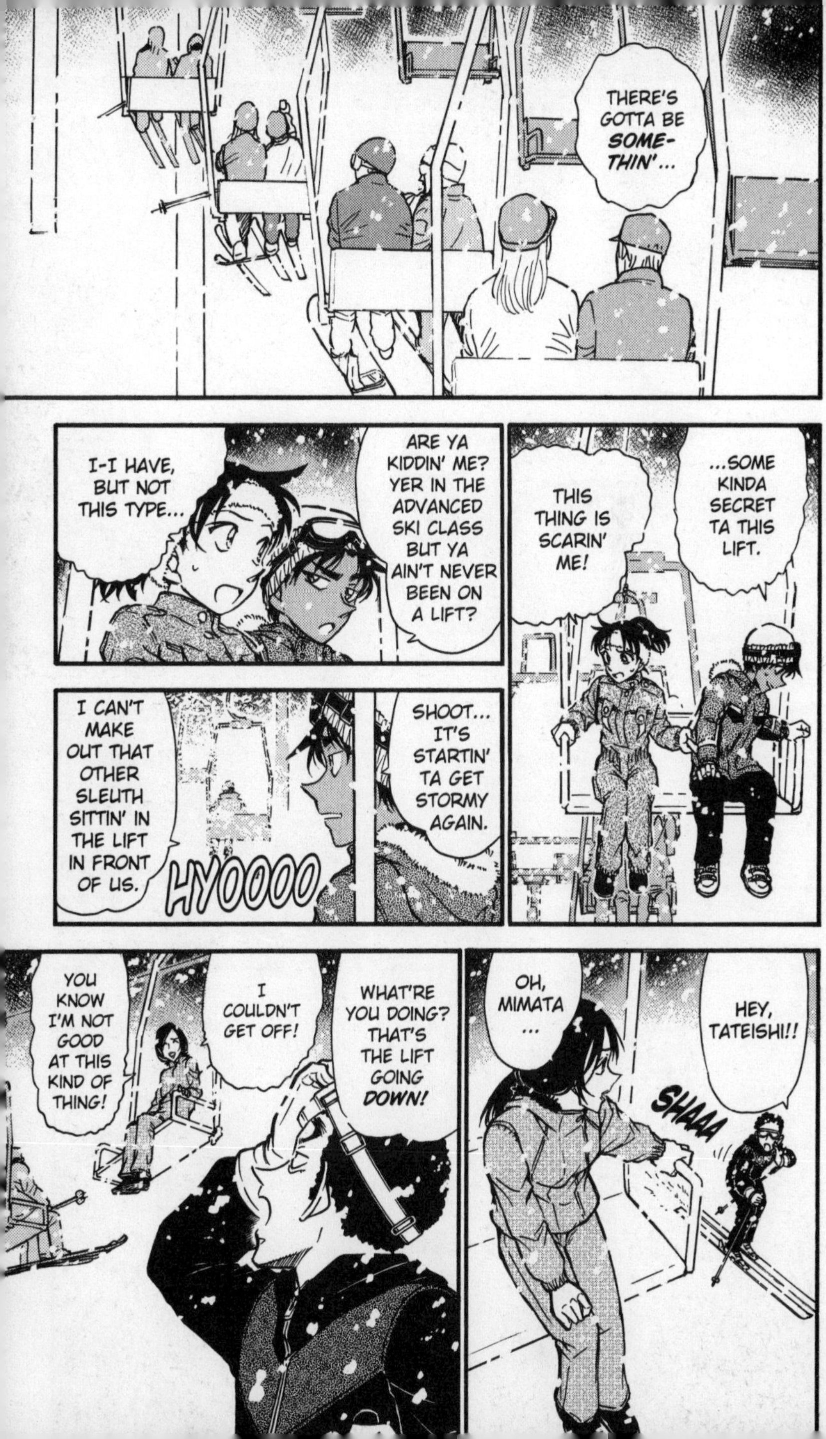
THERE'S GOTTA BE SOME-THIN'...
...SOME KINDA SECRET TA THIS LIFT.
THIS THING IS SCARIN' ME!
ARE YA KIDDIN' ME? YER IN THE ADVANCED SKI CLASS BUT YA AIN'T NEVER BEEN ON A LIFT?
I-I HAVE, BUT NOT THIS TYPE...
SHOOT... IT'S STARTIN' TA GET STORMY AGAIN.
HYOOOO
I CAN'T MAKE OUT THAT OTHER SLEUTH SITTIN' IN THE LIFT IN FRONT OF US.
HEY, TATEISHI!!
SHAAA
OH, MIMATA...
WHAT'RE YOU DOING? THAT'S THE LIFT GOING DOWN!
I COULDN'T GET OFF!
YOU KNOW I'M NOT GOOD AT THIS KIND OF THING!

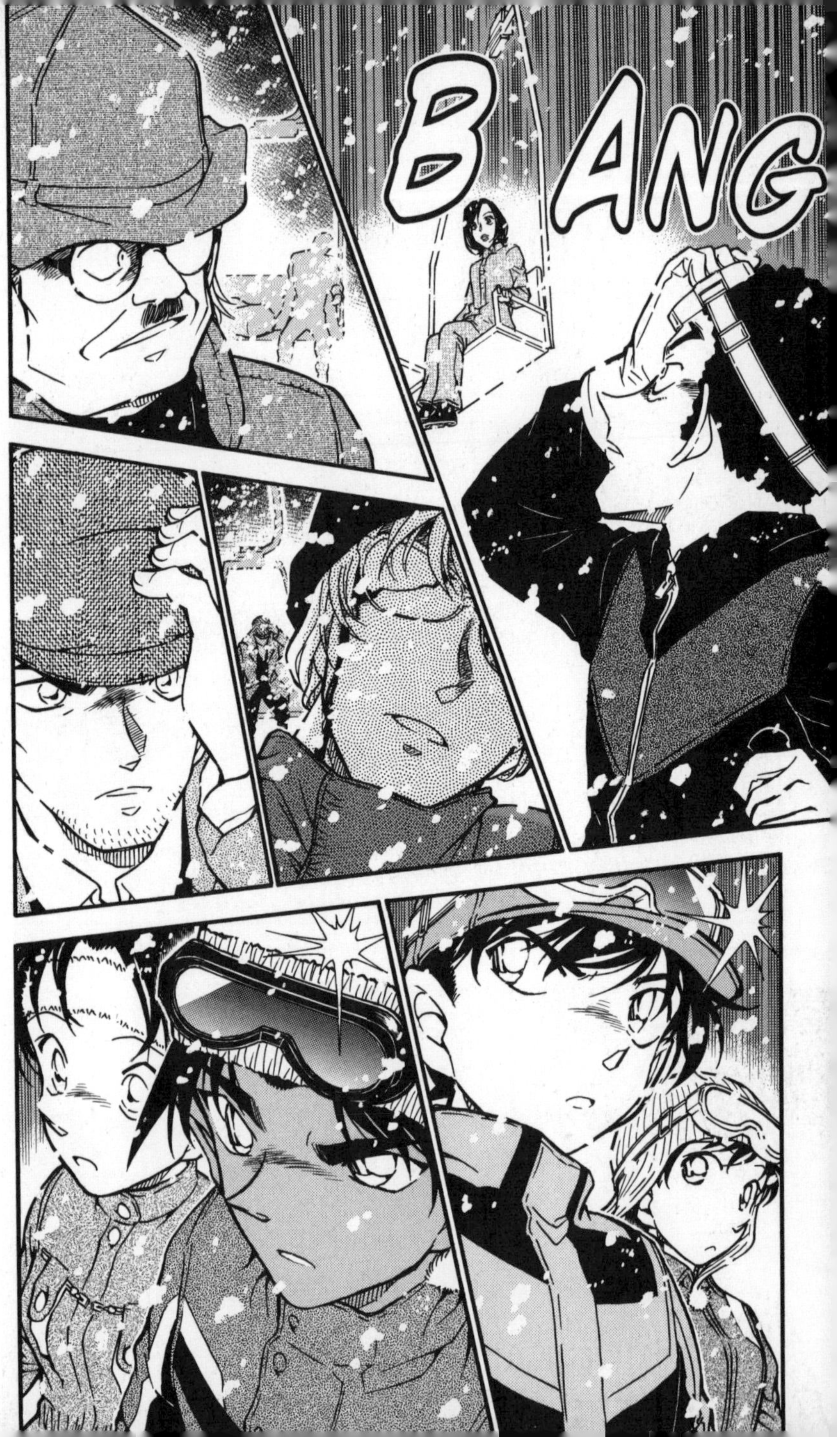
BANG

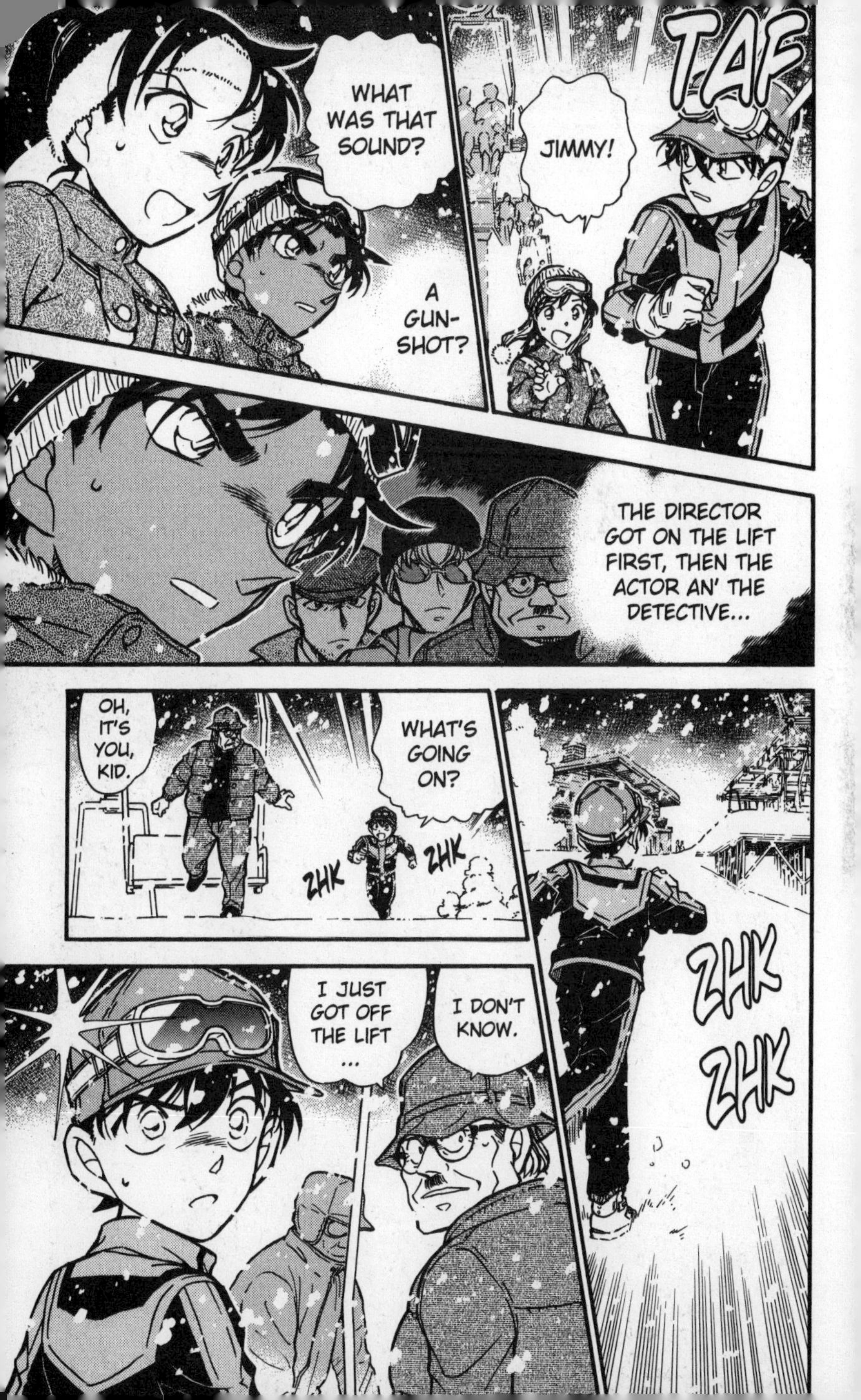
TAP
JIMMY!
WHAT WAS THAT SOUND?
A GUN-SHOT?
THE DIRECTOR GOT ON THE LIFT FIRST, THEN THE ACTOR AN' THE DETECTIVE...
ZHK
ZHK
WHAT'S GOING ON?
OH, IT'S YOU, KID.
ZHK
ZHK
I DON'T KNOW.
I JUST GOT OFF THE LIFT ...

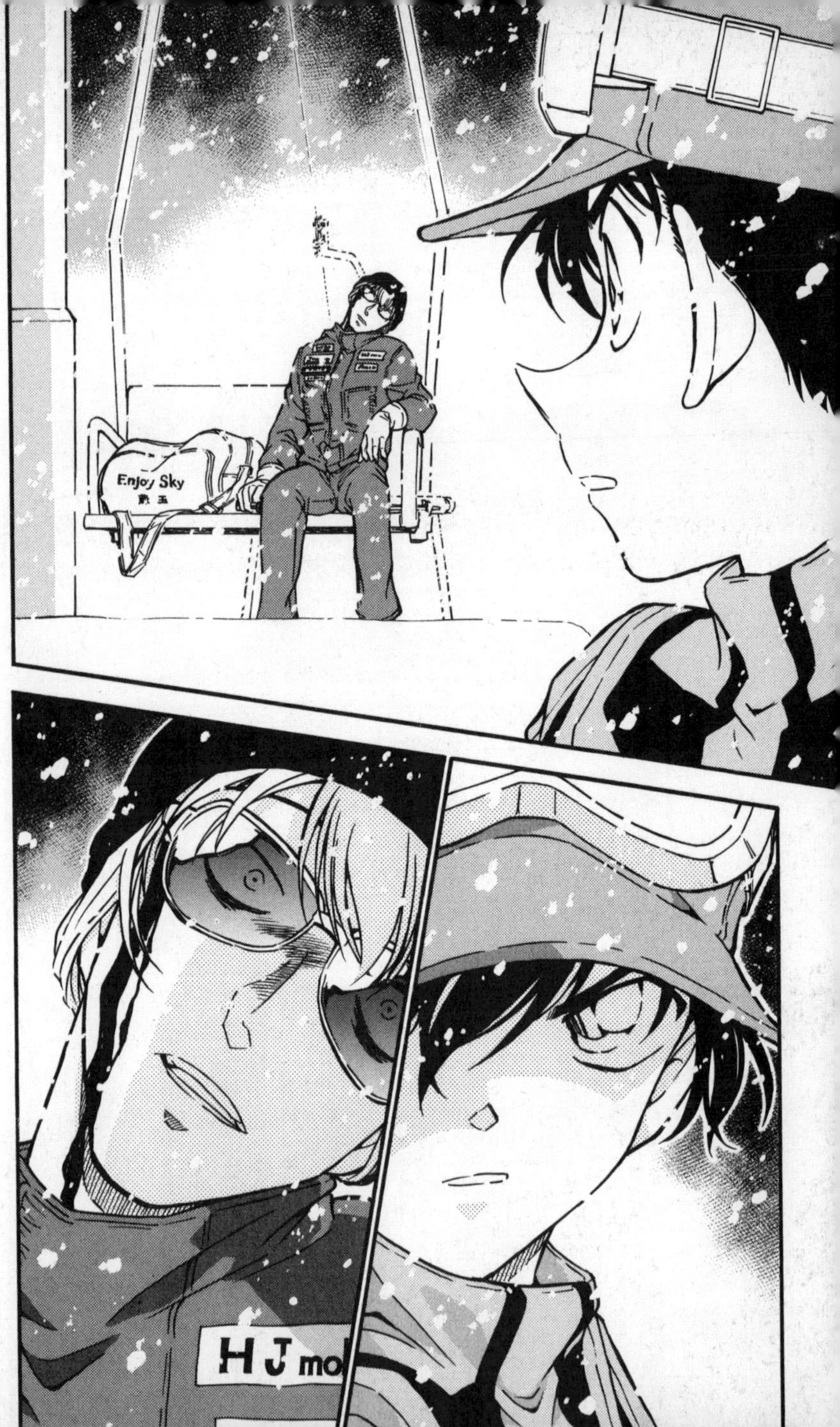
Enjoy Sky
H J mo

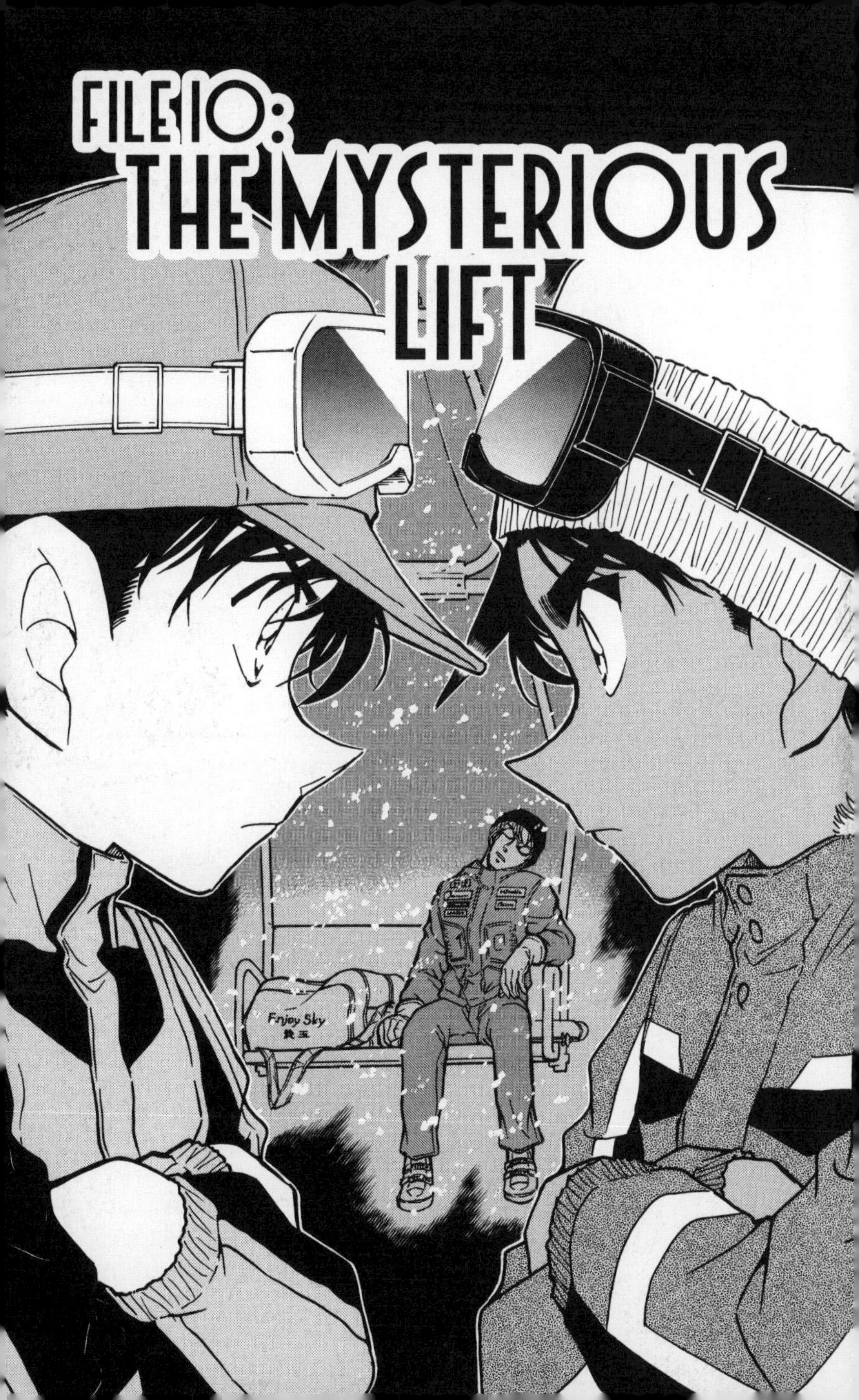
FILE 10:
THE MYSTERIOUS LIFT
Enjoy Sky

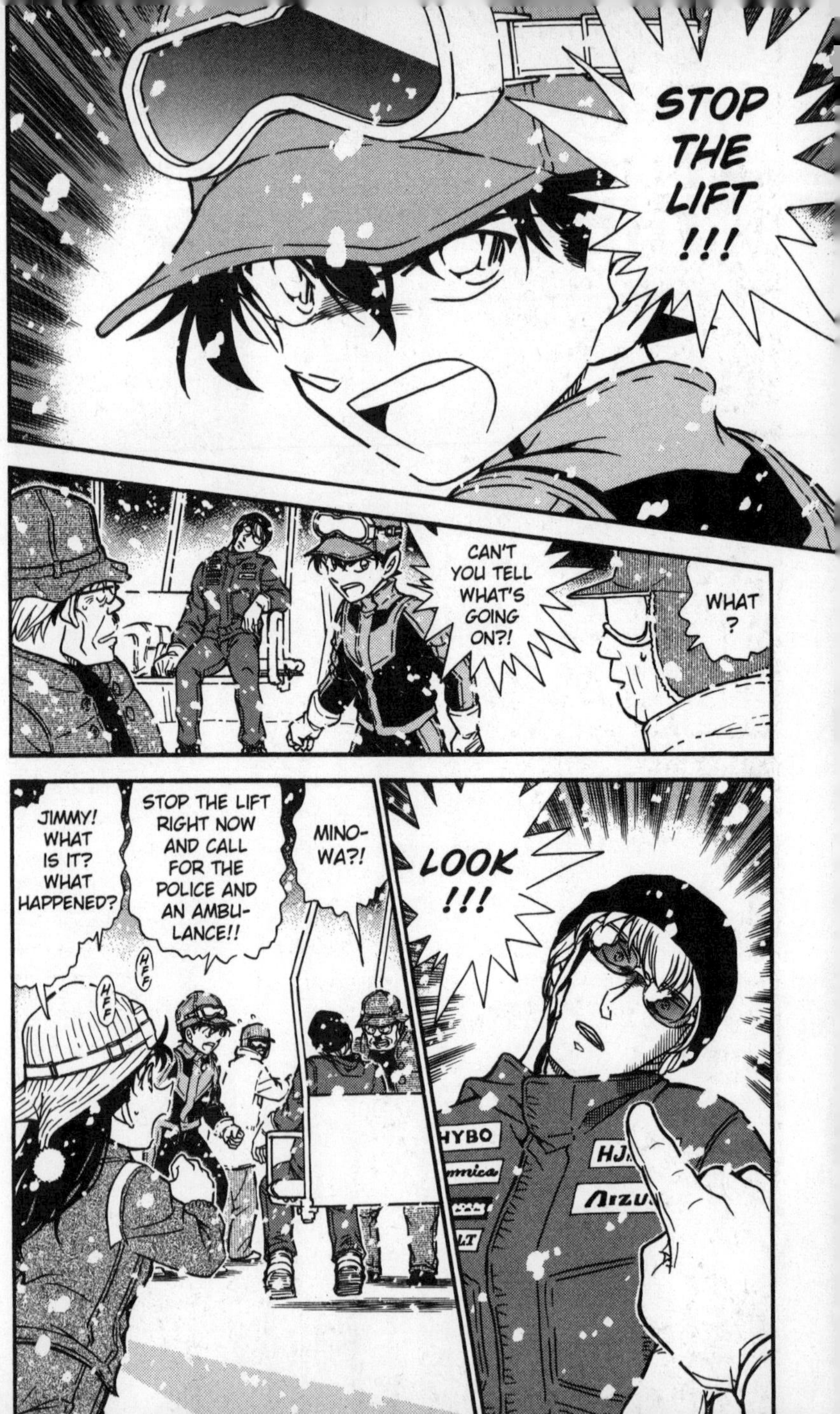
STOP THE LIFT !!!
WHAT ?
CAN'T YOU TELL WHAT'S GOING ON?!
LOOK !!!
MINO-WA?!
STOP THE LIFT RIGHT NOW AND CALL FOR THE POLICE AND AN AMBU-LANCE!!
JIMMY! WHAT IS IT? WHAT HAPPENED?
HEF
HEF
HYBO

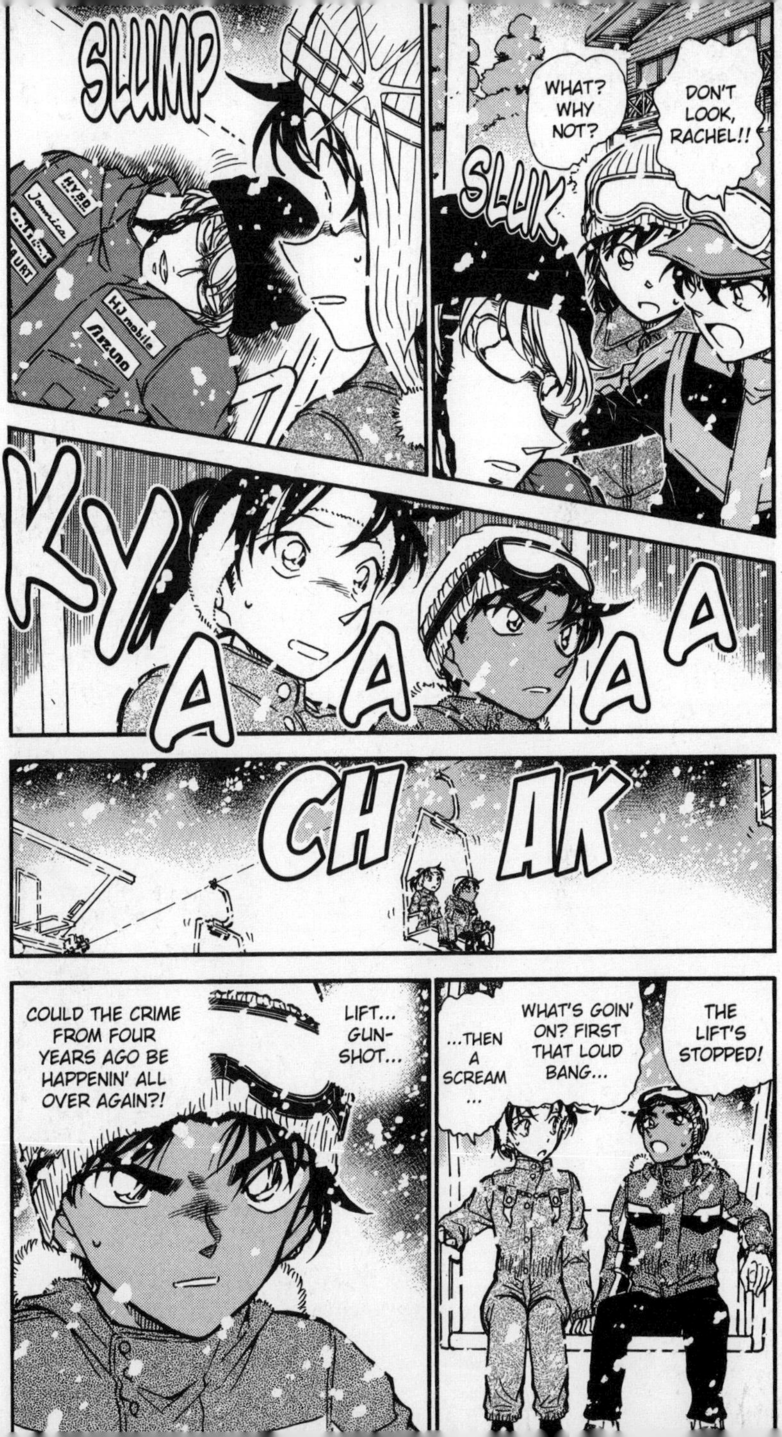
DON'T LOOK, RACHEL!!
WHAT? WHY NOT?
SLUK
SLUMP
KYAAAAA
CH AK
THE LIFT'S STOPPED!
WHAT'S GOIN' ON? FIRST THAT LOUD BANG...
...THEN A SCREAM...
LIFT... GUN-SHOT...
COULD THE CRIME FROM FOUR YEARS AGO BE HAPPENIN' ALL OVER AGAIN?!

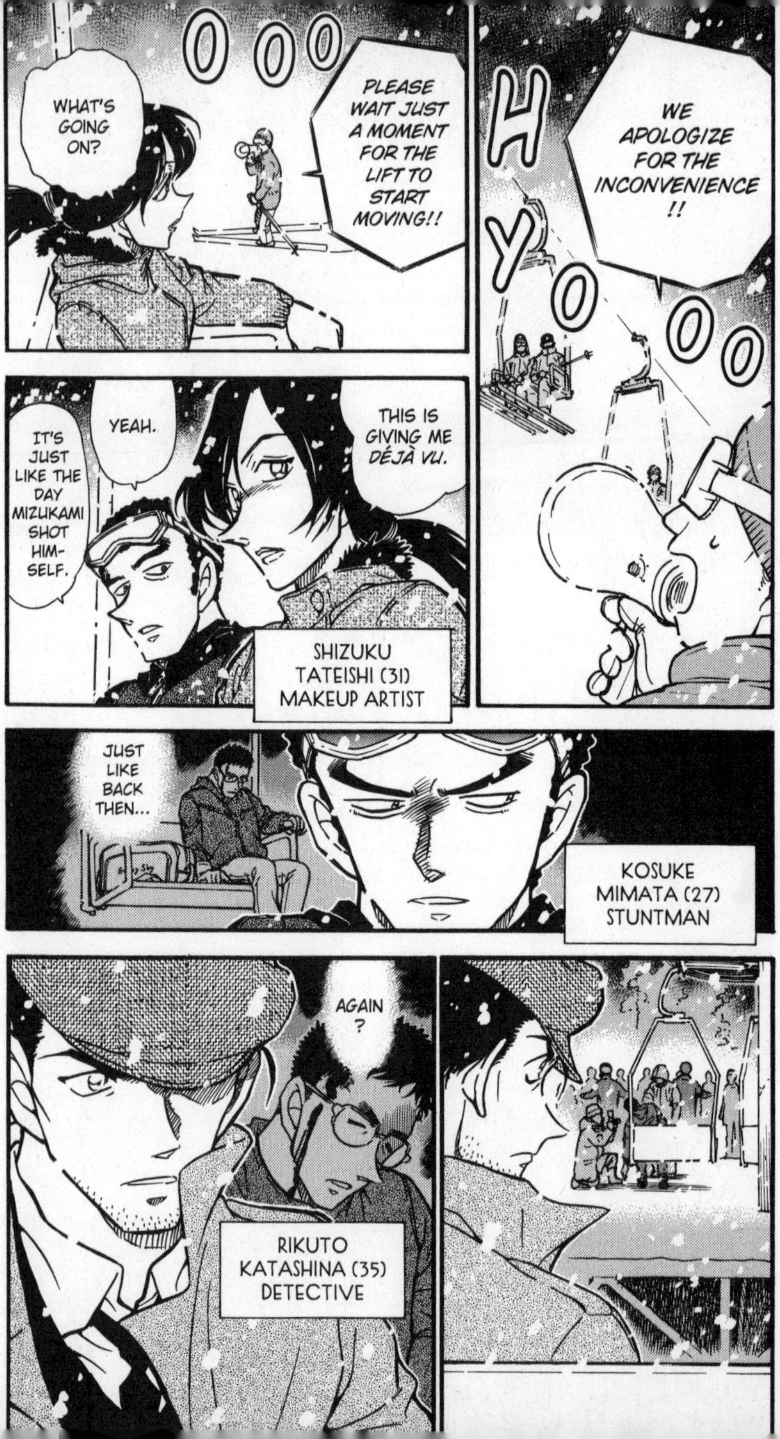

WE APOLOGIZE FOR THE INCONVENIENCE !!
HYOOO
OOO
PLEASE WAIT JUST A MOMENT FOR THE LIFT TO START MOVING!!
WHAT'S GOING ON?
THIS IS GIVING ME DÉJÀ VU.
YEAH.
IT'S JUST LIKE THE DAY MIZUKAMI SHOT HIM-SELF.
SHIZUKU TATEISHI (31) MAKEUP ARTIST
KOSUKE MIMATA (27) STUNTMAN
JUST LIKE BACK THEN...
AGAIN ?
RIKUTO KATASHINA (35) DETECTIVE

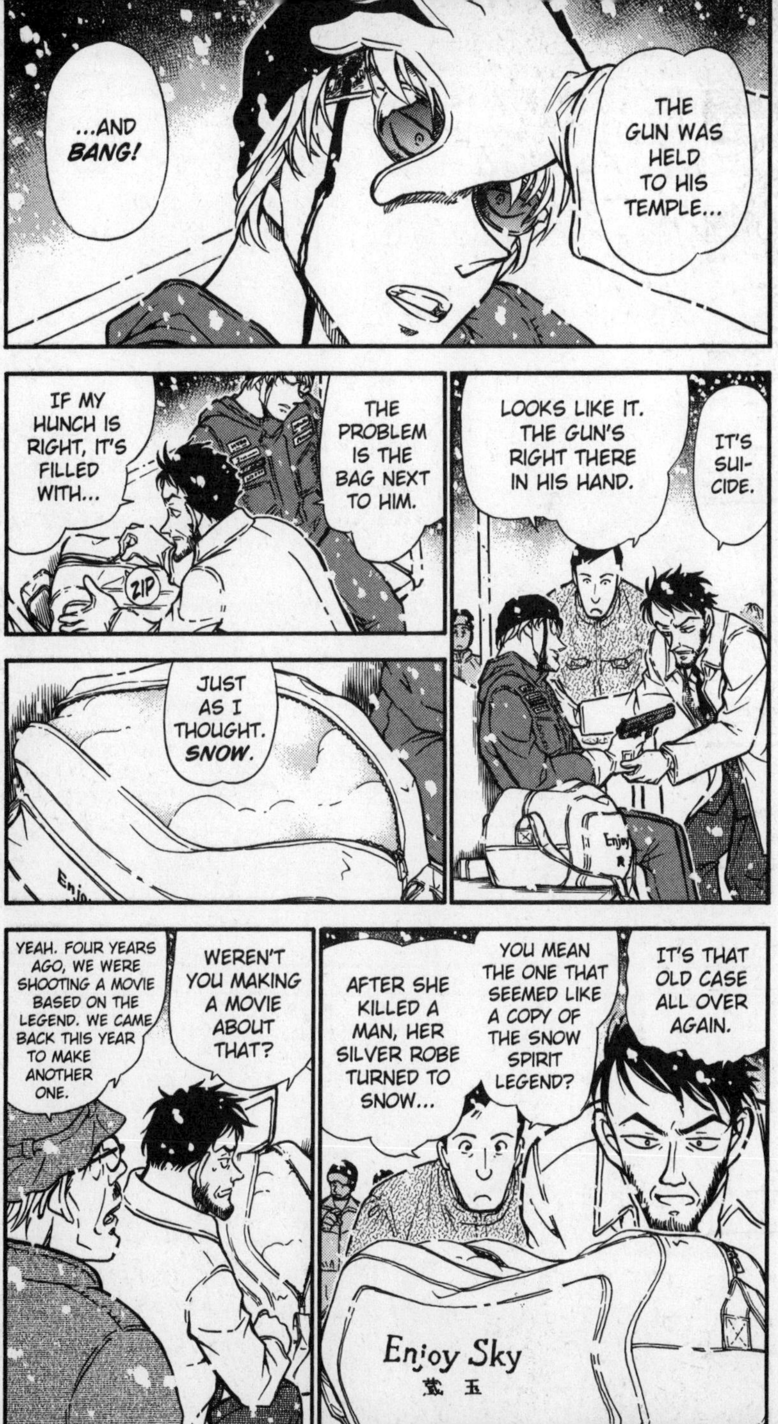
THE GUN WAS HELD TO HIS TEMPLE...
...AND BANG!
IT'S SUI-CIDE.
LOOKS LIKE IT. THE GUN'S RIGHT THERE IN HIS HAND.
THE PROBLEM IS THE BAG NEXT TO HIM.
IF MY HUNCH IS RIGHT, IT'S FILLED WITH...
ZIP
JUST AS I THOUGHT. SNOW.
IT'S THAT OLD CASE ALL OVER AGAIN.
YOU MEAN THE ONE THAT SEEMED LIKE A COPY OF THE SNOW SPIRIT LEGEND?
AFTER SHE KILLED A MAN, HER SILVER ROBE TURNED TO SNOW...
Enjoy Sky
WEREN'T YOU MAKING A MOVIE ABOUT THAT?
YEAH. FOUR YEARS AGO, WE WERE SHOOTING A MOVIE BASED ON THE LEGEND. WE CAME BACK THIS YEAR TO MAKE ANOTHER ONE.

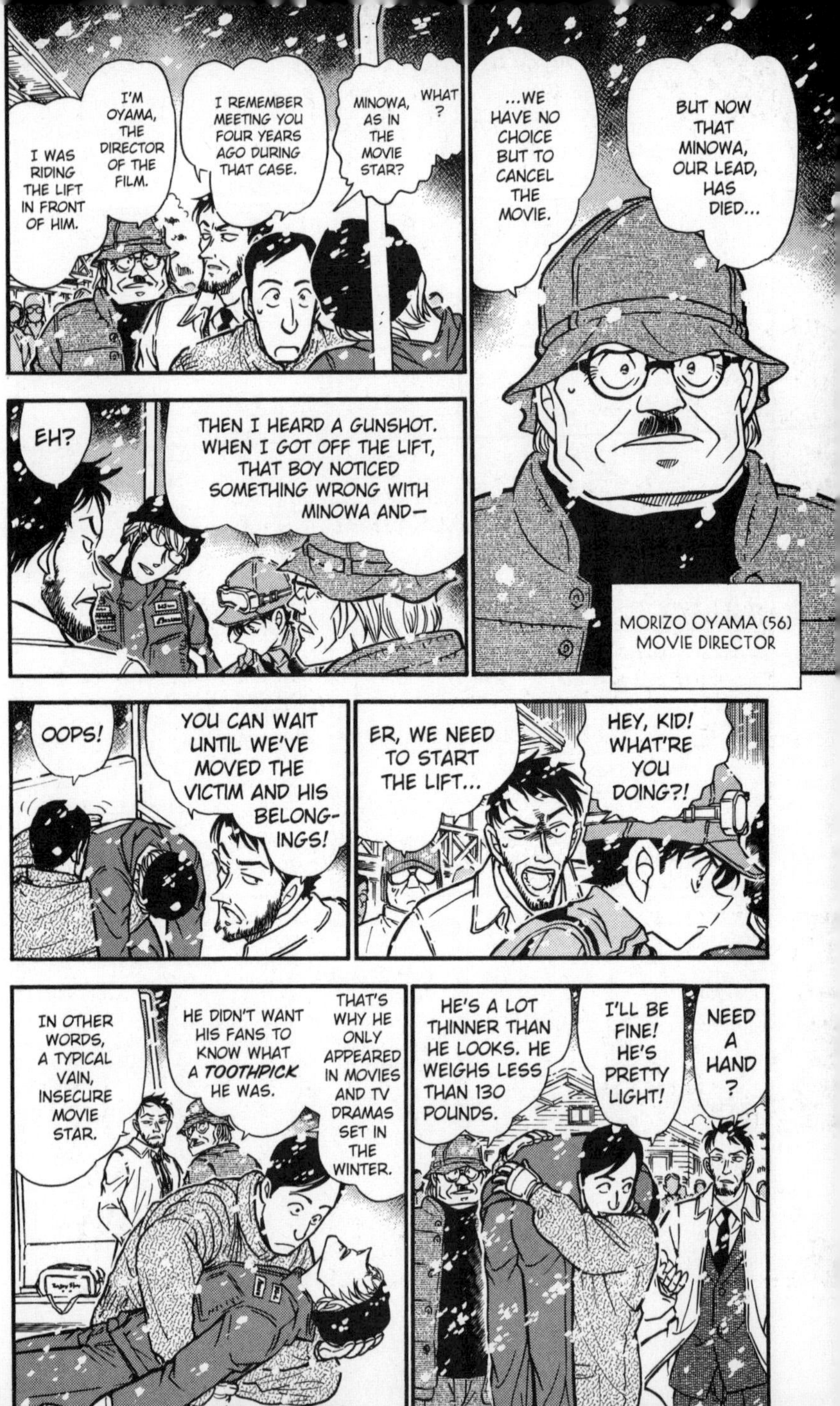
BUT NOW THAT MINOWA, OUR LEAD, HAS DIED...
...WE HAVE NO CHOICE BUT TO CANCEL THE MOVIE.
MORIZO OYAMA (56) MOVIE DIRECTOR
WHAT?
MINOWA, AS IN THE MOVIE STAR?
I REMEMBER MEETING YOU FOUR YEARS AGO DURING THAT CASE.
I'M OYAMA, THE DIRECTOR OF THE FILM.
I WAS RIDING THE LIFT IN FRONT OF HIM.
THEN I HEARD A GUNSHOT. WHEN I GOT OFF THE LIFT, THAT BOY NOTICED SOMETHING WRONG WITH MINOWA AND—
EH?
HEY, KID! WHAT'RE YOU DOING?!
ER, WE NEED TO START THE LIFT...
YOU CAN WAIT UNTIL WE'VE MOVED THE VICTIM AND HIS BELONGINGS!
OOPS!
NEED A HAND?
I'LL BE FINE! HE'S PRETTY LIGHT!
HE'S A LOT THINNER THAN HE LOOKS. HE WEIGHS LESS THAN 130 POUNDS.
THAT'S WHY HE ONLY APPEARED IN MOVIES AND TV DRAMAS SET IN THE WINTER.
HE DIDN'T WANT HIS FANS TO KNOW WHAT A ***TOOTHPICK*** HE WAS.
IN OTHER WORDS, A TYPICAL VAIN, INSECURE MOVIE STAR.

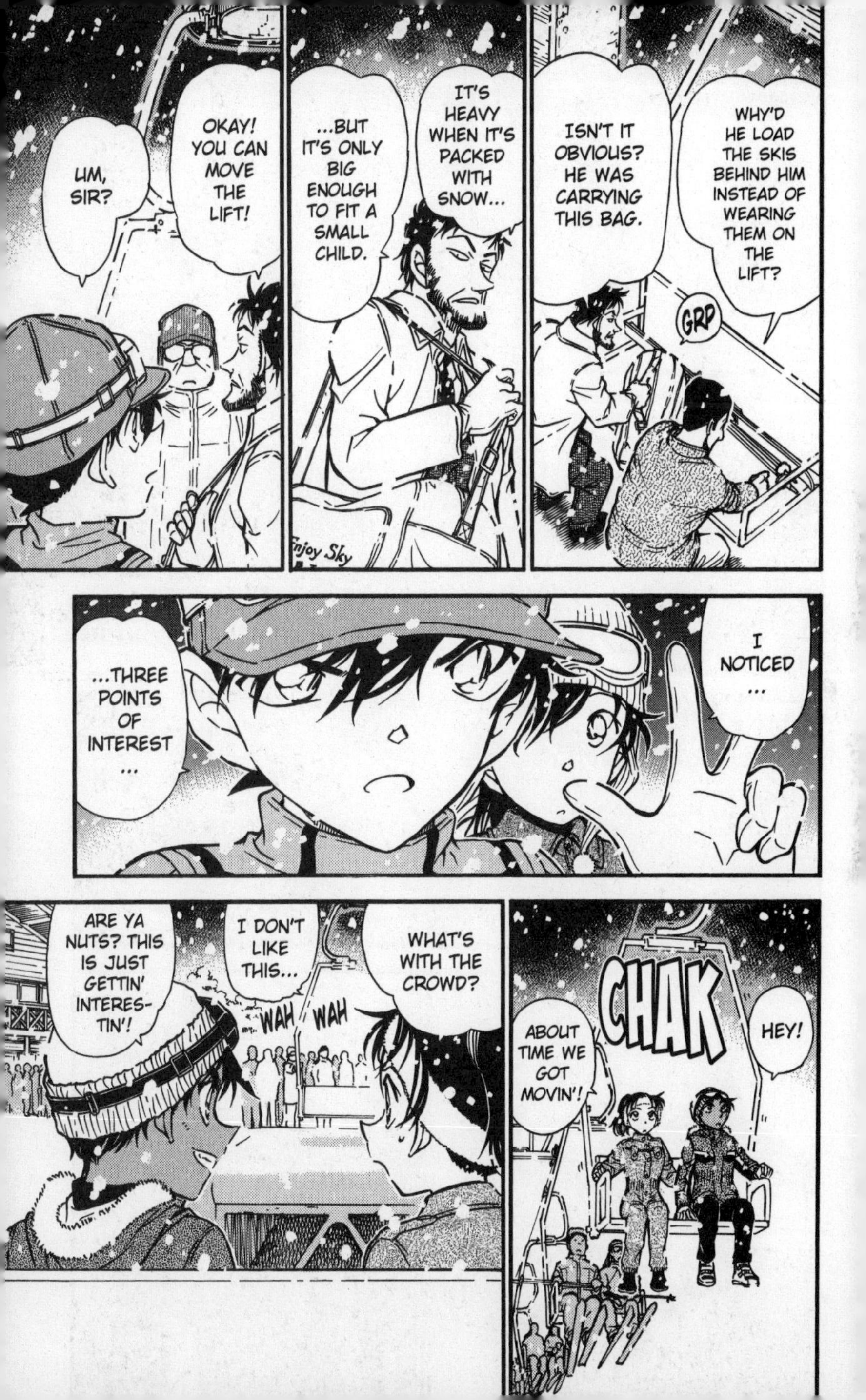
WHY'D HE LOAD THE SKIS BEHIND HIM INSTEAD OF WEARING THEM ON THE LIFT?
ISN'T IT OBVIOUS? HE WAS CARRYING THIS BAG.
GRP
IT'S HEAVY WHEN IT'S PACKED WITH SNOW...
...BUT IT'S ONLY BIG ENOUGH TO FIT A SMALL CHILD.
Enjoy Sky
OKAY! YOU CAN MOVE THE LIFT!
UM, SIR?
I NOTICED...
...THREE POINTS OF INTEREST...
HEY!
CHAK
ABOUT TIME WE GOT MOVIN'!
WHAT'S WITH THE CROWD?
I DON'T LIKE THIS...
WAH WAH
ARE YA NUTS? THIS IS JUST GETTIN' INTERES-TIN'!

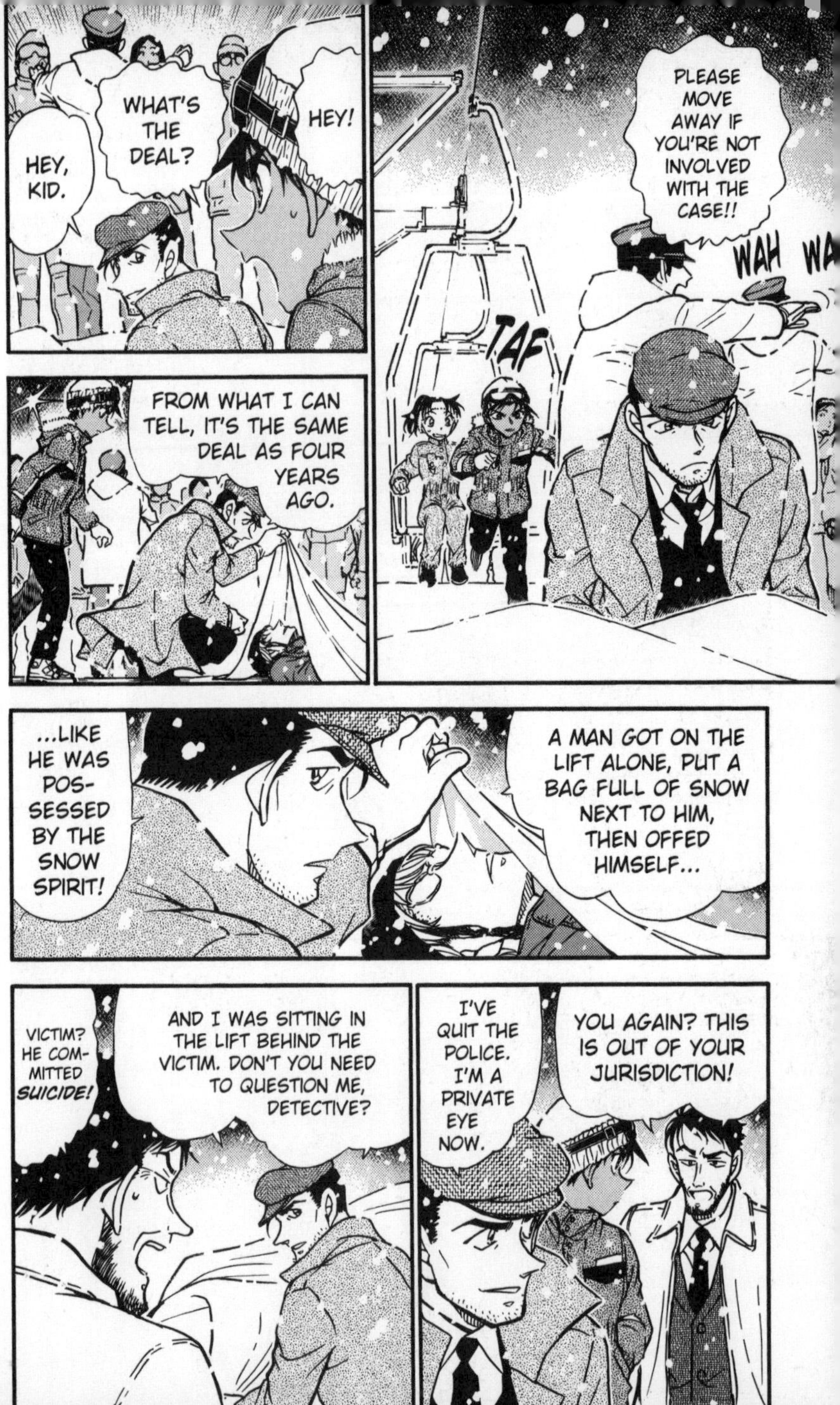
PLEASE MOVE AWAY IF YOU'RE NOT INVOLVED WITH THE CASE!!
WAH WA
TAF
HEY!
WHAT'S THE DEAL?
HEY, KID.
FROM WHAT I CAN TELL, IT'S THE SAME DEAL AS FOUR YEARS AGO.
A MAN GOT ON THE LIFT ALONE, PUT A BAG FULL OF SNOW NEXT TO HIM, THEN OFFED HIMSELF...
...LIKE HE WAS POS-SESSED BY THE SNOW SPIRIT!
YOU AGAIN? THIS IS OUT OF YOUR JURISDICTION!
I'VE QUIT THE POLICE. I'M A PRIVATE EYE NOW.
AND I WAS SITTING IN THE LIFT BEHIND THE VICTIM. DON'T YOU NEED TO QUESTION ME, DETECTIVE?
VICTIM? HE COM-MITTED SUICIDE!

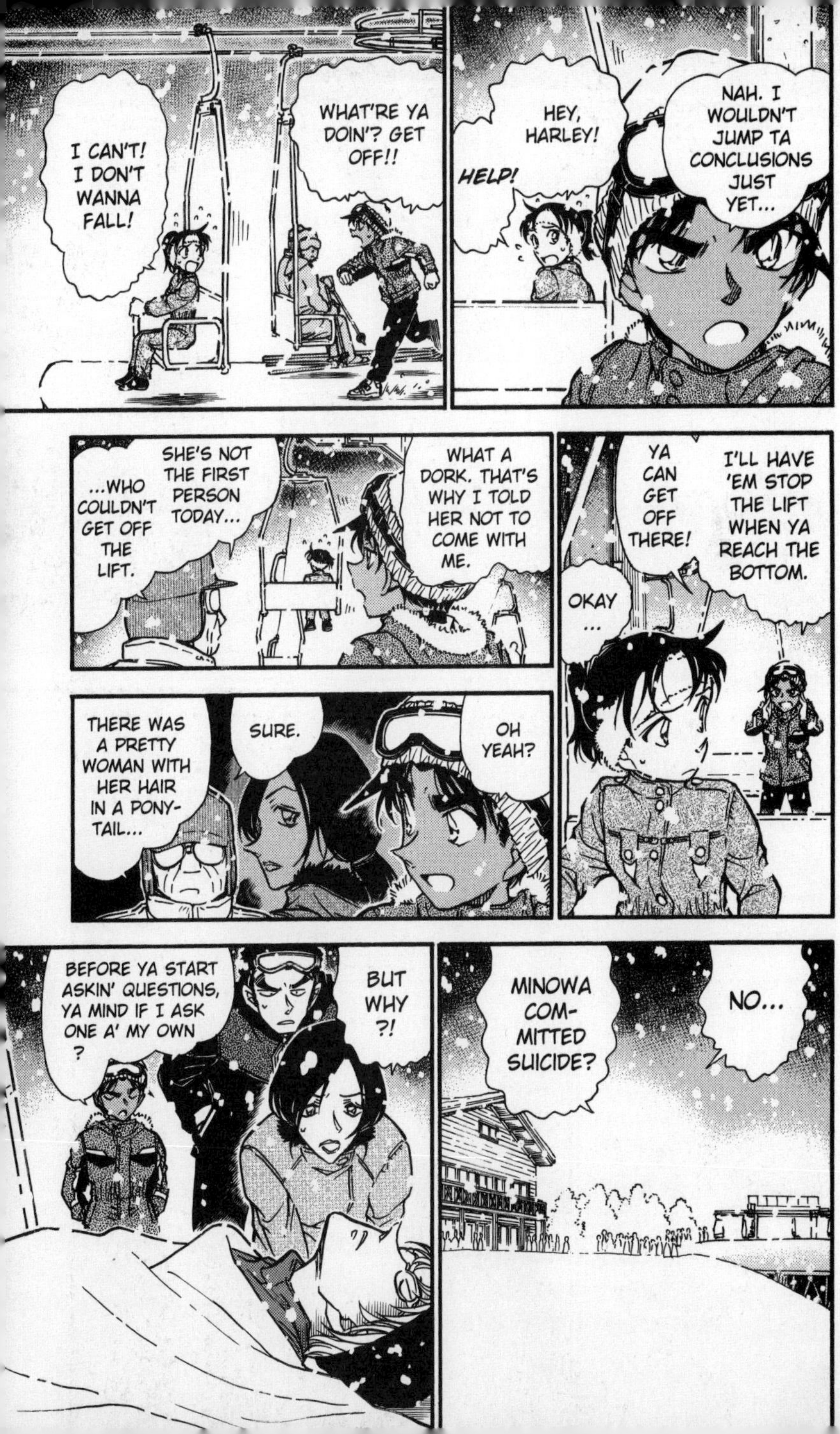
NAH. I WOULDN'T JUMP TA CONCLUSIONS JUST YET...
HEY, HARLEY!
HELP!
WHAT'RE YA DOIN'? GET OFF!!
I CAN'T! I DON'T WANNA FALL!
I'LL HAVE 'EM STOP THE LIFT WHEN YA REACH THE BOTTOM.
YA CAN GET OFF THERE!
OKAY ...
WHAT A DORK. THAT'S WHY I TOLD HER NOT TO COME WITH ME.
SHE'S NOT THE FIRST PERSON TODAY...
...WHO COULDN'T GET OFF THE LIFT.
OH YEAH?
SURE.
THERE WAS A PRETTY WOMAN WITH HER HAIR IN A PONY-TAIL...
NO...
MINOWA COM-MITTED SUICIDE?
BUT WHY ?!
BEFORE YA START ASKIN' QUESTIONS, YA MIND IF I ASK ONE A' MY OWN ?

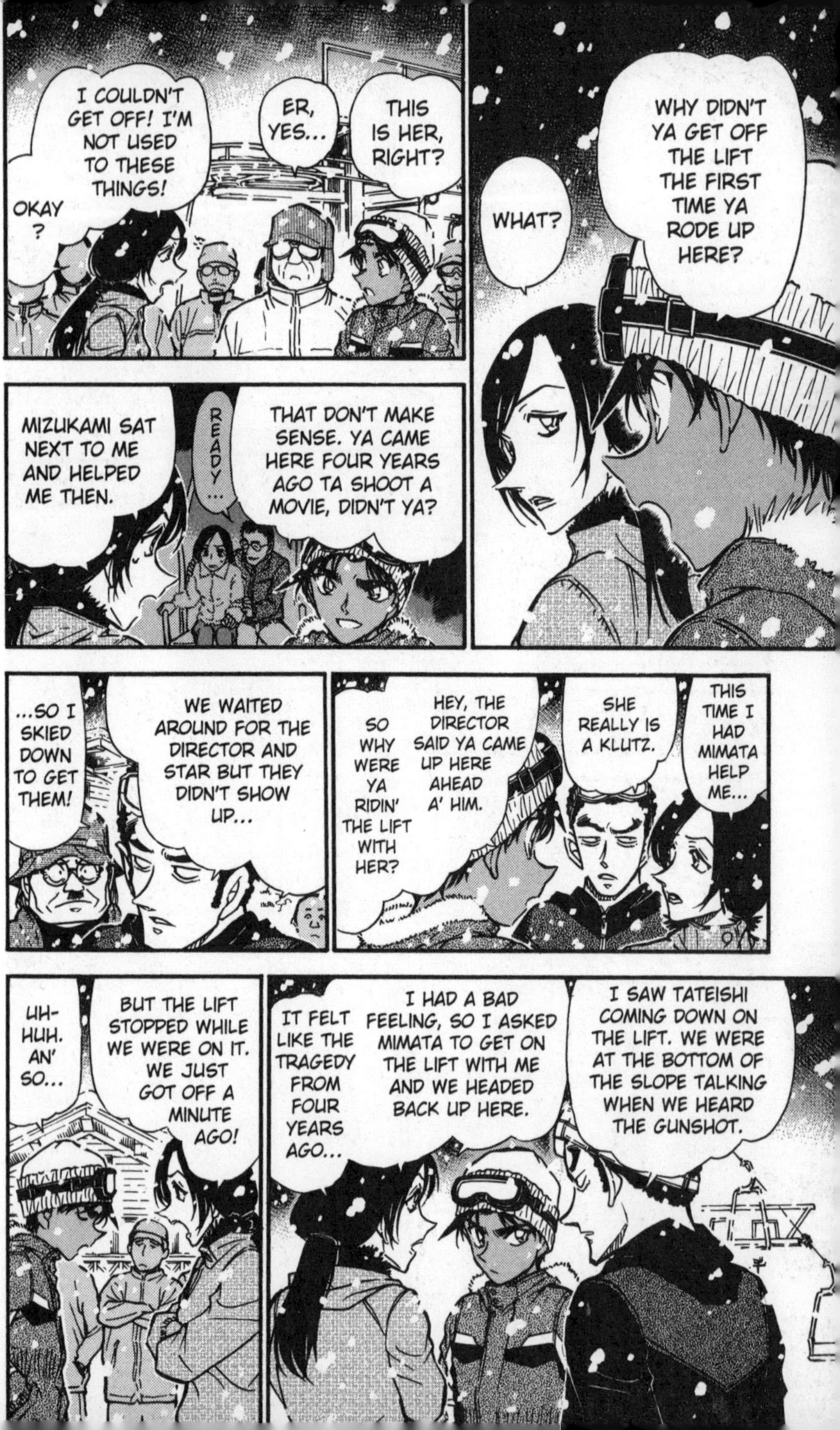
WHY DIDN'T YA GET OFF THE LIFT THE FIRST TIME YA RODE UP HERE?
WHAT?
THIS IS HER, RIGHT?
ER, YES...
I COULDN'T GET OFF! I'M NOT USED TO THESE THINGS!
OKAY?
THAT DON'T MAKE SENSE. YA CAME HERE FOUR YEARS AGO TA SHOOT A MOVIE, DIDN'T YA?
READY...
MIZUKAMI SAT NEXT TO ME AND HELPED ME THEN.
THIS TIME I HAD MIMATA HELP ME...
SHE REALLY IS A KLUTZ.
HEY, THE DIRECTOR SAID YA CAME UP HERE AHEAD A' HIM.
SO WHY WERE YA RIDIN' THE LIFT WITH HER?
WE WAITED AROUND FOR THE DIRECTOR AND STAR BUT THEY DIDN'T SHOW UP...
...SO I SKIED DOWN TO GET THEM!
I SAW TATEISHI COMING DOWN ON THE LIFT. WE WERE AT THE BOTTOM OF THE SLOPE TALKING WHEN WE HEARD THE GUNSHOT.
I HAD A BAD FEELING, SO I ASKED MIMATA TO GET ON THE LIFT WITH ME AND WE HEADED BACK UP HERE.
IT FELT LIKE THE TRAGEDY FROM FOUR YEARS AGO...
BUT THE LIFT STOPPED WHILE WE WERE ON IT. WE JUST GOT OFF A MINUTE AGO!
UH-HUH. AN' SO...

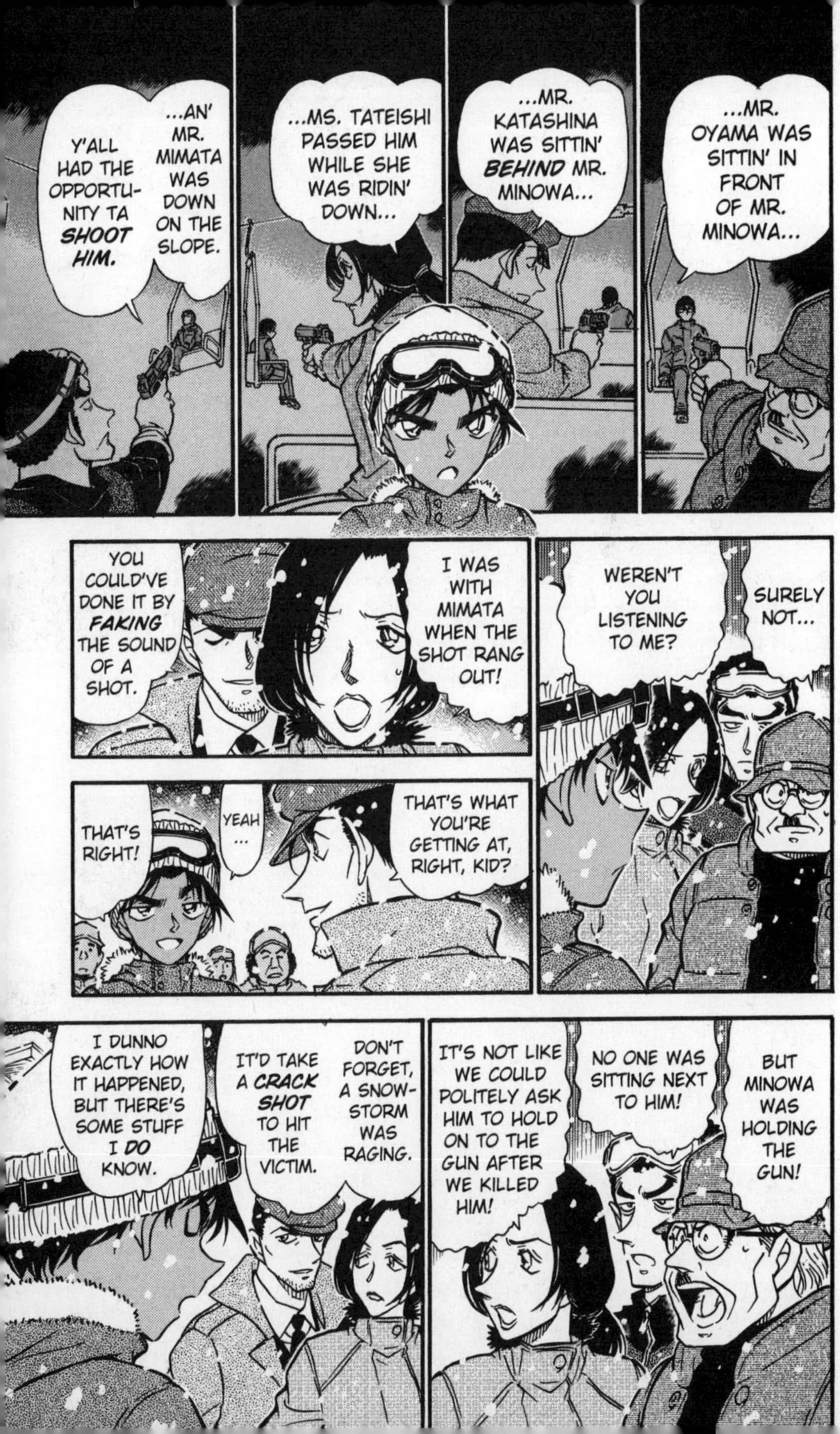
...MR. OYAMA WAS SITTIN' IN FRONT OF MR. MINOWA...
...MR. KATASHINA WAS SITTIN' BEHIND MR. MINOWA...
...MS. TATEISHI PASSED HIM WHILE SHE WAS RIDIN' DOWN...
...AN' MR. MIMATA WAS DOWN ON THE SLOPE.
Y'ALL HAD THE OPPORTU-NITY TA SHOOT HIM.
SURELY NOT...
WEREN'T YOU LISTENING TO ME?
I WAS WITH MIMATA WHEN THE SHOT RANG OUT!
YOU COULD'VE DONE IT BY FAKING THE SOUND OF A SHOT.
THAT'S WHAT YOU'RE GETTING AT, RIGHT, KID?
YEAH...
THAT'S RIGHT!
BUT MINOWA WAS HOLDING THE GUN!
NO ONE WAS SITTING NEXT TO HIM!
IT'S NOT LIKE WE COULD POLITELY ASK HIM TO HOLD ON TO THE GUN AFTER WE KILLED HIM!
DON'T FORGET, A SNOW-STORM WAS RAGING.
IT'D TAKE A CRACK SHOT TO HIT THE VICTIM.
I DUNNO EXACTLY HOW IT HAPPENED, BUT THERE'S SOME STUFF I DO KNOW.

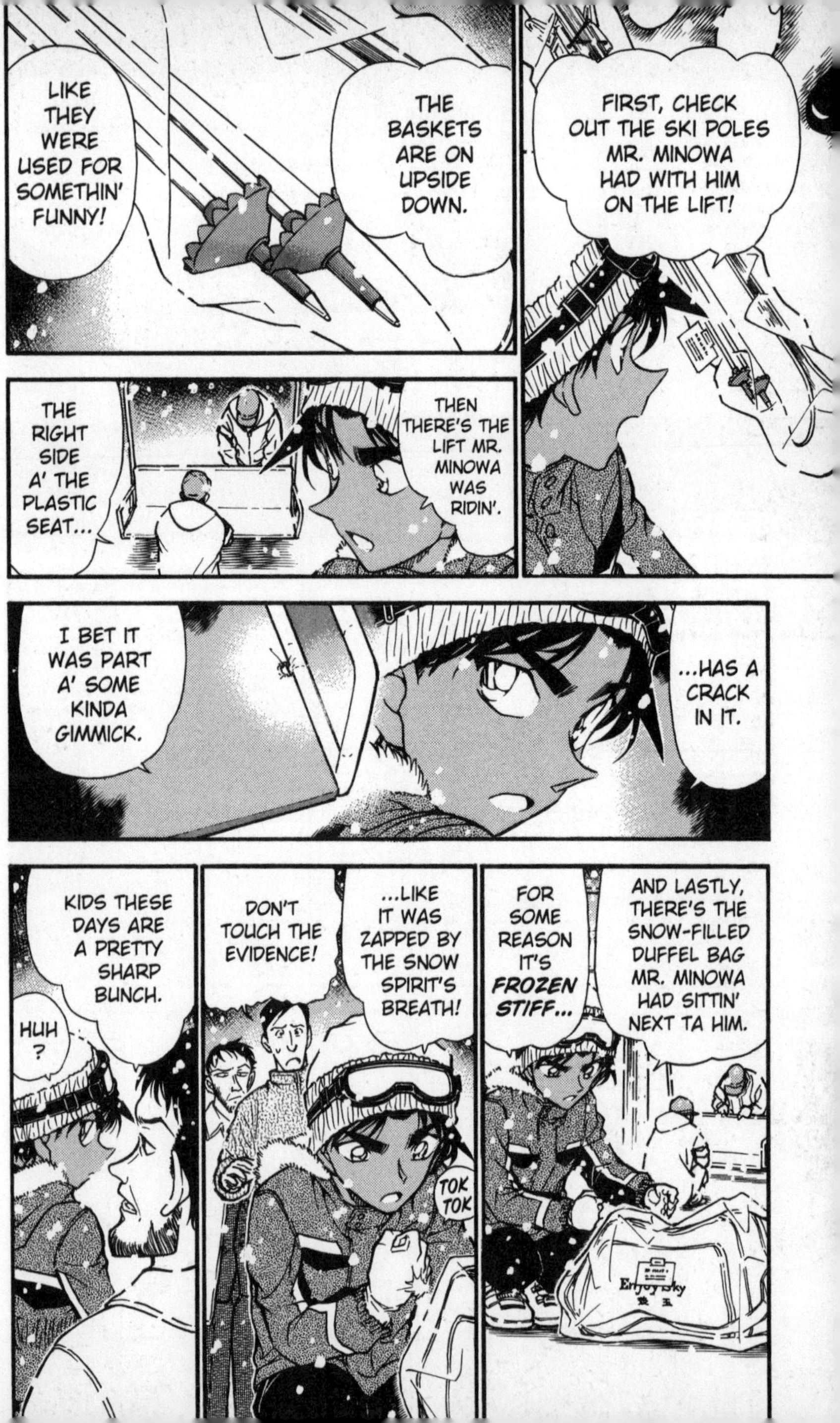
FIRST, CHECK OUT THE SKI POLES MR. MINOWA HAD WITH HIM ON THE LIFT!
THE BASKETS ARE ON UPSIDE DOWN.
LIKE THEY WERE USED FOR SOMETHIN' FUNNY!
THEN THERE'S THE LIFT MR. MINOWA WAS RIDIN'.
THE RIGHT SIDE A' THE PLASTIC SEAT...
...HAS A CRACK IN IT.
I BET IT WAS PART A' SOME KINDA GIMMICK.
AND LASTLY, THERE'S THE SNOW-FILLED DUFFEL BAG MR. MINOWA HAD SITTIN' NEXT TA HIM.
FOR SOME REASON IT'S *FROZEN STIFF*...
...LIKE IT WAS ZAPPED BY THE SNOW SPIRIT'S BREATH!
DON'T TOUCH THE EVIDENCE!
TOK TOK
KIDS THESE DAYS ARE A PRETTY SHARP BUNCH.
HUH ?

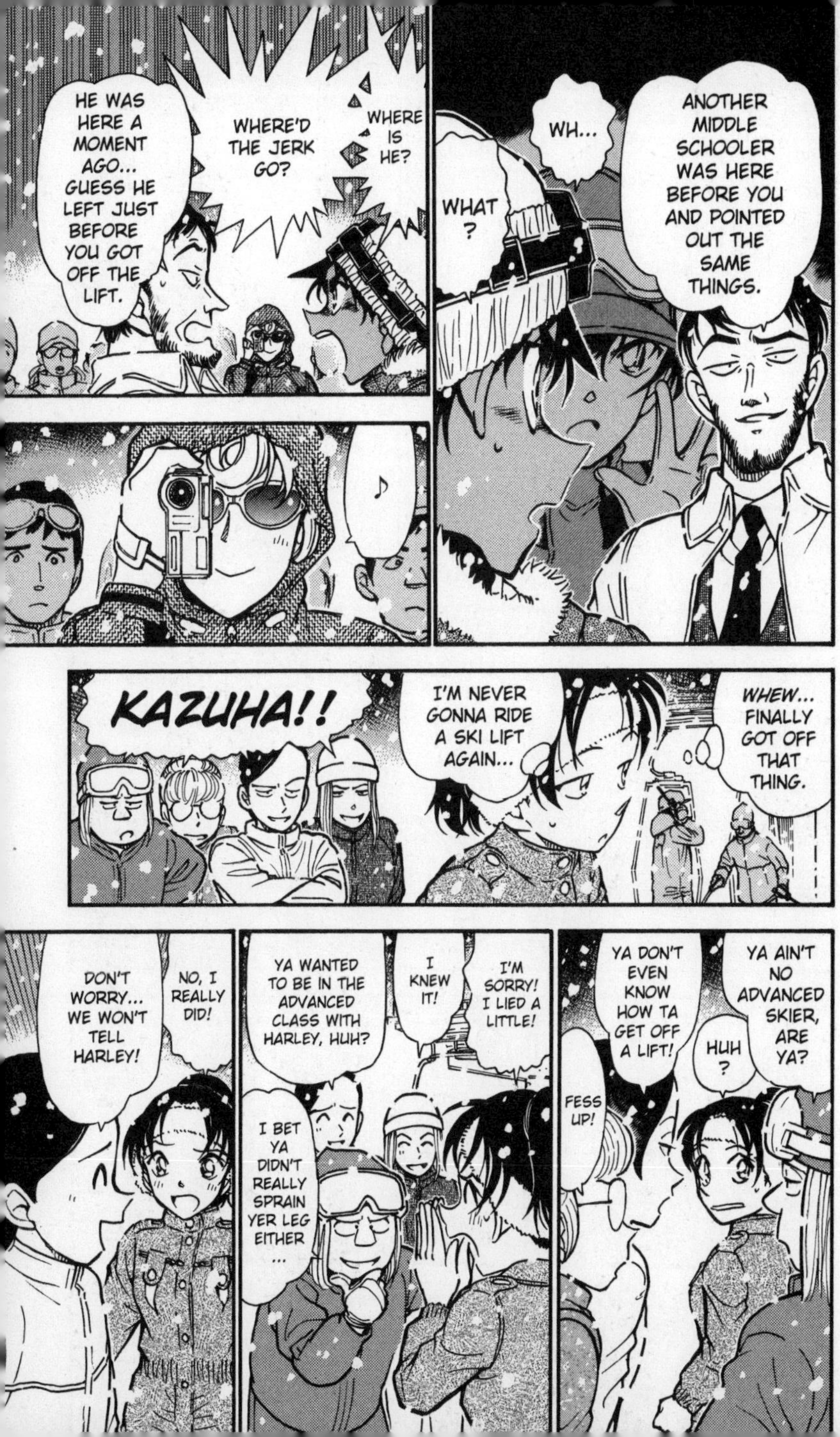
ANOTHER MIDDLE SCHOOLER WAS HERE BEFORE YOU AND POINTED OUT THE SAME THINGS.
WH...
WHAT?
WHERE IS HE?
WHERE'D THE JERK GO?
HE WAS HERE A MOMENT AGO... GUESS HE LEFT JUST BEFORE YOU GOT OFF THE LIFT.
♪
WHEW... FINALLY GOT OFF THAT THING.
I'M NEVER GONNA RIDE A SKI LIFT AGAIN...
KAZUHA!!
YA AIN'T NO ADVANCED SKIER, ARE YA?
HUH?
YA DON'T EVEN KNOW HOW TA GET OFF A LIFT!
FESS UP!
I'M SORRY! I LIED A LITTLE!
I KNEW IT!
YA WANTED TO BE IN THE ADVANCED CLASS WITH HARLEY, HUH?
I BET YA DIDN'T REALLY SPRAIN YER LEG EITHER...
NO, I REALLY DID!
DON'T WORRY... WE WON'T TELL HARLEY!

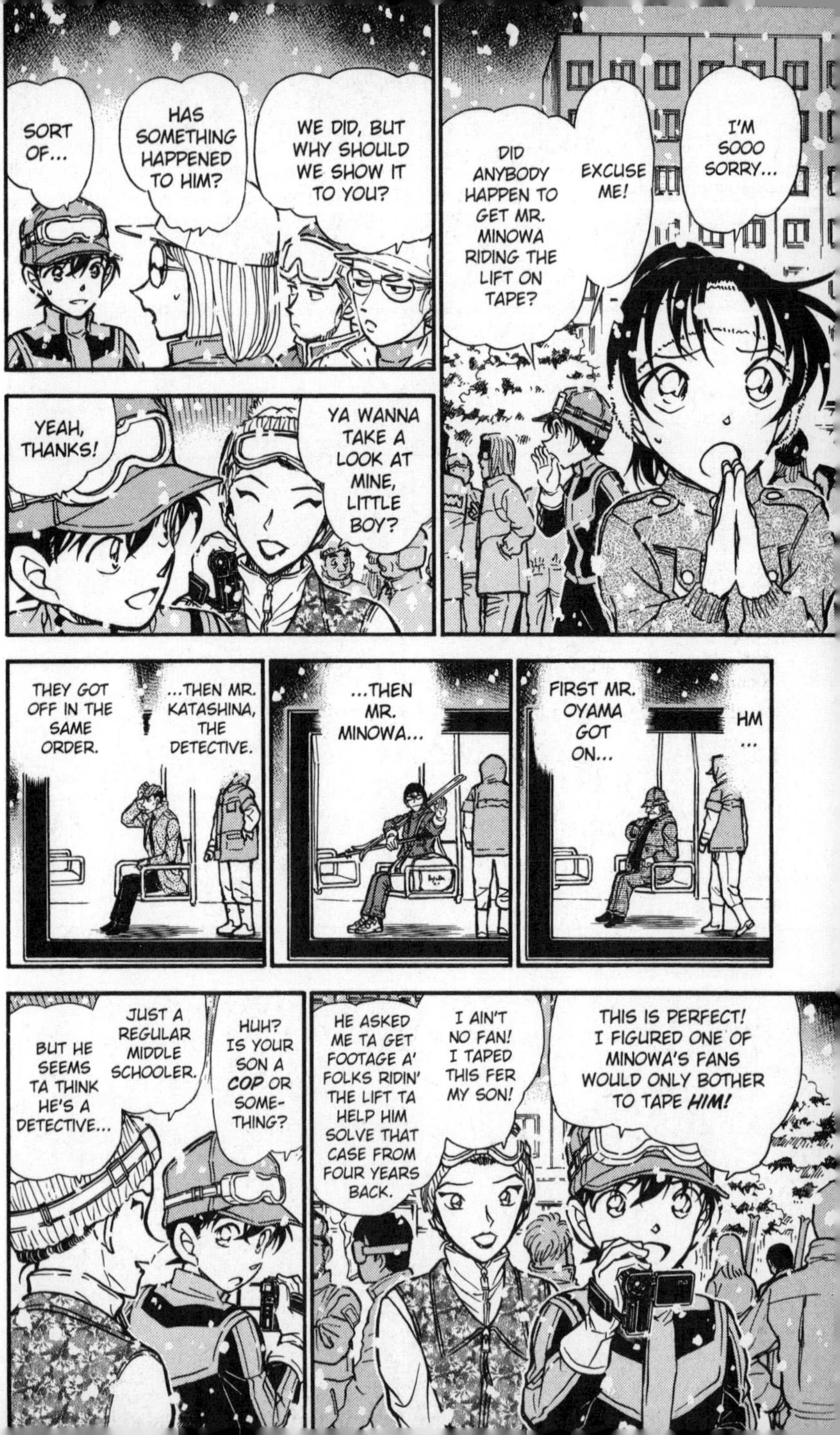
I'M SOOO SORRY...
EXCUSE ME!
DID ANYBODY HAPPEN TO GET MR. MINOWA RIDING THE LIFT ON TAPE?
WE DID, BUT WHY SHOULD WE SHOW IT TO YOU?
HAS SOMETHING HAPPENED TO HIM?
SORT OF...
YA WANNA TAKE A LOOK AT MINE, LITTLE BOY?
YEAH, THANKS!
HM...
FIRST MR. OYAMA GOT ON...
...THEN MR. MINOWA...
...THEN MR. KATASHINA, THE DETECTIVE.
THEY GOT OFF IN THE SAME ORDER.
THIS IS PERFECT! I FIGURED ONE OF MINOWA'S FANS WOULD ONLY BOTHER TO TAPE *HIM!*
I AIN'T NO FAN! I TAPED THIS FER MY SON!
HE ASKED ME TA GET FOOTAGE A' FOLKS RIDIN' THE LIFT TA HELP HIM SOLVE THAT CASE FROM FOUR YEARS BACK.
HUH? IS YOUR SON A *COP* OR SOME-THING?
JUST A REGULAR MIDDLE SCHOOLER.
BUT HE SEEMS TA THINK HE'S A DETECTIVE...

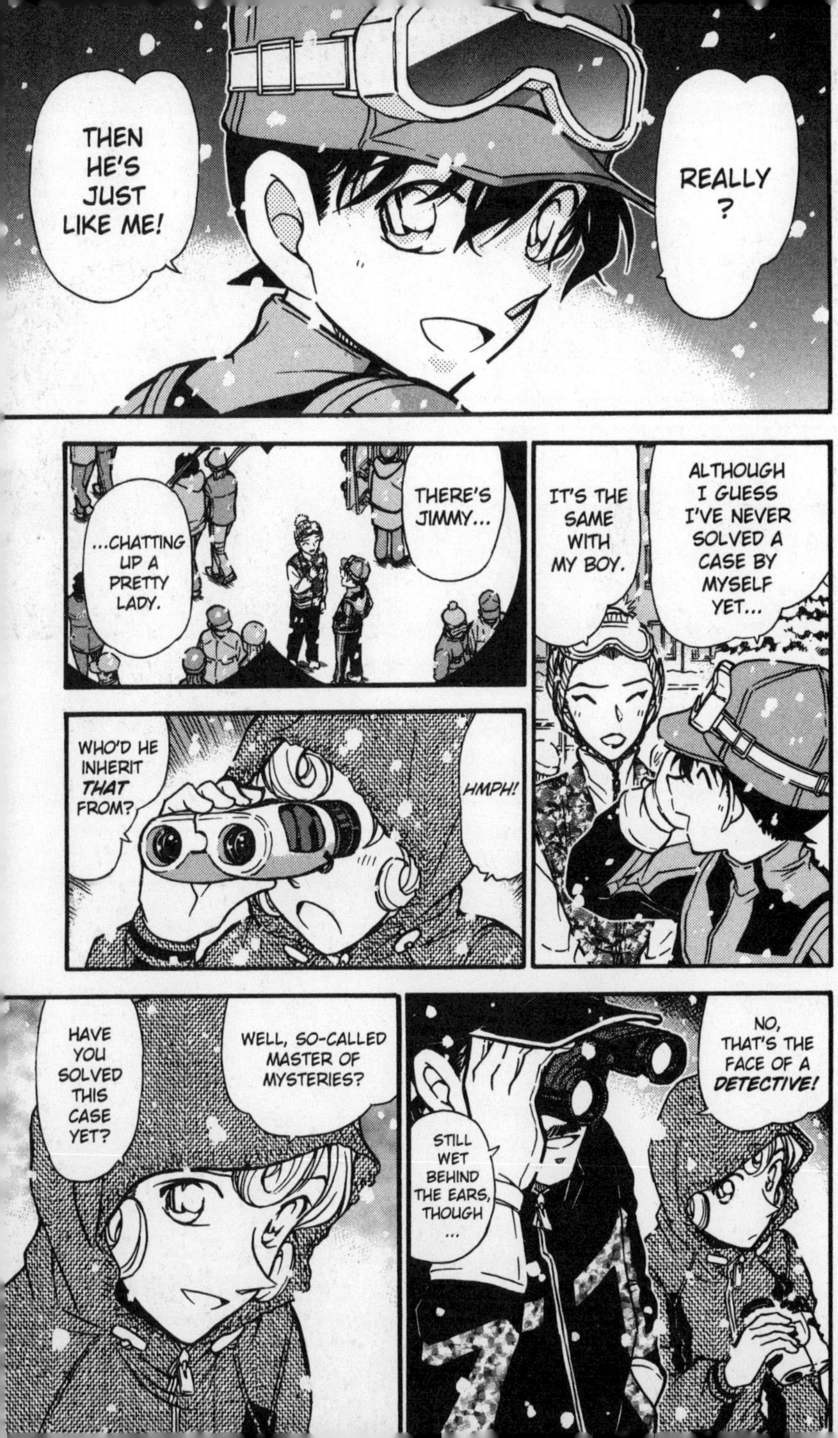
REALLY ?
THEN HE'S JUST LIKE ME!
ALTHOUGH I GUESS I'VE NEVER SOLVED A CASE BY MYSELF YET...
IT'S THE SAME WITH MY BOY.
THERE'S JIMMY...
...CHATTING UP A PRETTY LADY.
HMPH!
WHO'D HE INHERIT *THAT* FROM?
NO, THAT'S THE FACE OF A *DETECTIVE!*
STILL WET BEHIND THE EARS, THOUGH ...
WELL, SO-CALLED MASTER OF MYSTERIES?
HAVE YOU SOLVED THIS CASE YET?

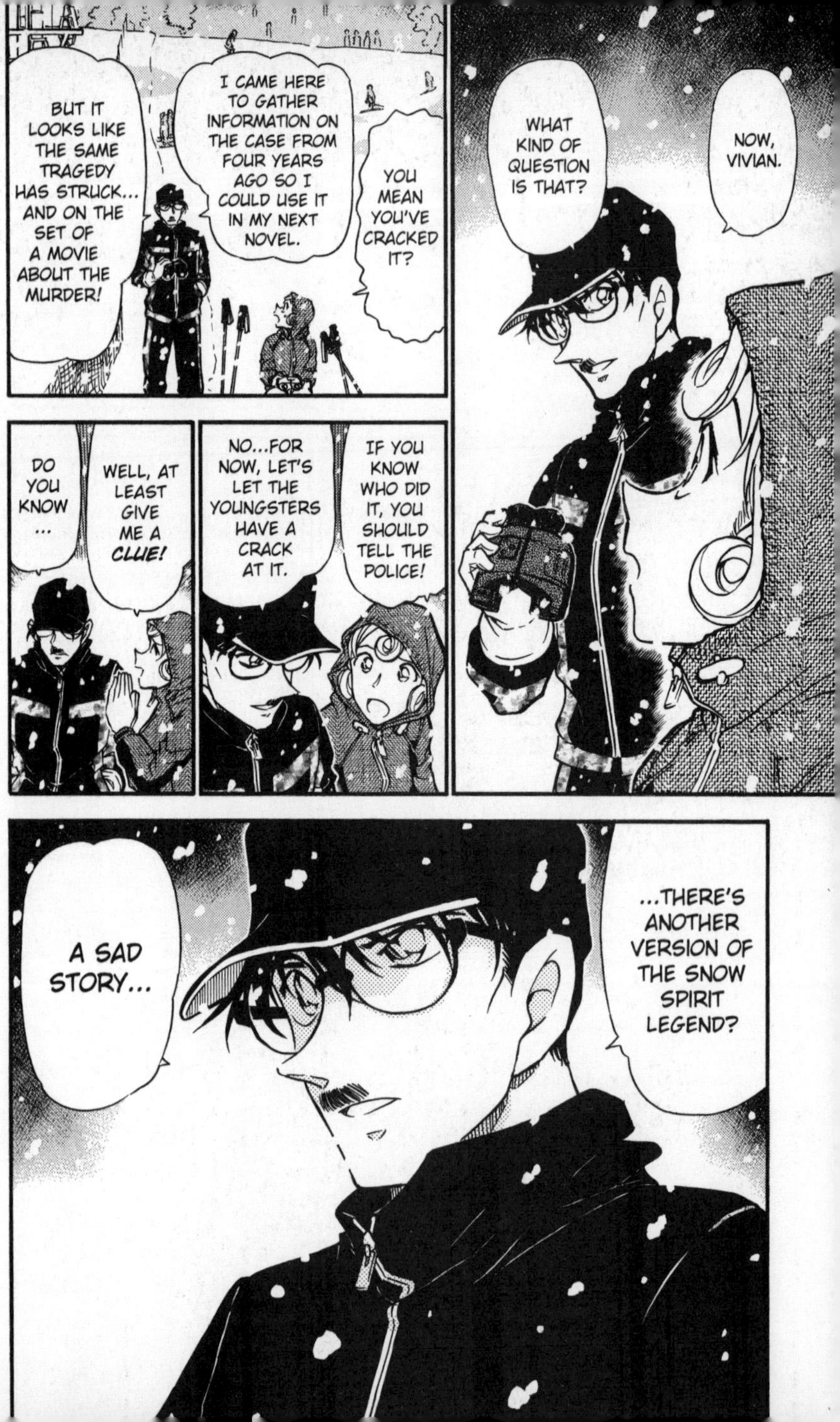
NOW, VIVIAN.
WHAT KIND OF QUESTION IS THAT?
YOU MEAN YOU'VE CRACKED IT?
I CAME HERE TO GATHER INFORMATION ON THE CASE FROM FOUR YEARS AGO SO I COULD USE IT IN MY NEXT NOVEL.
BUT IT LOOKS LIKE THE SAME TRAGEDY HAS STRUCK... AND ON THE SET OF A MOVIE ABOUT THE MURDER!
IF YOU KNOW WHO DID IT, YOU SHOULD TELL THE POLICE!
NO...FOR NOW, LET'S LET THE YOUNGSTERS HAVE A CRACK AT IT.
WELL, AT LEAST GIVE ME A CLUE!
DO YOU KNOW ...
...THERE'S ANOTHER VERSION OF THE SNOW SPIRIT LEGEND?
A SAD STORY...

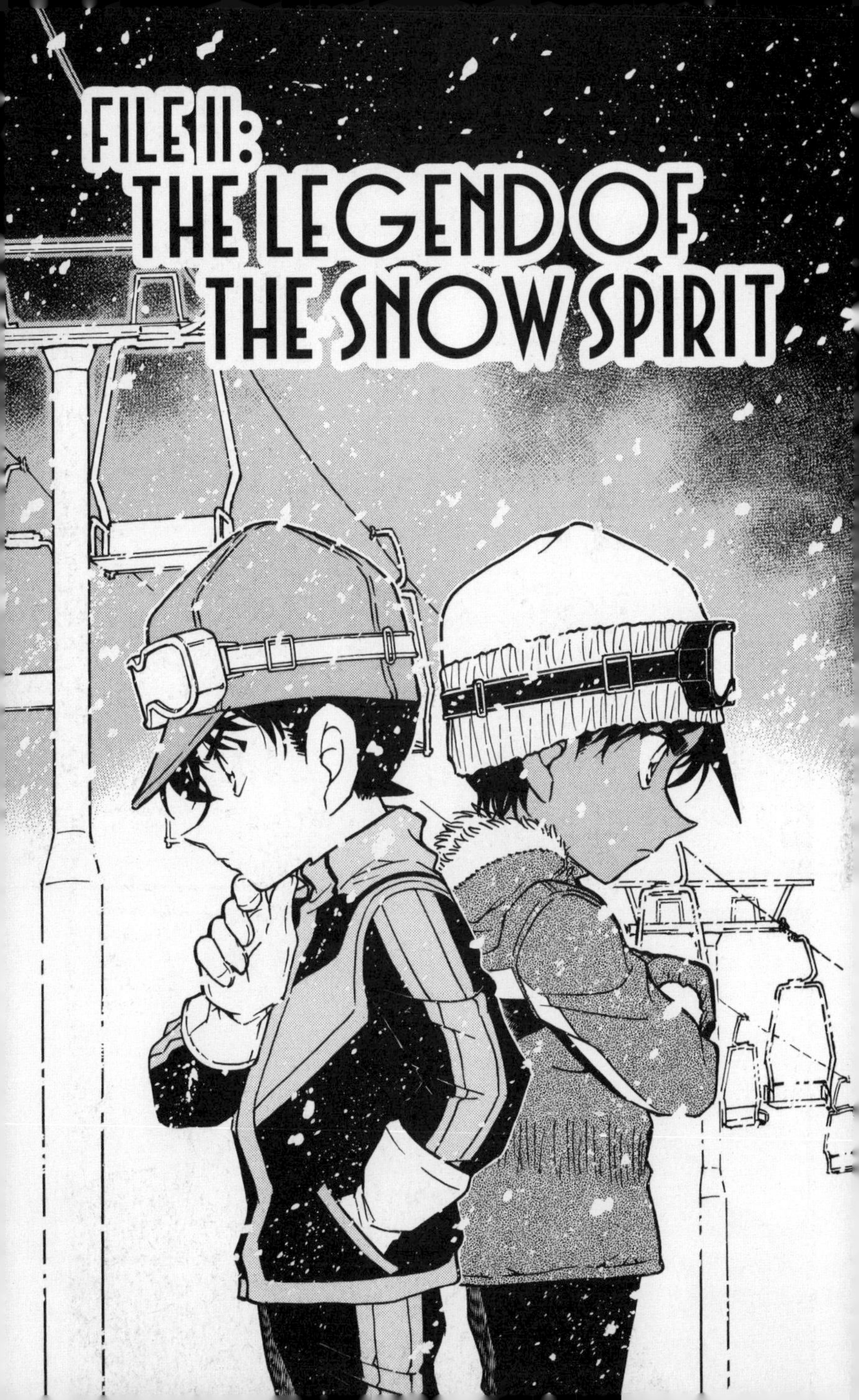
FILE 11:
THE LEGEND OF
THE SNOW SPIRIT

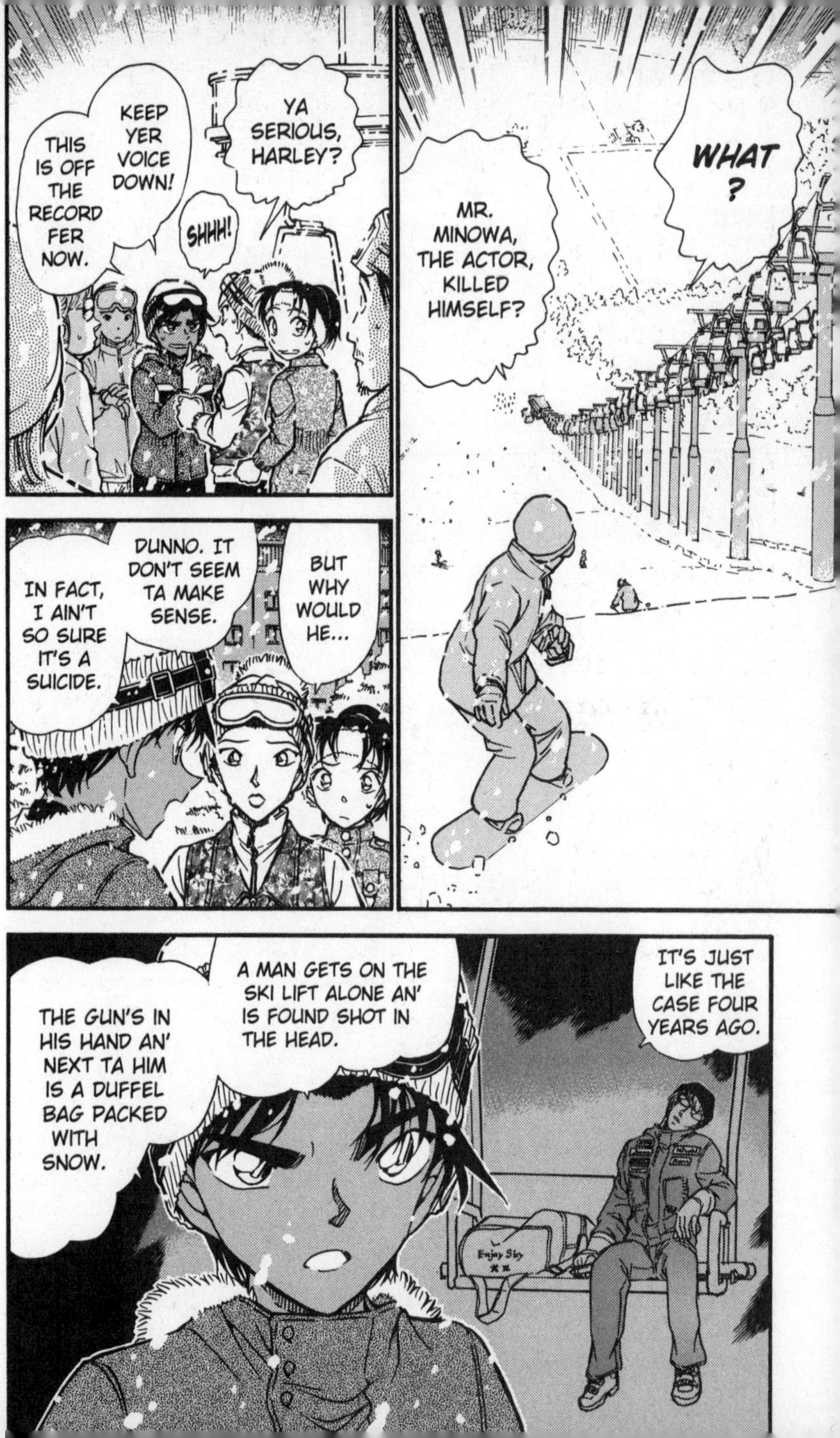
WHAT?
MR. MINOWA, THE ACTOR, KILLED HIMSELF?
YA SERIOUS, HARLEY?
KEEP YER VOICE DOWN!
SHHH!
THIS IS OFF THE RECORD FER NOW.
BUT WHY WOULD HE...
DUNNO. IT DON'T SEEM TA MAKE SENSE.
IN FACT, I AIN'T SO SURE IT'S A SUICIDE.
IT'S JUST LIKE THE CASE FOUR YEARS AGO.
A MAN GETS ON THE SKI LIFT ALONE AN' IS FOUND SHOT IN THE HEAD.
THE GUN'S IN HIS HAND AN' NEXT TA HIM IS A DUFFEL BAG PACKED WITH SNOW.
Enjoy Sky

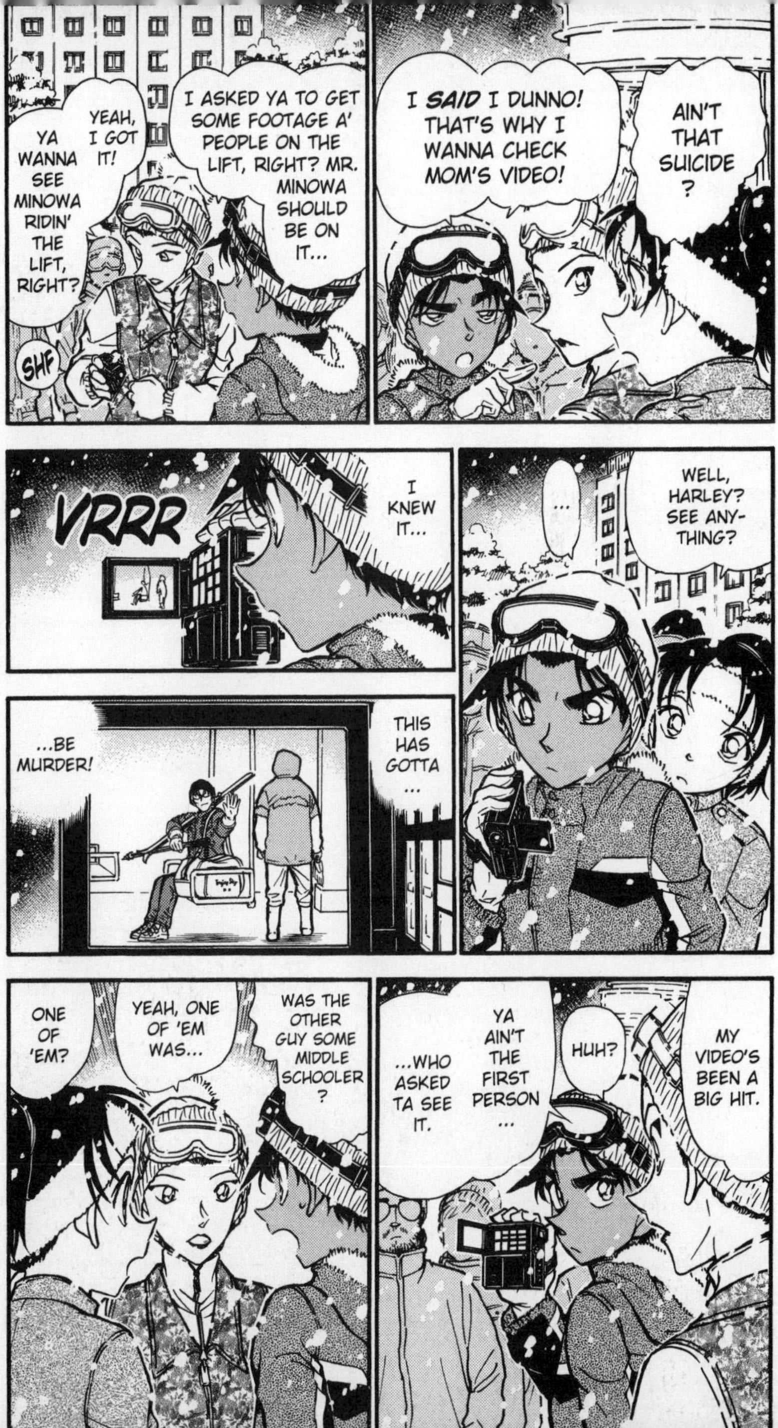
AIN'T THAT SUICIDE?
I *SAID* I DUNNO! THAT'S WHY I WANNA CHECK MOM'S VIDEO!
I ASKED YA TO GET SOME FOOTAGE A' PEOPLE ON THE LIFT, RIGHT? MR. MINOWA SHOULD BE ON IT...
YEAH, I GOT IT!
YA WANNA SEE MINOWA RIDIN' THE LIFT, RIGHT?
SHF
WELL, HARLEY? SEE ANYTHING?
...
I KNEW IT...
VRRR
THIS HAS GOTTA...
...BE MURDER!
MY VIDEO'S BEEN A BIG HIT.
HUH?
YA AIN'T THE FIRST PERSON...
...WHO ASKED TA SEE IT.
WAS THE OTHER GUY SOME MIDDLE SCHOOLER?
YEAH, ONE OF 'EM WAS...
ONE OF 'EM?

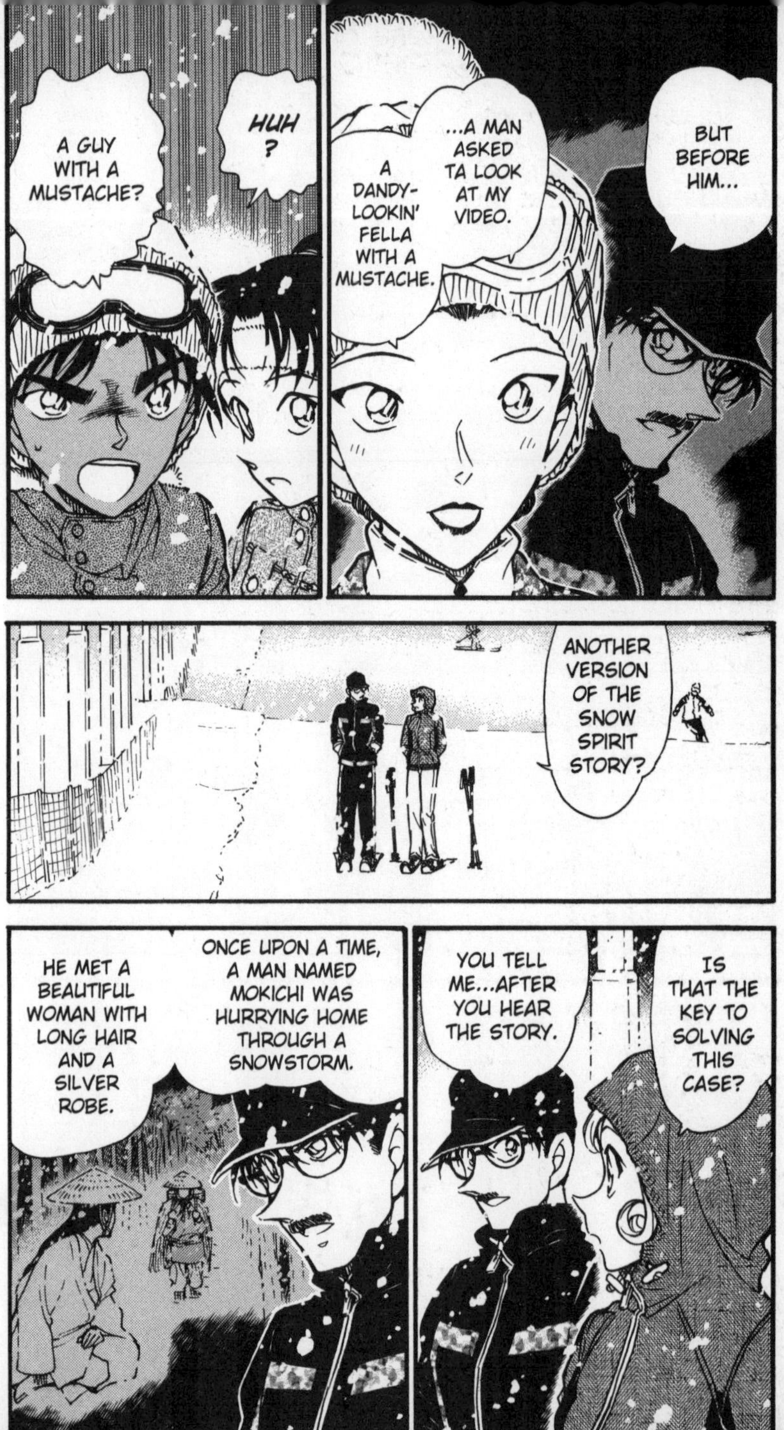
BUT BEFORE HIM...
...A MAN ASKED TA LOOK AT MY VIDEO.
A DANDY-LOOKIN' FELLA WITH A MUSTACHE.
HUH ?
A GUY WITH A MUSTACHE?
ANOTHER VERSION OF THE SNOW SPIRIT STORY?
IS THAT THE KEY TO SOLVING THIS CASE?
YOU TELL ME...AFTER YOU HEAR THE STORY.
ONCE UPON A TIME, A MAN NAMED MOKICHI WAS HURRYING HOME THROUGH A SNOWSTORM.
HE MET A BEAUTIFUL WOMAN WITH LONG HAIR AND A SILVER ROBE.

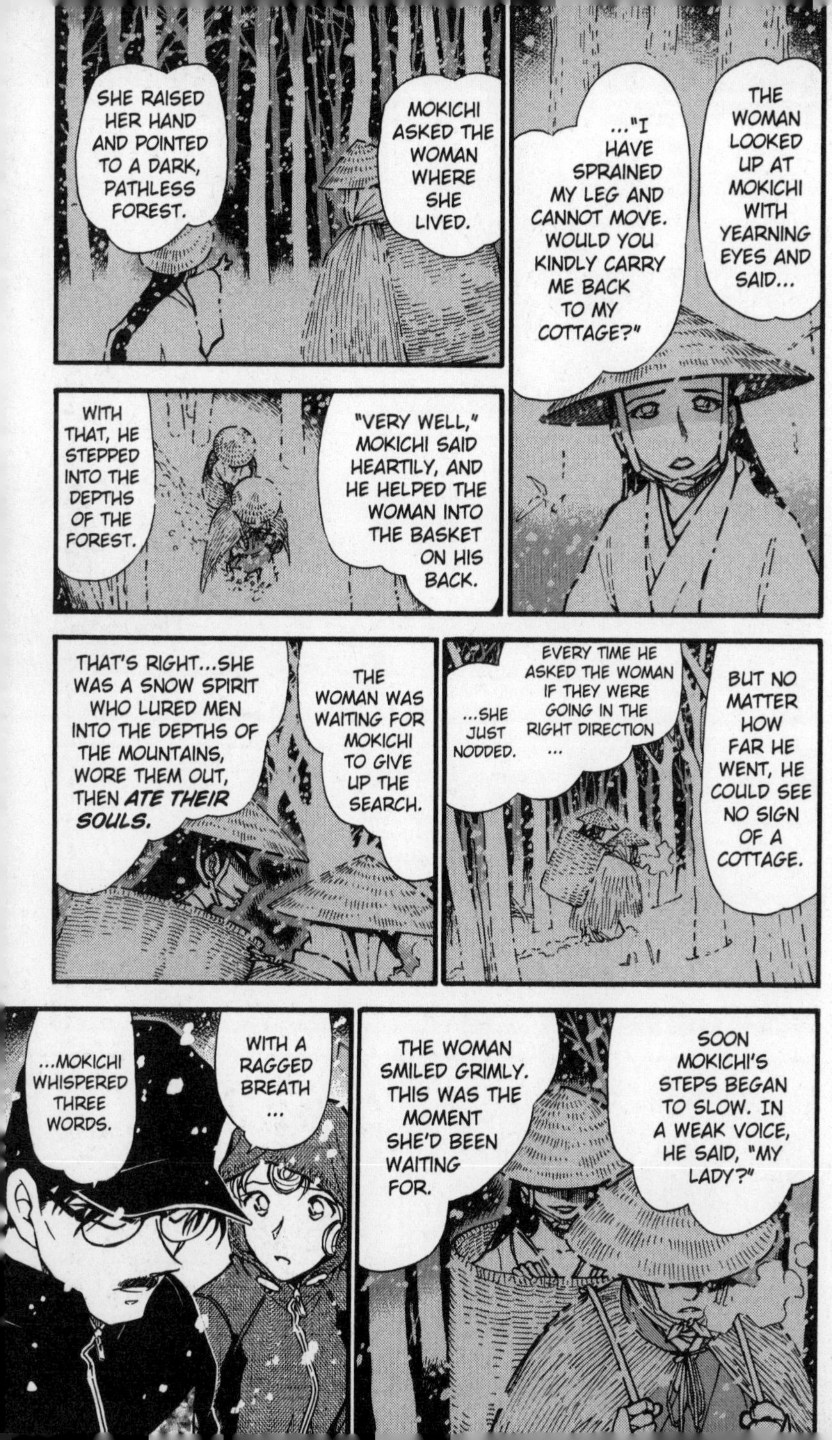
THE WOMAN LOOKED UP AT MOKICHI WITH YEARNING EYES AND SAID...
..."I HAVE SPRAINED MY LEG AND CANNOT MOVE. WOULD YOU KINDLY CARRY ME BACK TO MY COTTAGE?"
MOKICHI ASKED THE WOMAN WHERE SHE LIVED.
SHE RAISED HER HAND AND POINTED TO A DARK, PATHLESS FOREST.
"VERY WELL," MOKICHI SAID HEARTILY, AND HE HELPED THE WOMAN INTO THE BASKET ON HIS BACK.
WITH THAT, HE STEPPED INTO THE DEPTHS OF THE FOREST.
BUT NO MATTER HOW FAR HE WENT, HE COULD SEE NO SIGN OF A COTTAGE.
EVERY TIME HE ASKED THE WOMAN IF THEY WERE GOING IN THE RIGHT DIRECTION ...
...SHE JUST NODDED.
THE WOMAN WAS WAITING FOR MOKICHI TO GIVE UP THE SEARCH.
THAT'S RIGHT...SHE WAS A SNOW SPIRIT WHO LURED MEN INTO THE DEPTHS OF THE MOUNTAINS, WORE THEM OUT, THEN ***ATE THEIR SOULS.***
SOON MOKICHI'S STEPS BEGAN TO SLOW. IN A WEAK VOICE, HE SAID, "MY LADY?"
THE WOMAN SMILED GRIMLY. THIS WAS THE MOMENT SHE'D BEEN WAITING FOR.
WITH A RAGGED BREATH ...
...MOKICHI WHISPERED THREE WORDS.

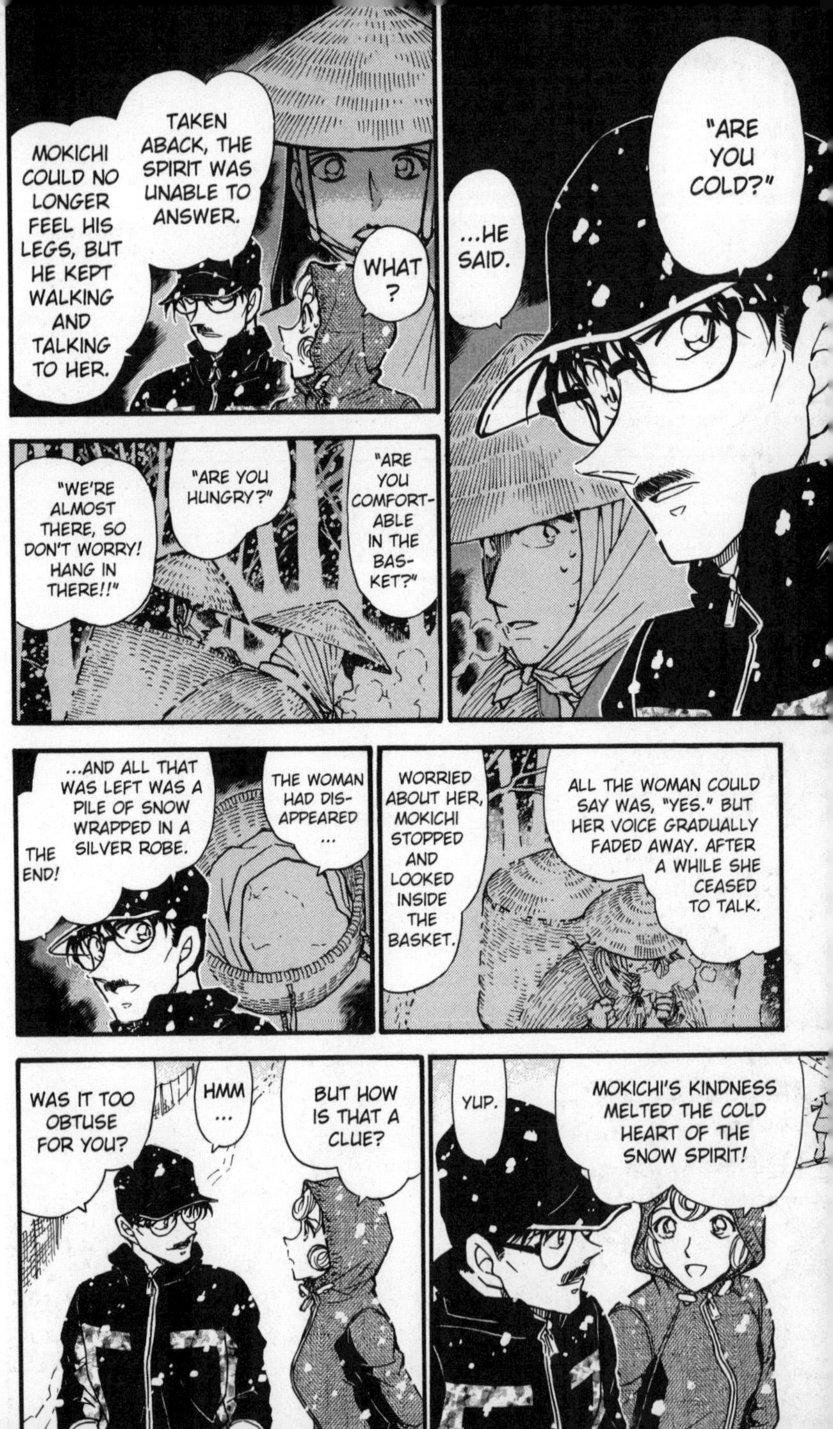
"ARE YOU COLD?"
...HE SAID.
WHAT?
TAKEN ABACK, THE SPIRIT WAS UNABLE TO ANSWER.
MOKICHI COULD NO LONGER FEEL HIS LEGS, BUT HE KEPT WALKING AND TALKING TO HER.
"ARE YOU COMFORT-ABLE IN THE BAS-KET?"
"ARE YOU HUNGRY?"
"WE'RE ALMOST THERE, SO DON'T WORRY! HANG IN THERE!!"
ALL THE WOMAN COULD SAY WAS, "YES." BUT HER VOICE GRADUALLY FADED AWAY. AFTER A WHILE SHE CEASED TO TALK.
WORRIED ABOUT HER, MOKICHI STOPPED AND LOOKED INSIDE THE BASKET.
THE WOMAN HAD DIS-APPEARED...
...AND ALL THAT WAS LEFT WAS A PILE OF SNOW WRAPPED IN A SILVER ROBE.
THE END!
MOKICHI'S KINDNESS MELTED THE COLD HEART OF THE SNOW SPIRIT!
YUP.
BUT HOW IS THAT A CLUE?
HMM...
WAS IT TOO OBTUSE FOR YOU?

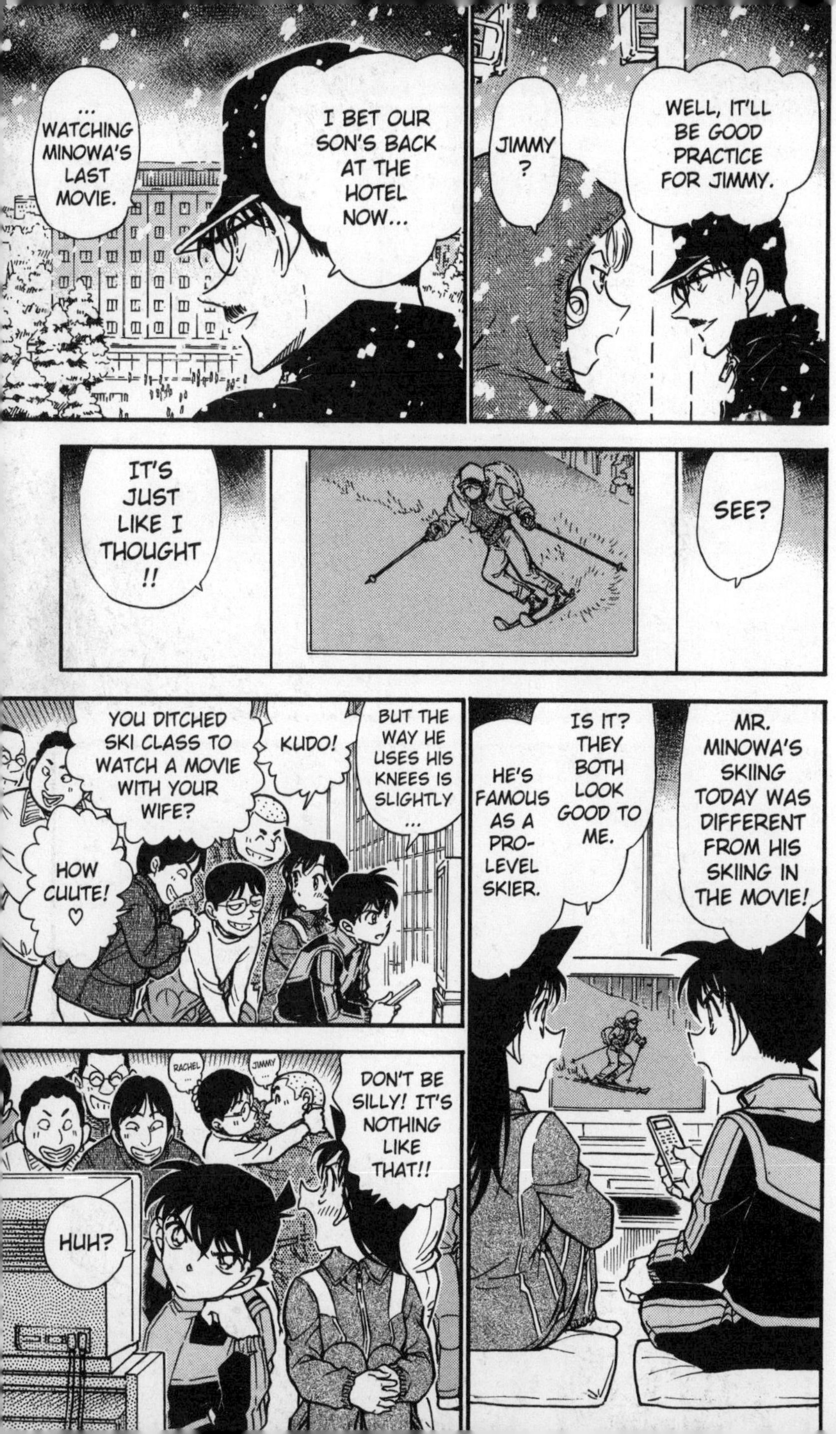
WELL, IT'LL BE GOOD PRACTICE FOR JIMMY.
JIMMY?
I BET OUR SON'S BACK AT THE HOTEL NOW...
... WATCHING MINOWA'S LAST MOVIE.
SEE?
IT'S JUST LIKE I THOUGHT!!
MR. MINOWA'S SKIING TODAY WAS DIFFERENT FROM HIS SKIING IN THE MOVIE!
IS IT? THEY BOTH LOOK GOOD TO ME.
HE'S FAMOUS AS A PRO-LEVEL SKIER.
BUT THE WAY HE USES HIS KNEES IS SLIGHTLY ...
KUDO!
YOU DITCHED SKI CLASS TO WATCH A MOVIE WITH YOUR WIFE?
HOW CUUTE! ♡
DON'T BE SILLY! IT'S NOTHING LIKE THAT!!
JIMMY ...
RACHEL ...
HUH?

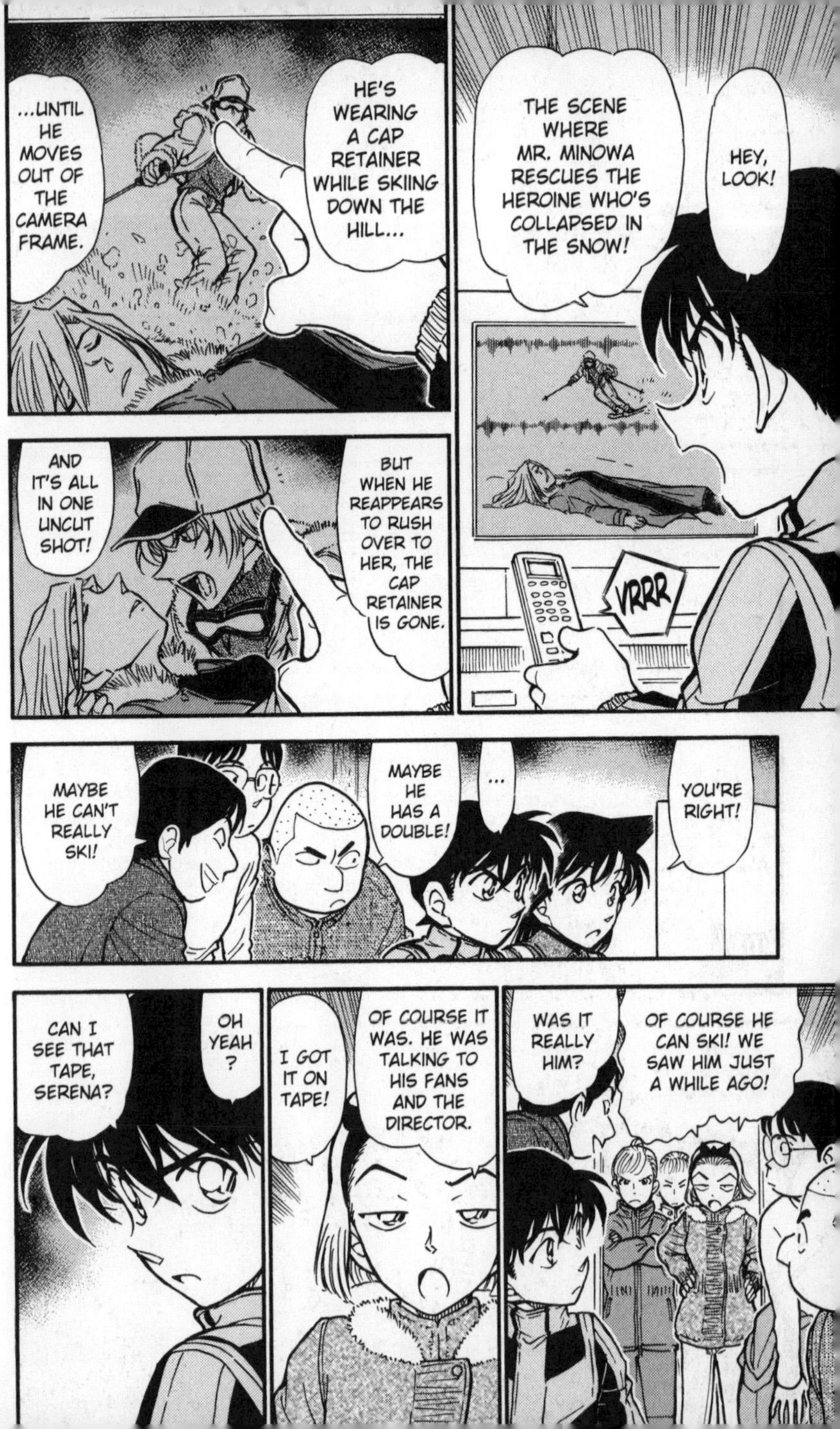
HEY, LOOK!
THE SCENE WHERE MR. MINOWA RESCUES THE HEROINE WHO'S COLLAPSED IN THE SNOW!
VRRR
HE'S WEARING A CAP RETAINER WHILE SKIING DOWN THE HILL...
...UNTIL HE MOVES OUT OF THE CAMERA FRAME.
BUT WHEN HE REAPPEARS TO RUSH OVER TO HER, THE CAP RETAINER IS GONE.
AND IT'S ALL IN ONE UNCUT SHOT!
YOU'RE RIGHT!
...
MAYBE HE HAS A DOUBLE!
MAYBE HE CAN'T REALLY SKI!
OF COURSE HE CAN SKI! WE SAW HIM JUST A WHILE AGO!
WAS IT REALLY HIM?
OF COURSE IT WAS. HE WAS TALKING TO HIS FANS AND THE DIRECTOR.
I GOT IT ON TAPE!
OH YEAH?
CAN I SEE THAT TAPE, SERENA?

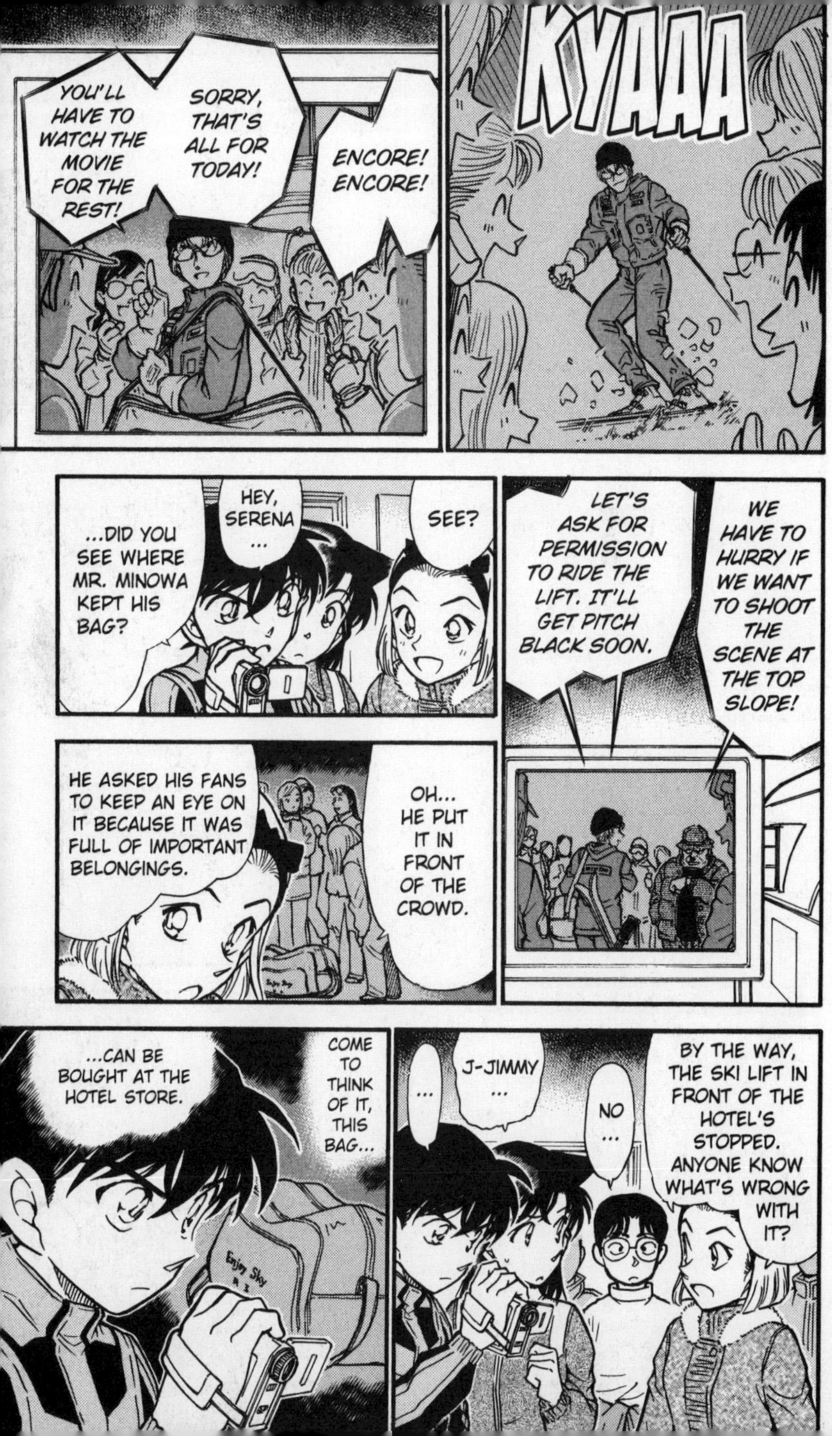
KYAAA
ENCORE! ENCORE!
SORRY, THAT'S ALL FOR TODAY!
YOU'LL HAVE TO WATCH THE MOVIE FOR THE REST!
WE HAVE TO HURRY IF WE WANT TO SHOOT THE SCENE AT THE TOP SLOPE!
LET'S ASK FOR PERMISSION TO RIDE THE LIFT. IT'LL GET PITCH BLACK SOON.
SEE?
HEY, SERENA ...
...DID YOU SEE WHERE MR. MINOWA KEPT HIS BAG?
OH... HE PUT IT IN FRONT OF THE CROWD.
HE ASKED HIS FANS TO KEEP AN EYE ON IT BECAUSE IT WAS FULL OF IMPORTANT BELONGINGS.
BY THE WAY, THE SKI LIFT IN FRONT OF THE HOTEL'S STOPPED. ANYONE KNOW WHAT'S WRONG WITH IT?
NO ...
J-JIMMY ...
...
COME TO THINK OF IT, THIS BAG...
...CAN BE BOUGHT AT THE HOTEL STORE.

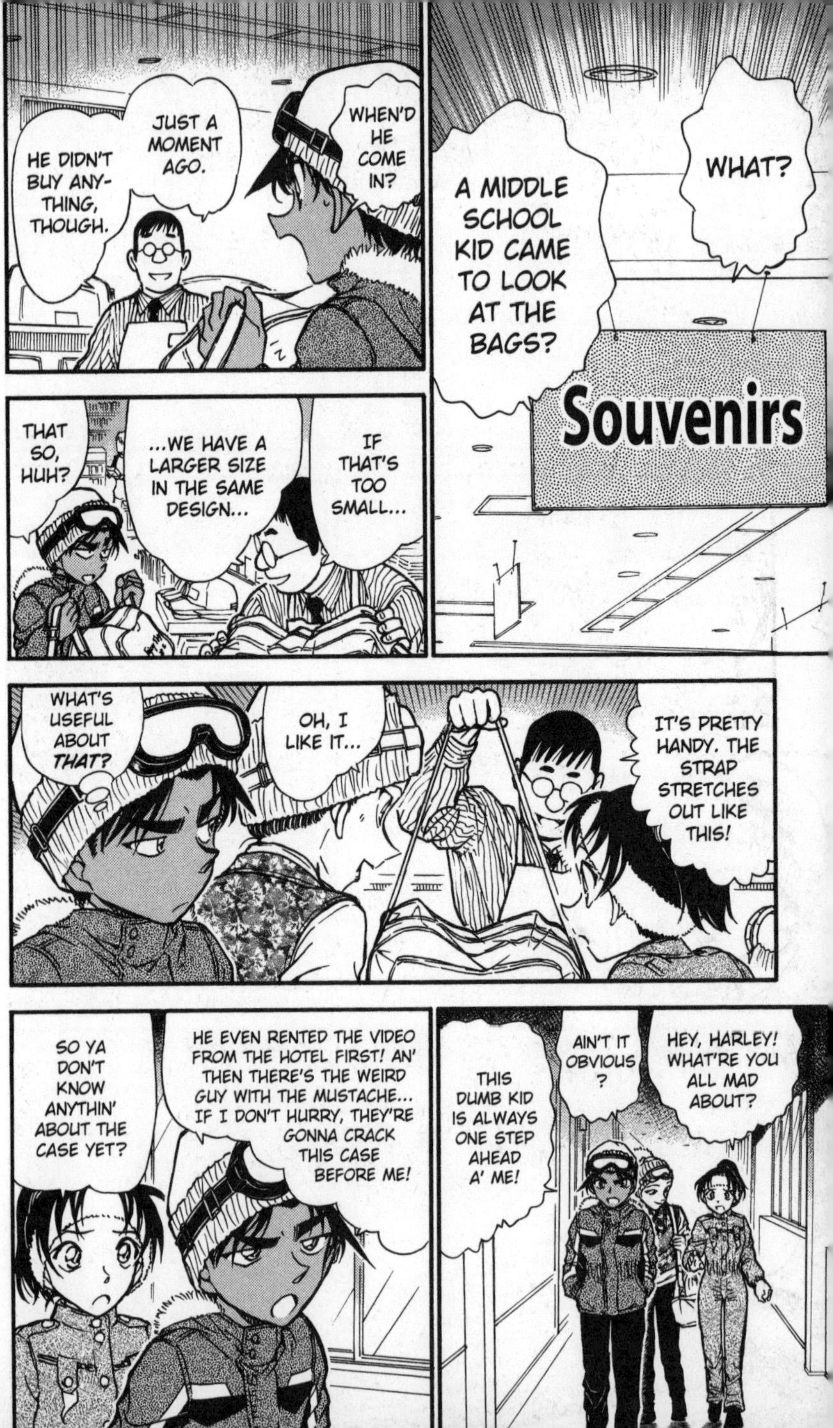
WHAT?
A MIDDLE SCHOOL KID CAME TO LOOK AT THE BAGS?
Souvenirs
WHEN'D HE COME IN?
JUST A MOMENT AGO.
HE DIDN'T BUY ANY-THING, THOUGH.
IF THAT'S TOO SMALL...
...WE HAVE A LARGER SIZE IN THE SAME DESIGN...
THAT SO, HUH?
IT'S PRETTY HANDY. THE STRAP STRETCHES OUT LIKE THIS!
OH, I LIKE IT...
WHAT'S USEFUL ABOUT *THAT*?
HEY, HARLEY! WHAT'RE YOU ALL MAD ABOUT?
AIN'T IT OBVIOUS?
THIS DUMB KID IS ALWAYS ONE STEP AHEAD A' ME!
HE EVEN RENTED THE VIDEO FROM THE HOTEL FIRST! AN' THEN THERE'S THE WEIRD GUY WITH THE MUSTACHE... IF I DON'T HURRY, THEY'RE GONNA CRACK THIS CASE BEFORE ME!
SO YA DON'T KNOW ANYTHIN' ABOUT THE CASE YET?

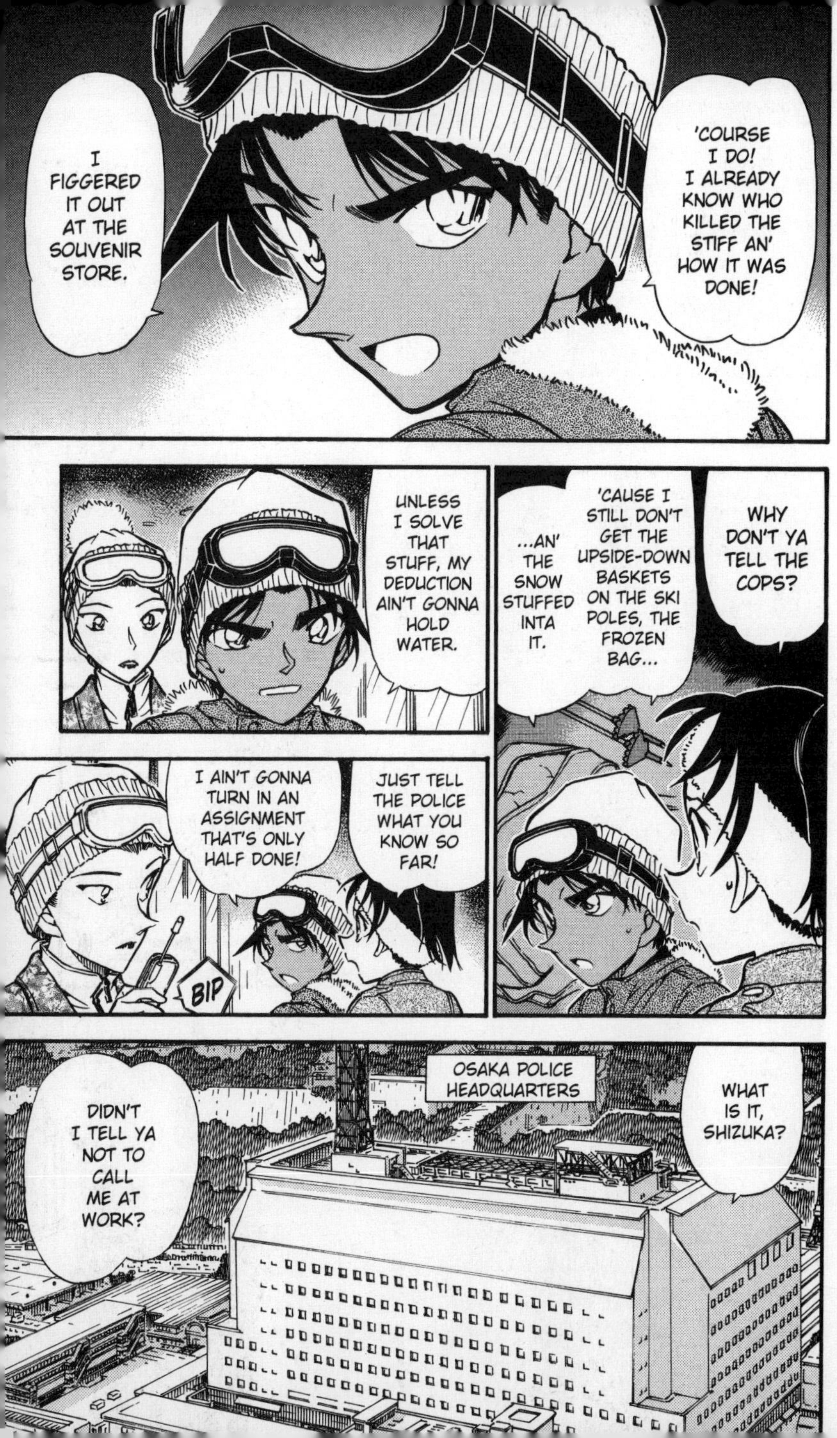
'COURSE I DO! I ALREADY KNOW WHO KILLED THE STIFF AN' HOW IT WAS DONE!
I FIGGERED IT OUT AT THE SOUVENIR STORE.
WHY DON'T YA TELL THE COPS?
'CAUSE I STILL DON'T GET THE UPSIDE-DOWN BASKETS ON THE SKI POLES, THE FROZEN BAG...
...AN' THE SNOW STUFFED INTA IT.
UNLESS I SOLVE THAT STUFF, MY DEDUCTION AIN'T GONNA HOLD WATER.
JUST TELL THE POLICE WHAT YOU KNOW SO FAR!
I AIN'T GONNA TURN IN AN ASSIGNMENT THAT'S ONLY HALF DONE!
BIP
OSAKA POLICE HEADQUARTERS
WHAT IS IT, SHIZUKA?
DIDN'T I TELL YA NOT TO CALL ME AT WORK?

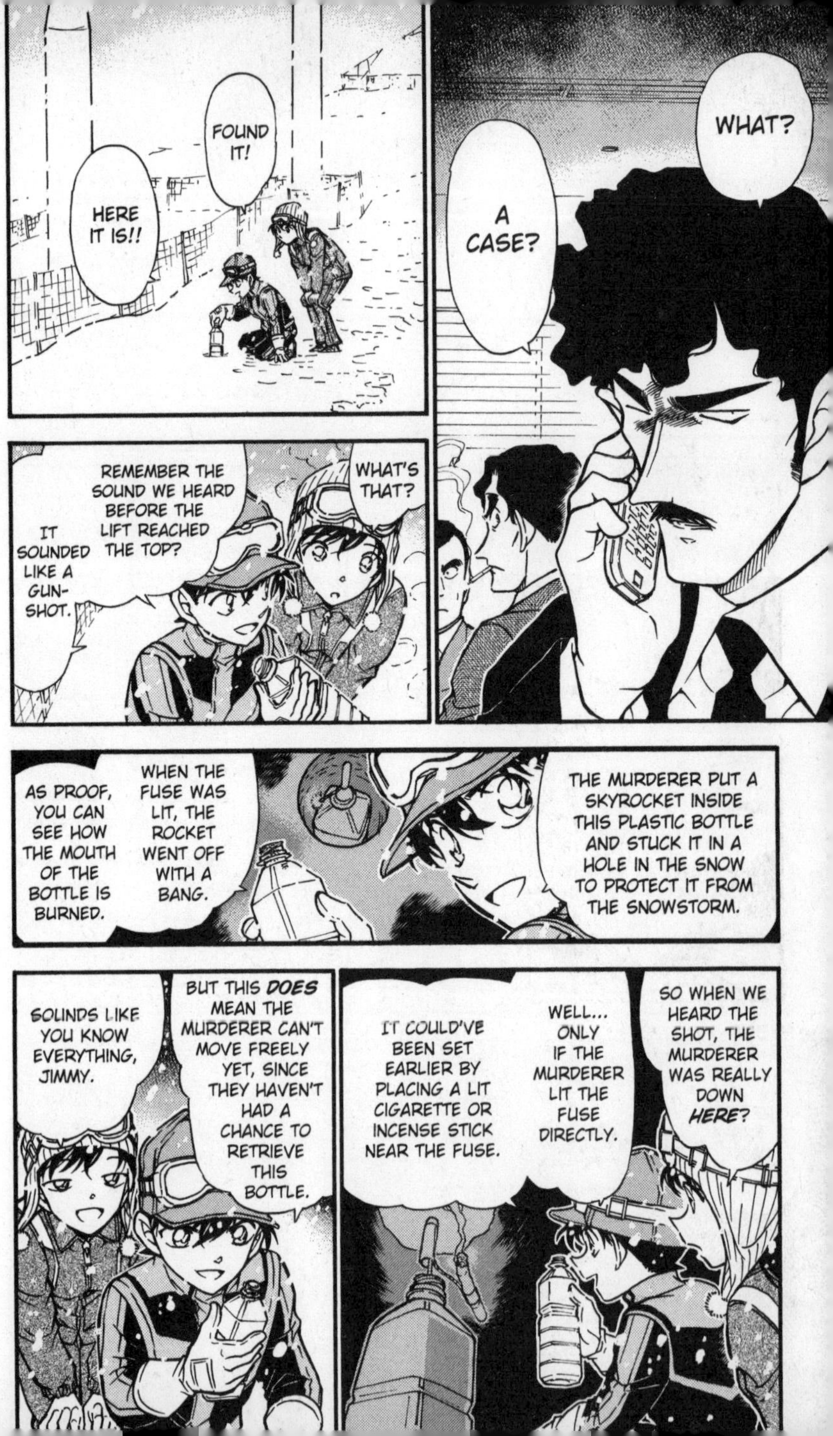
WHAT?
A CASE?
FOUND IT!
HERE IT IS!!
WHAT'S THAT?
REMEMBER THE SOUND WE HEARD BEFORE THE LIFT REACHED THE TOP?
IT SOUNDED LIKE A GUN-SHOT.
THE MURDERER PUT A SKYROCKET INSIDE THIS PLASTIC BOTTLE AND STUCK IT IN A HOLE IN THE SNOW TO PROTECT IT FROM THE SNOWSTORM.
WHEN THE FUSE WAS LIT, THE ROCKET WENT OFF WITH A BANG.
AS PROOF, YOU CAN SEE HOW THE MOUTH OF THE BOTTLE IS BURNED.
SO WHEN WE HEARD THE SHOT, THE MURDERER WAS REALLY DOWN *HERE*?
WELL... ONLY IF THE MURDERER LIT THE FUSE DIRECTLY.
IT COULD'VE BEEN SET EARLIER BY PLACING A LIT CIGARETTE OR INCENSE STICK NEAR THE FUSE.
BUT THIS ***DOES*** MEAN THE MURDERER CAN'T MOVE FREELY YET, SINCE THEY HAVEN'T HAD A CHANCE TO RETRIEVE THIS BOTTLE.
SOUNDS LIKE YOU KNOW EVERYTHING, JIMMY.

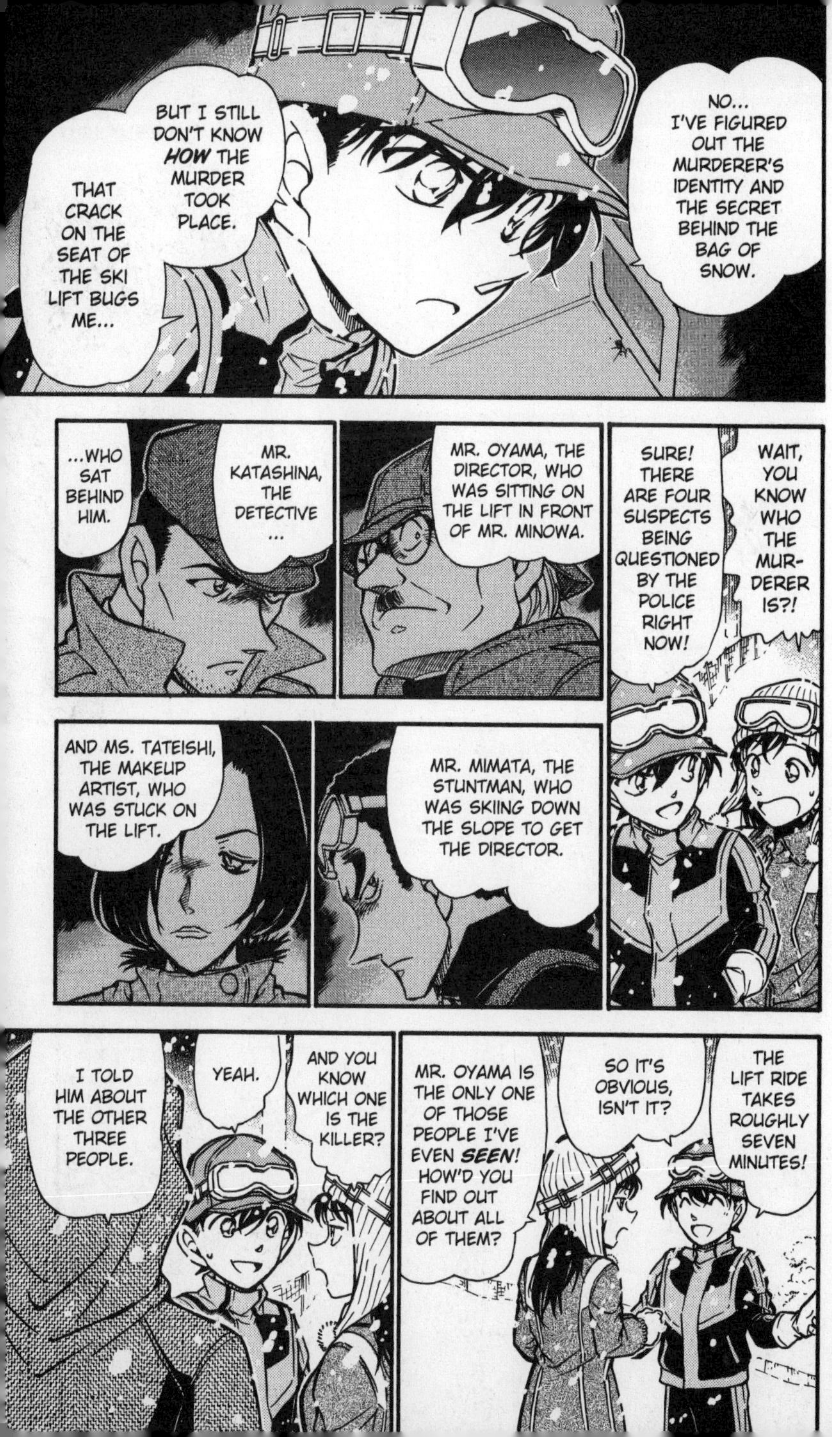
NO... I'VE FIGURED OUT THE MURDERER'S IDENTITY AND THE SECRET BEHIND THE BAG OF SNOW.
BUT I STILL DON'T KNOW **HOW** THE MURDER TOOK PLACE.
THAT CRACK ON THE SEAT OF THE SKI LIFT BUGS ME...
WAIT, YOU KNOW WHO THE MURDERER IS?!
SURE! THERE ARE FOUR SUSPECTS BEING QUESTIONED BY THE POLICE RIGHT NOW!
MR. OYAMA, THE DIRECTOR, WHO WAS SITTING ON THE LIFT IN FRONT OF MR. MINOWA.
MR. KATASHINA, THE DETECTIVE ...
...WHO SAT BEHIND HIM.
MR. MIMATA, THE STUNTMAN, WHO WAS SKIING DOWN THE SLOPE TO GET THE DIRECTOR.
AND MS. TATEISHI, THE MAKEUP ARTIST, WHO WAS STUCK ON THE LIFT.
THE LIFT RIDE TAKES ROUGHLY SEVEN MINUTES!
SO IT'S OBVIOUS, ISN'T IT?
MR. OYAMA IS THE ONLY ONE OF THOSE PEOPLE I'VE EVEN **SEEN**! HOW'D YOU FIND OUT ABOUT ALL OF THEM?
AND YOU KNOW WHICH ONE IS THE KILLER?
YEAH.
I TOLD HIM ABOUT THE OTHER THREE PEOPLE.

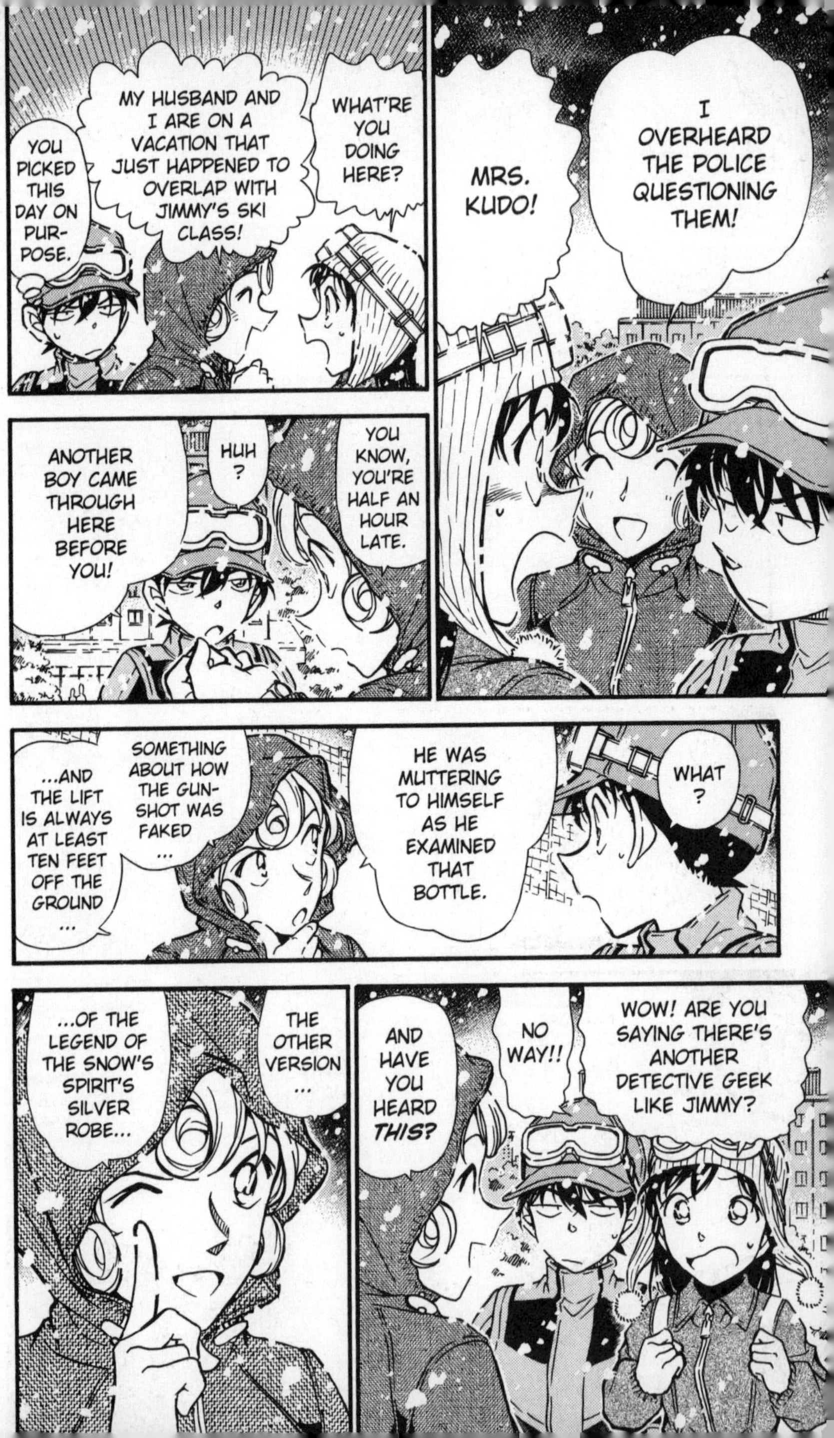
I OVERHEARD THE POLICE QUESTIONING THEM!
MRS. KUDO!
WHAT'RE YOU DOING HERE?
MY HUSBAND AND I ARE ON A VACATION THAT JUST HAPPENED TO OVERLAP WITH JIMMY'S SKI CLASS!
YOU PICKED THIS DAY ON PURPOSE.
YOU KNOW, YOU'RE HALF AN HOUR LATE.
HUH?
ANOTHER BOY CAME THROUGH HERE BEFORE YOU!
WHAT?
HE WAS MUTTERING TO HIMSELF AS HE EXAMINED THAT BOTTLE.
SOMETHING ABOUT HOW THE GUNSHOT WAS FAKED...
...AND THE LIFT IS ALWAYS AT LEAST TEN FEET OFF THE GROUND...
WOW! ARE YOU SAYING THERE'S ANOTHER DETECTIVE GEEK LIKE JIMMY?
NO WAY!!
AND HAVE YOU HEARD *THIS?*
THE OTHER VERSION...
...OF THE LEGEND OF THE SNOW'S SPIRIT'S SILVER ROBE...

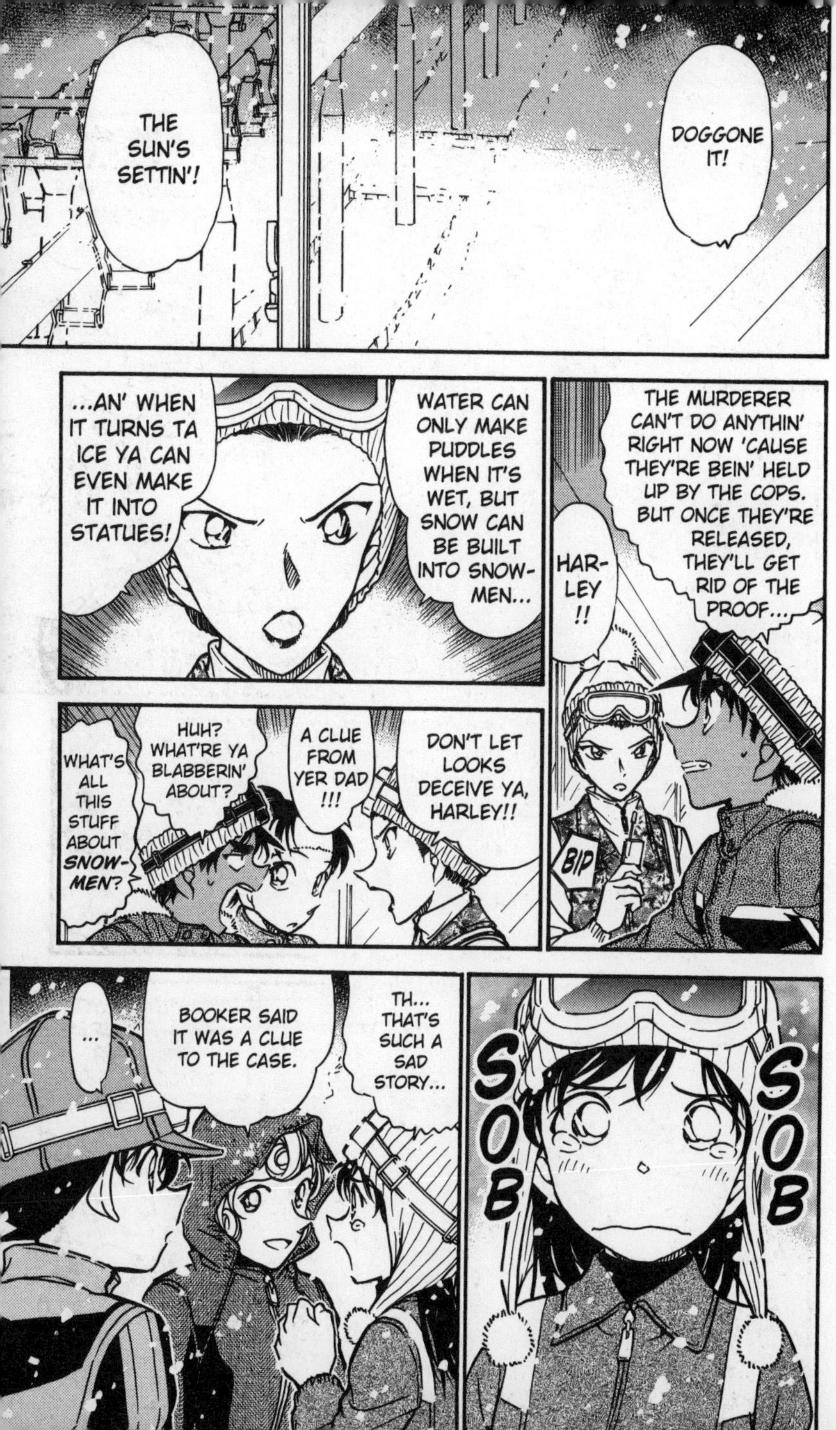
DOGGONE IT!
THE SUN'S SETTIN'!
THE MURDERER CAN'T DO ANYTHIN' RIGHT NOW 'CAUSE THEY'RE BEIN' HELD UP BY THE COPS. BUT ONCE THEY'RE RELEASED, THEY'LL GET RID OF THE PROOF...
HAR-LEY!!
BIP
WATER CAN ONLY MAKE PUDDLES WHEN IT'S WET, BUT SNOW CAN BE BUILT INTO SNOW-MEN...
...AN' WHEN IT TURNS TA ICE YA CAN EVEN MAKE IT INTO STATUES!
DON'T LET LOOKS DECEIVE YA, HARLEY!!
A CLUE FROM YER DAD!!!
HUH? WHAT'RE YA BLABBERIN' ABOUT?
WHAT'S ALL THIS STUFF ABOUT *SNOW-MEN*?
SOB
SOB
TH... THAT'S SUCH A SAD STORY...
BOOKER SAID IT WAS A CLUE TO THE CASE.
...

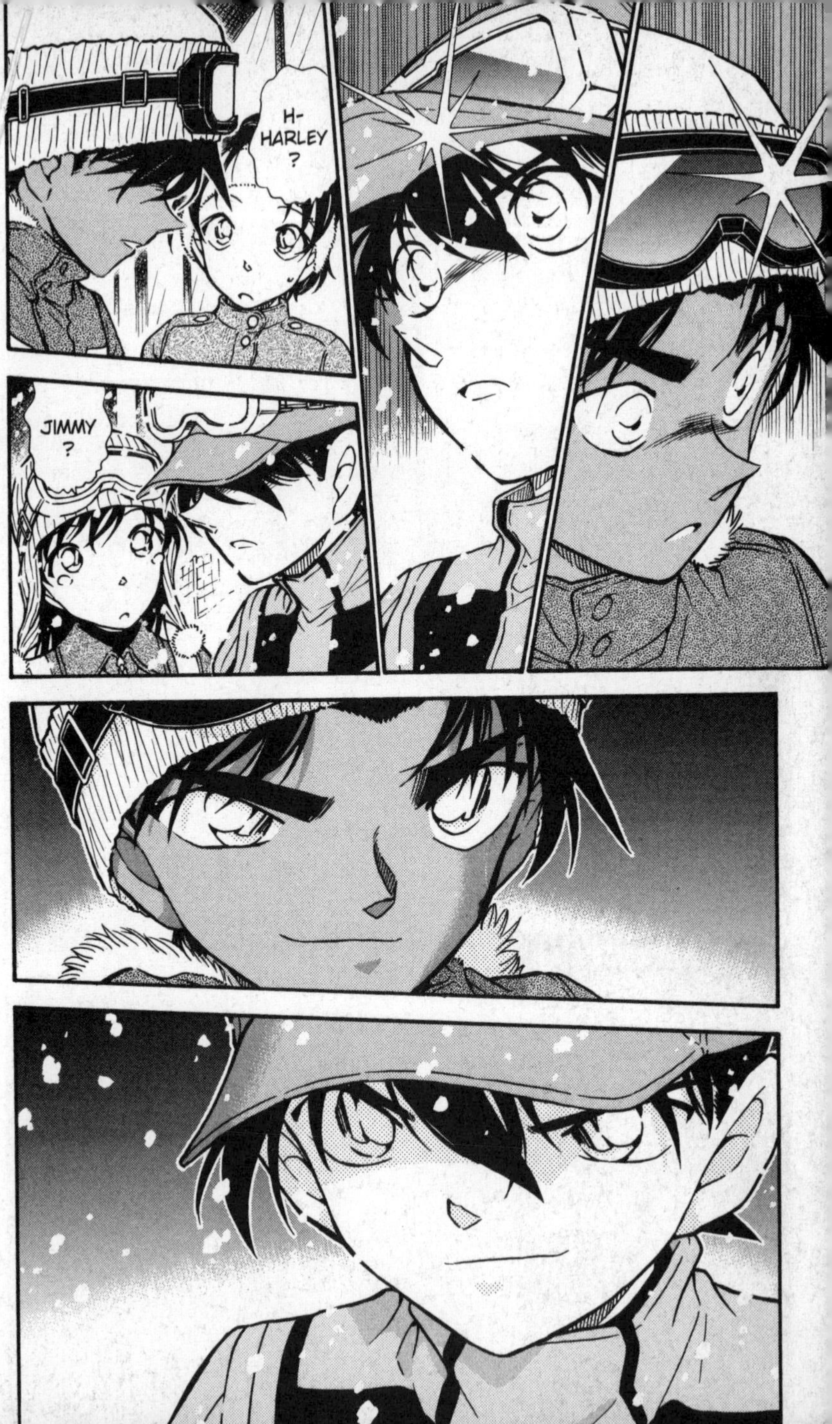
H-HARLEY?
JIMMY?

Hello, Aoyama here.

So we've finally arrived at volume 50! To commemorate the occasion, I've included a story about Jimmy and Harley in middle school! Well...the idea was nice, but being 42 years old, I couldn't really recall what it was like to be in middle school, so I had a hard time creating the story. Heh...

Gosho Aoyama's Mystery Library

50

HIDEO HIMURA

The reason he gives for his interest in crime is that "he once had the desire to kill someone." This rather dangerous character is the young researcher and detective Hideo Himura! Single and 32, he's an assistant professor at Eito University in Kyoto and a "clinical criminologist" who takes part in criminal investigations. But he's far from the typical image of a scholar with his loose tie and messy hair. When a crime occurs, he reveals his true potential by carefully walking around the scene of the crime to gather information and shed light on hidden truths.

Himura's partner, Arisu Arisugawa, is the narrator of the series. Despite his cutesy name, he's a grown man and has been Himura's partner since they were students. By the way, the author of the series uses "Arisu Arisugawa" as his pseudonym. It's a name you'll never forget once you hear it.

I recommend *The 46th Locked Room.*